ISBN 978-1-332-27232-7
PIBN 10307307

1 MONTH OF
FREE
READING

at

www.ForgottenBooks.com

By purchasing this book you are eligible for one month membership to ForgottenBooks.com, giving you unlimited access to our entire collection of over 700,000 titles via our web site and mobile apps.

To claim your free month visit:

www.forgottenbooks.com/free307307

English
Français
Deutsche
Italiano
Español
Português

www.forgottenbooks.com

Mythology Photography **Fiction**
Fishing Christianity **Art** Cooking
Essays Buddhism Freemasonry
Medicine **Biology** Music **Ancient**
Egypt Evolution Carpentry Physics
Dance Geology **Mathematics** Fitness
Shakespeare **Folklore** Yoga Marketing
Confidence Immortality Biographies
Poetry **Psychology** Witchcraft
Electronics Chemistry History **Law**
Accounting **Philosophy** Anthropology
Alchemy Drama Quantum Mechanics
Atheism Sexual Health **Ancient History**
Entrepreneurship Languages Sport
Paleontology Needlework Islam
Metaphysics Investment Archaeology
Parenting Statistics Criminology
Motivational

From a Photo by Gilbert & Bacon, Philad'a.

Yours fraternally
Saml. C. Upham,
a H 49er

From a Photo by Sarony, New York, Jan 19th, 1878.

NOTES OF A

VOYAGE TO CALIFORNIA

VIA CAPE HORN,

TOGETHER WITH

SCENES IN EL DORADO,

IN THE YEARS 1849-'50.

WITH AN APPENDIX

Containing Reminiscences of Pioneer Journalism in California—California Day
at the Centennial Exhibition Philadelphia, Sept 9th, 1876—Re-Unions
and Banquets of the Associated Pioneers of California, in New
York, January 18th, 1877 and 1878- Celebration of Admission Day, at Long Branch, N. J., Sept 8th, 1877—

Reception to GENERAL JOHN C. FREMONT, Aug. 1st, 1878, and to Hon. PHILIP A.
ROACH, June 19th, 1876—Dedication of the Lick Monument at Fredericksburg, Pa , April 22d, 1878—Extracts from the Manuscript Journal of the " KING's ORPHAN," in the
year 1843—Pioneer and Kindred
Organizations,

TOGETHER WITH THE

ARTICLES OF ASSOCIATION AND ROLL OF MEMBERS

OF

"THE ASSOCIATED PIONEERS OF THE TERRITORIAL DAYS OF CALIFORNIA."

By SAMUEL C. UPHAM.

WITH FORTY-FIVE ILLUSTRATIONS.

"ALL OF WHICH I SAW, AND PART OF WHICH I WAS."

PHILADELPHIA:
PUBLISHED BY THE AUTHOR.
1878.

Copy 2

From a Photo by Sarony, New York, Jan 19th, 1878.

NOTES OF A

VOYAGE TO CALIFORNIA

VIA CAPE HORN,

TOGETHER WITH

SCENES IN EL DORADO,

IN THE YEARS 1849-'50.

WITH AN APPENDIX

Containing Reminiscences of Pioneer Journalism in California—California Day
at the Centennial Exhibition, Philadelphia, Sept. 9th, 1876—Re-Unions
and Banquets of the Associated Pioneers of California, in New
York, January 18th, 1877 and 1878—Celebration of Admission Day, at Long Branch, N. J., Sept 8th, 1877—

Reception to GENERAL JOHN C. FREMONT, Aug 1st, 1878, and to Hon. PHILIP A.
ROACH, June 19th, 1876—Dedication of the Lick Monument at Fredericksburg, Pa , April 22d, 1878—Extracts from the Manuscript Journal of the "KING'S ORPHAN," in the
year 1843—Pioneer and Kindred
Organizations,

TOGETHER WITH THE

ARTICLES OF ASSOCIATION AND ROLL OF MEMBERS

OF

"THE ASSOCIATED PIONEERS OF THE TERRITORIAL DAYS OF CALIFORNIA."

By SAMUEL C. UPHAM.

WITH FORTY-FIVE ILLUSTRATIONS.

"ALL OF WHICH I SAW, AND PART OF WHICH I WAS."

PHILADELPHIA:
PUBLISHED BY THE AUTHOR.
1878.

Copy 2

PRESS OF
FRANKLIN PRINTING HOUSE,
38 HUDSON STREET.

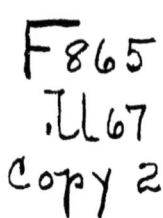

TO THE

PIONEERS OF CALIFORNIA,

WHO ENCOUNTERED DANGERS BY FLOOD AND FIELD,

AND WHOSE

BRAVE HEARTS AND WILLING HANDS

HAVE CAUSED THE ARID PLAIN AND THE WILDERNESS TO

"BLOSSOM AS THE ROSE,"

THIS VOLUME IS RESPECTFULLY DEDICATED BY

THE AUTHOR.

ACKNOWLEDGMENT.

———

To his esteemed personal friends, MR. FRANCIS D. CLARK and HON. JEREMIAH SHERWOOD, of New York; MR. COLIN M. BOYD, MR. WILLIAM WINTER, HON. PHILIP A. ROACH and DANIEL NORCROSS, Esq., of San Francisco, for their efforts in behalf of this volume; to the HON. DEMAS STRONG, of Brooklyn, N. Y., for his proffer of pecuniary aid; to the proprietors of the *Examiner* and the *Golden Era*, of San Francisco; *The Pioneer*, of San José, and the *News*, of San Diego, Cal., who published in their respective journals the Prospectus of this book, and especially to the following-named gentlemen, who had the courage to read the manuscript, comprising six hundred closely-written pages, the author returns his grateful acknowledgments:

Having been residents of California during the years 1849–'50, we cheerfully indorse the work written by Mr. Samuel C. Upham, of Philadelphia, and consider the volume in all respects a truthful and creditable history of that period in California, and of such a character as should especially interest all who formed a part of her population in those days of excitement and experience.

H. G. GIBSON, Brevet Brig.-Gen'l, U. S. A., Fort Wadsworth, N. Y.
THOS W. SWEENY,   "   "   "   314 East 120th Street, N. Y
DEMAS STRONG, ... 67 Broadway, Brooklyn, E. D.
JOHN SICKELS, ... 25 Pine Street, N. Y.
EDWARD F. BURTON, Deputy Surveyor, Custom-House, N. Y.
JOHN GAULT, ... 71 Broadway, N. Y.
BEVERLY C. SANDERS,   .   .   . 71 Broadway, N. Y.
W. C. ANNAN, ... 160 Fulton Street, N. Y.
WM. M. WALTON, ... 19 Dey Street, N. Y
STEPHEN L. MERCHANT,   .   .   . 53 Broadway, N. Y.
ROBERT W. DOWLING,   ,,   .   . 105th St. and Eleventh Ave , N. Y.
A. T. GOODELL, ... 451 East 57th Street, N. Y.
GEO. F. SNIFFEN, Sec'y Knickerbocker Life Ins. Co., N. Y.

(viii)

PREFACE.

PREFACE—the last part of a book written and the first read. A book without a preface is like a coach without horses—an engine without steam.

When the news of the discovery of gold in California reached the Atlantic States, in the summer of 1848, I held a somewhat lucrative situation in the counting-house of a mercantile firm in the city of Brotherly Love. The early reports were of so vague a character as scarcely to be credited by the most enthusiastic, and were pronounced by the skeptical as visionary—schemes gotten up by the powers at Washington to encourage emigration to California and Oregon. But when, in the fall of that year, the dispatches of Commodore Jones, Colonel Mason and Thomas O. Larkin were officially announced by President Polk's Cabinet, and their statements indorsed by the President himself, soon after, in his message to both Houses of Congress, the existence of the gold-mines of California was acknowledged a fixed fact, and thousands started at once for the new *El Dorado*, and among them the reader's humble servant. When I resigned the quill for "the pick and the spade," it was my intention to have gone to California *via* the Isthmus of Panama, but on the eve of my departure, a communication appeared in the *New York Herald*, in which the writer depicted in such vivid colors the "hair-breadth 'scapes" by that route, that

(ix)

I abandoned my original intention and engaged passage *via* Cape Horn.

My time, during the two weeks prior to my departure, was mostly employed in making the necessary arrangements for the voyage. Expecting to remain at least one year in the gold-diggings, I purchased and shipped the requisite provisions for my subsistence during that time. I also stowed away in a large camp-chest, purchased expressly for that purpose, sundry dozens of flannel and "hickory" shirts, several pairs of inexpressibles, half a dozen hats, of the latest California styles, one of Krider's incomparable rifles, a six-shooter, with ammunition to match, and last, though not least, one of those indispensable articles in a new country— an Arkansas "tooth-pick." As I was on the eve of starting, I added to my outfit a chest of medicine, accompanied by a book containing directions, which, if strictly adhered to, would cure all the ills which flesh is heir to. My mining implements consisted of a pick, spade and crowbar, a nest of sieves, a large tin pan and three patent gold-washers, each of a different pattern—first-class humbugs! I also purchased an India-rubber *water-proof* suit—which was anything else than what it purported to be—consisting of coat, cap, long boots and gauntlets, together with a tent of the same material, another proof of the old adage—a fool and his money are soon parted. But I was not alone in my folly. Many of my fellow-voyagers were equally burthened with "traps," which, on their arrival in California, proved to be quite as useless.

I do not claim for these Reminiscences any great literary merit, nor do I expect to "put money in my purse" by their publication. They have been written amid the hurly-burly of a busy mercantile life, from notes taken at the time the incidents treated of transpired—their principal merit being a narration of *facts*, not *fancies*. I have devoted considerable space to the early history of Sacamento City, where, during the spring and summer of 1850, I was engaged in the publication of the *Sacramento Transcript*, and from the columns of that journal I have made frequent drafts. Should the reader become weary of the monotony of the long sea-voyage, let him turn to the portrayal of scenes in Rio de Janeiro or Concepcion, or to the more stirring events in Sacramento City, during the Squatter riots in the month of August, 1850. In conclusion, permit me to say, should anything in this volume add to the hitherto unwritten history of California, my labor will not have been in vain; and I will also state, that throughout these pages my chief aim has been to

> " A round, unvarnished tale deliver,
> Nothing extenuate, nor set down aught in malice."

SAMUEL C. UPHAM.

Philadelphia, October 5th, 1878.

CONTENTS.

CHAPTER I.

CHAPTER II.

CHAPTER III.

CHAPTER IV.

CHAPTER V.

CHAPTER VI.

CHAPTER VII.

CHAPTER XIX.

CHAPTER XX.

CHAPTER XXI.

CHAPTER XXII.

APPENDIX.

PIONEER JOURNALISM IN CALIFORNIA.

"CALIFORNIA DAY" AT THE CENTENNIAL EXHIBITION.

SECOND ANNUAL RE-UNION AND BANQUET OF "THE ASSOCIATED PIONEERS OF THE TERRITORIAL DAYS OF CALIFORNIA."

CELEBRATION OF "ADMISSION DAY" AT LONG BRANCH, N. J.

THIRD ANNUAL RE-UNION AND BANQUET OF "THE ASSOCIATED PIONEERS OF THE TERRITORIAL DAYS OF CALIFORNIA."

RECEPTION TO GENERAL JOHN C. FREMONT.

RECEPTION TO HON. PHILIP A. ROACH.

DEDICATION OF THE LICK MONUMENT AT FREDERICKSBURG, PA.

ILLUSTRATIONS.*

* The illustrations in this volume are from Original Sketches, Daguerreotypes, Photographs, the "Annals of San Francisco," and "California Illustrated." The two latter were published soon after the discovery of gold in California, and are now nearly out of print. Dr. John H. Gihon, a Philadelphian, and one of the authors of the *Annals of San Francisco,*" died in one of the Southern States, three or four years ago. Frank Soulé and James Nisbet, his associates, are, I believe, still living in San Francisco. Mr. J. M. Letts, author of *"California Illustrated,"* is a resident of Staten Island, N.Y. The illustrations of San Francisco, Sacramento City, Stockton and the mining scenes were re-drawn and enlarged by Mr. F. E. Lummis, and engraved by David Scattergood. The Portraits were engraved by David Scattergood and C. H. Reed.

CHAPTER I.

Monday, January 15, 1849.—Carried my baggage on board the brig *Osceola*, Captain James Fairfowl, bound from Philadelphia to San Francisco, California. At eleven o'clock, P. M., bade adieu to wife, child and friends, and went on board the brig to spend the night, expecting to sail early the next morning. The weather being cold, and no fire in cabin or steerage, I slept very little during the night. Two brothers of the name of Kelly, companions *en voyage*, accompanied me on board.

Tuesday, Jan. 16.—At eight o'clock, A. M., the City Ice-boat made fast to the *Osceola*, and we were soon passing slowly down the Delaware. In consequence of the early hour at which we got under way, not more than one-half of our passengers were on board when the Ice-boat made fast to us. We had not, however, gotten fairly into the stream, before the belated passengers might be seen at different points along the wharves, swinging their hats and

(23)

caps, and yelling at the highest pitch of their voices for the *Osceola* to slacken her speed and take them on board. One of the passengers, a corpulent individual, whom I shall designate as the Doctor, went shouting along the wharves until his safety-valve collapsed, and his steam and gas having become exhausted, he availed himself of the facilities offered by a boatman and came on board wheezing like a person afflicted with the asthma. Passengers came off to the brig at different points along the Delaware between Race Street and the Navy Yard, and at the latter place the last straggler arrived.

The following is a list of the *Osceola's* passengers: Dr. Cassady, William Bassett, W. H. Bunn, Wm. Freed, H. W. Gillingham, C. H. Bennett, J. Slaughter, A. Mecartney, W. McPherson Hill, George Guier, Jr., M. D., John A. Lessig, Pat. Langton, George W. Hart, C. W. H. Solinsky, Abram Powell, Wm. H. Graham, John E. Wainwright, G. H. Weaver, T. P. Kleinhans, W. Wack, T. P. Dougherty, T. B. Butcher, Wm. Butcher, T. H. Russell, S. K. Harman, Samuel Christ, H. B. Good, J. J. Cowden, J. A. Banks, Samuel C. Upham, Amos S. Kelly, Chas. S. Kelly, J. W. Folwell, T. J. Folwell, J. M'Clelland, David L. Munns, E. Boehme, Henry Prior, H. Shoenfield, H. Courvoisier, F. Dekirt, W. Arnold, J. Falls, John A. McCoy, J. Kellum, William Beenkin, C. Beenkin, F. Miller, J. Kimmell, J. Moore, J. Kepheldt, F. Kline, H. Limberg, J. Hortsman, Hugh Brady, J. Hewdegan, George Dreka, John Heyberger, T. S. Berger, Wm. Fetters, George Wilson,

H. K. Cummings, R. M. Patterson, Charles Welding, Henry Hyde—65 passengers: Captain, mates and crew, 15, making together 80 souls on board.

At seven o'clock, P. M., we arrived at New Castle, Del., where we made fast alongside the wharf for the night. During the evening a majority of the passengers went on shore for the purpose of having a jollification, prior to a six months' cruise at sea. They came on board about two o'clock next morning as mellow as peaches, and several of them will remember for a long time the last night on *terra firma* previous to leaving for San Francisco. Moderate breeze from S. W. Weather clear and cold.

Wednesday, Jan. 17.—At seven o'clock, A. M., the Ice-boat got under way, and we proceeded down the river. At seven o'clock, P. M., we cast off and came to anchor inside the Delaware Breakwater, with thirty-five fathoms of chain. The Iceboat, in coming alongside with Captain Fairfowl, ran into us and stove our larboard main-rail badly. Passengers have been busily engaged during the afternoon writing letters to their wives, sweethearts and friends, with a view to sending them on shore by the pilot, who is expected to leave us to-night. After several efforts, I finally succeeded in scribbling a note to my wife, using my hat-box for a writing-desk. Weather cloudy and very cold. Wind S. W.

Thursday, Jan. 18.—At half-past eleven o'clock, A. M., weighed anchor and stood out to sea, and at twelve o'clock, M., discharged the pilot. On leaving the brig he received three hearty cheers from the passengers, and when his boat receded from our view the last link that bound us to *terra firma* was severed. A fine breeze springing up toward night enabled us to lay our course and scud along at the rate of ten knots an hour. Strong breeze from N. W. Clear and cold.

Friday, Jan. 19.—Wind still fair, but the weather is cloudy and cold. Of the sixty-five passengers, all are sea-sick with the exception of three. The lee-rail is completely lined with demoralized passengers, who are paying their tribute to old Neptune. Those who are not able to pay their respects to the deity of the great deep over the rail, are casting up their accounts in buckets, wash-basins and spittoons. In consequence of the coldness of the weather, I remained in my berth all day. Considerable excitement was caused to-day in consequence of the man at the wheel being found slightly inebriated. This led to an investigation of the matter, and in searching the forecastle a jug of whisky was found in the chest of one of the sailors, which the Captain ordered thrown overboard. Distance sailed, 184 miles. Latitude 37° 47'.

Saturday, Jan. 20.—This morning wind light and baffling, being barely sufficient to keep the brig steady. At ten o'clock, A. M., passed the ship *St. Louis*, bound west. Sea-sick passengers look better this morning. Those that are able to crawl out of their berths are on the poop-deck taking the benefit of a little sunshine. D. L.

Munns and S. C. Upham were to-day appointed by the Captain to divide the steerage passengers into messes. They were accordingly arranged into four messes of nine persons each—two occupying the starboard and two the larboard side of the steerage. Several squalls during the afternoon, accompanied by hail. Distance sailed, 109 miles. Lat. 36° 41'. Thermometer at M. 25°.

Sunday, Jan. 21.—Eight o'clock, A. M. The wind has been blowing a perfect gale from S. S. E. since midnight; brig laboring and straining very much, and shipping heavy seas. Owing to the rough weather, the passengers are nearly all seasick again. No cooking and but little eating done to-day in consequence of the galley having been unshipped by a heavy sea. Distance sailed, 128 miles. No observation. Therm. at M. 27°.

Monday, Jan. 22.—Wind still continues blowing fresh from S. S. E., accompanied by rain. Cook's galley fitted up to-day; started a fire, and the cook commenced operations in the culinary line. The steerage passengers complain bitterly of a scanty allowance of food, also of the manner in which it is cooked. A small codfish and two dozen potatoes were served up to-day for dinner for thirty-six steerage passengers. This circumstance being reported to the Captain, he promises that all shall be right on this score hereafter. Distance sailed, 116 miles. Lat. 35° 53''. Therm. at M. 26°.

Tuesday, Jan. 23.—Seven o'clock, A. M. Fine breeze from the N. E., which enables the brig to lay her course and make about eight knots an hour.

Have had several light showers during the day, but the atmosphere is delightful. The passengers have nearly all recovered from their sea-sickness, and are lounging about the decks amusing themselves in various ways. They have not yet gotten their sea-legs on, consequently, cannot walk about the decks very readily. Passed a brig to-day, bound west, but could not make her out. Distance sailed, 176 miles. Lat. 34° 23'. Therm. at M. 25°.

Wednesday, Jan. 24.—Wind from the north; brig rolls lazily over the water, making little headway. Have been visited to-day by rain and sunshine, alternately. Several of the steerage passengers have spread their mattresses and blankets on deck for the purpose of drying them in the sun. Owing to the leaky condition of the deck, the upper tier of steerage berths have been saturated with water since leaving Philadelphia. The Captain and second mate had an altercation this morning, in which they called each other everything but gentlemen. This war of words ended by the Captain sending the mate below and putting him off duty. Passed three vessels during the day. Distance sailed, 157 miles. Lat. 34° 11'. Therm. at M. 28°.

Thursday, Jan. 25.—Fine breeze from the N. E. and weather clear. All sails set by the wind. The steerage passengers still complain of their accommodations. They have been grossly imposed upon by Burling & Dixon, owners of the brig. A large portion of the steerage is occupied with freight and luggage belonging to the cabin passengers. Bills of lading having been executed for the freight it should have been stored in the hold of the brig or left on shore. A flying-fish was found on deck this morning, it having flown on board during the night. It was cooked and eaten by one of the passengers. Distance sailed, 143 miles. Lat. 32° 41'. Therm. at M. 27°.

Friday, Jan. 26.—Throughout the last twenty-four hours heavy squalls accompanied by rain. Brig laboring and straining very much, and shipping heavy seas. The jib was split to-day during a severe squall. The steerage passengers assisted the crew in shortening sail. The *Osceola* left Philadelphia without a full crew, having only six men and two boys before the mast to work a brig of two hundred and seventy-six tons burthen, around Cape Horn. Distance sailed, 140 miles. Lat. 31° 21'. Therm. at M. 33°.

Saturday, Jan. 27.—Gale still continues with increased violence. Top-sails double-reefed; sea running very high and brig straining badly. In the afternoon, the crew commenced shifting deck-load, which was somewhat wet and damaged. Found that the water in one cask had entirely leaked out, and another cask was only one-third full. Burling & Dixon, in their hurry to get the brig to sea, caused the water-casks to be filled without having the hoops tightened, hence the result. If the casks in the hold are in the same condition as those on deck, we shall most certainly be on a short allowance of water in the tropics. Distance sailed, 72 miles. Lat. 30° 41'. Therm. at M. 36°.

Sunday, Jan. 28.—Morning, wind light and baffling; meridian, wind has died away and it is nearly
a dead calm. Afternoon, light squalls accompanied
by rain. For several days past, a few of the steerage passengers have been in favor of having their
rations weighed out, while others have opposed the
measure. This morning the Captain gave the first
mate orders to serve out naval rations to the steerage passengers until further orders. Passengers
and crew served with water this morning—three
quarts to each person. This afternoon the crew
removed the "iceboards" from the bow of the brig.
Distance sailed, 31 miles. Lat. 30° 52'. Therm.
at M. 40°.

Monday, Jan. 29.—At daylight this morning the
wind suddenly increased to a gale. We were compelled to hard-up the helm in order to get the canvas off the brig. At eight o'clock, A. M., hove to
under close-reefed maintop-sail and stay-sail, with
a heavy sea running, which caused the brig to
strain very much. To add to our peril, the forward cabin now began to work with the strain of
the deck-load. The safety of the brig compelled
the Captain to give orders to heave overboard the
principal part of the deck-load to ease her. With
the exception of a few ship's stores, it belonged to
the passengers, and consisted of provisions, brandy,
house-frames and gold-washers. Unfortunately,
several of the passengers had their entire freight on
deck, consisting of provisions for their subsistence
in California. Poor fellows! they will be in a sad
plight on arriving in San Francisco, almost penni-

less and without provisions. The throwing overboard a cargo at sea for the purpose of saving the ship is anything but agreeable when nothing but a plank separates one from eternity. During the gale the following ludicrous incident occurred: While all hands, passengers and crew, were busily engaged staving in the heads and throwing overboard brandy, molasses and vinegar casks, a fellow-passenger, who had

" Done the State some service "

during the late war with Mexico, and being withal a great lover of whisky, caught up from off the deck both hands full of a mixture of brandy, molasses, vinegar and salt water, and after taking a hearty swig, exclaimed, "*Jimminy, boys, this is first-rate swankey.*" The same individual, during the destruction of the brandy casks, labored extremely hard to preserve one from the general wreck, which on being broached, proved to be, to his great chagrin, a brandy cask filled with pilot-bread.

While the casks composing the deck-load were waltzing to one of the tunes of old Boreas, the two ship's boys and one of the passengers had their propellers slightly injured. Distance sailed, 116 miles. Lat. 31° 45′. Therm. at M. 44°.

Tuesday, Jan. 30.—Went on deck at six o'clock this morning and found the gale still raging; brig under close-reefed sails. The main-hatch was broken out to-day for the purpose of getting at the water, all on deck having been used. In consequence of the leaky condition of the casks, one-third of the water was found to have leaked out of each of the five casks broken out. We shall most certainly suffer for the want of fresh water before reaching Rio de Janeiro.

Owing to the crowded state of the brig, the accommodations in cabins and steerage are miserable. The passengers belonging to the latter, in particular, have been shamefully imposed upon by the owners, as the following facts will fully demonstrate:—

When the steerage berths were taken, a table was fitted up for the use of the passengers, at which thirty persons could be comfortably seated, and the steerage was tolerably well lighted by sky-lights. When the *Osceola* was on the eve of leaving the port of Philadelphia, the table and seats were removed by order of the owners of the brig, and the space occupied by them stowed with cases chests and trunks, a large portion of which belonged to the cabin passengers; consequently, the steerage passengers have been compelled to mess on chicken-coops, pig-pens, water-casks and trunks, subjected to almost every imaginable inconvenience. In fact, the brig has been a perfect *Hades* since she sailed from Philadelphia. The steerage of the brig contains less than six hundred and fifty superficial feet, and there are forty-four souls, including mates, stewards and cooks, who sleep in it, which is twelve persons more than is allowed by the laws of the United States to passenger vessels passing through the tropics. Distance sailed, 124 miles. Lat. 31° 07'. Therm. at M. 49°.

Wednesday, Jan. 31.—Went on deck this morning at seven o'clock and found the brig jumping through the water at the rate of eight knots an hour, with starboard studding-sails all set. This is the most delightful day experienced since leaving Philadelphia. We had a partial break-out in the steerage to-day, which has added very much to the convenience of the passengers. The Captain ordered the booby-hatch removed for the purpose of more thoroughly ventilating the steerage. The brig has no wind-sails on board, but the Captain has promised to have one made for the steerage at once. Distance sailed, 49 miles. Lat. 30° 44'. Therm. at M. 56°.

Thursday, Feb. 1.—Eight o'clock, A. M., fine breeze from W. S. W. and clear. Studding-sails set below and aloft, and brig making eight knots an hour, which is all we can get out of the old tub. This being duff-day, the flour and raisins were served out last evening to the caterers of the steerage messes for their duff. The ingredients were accordingly mixed and taken to the cook last evening in order that they might be put into the coppers early this morning to boil for dinner; but the boys, on going to the galley for their coffee, were taken all aback by the cook's presenting them with their duff *for breakfast*, piping hot, a mistake chargeable to the misplaced zeal of the son of a sea-cook! The circumstance was reported to the Captain, who gave the cook orders in future not to *boil duff for breakfast!* Distance sailed, 158 miles. Lat. 30° 55'. Therm. at M. 63°.

Friday, Feb. 2.—This is my birthday. Thirty

years old to-day. Have been a rolling-stone all my life, consequently have gathered no moss. Am now in search of "the golden fleece," and may return shorn. *Nous verrons!* At eleven o'clock last night the wind commenced blowing a gale from N. N. E. At twelve o'clock split foretop-sail; soon after sent down royal-yards and hove the brig to. At eight o'clock this morning repaired top-sail and let the close reef out of the maintop-sail. At meridian, the storm abated somewhat, but the sea is still running very high, causing the brig to labor heavily and ship an occasional sea. Commenced reading to-day a work entitled "WHAT I SAW IN CALIFORNIA," by Edwin Bryant, in which I am deeply interested. Mr. Bryant traveled the overland route to California, *via* Independence, Missouri; and I regret very much that I did not take the same route in preference to this, *via* Cape Horn. Descriptions of a "life on the ocean wave" read very prettily on shore, but the *reality* of a sea voyage speedily dispels the romance. Distance sailed, 84 miles. Lat. 29° 55′. Therm. at M. 68°.

Saturday, Feb. 3.—Went on deck at six o'clock this morning, found the reefs all let out and the light sails set; brig sailing six knots an hour. The wind continuing fair in the afternoon, the Captain ordered the larboard topmast and top-gallant studding-sails set, which caused the brig to bound merrily over the water, shortening the distance between us and the golden land to which we are bound. God grant that we may have a safe and speedy passage to our port of destination, and that, on our arrival, our most sanguine expectations may be realized. Distance sailed, 166 miles. Lat. 30° 17'. Therm. at M. 71°.

Sunday, Feb. 4.—To-day, wind light and baffling, but the weather is delightfully pleasant. Being religiously inclined I borrowed a Bible from a fellow-passenger—not being provided with one myself—read a chapter, and cogitated in my mind a sermon suited to the occasion. I regret exceedingly that I did not bring a Bible and Prayer-Book with me, for I expect to do my own preaching during the next two years. California will probably be better supplied with mosquitoes than ministers. Distance sailed, 125 miles. Lat. 29° 55'. Therm. at M. 67°.

Monday, Feb. 5.—Fine breeze from W. S. W., weather clear and pleasant. Passengers assisted the crew in breaking out the main-hold for water and provisions. Found the water in two of the casks nearly half leaked out, which fully confirms in my mind a previously-expressed opinion that we shall run short of fresh water before reaching Rio de Janeiro. Several of the passengers have already become weary of a sea voyage, and have been talking very strongly to-day of leaving the *Osceola* at Rio, crossing the Andes to Valparaiso, and awaiting there the arrival of the brig, thus avoiding the passage around Cape Horn. I consider the project an insane one, one which I would not attempt for any earthly consideration, and shall use my best endeavors to dissuade others from hazarding their lives in an undertaking so futile and foolhardy.

The distance across from Rio to Valparaiso is far
greater than at any other point on the continent of
South America, and the journey would be attended
with incredible hardship and suffering.   Having
paid my passage to San Francisco on board the
brig *Osceola*, I intend, if my life be spared, to
remain by her until she reaches that port or goes to
Davy Jones's locker.   Distance sailed, 92 miles.
Lat. 28° 27'. Therm. at M. 78°.

Tuesday, Feb. 6.—This morning, at daylight,
weather fair with a fresh breeze from N. N. E.
The brig is making nine knots an hour, which is
something remarkable for her, and all hands, including the cook, feel jolly. At ten o'clock, A. M.,
we exchanged signals with a French brig steering
N. N. W. The crew, assisted by the passengers,
broke out the main-hold again to-day in search of
water.   More leaky casks found, in consequence of
which the Captain has put all hands on an allowance of five pints of water to each person. Yesterday, we struck the "trades," in longitude 37° 20'.
Distance sailed, 182 miles. Lat. 26° 31'. Therm.
at M. 71°.

Wednesday, Feb. 7.—Throughout to-day, fresh
breeze from N. E., with occasional squalls and light
rain.   The cabin passengers have been growling
for some time about their miserable accommodations, and to-day have declared war to the knife.
They have resolved to hold an indignation meeting,
and on their arrival at Rio de Janeiro to report the
proceedings with their grievances to the American
consul at that port, and ask his interference in the

matter. They swear by all the saints in the calendar that the *Osceola* shall not leave Rio until matters are adjusted to their entire satisfaction. Both cabin and steerage passengers have much cause for complaint, and I sincerely hope that justice may be done to all on board before the *Osceola* leaves Rio. Distance sailed, 190 miles. Lat. 24° 22'. Therm. at M. 69°.

Thursday, Feb. 8.—We crossed the Tropic of Cancer to-day and may expect excessively hot weather until we cross Capricorn. Last evening an altercation occurred between the Captain and first mate, Mr. Howell, in relation to the pumps, which resulted in the latter being put off duty. During the controversy they were not very choice in their selections from the King's English. The opinions of the passengers, in relation to this matter, appear to be about equally divided, although I am inclined to the belief that were a vote of all on board registered, a majority would be found in favor of the mate. To-day we have been favored with a fair breeze from the north-east, and all drawing sails have been set. Distance sailed, 176 miles. Lat. 22° 15'. Therm. at M. 71°.

Friday, Feb. 9.—The weather this morning is as clear and balmy as a May morning in Philadelphia, and the brig is gliding along at the rate of eight knots an hour.

In consequence of the first mate being off duty, the first watch last night was kept by one of the passengers, who in early life had served on board a man-of-war. There is nothing, in my opinion,

3

more essential to the safety of a vessel and the lives of her passengers than harmony among her officers. The Captain and mates of the *Osceola* have been at loggerheads since leaving Philadelphia, and God only knows how much longer this asperity of feeling will continue to exist between them.

A brig, supposed to be the *Oniota*, bound for San Francisco, which sailed from Philadelphia five days ahead of the *Osceola*, has been on our weather-quarter, five miles distant, during the afternoon, but we are now rapidly leaving her astern. We are to-day in the latitude of the Cape de Verde Islands, and about thirty hours' sail, *Osceola* time, to the westward of them. Distance sailed, 174 miles. Lat. 19° 53'. Therm. at M. 72°.

Saturday, Feb. 10.—Went on deck at seven o'clock this morning, and found the weather delightfully pleasant. The brig is being wafted along by the trade-winds at the rate of eight knots an hour. The Captain flogged one of the sailors this morning for a trifling misdemeanor, and the passengers have been gathered in knots about the deck, during the forenoon, discussing the matter. The majority appear to be opposed to corporeal punishment, but are willing to admit that the safety of the brig depends on the maintenance of strict discipline.

During the twenty-four hours ending at twelve o'clock, M., to-day, the *Osceola* has sailed 205 miles, being a greater distance than she has made during any previous day since leaving the Capes of the Delaware. Three cheers for the *Osceola!* She certainly smells land. Several flying-fish came on board during last night. I have preserved one of their wings as a memento of the tropics. Lat. 16° 52'. Therm. at M. 75°.

Sunday, Feb. 11.—Although it has been hazy to-day, the weather has not been oppressive in consequence of the trade-winds, which in this latitude are bracing and invigorating. This morning, Mr. Howell, the first mate, presented me with a Bible, for which I feel very grateful. Law and physic have several votaries on board the *Osceola,* but divinity has not a single representative. During the day I have noticed several flocks of "Mother Cary's chickens" flying around the brig and skimming over the surface of the water. These little messengers of the deep are of the size and color of a swallow, and are regarded by most sailors with feelings of superstition and reverential awe. Some mariners fully believe them to be the winged spirits of their departed comrades, and consider it a great sacrilege to attempt to capture or kill them. Distance sailed, 202 miles. Lat. 13° 53'. Therm. at M. 76°.

CHAPTER II.

Monday, February 12.—The weather continues
close and hazy, with strong indications of rain.
The trade-winds are gradually dying away, and we
shall probably be becalmed before reaching the
equator.

As we were nearing the head-quarters of old
Neptune yesterday afternoon, a letter addressed to
His Highness was thrown overboard by one of his
subjects, informing him that there were several
candidates for initiation on board the *Osceola*.
Early this morning a reply was received from
the old salt, stating that he would board us as we
" crossed the line " of his dominions, for the express
purpose of performing the " awful and terrifying "
ceremonies of initiation, and requesting the candidates to be in readiness, as he could not be detained
long from home, in consequence of the ill-health of
Mrs. Neptune. Distance sailed, 192 miles. Lat.
11° 04′. Therm. at M. 77°.

Tuesday Feb. 13.—The weather is as warm to-day as it is in Philadelphia in midsummer, and were it not for the trade-winds the heat would be very oppressive. To-day the caterers of the steerage messes made a complaint to the Captain in relation to the quality and quantity of provisions received by them from the cook. He has promised to provide the steerage passengers with a cook and galley, on the arrival of the brig at Rio. If this promise is not adhered to, a full report of our grievances will be made to the American consul. Distance sailed to-day, 225 *miles!* Best time yet made. Hurrah for the old tub! Lat. 7° 45′. Therm. at M. 80°.

Wednesday, Feb. 14.—Owing to the excessive heat, I slept very little last night, and throughout the day the weather has been very oppressive. Several of the passengers remained on deck last night rather than submit to a vapor-bath in their berths. Took a salt-water bath this evening, and feel very much refreshed. Distance sailed, 184 miles. Lat. 4° 41′. Therm. at M. 82°.

Thursday, Feb. 15.—When I went on deck, at six o'clock this morning, the wind was light and baffling, with every indication of a calm. The brig has not made more than four knots an hour during the night. At twelve o'clock, M., it was nearly a dead calm, and the sails flapped lazily against the masts. In the afternoon we had a light fall of rain, accompanied by baffling breezes. This forenoon saw a hermaphrodite brig steering south by west, probably bound for Rio de Janeiro. This afternoon ran into a school of skip-jacks, a species of the finny tribe found in abundance in this latitude. They are about two feet in length when full grown, very plump, and of a deep purple color. The morning watch was kept by one of the ship's boys—a *juvenile watch officer!* Distance sailed, 134 miles. Lat. 2° 28'. Therm. at M. 81°.

Friday, Feb. 16.—We have been becalmed all day within one hundred miles of the equator. Last night the weather was so excessively hot that a majority of the passengers slept on deck. During the night, four of the first cabin passengers, not having the fear of "*delirium triangles*" before their eyes, took it into their heads to have a jollification. They made night hideous with their drunken revelry, to the great annoyance and disgust of those who were more quietly disposed. To cap the climax, one of the revelers had an attack of *mania a polu* this morning, which I think will have a tendency to check his bacchanalian propensities in future. Distance sailed, 58 miles. Lat. 1° 30'. Therm. at M. 86°. "Jerusalem, my happy home," how hot it is!

Saturday, Feb. 17.—We are still north of the equator, having been becalmed during last night and this forenoon. I slept on top of the cabin last night with nothing but the canopy of heaven for covering. Early this morning the mate caught an albicore, being the first fish caught with a hook and line during the passage, although several lines have been trailing over the stern of the brig the past ten days. During the last week we have seen small fish in abundance, but they do not seem to be very hungry. It has been rainy and squally all the afternoon, still it remains very hot and oppressive. Distance sailed, 30 miles. Lat. 1° 13'. Therm. at M. 84°.

Sunday, Feb. 18.—It rained incessantly throughout last night. It seemed as though the flood-gates of heaven had been opened especially for our benefit. The rain ceased at daylight, and a fresh breeze from W. S. W. has enabled us to glide along at the rate of seven knots an hour this forenoon. During the night we caught a barrel of rain-water, which has enabled the passengers to indulge in the luxury of a *fresh-water wash*—the first since leaving Philadelphia. This morning one of the passengers caught a bonito weighing thirty pounds, which was served up for dinner. A large school of blackfish passed us this morning to the leeward, half a mile distant. We crossed the equinoctial line about ten o'clock, in longitude 25° 40'. Neptune did not honor us with a visit, in consequence, I presume, of its being Sunday. Distance sailed, 83 miles. Lat. 0° 11' south. Therm. at M. 80°.

Monday, Feb. 19.—Another dead calm throughout to-day. It seems as though we were never to get out of the "horse latitude." Yesterday evening a bark was discovered to the windward heading for Rio. Early this morning we exchanged colors with her, and at ten o'clock, A. M., our stern boat was lowered and manned with passengers, for the purpose of boarding her. At one o'clock, P. M., our boat returned with a dozen passengers from the stranger, which proved to be the bark *Croton*, Cap-

tain D. V. Souillard, which sailed from New York
on the 16th ultimo, bound for San Francisco, with
fifty-four passengers on board. During the afternoon, the boats of both vessels have been busily
engaged carrying the passengers to and fro. Some
fifteen or twenty of the *Croton's* passengers dined
with us, and about the same number of our passengers partook of a collation on board that vessel.
The wine bottle passed merrily around, and wit,
sentiment and song imparted zest to the scene.
Mirth and hilarity reigned pre-eminent, and everything went as

"Merry as a marriage bell,"

until toward night one of our passengers, who had
imbibed too much whisky, kicked up a row on
board the *Croton*, which resulted in his being
brought on board the brig by his shipmates and
placed in durance. The accommodations of the passengers on board the *Croton* are most admirable.
They are so much superior to ours, that one of our
passengers offered $150 to any one on board that
vessel who would exchange berths with him. The
offer was not accepted. Distance sailed, 35 miles.
Lat. 0° 28'. Therm. at M. 85°.

Tuesday, Feb. 20.—The brig's awning was spread
to-day for the first time during the passage, although
for the past ten days we have, when on deck, been
exposed to the broiling rays of a tropical sun. We
are still within one degree of the equator, having
made only five minutes of latitude during the past
twenty-four hours. In consequence of the con-

tinued calm and the low state of our fresh water, each person to-day received his allowance of water separately, which called into requisition all the empty bottles, jugs and jars that could be found on board the brig.

This morning one of the passengers caught a shark seven feet in length, and in less than twenty minutes after having been landed on deck, he was literally "used up." Never was a shark more thoroughly dissected. His vertebræ were cut out and divided among the passengers, each receiving a joint as a memento of his sharkship. Distance sailed, *only eight miles!* Lat. 0° 33'. Therm. at M. 84°.

Wednesday, Feb. 21.—Since sunrise we have been favored with a light but fair breeze from E. S. E. God grant that it may continue until we reach Rio. Yesterday morning, I was appointed one of a committee of three to present to Captain Fairfowl a petition signed by fifty-one of our passengers, protesting against the first mate's watch being kept by incompetent persons, thereby endangering the lives of all on board; also requesting in respectful terms the restoration of the first mate to duty. This afternoon a written reply was received from the Captain, stating that he hoped to reach Rio in safety, but would not comply with our request in relation to the mate, refusing in positive terms to restore him to duty so long as he (the Captain) "breathed the breath of life."

The sun being obscured to-day, the old skipper

was unable to take an observation. Distance sailed, as per log, 45 miles. Therm. at M. 80°.

Thursday, Feb. 22.—Last night, at twelve o'clock, we made the south-east "trades," and to-day we have been skimming along at the rate of six knots an hour. In consequence of the excessively hot weather, and want of exercise, two of the first-cabin passengers have had an attack of the *rabies*, and not having the fear of man before their eyes, have concluded to have coffee and pistols for two served up on their arrival in Rio. A challenge has been given and accepted, and all the preliminaries arranged by the seconds, to the apparent satisfaction of both parties.

> "It has a strange, quick jar upon the ear,
>   That cocking of a pistol, when you know
> A moment more will bring the sight to bear
>   Upon your person, twelve yards off, or so;
> A gentlemanly distance, not too near,
>   If you have got a former friend or foe;
> But after being fired at once or twice,
>   The ear becomes more Irish, and less nice."

To-day being the anniversary of the birth of Washington, the ensign and pennant of the *Osceola* have been flying in the breeze since daylight this morning. At meridian, a salute with small-arms was fired by the passengers in honor of the day, and several National airs were played by the "El Dorado Band." During the afternoon, speeches appropriate to the occasion were delivered by five of the passengers. The jubilee was kept up until a late hour in the evening. Distance sailed, 120 miles. Lat. 3° 32'. Therm. at M. 84°.

Friday, Feb. 23.—Fair wind continues. Brig making seven knots an hour. In compliance with the Captain's request, I have to-day written out a list of provisions for thirty-six steerage passengers for seventeen weeks, as per scale of U. S. Naval rations, and, on our arrival at Rio, he has promised to purchase such provisions as are deficient, in order to complete the list. An altercation occurred this morning between the Captain and several of the steerage passengers in relation to their ration of Irish potatoes. The Captain and steerage passengers are continually at loggerheads. Scarcely a day passes without a shindy being kicked up between them. Saw two vessels to-day to leeward; one a brig bound south, the other a Belgian bark homeward bound. Distance sailed, 200 miles. Lat. 5° 43'. Therm. at M. 84°.

Saturday, Feb. 24.—The atmosphere is clear to-day, and the weather as balmy as a June day in Yankee land. The trade wind is wafting us along at the rate of eight knots an hour. The skirmish that commenced yesterday between the Captain and the steerage passengers, in relation to potatoes, assumed a more warlike aspect this morning, and the old skipper has given orders to the cook to cook no more potatoes for the steerage passengers. He also said he would throw the potatoes overboard rather than have them served to the steerage messes. This last straw has broken the camel's back, and a spirit of indignation prevails throughout the brig in regard to Captain Fairfowl's treatment of the steerage passengers. He is a sea-tyrant, and totally unfit to command a passenger vessel. The dinner for the steerage passengers to-day consisted of *boiled codfish and hard tack*—all told! If a more *rascally* dinner was ever placed before a like number of *Christians* when on a short allowance of water in a tropical climate, with the thermometer at 85° in the shade, and when surrounded with provisions in abundance, I have yet to learn what it consisted of. The truth of the matter is, there is the d—— to pay, and no Irish potatoes to cancel the debt! Distance sailed, 173 miles. Lat. 8° 21′. Therm. at M. 85°.

Sunday, Feb. 25.—The trade winds continued throughout last night and this forenoon. Sunday has proved a very lucky day to me ever since leaving Philadelphia. Two weeks ago to-day, I was presented with a Bible, and to-day a fellow-passenger of the name of Patterson, a relative, I presume, of Billy P. of pugilistic memory, presented me with an Episcopal Prayer-Book, which I have been reading nearly all day. Should I have the good luck to obtain a Hymn Book before reaching California, I shall, on my arrival in that far-off land, possess the requisite documents for commencing the profession of itinerant preacher. This afternoon, one of the steerage passengers shot a ganet as it was flying over the brig, but it fell overboard and was lost. The ganet is of the fish-hawk genus, and in size and color of plumage resembles that bird very closely. The potato war that raged with so much fury yesterday, has gradually subsided. Distance sailed, 163 miles. Lat. 10° 33'. Therm. at M. 84°.

Monday, Feb. 26.—Our water, which has been remarkably good until within the past few days, is undergoing the process of fermentation, which renders it very unpalatable. The potato war broke out again to-day, in consequence of no dinner being cooked for the steerage passengers. The circumstance was reported to the Captain, who imputed the fault to the cook, and he in return swore pointblank that he had received no orders to cook dinner for the steerage passengers! The dinner, however, was ordered to be cooked, and, at the fashionable hour of four o'clock, P. M., we dined on bean soup and pork, confident in the belief that a late dinner was better than no dinner at all. The brig has been steering her course to-day at the rate of seven knots an hour. During the day we have sighted four vessels; two bound north-east, and with one, an American whaler, homeward bound, we exchanged colors. One of the other vessels was bound south-east, for the Cape of Good Hope; the other was a bark, bound north-east, with her we exchanged colors, but could not make out her nationality. Distance sailed, 170 miles. Lat. 12° 50'. Therm. at M. 84°.

Tuesday, Feb. 27.—The wind has been very light to-day, causing the brig to "make haste very slowly." During the last three days all hands have been elated with the idea of reaching Rio on Sunday next, but we shall most certainly be disappointed unless favored with a stronger breeze than that of to-day. We are at this time 900 miles north-east of Rio, yet an eight-knot breeze would waft us there in five days very easily. Some old sails have been spread above our heads to-day as a substitute for an awning, and the passengers have been amusing themselves by playing cards, dominoes, backgammon, checkers, and reading, writing, singing, fiddling and dancing. The Captain being asleep and the first mate off duty, no observation was taken at meridian to-day! To relieve the tedium of the voyage, the passengers have introduced a new game this afternoon—pitching pennies, and while I am writing, the pennies are rattling on the deck over my head. Distance sailed, per log, 170 miles. Therm. at M. 86°. Shades of Lucifer! it has been hot to-day. If I could only divest myself of flesh and sit in my bones for an hour or so, wouldn't it be altogether lovely?

Wednesday, Feb. 28.—Last day of February and fifty-three days at sea! Rio not reached yet. Since sunrise, this morning, the brig has been rolling lazily along, scarcely making three knots an hour, which does not look much like reaching Rio this week. Captain Fairfowl has experienced a very sudden change of heart! Yesterday afternoon full naval rations, with the exception of cheese, were served to the steerage passengers, for the first time since leaving Philadelphia. We received no cheese for the very best of reasons—there was none on board the brig. The Captain has promised the steerage passengers full naval rations when they arrive at Rio, if the articles of which we are defi-

cient can be had in that port. Among the rations
served out yesterday, were butter, pickles and vinegar, the first tasted during the passage.

Our cook is possessed of a devil as large as a
ground-hog. The soup for the steerage passengers
was served up to-day in the following novel manner: A large boiler, from the galley, was placed in
the lee gangway, exposed to the broiling rays of the
sun, and the passengers were called to help themselves as best they could. This scene reminds me
of one witnessed in a Spanish barracks, at Port
Mahon, in the Mediterranean, where the soldiers
were marched up to a large kettle of soup, and the
foremost after partaking of three spoonfuls fell
back, and the person next to him advanced for his
share of the spoils, and so on in turn, until all were
served.

This morning, a committee of three, consisting of
Dr. George Guier, Jr., T. B. Butcher and S. C.
Upham, was appointed by the passengers to wait
on Captain Fairfowl, state their grievances, and
request that they be remedied by him on the arrival
of the *Osceola* in Rio. At three o'clock, P. M.,
the committee had an interview with the Captain,
and he acceded to the following propositions:

On the arrival of the *Osceola* in Rio, a waiter
shall be shipped to attend to the wants of the first
and second cabin passengers; a galley shall be
erected and a cook shipped exclusively for the
steerage passengers; a table shall also be fitted
up in the steerage for their especial use and benefit,
and stores shall be purchased to complete the full

naval ration, which shall be served regularly thereafter. Potatoes shall be served alike to cabin
and steerage passengers. The committee are to
be allowed the privilege of seeing that the stores
purchased for the vessel are of a good quality, and
that the other arrangements are carried into effect
before sailing from Rio. Distance sailed, 169
miles. Lat. 16° 55'. Therm. at M. 85°.

Thursday, March 1.—During yesterday and
to-day the *Osceola* has been bowling along with
square yards, and studding-sails set below and aloft.
Gambling has again broken out on board the brig
—this time, in the form of an epidemic. Poker,
monté and "rattle-and-snap" have been the order
of the day during the past week, and to-day, by
way of change, two raffles came off, one for a gold
guard-chain, and the other for a gold watch. Both
prizes were won by the "gentlemen of honor," who
are to partake of pistols and coffee for two on their
arrival in Rio. The forward cabin and steerage
passengers have been playing cards and dominoes
for dinners, oranges and monkeys, to be purchased
in Rio by the losing parties. If the bets are all
paid, there will be a scarcity of the raw material in
the monkey market. A vessel was reported from
the maintop this morning, bound north. Distance
sailed, 173 miles. Lat. 19° 21'. Therm. at M. 87°.

Friday, March 2.—This morning the rain poured
down in torrents, accompanied by thunder and
lightning. Just before the storm commenced two
jack-o'-lanterns paid us a visit. One was stationed
on the maintop-gallant-yard-arm, and the other

on the fore-truck, where they remained until vanquished by the rain-storm. The storm has been succeeded by a calm, and disappointment is depicted in the countenances of all on board.

Early this morning a brown butterfly and a small land-bird came on board, and their visit was hailed with pleasure by all hands. The butterfly was retained a prisoner, but the little bird, after fluttering about the masts and rigging a few moments, bade us adieu, and turning his head in the direction of the land, was soon lost to view. During to-day the surface of the water has been covered with a green substance, not unlike that which may be seen on a frog-pond. The sperm-whale is said to subsist on this floating scum. If so, I imagine they will never be troubled with dyspepsia or gout in consequence of high diet. This afternoon a sail was reported on our weather-bow, heading the same direction with us. Distance sailed, 130 miles. Lat. 21° 15'. Therm. at M. 82°.

Saturday, March 3.—Another severe rain-storm at three o'clock this morning. At the commencement of the rain several of the passengers were asleep on top of the after-cabin, but they were soon compelled to take up their beds and walk. The storm was succeeded by an eight-knot breeze, which we have carried all day. Should this breeze continue until eight o'clock to-morrow morning, we shall make Cape Frio, which is seventy miles to the northward of Rio de Janeiro.

Two of the passengers, carpenters by profession, have been engaged during the day constructing a galley for the use of the steerage passengers, which, when completed and manned by a competent cook, will add much to their comfort. Distance sailed, 116 miles. Lat. 22° 28'. Therm. at M. 82°.

Sunday, March 4.—A dead calm prevailed throughout last night and to-day. Went on deck this morning at six o'clock and saw Cape Frio directly ahead, about thirty miles distant. To the leeward of us lie the Papagayos, Anchor and St. Ann's Islands, Cape Busios, St. John's Hill and Cape St. Thomas. Cape Frio, looming up in the distance, recalled vividly to mind recollections of my boyhood's home, in consequence of its close resemblance to the Camel's Hump, one of the highest peaks of the Green Mountain range.

During the afternoon the brig has drifted so near the shore that the light-house on Cape Frio can easily be discerned without the aid of a glass. A half-dozen vessels can be seen from our deck, standing in the same direction with us. A large green turtle was seen on our weather-bow early this morning, about thirty yards distant, making toward us with head erect. When within fifteen yards of the brig he bade us adieu by shaking his head and

"Diving down below, down below."

Distance sailed, 35 miles. Lat. 23° 03'. Therm. at M. 80°.

Monday, March 5.—Last night a light breeze sprang up from the north-west, which enabled us to double Cape Frio. At daylight this morning the wind died away, and during the day we have been rolling about within thirty miles of the harbor of Rio, surrounded by half a dozen vessels similarly situated. The highlands and mountains of Brazil can be seen along the horizon in the direction of Rio, as far as the eye can scan, and from our main-royal-yard can be seen the Sugar Loaf, a high conical-shaped promontory near the entrance to the harbor.

The passengers have been busily engaged to-day, shaving, shearing and clipping, which has called into requisition all the razors, scissors, hair-dyes, oils and pomades that can be mustered. They are all desirous of captivating the dark-eyed *señoritas* on their arrival in Rio. In consequence of the disappointment occasioned by the *Osceola's* not reaching Rio to-day, two of our passengers have adopted the whisky treatment in order to drown their sorrows. Whether they will succeed in calming their troubled spirits remains to be seen, but they have succeeded in making themselves uproariously drunk.

We spoke a Brazilian brig this afternoon, bound out of Rio for Pernambuco, with an assorted cargo. Distance sailed, *six miles!* Lat. 23° 09'. Therm. at M. 82°.

Tuesday, March 6.—At nine o'clock last night we made the light on Razor Island, at the entrance of the harbor of Rio. We continued our course toward the light until two o'clock this morning, when the wind died away and left us within three miles of a rock-bound shore, which was being lashed furiously by the angry waves. Fortunately, the tide set us off shore, and at daylight the roaring of the breakers was scarcely audible, although the coast for many miles in extent was distinctly in view. Soon after daylight a light breeze sprang up, which enabled us to steer direct for the entrance to the harbor of Rio, which we entered at four o'clock, P. M., and after passing Fort Santa Cruz on the right and the battery at the base of the Sugar Loaf on the left, we dropped anchor about one and a half miles below the principal landing of the city, at five o'clock, P. M. While passing up the harbor, we spoke the bark *Elvira*, of Boston, bound out for San Francisco, with sixty-three passengers. Suspended from her main-stay, were several bunches of bananas, which looked very inviting, as I had not tasted fruit of any description for more than forty days. As we passed Fort Santa Cruz, we were hailed in broken English by a Portuguese official, who thrust his curly head above the ramparts and bellowed through a dilapidated tin trumpet in a Boanergean voice. What he said, we knew not and cared as little, and the reply of our Captain was probably received with like indifference. The custom of hailing vessels from this fort is

"More honored in the breach than in the observance."

The scene presented from the deck of a vessel on entering the harbor of Rio de Janeiro is unrivaled. The most romantic imagination can picture nothing more magnificent than this beautiful harbor, sur-

HARBOR OF RIO JANEIRO

rounded by innumerable conical hills clothed to
their summits with luxuriant tropical verdure, and
the valleys dotted with beautiful white villas standing out in bold relief and contrast with the eternal
green of the hills. Our anchor was scarcely down,
before the news-boat came alongside. Soon after,
we were visited by the Port Physician and the
Custom-house officer. They had scarcely left us,
before half a dozen shore-boats were alongside
manned by half-naked negroes and Portuguese.
The boats were soon filled to their utmost capacity
by the passengers—scarcely a dozen remaining on
board—and the word *vamose* being given, we soon
passed the guard-ship and were landed on shore at
the foot of Palace Square.

Immediately after landing, I went by invitation
to the counting-house of Mr. Philip Hue, grocer
and wine merchant, No. 14 Rua Direita, where I
wrote letters to my friends in the United States.
A mail-bag was to leave on the following day, on
board the bark *Hope*, Captain Hall, bound for
Philadelphia. Having finished my correspondence,
I repaired to the Hotel Pharoux, accompanied by
three friends, and ordered supper for four. The
supper, consisting of cold chicken, coffee and rolls,
was soon dispatched and the bill called for, which
was presented by a very pretty French bar-maid.
On examining the bill, I was thunder-struck! It
footed up, as I supposed, *seven dollars and eighty
cents!* I handed the bill to my companions, who
exclaimed, simultaneously, "robbers! pirates! vil-
lains!" I inquired for the proprietor of the hotel,

for the purpose of ascertaining the price of chickens by the dozen. If they were two dollars each cooked, I desired to learn the price of the *raw material!* The landlord soon made his appearance, and an explanation followed which soon placed matters in their true light. Our bill was four millreis and 780 reis, instead of $7.80, being about sixty-two cents each, but enough for cold chicken and coffee. There are at the present time in Rio fully one thousand Americans belonging to California passenger vessels, which has caused the boatmen, hotel and livery-stable keepers to increase their tariff of prices fully one hundred per cent. Not wishing to pay fifty cents for the privilege of sleeping on the soft side of a billiard table, I went on board the brig at eleven o'clock, P. M., not overly elated with life in Rio.

CHAPTER III.

Wednesday, March 7.—Went on shore at eight o'clock, A. M., and after breakfasting at the Hotel Pharoux, visited the market-house, situated on the north side of Palace Square. The walls of the market are composed of stone, rough-cast, and the interior forms a hollow square. There are three arched gateways, or entrances, the principal of which, fronting Palace Square, is surmounted by an astronomical globe bearing a crown and cross, the Brazilian coat of arms. The eastern portion of the market is occupied by the fish-mongers, and on their stalls is displayed the greatest variety of the finny tribe I have ever seen, and I question whether the fish-market of Rio is excelled in variety by any other in the world. In the northern and western portions of the market are exposed for sale tropical fruits in all their varieties, and vegetables of various

(61)

kinds.   Most of the stalls are attended by female slaves, many of whom have their little ones lashed to their backs with a strip of cotton cloth.   The little pickaninnies remain as quiet in this position

MODE OF NURSING CHILDREN IN RIO.

as would an American child in a cradle or baby-jumper, and allow their mammas to perform their avocations without hindrance.

After having spent two or three hours in the market, I sauntered down toward the southern part of the city and visited the Passeio Publico, a beautiful square inclosed by a substantial stone wall ten feet high.   At the entrance, which is surmounted by a marble bust of the late queen, Donna Maria I, were

stationed two guards, to whom I tipped my Panama
on entering, and walked leisurely about for an hour,
viewing the trees, plants and flowers growing here
in all their splendor. Among the trees under which
I strolled were the genepa, tamarind, casuarina,
bread-fruit, joboticaba and cocoa; and among the
rare plants I noticed the spiral aloe unfolding its
long sword-shaped leaves. The flowers, of which
there were many rare and beautiful specimens, were
in square beds neatly arranged, and surrounded by
a light and tasteful iron railing. Between the stairs
leading to the terrace, at the southern extremity of
the Passeio Publico, is a granite fountain standing
on the backs of two huge brazen crocodiles. The
terrace was decked with numerous urns and busts,
and at the fountain a little leaden angel held by the
tail a turtle of the same metal, from whose distended
mouth issued a stream of pure fresh water into a
marble reservoir beneath. On either side of the
fountain, a little to the northward, is a triangular
obelisk of granite, about thirty feet high, on which
is the following inscription: "*Au saudad de Rio—
au amor publico.*" "To the health of Rio, and to
the public love." Around the southern wall of the
terrace are marble seats, the wall above being inlaid
with variegated porcelain. At each end of the terrace is an octangular-shaped tower about thirty feet
high; the basement and space between the two
towers being a tessellated marble pavement of much
beauty.

From the Passeio Publico, I went to the butchery
of Santa Lucia, a block of low buildings bordering

on the harbor, about half a mile above the Passeio Publico. At this place is slaughtered all the meat for the consumption of the city and its suburbs. At the time I was at the butchery, eleven o'clock, A. M., all the beeves for that day, about two hundred, had been killed, and the knights of the knife and steel were busily engaged divesting them of their hides. The butchers were all slaves, and among them I noticed several drivers with pointed sticks, with which they prodded those that were inclined to lag behind. The beef was carried on the heads of slaves to the carts of customers waiting in front of the butchery. I next went to the Hotel de Norte, where I partook of a tolerable dinner, for which I paid seventy-five cents. After dinner, accompanied by four or five friends, I visited Telegraph Hill, from which I had a fine view of the city, harbor and surrounding country. From this elevation, the scenery, as far as the eye can scan, is the most magnificent I have ever witnessed. Groves of oranges, limes, bananas and tamarinds meet the eye in every direction and perfume the air with their fragrant odors.

The city of Rio is situated on the west side of the Rio de Janeiro, or River of January, about ten miles from its mouth or entrance into the ocean, and is surrounded on three sides by a range of conical hills, most of which are covered to their summits with fruits, flowers and luxuriant herbage. In the dim distance can be seen the Organ Mountains, raising their majestic heads far above the clouds as if eager to kiss the blue vault of heaven.

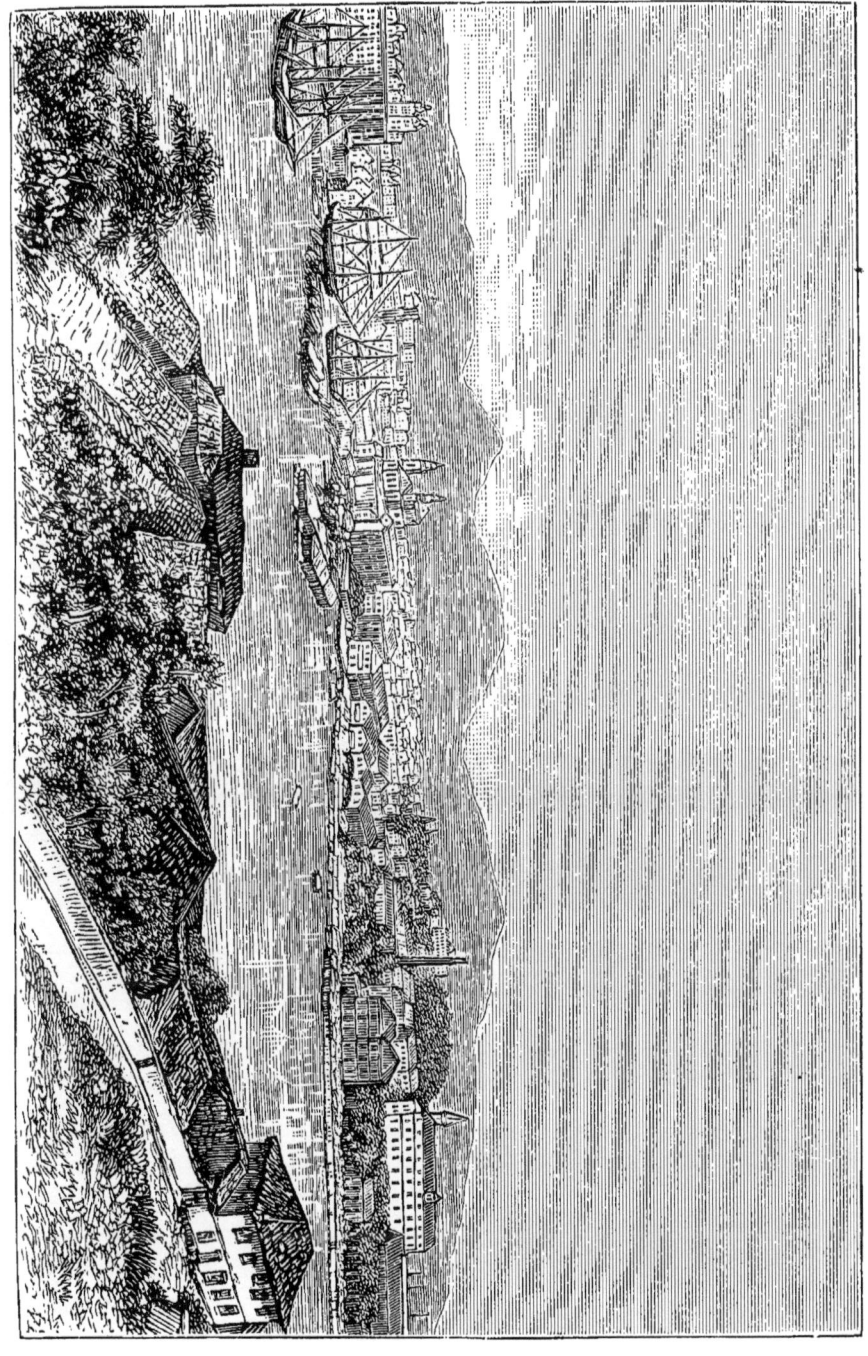

GENERAL VIEW OF RIO JANERIO.

Rio is very compactly built, and with its suburbs contains nearly as many inhabitants as New York, but does not occupy as much ground as Philadelphia. The streets, which are narrow, mostly cross each other at right angles. There are in the city several public squares, or palazas, the principal of which are the Palace Square and the Campo Santa Anna, in each of which there is a public fountain, composed of granite and surmounted by the globe, crown and cross, the Brazilian coat of arms. The Rua de Ouvidor, the Broadway of Rio, is scarcely three paces wide, without curb or sidewalks. The buildings are composed of stone, with tile roofs, the walls rough-cast, and generally two stories high. In this city, as well as in all Catholic countries, the cathedrals, convents and nunneries attract the attention of strangers. I have to-day visited several of these institutions, and the cowled monks and veiled nuns have brought vividly to mind scenes from the " Mysteries of Udolpho " and the " Children of the Abbey." The palaces of the Emperor are externally by far the most beautiful edifices in the city or suburbs.

In the evening I visited the theatre San Januaria, for the express purpose of seeing the Emperor and Empress of Brazil; but, for reasons best known to themselves, they did not appear in their box to be gazed at by the *los Americanos*. The first part of the entertainment consisted of feats on the tight-rope by the far-famed Ravel family, after which was performed a pantomime by the stock company, which amused me very much. The after-piece was a comedy, in the Portuguese language, not one word of which was intelligible to me. At the close of the performance I went to a public-house near by, kept by a German, where I invested fifty cents for the privilege of *trying* to sleep on a dilapidated sofa until daylight.

Thursday, March 8.—This morning, after breakfasting at the Hotel de Universe, I visited the Emperor's church, on the west side of Rua Direita, near the palace. An arched causeway or passage leads from the palace to the church, through which the Emperor, Empress and suite are admitted to mass. Externally, the church has a very dingy appearance, but its interior arrangements are more pleasing to the eye. As I crossed the threshold the first object that met my eye was one of the emperor's guards, whose complexion was a shade lighter than the ace of spades, with a musket at his shoulder, and stationed near the altar, at which were a dozen priests and friars, with shaven heads and black gowns, ducking and bobbing around a large silver crucifix, placed in front of a wax statue of Him who died to atone for the sins of the world. Worshipers of all ages, complexions and conditions were kneeling about the church and around the altar, there being no seats, saying mass. The walls and ceiling of the church are elaborately carved and handsomely gilded, and on each side are niches, occupied by statues of the various saints of the calendar. Around the church walls, near the ceiling, are suspended in gilt frames pictures of the apostles and scriptural paintings, several of which were executed by the old masters.

At ten o'clock, A. M., at the solicitation of Mr. Howell, our first mate, I accompanied him to the office of the American consul, for the purpose of hearing the charges to be preferred against him by Captain Fairfowl. After listening to the charges and the mate's defense, the consul discharged him from the brig. The captain and passengers of the ship *Pacific*, from New York, now in this port, are at loggerheads, and to the great joy of the passengers, the consul has given Captain Tibbets his " walking papers."

During the forenoon I visited the store of Messrs. Southworth & Sands, of New York, who have recently established themselves in Rio. The junior partner, is the son of Dr. Sands, of sarsaparilla fame, and their store is a curiosity-shop to the natives, it being a receptacle of all kinds of Yankee notions, from a jew's-harp to a Troy-built omnibus! With the gentlemanly proprietors of this establishment I spent an hour very agreeably, examining their stock of notions and chatting about matters in the United States.

In the afternoon it commenced raining, and after purchasing a few articles of tinware, for which I paid three times their value in the United States, I concluded to go on board the brig. The market being on my route to the landing, I purchased a handkerchief full of oranges at half a cent each, which fully made up the loss incurred on tinware. On arriving at the landing I was completely surrounded by the boatmen, anxious to row me off to the brig. I paid an old Portuguese five "dumps," a copper coin a trifle larger than an American dollar, to take me on board the *Osceola*, where I remained during the remainder of the afternoon and night.

Friday, March 9.—I went on shore at eight o'clock, A. M., and after breakfasting at the Hotel Pharoux, joined a party of friends who were about visiting Praya Grande, a delightful little village on the east side of the harbor and directly opposite the city of Rio. The preliminaries for our departure being arranged, we went to the ticket office at the steamboat pier, purchased tickets, fare two dumps, and seating ourselves on board the boat, were landed in thirty minutes at the south or lower landing of Praya Grande. On board the boat were several Brazilian ladies and gentlemen with their children and servants. After landing we strolled along the beach toward the northern part of the town, passing on the way orange groves and several beautiful cottages. From one of the latter issued the tones of a piano, which brought vividly to mind,

"Home, sweet home."

Passing a café, we were hailed in English by a dapper little gentlemen, who scraped and bowed like a French dancing-master. We entered his café, and after drinking a bottle of claret wine, engaged him as guide to accompany us during the remainder of the day. At the foot of a mountain, at the extreme northern part of the town, we entered, by invitation, the garden of a Frenchman, once a resident of the

United States, but of late years a sojourner in Brazil. Having passed through the garden, fragrant with the sweet odors of tropical flowers, we visited an orange grove attached thereto, containing upwards of a thousand orange, lime, lemon and pitanga trees, laden with ripe and luscious fruit, of which we were invited to partake freely, "without money and without price." That scriptural order was religiously obeyed! On leaving the orange grove, we passed a wash and spring-house, in which was a lusty wench elbow deep in soap-suds, with a little yellow-skin lashed to her back, who rolled up his white eyes and grinned a ghastly smile as we passed by him.

After leaving the cottage of the Frenchman, we stopped at a café and lunched on coffee, rolls and rancid butter. Price thirty-eight cents each. Being ready to resume our peregrinations, we looked for our guide, and were informed by the proprietor of the café that he had vamosed, for the purpose of enjoying his accustomed after-dinner *siesta*. During the afternoon we visited St. Domingo, the southern suburb of Praya Grande, for the purpose of purchasing syrups and jellies, which we were told were manufactured by a confectioner at that place. We strolled around until nearly night before we found the syrup and jelly establishment. Every one of whom we inquired seemed to put us on the wrong track. The jelly shop was kept by a French lady who had resided in New York and Philadelphia, and who spoke the English language fluently. We purchased about twenty dollars' worth of her commodities at very reasonable prices. We now chartered a sail-boat, and after placing our goods on board, bade the French lady adieu, and went on board the brig well satisfied with the first day spent in Praya Grande.

Saturday, March 10.—I went on shore this morning for the purpose of visiting the Brazilian Navy Yard, convent of St. Benedict and other places of interest. At nine o'clock, A. M., accompanied by a party of friends, I passed up the Rua Direita, crossed the Rua Piscadore, entered the Navy Yard gate, and was soon in the midst of ship-carpenters, blacksmiths, boat-builders, armorers and machinists. The Navy Yard is of an oblong form and occupies about as much ground as the United States Navy Yard at Philadelphia. There is but one ship-house in the yard, where is being constructed a sloop of war which I learned had been on the stocks for three years. In the boat-shed they were building several boats, some of which were beautiful models. The building occupied by the machinists and blacksmiths appeared to have been recently constructed, and the lathes and other machinery were imported from England, the manufacturer's name and residence being stamped on each article. In the blacksmith's shop we made the acquaintance of two of the workmen who spoke the English language—one a Scotchman, and the other a German, both of whom had visited the United States. We next visited the shot and shell foundry, in which we saw several tons of shot just turned out of the moulds. In the armory, the workmen were busily engaged manufacturing fire-arms for the use of the soldiers and marines of the Brazilian service.   As we were about passing through the yard-gate on our return, my attention was arrested by two females seated on the ground, a few yards to the left, in front of a one-story stone building with grated doors and windows.

On approaching them we learned by gestures that the building was a guard-house, and two of its inmates were their husbands.   I looked through the grated door and saw several prisoners lying on a rough deal table, on which was standing a jug of water, and by its side were two or three loaves of brown bread.   This scene having convinced me that there were persons in this wicked world whose conditions were worse than my own, I turned from the prison and the females seated at the door, and ascending the hill of San Bempo by a crooked and roughly-paved walk, soon stood before the convent of St. Benedict.

The St. Benedict is one of the oldest convents in Rio, having been erected in 1761, as I learned from an inscription over the door of the main entrance. On entering the convent, we were accosted by a monk who beckoned us to proceed to the second floor, which we reached by a heavy, antiquated flight of stairs, and passing to the left through a long, dimly-lighted hall, entered the choir, where we met a servant dusting the seats occupied by the jolly fat friars.   After examining the choir, the walls of which were nearly covered with scriptural paintings by the old masters, we went into the side galleries, from which we had a fine view of the interior of the church with its richly gilded and carved

5

mouldings, which lined the walls and ceiling, and displayed vines loaded with grapes and mingled with flowers. Standing in niches in the walls were statues of the saints gorgeously dressed, and from the frescoed ceiling were suspended two massive silver lamps somewhat dusty with age. From the church we passed into the courtyard, one hundred and fifty feet square and covered with granite flags, under which repose the dead. From the convent windows we had a magnificent view of the harbor, the Island of Cobras, the city, its evergreen hills, the azure mountains in the distance, and the vast ravines furrowing their sides. From the convent we descended a zigzag path to the street, and after a walk of twenty minutes, reached the Hotel Pharoux.

Casting my eyes in the direction of the Emperor's church, I noticed a hearse drawn by six plumed horses coming to a halt in front of it. Before I reached the church, the gold-laced coffin had been removed from the hearse and placed on a bier or altar in the middle of the floor, and the corpse exposed to view by opening the hinged lids. On each side of the coffin were half a dozen priests and friars in black gowns trimmed with white, holding in their hands lighted wax candles four feet long and two inches in diameter, the lower ends resting on the tile floor and the tops inclining slightly forward. There was also a long file of gentlemen dressed in black bearing *blazing wax candles*, on each side of the passage leading from the hearse to the bier, although it was broad *daylight!* During the funeral ceremony, the officiating priest sprinkled holy water over the corpse several times from a silver instrument somewhat resembling a child's rattle; then shook over it a censer of burning incense, which diffused its odor through the church. The ceremony being over, the priests retired from the church, and the gentlemen in black extinguished their candles and placed them in a rack. Some left the church; others removed the coffin from the bier and carried it into the receptacle for the dead, a court attached to the church. An excavation had been made in the wall, before which the coffin was placed and the lids again thrown open by the sexton. Holy water and quicklime were now thrown upon the corpse by the mourners. This part of the exercises being concluded, a requiem was chanted and the corpse left to be placed in the *hole in the wall* by the sexton and his black attendant. Having witnessed the commencement of the ceremony, curiosity prompted me to see the finale. Despite the surly looks of the sexton, I remained behind, with five or six other Americans, for the purpose of seeing the deceased placed in his narrow cell. The coffin, on being raised to the niche, was found too large for admission, but, with the aid of a crowbar, it was quickly reduced in size by knocking in the head-board and pressing down the lid upon the breast of the corpse! It was soon adjusted to the satisfaction of the sexton, and the entrance closed by a mason.

Remained on shore during the night, and slept on the soft side of a billiard-table, all the beds in the hotel being double-banked.

CHAPTER IV.

Sunday, March 11.—This forenoon, accompanied
by two friends, I visited the museum, situated on
the eastern side of the Campo Santa Anna, which
is open every Sunday from ten o'clock, A. M., until
two o'clock in the afternoon—admission free. The
museum was founded by King John VI, in the
year 1821, and is a large two-story edifice, comprising a main building and two wings. The
entrance is guarded by soldiers, and there are
attendants inside to see that no improper conduct
takes place. The museum contains eight communicating rooms. Two are devoted exclusively to
minerals of the empire, which are locked in taste-
fully-arranged mahogany cases with glass doors.

Among the minerals in the cases are ores of gold,
silver, copper, carbonates, muriates, phosphates and

(76)

sulphurets of lead, ores of iron, jasper, agate, quartz, talc, mica, coral and limestone of various kinds. There are diamonds, and also crystals of white transparent quartz two or three inches in length. The most wonderful mineral is a crystalized quartz of a hexangular shape, fifteen inches in thickness and nearly three feet in length. Its weight is not less than two hundred pounds.

The specimens of the animal kingdom belong chiefly to the empire, and consist of the gray, black and scaly ant-eater, leopard, wolf, paca, guinea-pig, besides a great variety of the monkey tribe. There is also a fine collection of sea-shells, bugs and butterflies. The collection of birds is very large, mostly natives of Brazil. Among them may be mentioned the parrot, goney, joao, grande, turdus-regius, pavao of Matogosso, crax-galiata and anherma unicorne, bemtivi, torecans and gulls. The Brazilian reptiles are also largely represented, the boa constrictor and coral-horned crotalus being the most prominent. Two live specimens of the former are at the entrance to the museum, on the first floor. The specimens of fish are all dried preparations.

In the room containing the Chinese and Indian curiosities is a cabinet of gold, silver, brass, bronze and copper coins and medals. Among the latter are likenesses of Marc Antony, Seneca, Cicero, Francis and Maria de Medicis, Cardinal Mazarin, Pope Innocent II, Henry IV of France, Marquis Cornwallis, George IV, Louis XVI, Maria Antoinette, Anne of Austria, Charles III of Spain,

Ferdinand VII, Lord Howe, and many other noted personages. In one of the rooms is the most perfect specimen of an Egyptian mummy ever exhibited.

On my return from the museum, I noticed that nearly all the stores and shops were open, and business was being transacted the same as on any other day of the week. Carpenters and cabinet-makers were shoving the plane and saw, and the sons of St. Crispin were plying the thread and bristle as briskly as ever. The inhabitants of Rio do not keep the Sabbath more holy than any other day of the week. They generally attend mass in the morning, and act as fancy dictates during the remainder of the day.

Understanding that there was to be a bull-fight in the Campo Santa Anna in the afternoon, I repaired thither for the purpose of witnessing it, but for some unexplained reason it did not take place. At the fountain in the Campo Santa Anna were a score of black wenches doing their week's washing, and the way they made the soap-suds and shirt-buttons fly was a caution to washing-machines!

Monday, March 12.—During the forenoon I visited the Academy of Fine Arts, a large two-storied stone edifice, to which visitors are admitted free. On the first floor are six ordinary sized rooms, which lead out of a spacious hall running lengthwise of the building. The walls of three of the rooms are covered from floor to ceiling with paintings, most of which are portraits of distinguished persons and citizens. There are several scriptural paintings by eminent artists. An equestrian picture of Dom Pedro II, the present Emperor of Brazil, and a full-length portrait of one of the Empress's maids of honor are the most artistic and beautiful specimens of modern oil painting I have ever seen. Two of the remaining three rooms on the first floor contain statuary in marble and plaster, none of which deserve particular notice. On the second floor I gained admission to two rooms, in one of which were mahogany cases with glass lids, containing the dies and medals of the empire. The other was hung with portraits of monks, and friars, and scriptural paintings, and had the appearance of being used as a studio, as I noticed several unfinished pictures on easels around the room. The unfinished pictures were all copies, and several compared favorably with the originals. Having examined everything worthy of notice, I passed the guard stationed at the door, and crossing Theatre Square, soon entered the Rua de Ouvidor, which I followed down to the Rua Direita, crossed the palace square, and reached the Hotel Pharoux, where I dined.

In the afternoon a party was made up, myself being one of the number, to visit the Strangers' Burial-ground, and the Emperor's Garden at St. Christoval. Taking seats in the St. Christoval omnibus, in about thirty minutes we were set down near the entrance to the Strangers' Burial-ground, which is situated on the southern declivity of a hill facing an arm of the bay of Rio de Janeiro.

The yard is inclosed by a substantial stone wall about ten feet high, and the principal entrance is through a ponderous iron gate, which was locked. Our guide soon found the sexton, and we were admitted. After sauntering about for an hour, viewing the tombstones and monuments of those who had fallen victims to disease in a foreign land, we passed out of the yard, and engaging a boat on the beach, were soon landed at St. Christoval. On stepping from the boat, the first object that met my eye was an old negro woman seated on the ground near a small fire roasting Indian corn. I purchased an ear, piping hot, and while eating it my thoughts reverted to Philadelphia and her hot-corn vendors. Passing along a little further, we met an American lady and gentleman returning from the Emperor's Garden. After a hearty shake of the hand all around, the lady informed us that herself and husband were passengers on board the ship *Architect*, from New Orleans bound for San Francisco. She also informed us that there were five other lady passengers on board the *Architect*, two of whom had lost their husbands by cholera since their departure from New Orleans. I requested her to console the widows with the fact that they were bound for a country where wives were scarce and husbands plenty. I have no positive proof that my message was delivered; but I had the consolation of knowing that, as one of Job's comforters, I did my duty. Each bidding the other adieu, and hoping to meet again in California, we parted, the lady and gentlemen returning to the city, and we continuing our walk toward the garden. We soon reached the palace yard or square, in which were lounging fifteen or twenty of the Emperor's guards in undress uniform. The palace originally consisted of a main building and two wings. The main building has recently been razed to the ground for the purpose of erecting on its site another of a different style of architecture, which, when completed, will be an imposing stone structure, four stories high with a tile roof.

The garden attached to the palace is the most beautiful in the vicinity of Rio, and is about five miles in circumference. Near the palace is a small lake, on the bosom of which the Emperor, when a flaxen-haired urchin, took his first nautical lessons, and the hull of his favorite yacht is still to be seen at the east end of the lake, high and dry on *terra firma*. Through the centre of the garden runs a stream of water over which is erected an aqueduct of solid masonry supported by innumerable arches and piers. In the garden are beautifully graveled walks which cross each other at right angles, and in many places are shaded on either side by rows of bamboos, whose tops unite and form magnificent bowers. It also contains a great variety of fruit-trees and plants, among which are the pintanga, cardo, maracaja, guava, banana, culambota, cocoa, mango, lemon, lime, caja, breadfruit, papaw arbacate, aresa, fruto de conte, genepa, sapucaia, fig, orange, palm, espinatree, legume, coffee, tea, and many plants both rare and curious, natives of the East Indies.

There was also a great variety of roses in full
bloom, which diffused a grateful fragrance through
the garden. As night was fast approaching, we
passed through the eastern gate and soon reached
the road leading to the city. The omnibus not
having arrived, we walked two miles before it overtook us, then getting on board, Jehu plied his whip
to the mules in a lively manner, and we were soon
rattling over the pavements of the city. After
supper, four of our party, myself among the number, engaged a private box at the theatre, and took
our seats early for the purpose of witnessing the
entrée into the royal box of their Majesties the
Emperor and Empress of Brazil. The Emperor's
box is on the same floor as the second tier of boxes,
and directly in front of the stage. It extends from
the floor of the second tier to the proscenium, and
has a frontage of about fifteen feet. In front was a
damask curtain looped up on each side, and the
box was surmounted by the Brazilian coat-of-arms
handsomely gilded. In the box were arranged
arm-chairs for the use of the Emperor, Empress
and suite. At a quarter before nine o'clock, the
Emperor, Empress, officers of the imperial household and maids of honor made their appearance,
the entire audience rising and remaining in that
position until the imperial family were seated.

The Emperor is an intelligent, modest-looking
young man, twenty-four years of age, fully six feet
high, with light-brown hair and whiskers, blue
eyes and florid complexion. He was dressed in a
plain black suit, with no other insignia of royalty

than a star or rosette on his left breast. He is greatly beloved by his subjects, and his constant endeavors to ameliorate their condition have gained for him the encomiums of the civilized world. I am neither a prophet nor the son of a prophet, but I predict that Dom Pedro II will make a mark on the finger-board of the nineteenth century not easily effaced.

The Empress is rather below the medium size, and looks somewhat older than her liege lord. Her eyes are blue and complexion light; hair light auburn, curling beautifully around her neck and falling in graceful ringlets on her shoulders. Her nose is large, which somewhat mars her features. When walking she inclines slightly forward. She wore a black satin dress with sleeves scarcely extending to the elbows, the edges of which, as well as the neck, were trimmed with lace edging. She wore neither rings nor bracelets, and was one of the most democratic specimens of feminine royalty I ever expect to see. The toilets of her maids of honor were gotten up more elaborately. Having become weary of gazing on royalty and a Portuguese pantomime, I left the theatre at eleven o'clock, P. M., and engaged lodgings for the night at the Hotel Pharoux.

[*Twenty-seven years later.* After the lapse of more than a quarter of a century since the foregoing was written, I have had the pleasure of again seeing the Emperor and Empress of Brazil (this time during the Centennial year in my own country), and I am happy to say that my early impressions and predictions have been fully verified. By his unostentations and gentlemanly demeanor during his brief sojourn in the United States, Dom Pedro II has won "golden opinions" from all classes of men— snobs excepted! His kindness to the California-bound passengers while in Rio will ever be held in grateful remembrance by the author of this humble tribute to a *great and good man.*

> "The rank is but the guinea's stamp,
>   The man's the gold for a' that."

Vive la Dom Pedro II!]

Tuesday, March 13.—I went on board the *Os-ceola* early this morning, and found the sailors busily engaged breaking out the hold preparatory to receiving water on board. I discovered among the cargo two barrels of pilot-bread belonging to myself with their heads stove in. After coopering the bread barrels I went below and spent the remainder of the day writing to friends in the United States. I also wrote a communication for the *New York Herald* over the signature of "S. Curtis"— my Christian name—giving a brief history of our voyage to this port, treatment of the passengers, etc., in which I went for the owners and captain of the *Osceola* in a lively manner, and concluded by giving a list of the California passenger vessels lying in the harbor of Rio.

The following passenger vessels from the United States bound for California, have put into this port for provisions and water, during the past three months:

From New York. Ships—*Sutton,* 55 days;

From a Photo taken in Philadelphia, 1876.

DOM PEDRO II., EMPEROR OF BRAZIL.

Christoval Colon, 51 days; *South Carolina,* 39 days; *Tarolinta,* 50 days; *William Ivey,* 42 days; *Pacific,* 42 days; *Apollo,* 53 days. Barks—*Josephine,* 45 days; *Express,* 52 days; *Harriet Newell,* 55 days; *Cordelia,* 39 days; *Peytona,* 54 days. Brigs—*Mary Stuart,* 42 days; *Eliza,* 43 days. Schooners—*Roe,* 39 days; *Olivia,* 48 days; *George Emory,* 43 days; *Joseph Newell,* 40 days; *Laura Virginia,* 38 days; *William G. Hackstaff,* 39 days.

From Boston. Ship—*Capitol,* 43 days. Barks —*Oxford,* 47 days; *Maria,* 57 days; *Elvira,* 47 days. Schooner—*Anonyma,* 38 days.

From Baltimore. Ship—*Jane Barker,* 42 days. Schooner—*Eclipse,* 47 days.

From New Orleans. Ship—*Architect,* 45 days.

From Norfolk, Va. Brig—*John Petty,* 50 days.

From New London, Conn. Ship—*Mentor,* 38 days.

From New Haven, Conn. Schooner—*Montague,* 40 days.

Wednesday, March 14.—During the forenoon I wrote several letters for the brig's cook and steward. A part of the brig's stores came on board this morning, which on examination proved to be of an inferior quality. The hams and bologna sausages were tainted and mouldy. At eleven o'clock, A. M., the government water-tank came alongside, and we soon filled our water-casks, barrels and buckets with fresh water, which I hope will last until we reach San Francisco.

A Russian bark, bound for St. Petersburg, arrived in this port to-day direct from California and *reports eight barrels of gold-dust* on board, taken from the *placers* of the Sacramento. The intelligence received by the bark corroborates all previous accounts in relation to the extent and richness of the California gold-mines. All hands are highly elated, and every man expects soon to become a millionaire. The Brazilians have also been attacked with the gold fever, and there are now in this port several vessels up for San Francisco. Fare $250.

After dinner I went on shore and deposited my letters in the letter-bag of a vessel which will sail for New York to-morrow. While on shore I saw a negro who was afflicted with the elephantiasis, one of the most loathsome diseases imaginable, but quite common in this country. His left leg was swollen to nearly the size of his body, and from the knee downward, protruded excrescences as large as English walnuts. The skin of the diseased limb appeared rough and scaly, and several of the toes had dropped off the foot. I saw others afflicted with this disease who had lost their lips and noses.

At sundown I purchased two bottles of wine for *medicinal purposes* and a handkerchief full of oranges, and went on board the brig.

Thursday, March 15.—Ship-carpenters and sail-makers have been on board to-day, caulking the deck and repairing the old sails. The mechanics here are mostly slaves, consequently they do not work very rapidly. A Yankee mechanic would perform as much labor in one day as two slaves in the same length of time. The slaves in this city appear to be well treated and seem happy. I asked several if they would like to return to Africa. Their reply was: *"Me no like to go back to Africa among the nigger thieves!"* The industrious slaves here, as in the United States, frequently save sufficient money to purchase their freedom. The free negroes in Rio wear shoes; the slaves invariably go barefooted.

I shaved myself to-day for the first time in two months, and, if my looking-glass does not deceive me, I look one hundred per cent. better than I did before performing the tonsorial operation. Before I applied the razor to my face it would have puzzled a physiognomist to determine which I resembled most, a man or a monkey.

In the early part of this week I purchased a shot-gun, which I left with Messrs. Garrett & Co., who are furnishing the sea-stores for the *Osceola*, and they promised to obtain a permit from the custom-house and send it off with the stores this morning. The stores were sent on board the brig but the gun did not accompany them. I engaged a boat from along-side the brig and went ashore to ascertain what had become of my gun. Mr. Garrett informed me that when the stores were sent on board the gun was forgotten, which he regretted very much, and would send it on board the next morning. Expecting to sail on the following day, I concluded to run the risk of carrying the gun on board myself. I accordingly placed it on my shoulder, walked down to the boat, was soon on board the brig and had the gun safely deposited under my mattress.

Friday, March 16.—It has been raining incessantly during the greater part of last night and to-day. During the storm last night two of our sailors deserted from the brig, bag and baggage. Our Captain is very unpopular with the crew, as well as with the passengers, and I am fearful he will not be able to ship men in this port to fill the vacancies occasioned by the discharges and desertions from the brig. We are now short two mates and three men before the mast.

The steerage passengers have learned that their table cannot be constructed unless they double-bank the second tier of berths and stow the lower tier with trunks and other baggage, in order to clear a space amidships for that purpose. The passengers have all agreed to this arrangement, and to-morrow the table will be rigged up.

At one o'clock, P. M., the steamship *Panama*, Lieutenant-Commanding Porter, twenty-six days from New York, bound for San Francisco, put into this port for the purpose of taking on board coal, water and provisions. The *Panama* is one of the line of Pacific Mail Steamers belonging to Howland & Aspinwall of New York, and on her arrival in the Pacific will ply between Panama and the mouth of the Columbia River, touching at Acapulco, Mazatlan, San Francisco and intermediate ports. By the *Panama* we received New York papers of the 17th of February, being nearly a month later than previous accounts from the United

States. The papers received were a New York *Herald* and a *Police Gazette*, which after going the round of the brig were pretty thoroughly used up. Captain Fairfowl came on board about eight o'clock, P. M., very much *fatigued !*

Saturday, March 17.—I assisted in the steerage to-day, breaking out trunks and other baggage and arranging the table. On examination we find that only twenty-six persons can be seated at the table at the same time; therefore, first come first served will be the order of exercises hereafter. We have engaged one of the passengers to act in the capacity of steward during the remainder of the voyage, for which we agree to pay him one dollar each on our arrival at San Francisco. We have inaugurated our new cook and new galley. The former answers our expectations, but the latter has been tried and found wanting. The boilers are too long. They run through the plate or top of the galley so far that there is not sufficient space for fuel, and unless this defect is remedied we shall be compelled to eat badly-cooked food until we reach San Francisco. The Captain has succeeded to-day in shipping a first and second mate and one man before the mast, which will enable us to put to sea to-morrow. The following California-bound vessels, having taken on board water and provisions, sailed to-day : ships, *Capitol* and *Jane Barker;* brig *John Petty,* and schooner *Laura Virginia.*

6

CHAPTER V.

Departure from Rio—Vessels bound for El Dorado—Auction sale at sea—A *pampero*—Its consequences—Putting a little whisky where it would do the most good—Hail-storm— Raffle for a monkey—Melee between a passenger and the steward—School of porpoises—Sudden change in the atmosphere—Its effects—All hands on an allowance of water —Horrors of a passage around Cape Horn subsiding—All-Fools' Day—"The Perseverance Mining Company"—Articles of agreement.

Sunday, March 18.—At nine o'clock, A. M., we hove up anchor, got under way and stood out of the harbor with a fair but light breeze. As we passed Fort Santa Cruz, we were hailed by the sentinel for the pass-word, which being given by the Captain, we glided along past the Sugar-Loaf, Razor Island, and were soon outside ploughing along toward our port of destination. Toward night-fall I went on deck for the purpose of bidding farewell to the highlands surrounding the harbor of Rio. The Sugar-Loaf and Sir Hood's Nose were scarcely discernible, and the highlands to the southward along the coast were fast fading from view. I bade them adieu and went below to construct airy castles and picture imaginary scenes in the far-off golden land to which I am bound.

The ship *Architect*, bark *Harriet Newell* and

brig *Mary Stuart*, bound for California, accompanied us to sea this morning. At sundown the *Architect* and *Mary Stuart* were five or six miles ahead of us, and the *Harriet Newell* about the same distance astern. Distance sailed, 25 miles. Lat. 23° 05'. Therm. at M. 78°.

Monday, March 19.—Last night a fine breeze sprang up from the eastward, which we have carried during the day. When I went on deck this morning the *Harriet Newell* was the only sail to be seen, the *Architect* and *Mary Stuart* had, during the night, left us far astern.

During the forenoon an auction sale was held by one of the forward-cabin passengers for the purpose of disposing of sundry lots and parcels of nuts, fruits and candies, which, as caterer, he had purchased for his mess, but several members thereof being somewhat impecunious, he was compelled to resort to this expedient to reimburse himself for the amount expended for the articles. Most of the goods sold at an advance of one hundred per cent. over their original cost, which left a large surplus in the pocket of the purchaser. I had knocked down to myself a box of raisins, five pounds of almonds and three pounds of filberts. The raisins, on examination, proved to be rather too highly spiced with bugs and worms to suit my taste, I therefore closed the box and put it up at raffle— eight chances, at twenty-five cents each. I did not envy the winner of the prize. I stowed the nuts in my hat-box, and flatter myself that for some time to come I shall have a dessert after each dinner of salt beef and hard-tack. Distance sailed, 140 miles. Lat. 24° 26'. Therm. at M. 80°.

Tuesday, March 20.—During last night and to-day we have been favored with an eight-knot breeze. Now that the steerage passengers have a table to eat off of, they are no better satisfied than when mess-ing on pig-pens, chicken-coops and water-casks. One thinks his messmate has more elbow-room than himself at the table; another, that he is not treated by the steward with the same degree of attention as his companion; and others imagine that a seat at the head of the table is preferable to one lower down.

Early this morning the bark *Harriet Newell* was on our lee-quarter, distant about five miles, and at sundown she was so far astern that she was scarcely discernible by the aid of a glass. Three or four of the passengers are on the sick-list, in consequence of having lived too fast while in Rio. Distance sailed, 184 miles. Lat. 27° 20'. Therm. at M. 82°.

Wednesday, March 21.—The breeze of yesterday continued throughout last night and this forenoon, and has placed us 200 miles nearer to San Fran-cisco. The two mates shipped in Rio have already become dissatisfied with the Captain, in consequence of his interference with their duty while in charge of the deck. I predict that both will be relieved from duty before we arrive in California.

At three o'clock, P. M., the western horizon became suddenly overcast with black clouds, and every indication of a *pampero* was visible. Studding-sails were accordingly taken in, royals and top-gallant-sails furled, top-sails double reefed, the spanker brailed up and everything made ready for the approaching gale, which was soon upon us in all its fury. The rain descended in torrents, and the wind burst upon us with such violence that every rag of canvas was taken off the brig and she was hove to under bare poles, in which condition she remained during the night. The gale was the most severe that we have encountered during the passage, and I have no anxiety to witness another of the same sort. The brig shipped heavy seas during the night, which completely deluged the cabins. The steerage was dry, but such another waltzing of trunks and boxes, crashing of crockery and jingling of tin pans, pots and spoons, I never before heard. Passengers, as well as baggage and dishes, were in commotion. Some of the former were gliding about clothed in a single garment; others in a state of nudity, genuine model artists, looking as ghastly as ghosts and trembling with fear. I remained in my berth, but as I could not sleep in consequence of the constant rolling and pitching of the brig, consoled myself by occasionally putting a little whisky where I thought it would do the most good. Distance sailed, 179 miles. Lat. 30° 02'. Therm. at M. 78°.

Thursday, March 22.—At daylight this morning the storm having somewhat abated, the storm stay-sail was set and the brig put before the wind. Other sails were set during the forenoon, but owing to the heavy sea, we have made very little progress. The wind at the present writing is blowing very

fresh and the waves are running mountain-high.
During the rough weather last night the steerage galley broke loose from its fastenings, and we
have had great difficulty in placing it in its former
position, in consequence of the rolling and pitching
of the brig. A sail was reported on our lee bow
this morning, bound northward. Distance sailed,
30 miles. Lat. 30° 28'. Therm. at M. 76°.

Friday, March 23.—Head-winds and cross-seas
during the last twenty-four hours have prevented
our making much progress toward our port of destination. The *pampero* has been succeeded by the
equinoctial storm, and we may be detained in these
latitudes several days by adverse winds. By way
of variety, we were treated this forenoon to an old-
fashioned hail-storm. This morning, soon after the
cook had kindled a fire in the galley, we shipped a
sea forward which extinguished it so effectually
that it could not be rekindled for several hours.
This caused a late breakfast and sour looks among
the passengers.

While in Rio, two of our passengers purchased a
monkey in copartnership, and his deviltry has
kept them constantly at loggerheads with the Captain and mates. This morning his monkeyship
took possession of the nail locker, and the mate
threatened him with decapitation should he visit it
again. This sanguinary threat having reached the
ears of his owners, they informed the mate that
they would like to be present when the operation
was performed! Distance sailed, *five miles!* Lat.
30° 23'. Therm. at M. 75°.

Saturday, March 24.—At two o'clock this morning the wind hauled around to the north, which has enabled us to steer our course. The sea to-day has been smoother and the brig has rolled less. We are off the mouth of the River La Plata, and may expect at any moment to be visited by another *pampero.*

This afternoon the owners of the monkey came to the conclusion that their pet was neither as agreeable a companion nor as profitable an investment as they first imagined, therefore they put him up at raffle, and he was won by the first mate. Distance sailed, 154 miles. Lat. 32° 13'. Therm. at M. 74°.

Sunday, March 25.—The wind to-day has been light and baffling, and the brig has headed as many different ways as there are points of the compass. The weather is becoming gradually cooler, and the breezes are bracing and invigorating. Large flocks of gulls have been flying around the brig all day.

This afternoon a large shark, a regular man-eater, was observed following the brig at the distance of about twenty yards, which caused a lively time on board. The shark-hook not being at hand, a mackerel-hook baited with pork was attached to a piece of marline and thrown overboard. His shark-ship, after swimming around the bait several times, approached it cautiously and turning quickly on his side swallowed the hook with a yard of the line and disappeared beneath the water.

Considerable excitement was occasioned this afternoon in consequence of a melee between one of the steerage passengers, a Philadelphia b'hoy, and the second steward. The former accused the latter of mixing the duff with water from the bathing-tub, which he said was

> "A lie, a d—— infernal lie,
> Upon his soul a lie!"

This somewhat excited the b'hoy's ire, and he gave the steward a blow alongside his visage which caused him to see stars at midday. Distance sailed, 139 miles. Lat. 34° 08'. Therm. at M. 68°.

Monday, March 26.—I went on deck at seven o'clock, A. M., and found the brig gliding briskly along with all drawing sails set. Since yesterday, the water has changed from a dark green to a light blue color, but whether caused by the commingling of the water of the Rio de la Plata or other causes, I am unable to state. This forenoon, while below writing, I heard a tremendous huzzaing on deck, and hurrying up I saw a short distance ahead of the brig a school of porpoises numbering several hundred, puffing, blowing, jumping, skipping and performing all manner of gymnastics. After having amused us half an hour with their feats of agility, they made their exit, playing leap-frog over each other's backs.

At one o'clock this afternoon the brig was struck by a flaw of wind, which carried away her main-royal yard. The broken yard was immediately sent down and a new one rigged and sent up. A broken spar floated past us to-day, which had probably been lost by a vessel off Cape Horn. We have to-day seen five vessels bound northward. Distance sailed, 115 miles. Lat. 35° 43'. Therm. at M. 67°.

Tuesday, March 27.—During to-day we have been surrounded by a thick fog, and the weather has been quite chilly. Flannel shirts and drawers, cloth pants and coats, which have been stowed away during the past forty days, made their appearance on deck this morning, and judging from my own personal experience, they were very acceptable. During the morning we had a fair but light breeze, which died away at one o'clock, and this afternoon the brig has been rolling and the sails flapping against the masts.

An albatross, measuring probably ten feet across its wings, has accompanied us all day, occasionally resting on the surface of the water for a few moments. The Captain being in a very bad humor with himself this afternoon, and wishing to curdle the milk of human kindness in the breasts of others, has put all hands on an allowance of water. Distance sailed, 189 miles. Lat. 38° 44'. Therm. at M. 63°.

Wednesday, March 28.—The wind to-day has been blowing fresh from S. S. W., dead ahead, and the weather has been uncomfortably cold, the thermometer having fallen twenty degrees during the past four days. If the mercury in the thermometer continues to fall in this ratio, it will be frozen in the bulb before we reach Cape Horn. Those of the passengers who did not break out their flannels yesterday, have to-day donned their red shirts and California mining boots. Owing to a strong head-wind the brig has rolled worse and shipped heavier seas to-day than on any previous occasion during the passage, which has kept both passengers and baggage constantly rolling and sliding about.

Several of the passengers have been amusing themselves by shooting gulls, albatross and other sea-birds which have been hovering around the brig throughout the day. All the birds killed fell overboard, not one was saved. Distance sailed, 94 miles. Lat. 40° 12′. Therm. at M. 55°.

Thursday, March 29.—The wind has been nearly dead ahead all day, which has kept the brig six or seven points off her course. The sea is smoother than it has been for several days past, but the weather is quite winterish. The crew has been engaged to-day preparing the brig for Cape Horn. The foretop-gallant-mast was condemned and sent down, and a new spar sent up in its place. Sails split and torn since leaving Rio have been repaired, and everything made ready for the coming rough weather.

A hook and line baited with pork, was made fast to the stern-boat this morning for the purpose of catching albatross. About ten o'clock, A. M., one was hooked, but broke loose before the line could be hauled in. This afternoon, a school of whales, numbering forty or fifty, was discovered on our weather-quarter, distant about three miles. They accompanied us until sundown, at about the same relative distance as when first discovered. Distance sailed, 85 miles. Lat. 39° 29′. Therm. at M. 53°.

Friday, March 30.—Throughout to-day we have been favored with a fair wind, and the weather is much milder. During the past four days, I have been eating salt pork and hard-tack with a relish that would astonish both Jews and Gentiles. If I carry my present appetite to California, it will be a very expensive companion, with flour at $60 a barrel and beefsteak at $1 a pound!

This afternoon, the passengers have been gathered about the deck in knots amusing themselves by playing cards, dominoes, backgammon and checkers.

A humpbacked whale made his appearance this morning within 100 yards of the brig, and after blowing several times, shook the spray from his tail and disappeared. Distance sailed, 29 miles. Lat. 39° 34'. Therm. at M. 56°.

Saturday, March 31.—The wind freshened gradually during the night, and throughout to-day has been blowing an eight-knot breeze, which is rapidly hastening us into colder weather. The weather during the past week has been very much like that of New England in the month of October—cold, but bracing and invigorating.

At the commencement of the voyage, the thoughts of doubling Cape Horn in the winter caused

"Each particular hair to stand on end,
Like quills upon the fretful porcupine;"

but the nearer I approach it, the less danger I apprehend in doubling it. We are now within 800 miles of Cape Horn, and the sea is as smooth as it was off the Cape de Verde Islands. Should the sea remain smooth and the wind continue in the same quarter as now during the next eight days, we shall have passed Cape Horn and reached the placid waters of the Pacific. Distance sailed, 128 miles. Lat. 41° 13′. Therm. at M. 54°.

Sunday, April 1.—Throughout last night, and up to meridian to-day, the wind has been light and baffling. At one o'clock, P. M., the barometer fell suddenly, and strong indications of a storm were observable, which caused the Captain to shorten sail forthwith. The men had scarcely laid down from aloft before we were struck by a white squall, which brought the brig down to her bearings and caused the spars and rigging to creak piteously. The gale soon subsided, and we were again gliding briskly over a smooth sea.

The steerage steward informed the passengers this morning that they were to have "fritters" for dinner, which caused them to eat a light breakfast and wait impatiently for the anxiously wished-for meal. At half-past twelve o'clock, the steward took his accustomed place at the steerage hatch, and placing his arms akimbo, cried out at the top of his voice: "Steerage passengers will please lay below and get their dinner!" This summons had scarcely ceased echoing through the rigging, before two-thirds of the mess were below gazing upon an *empty table.* After the rattling of boots on the ladder had ceased, the steward thrust his phiz below the hatch and asked the steerage gents if they were aware that the *first day of April* had arrived. Some relished the joke, others preferred "fritters;" but all acknowledged themselves sold. The steward, however, soon set matters to rights by providing each person with a panful of "fritters" well slicked over with molasses. Distance sailed, 102 miles. Lat. 42° 30'. Therm. at M. 56°.

Monday, April 2.—I went on deck at seven o'clock this morning, and found the brig steering her course with yards square and studding-sails set below and aloft. The weather, strange to say, instead of growing colder as we approach Cape Horn, is gradually becoming milder. The thermometer has risen four degrees during the past three days. This afternoon the wind has been blowing very fresh, and the sea has been rougher than usual, which has caused the brig to roll heavily and ship frequent seas.

The brothers Kelly and myself have to-day joined the "PERSEVERANCE MINING COMPANY," which increases its membership to seven persons. I think we are now as well prepared for mining as any company bound for *El Dorado*. The joint stock of the company consists of twelve months' provisions, three tents, two batteaux, with mining implements of all descriptions and of the best quality. The following are the articles of agreement :—

"Know all men by these presents, that the undersigned have associated themselves together under the name and title of the 'PERSEVERANCE MINING COMPANY,' for the purpose of transacting business in California, and have mutually agreed upon and adopted the following rules and regulations, by which they mutually pledge themselves to be governed :

"ARTICLE I. It is agreed that there shall be one of the company chosen, by a majority of its members, who shall be styled Director, and who shall perform the duties of President.

"ART. II. It is agreed that one other member shall be chosen as Treasurer of the company, who shall have in charge all moneys and property of the company.

"ART. III. It is also agreed that there shall be one other member chosen as Secretary of the company, who shall keep the books and accounts of the same.

"ART. IV. It is agreed that the foregoing officers shall account to the company, at all times when requested to do so, and shall also be liable to removal at any time by a majority of said company.

"ART. V. It is agreed that each member of the company shall bear his own expenses until he arrives in California.

"ART. VI. It is agreed that each member shall contribute an equal proportion of the amount required to increase the stock of mining implements, provisions, etc., for the conducting of business on their arrival in California, which shall belong to the joint stock of the company.

"ART. VII. It is agreed that any member who shall withdraw from the company, after his arrival in California, shall receive only such portion of the joint stock as may be awarded to him by a vote of two-thirds of the members of said company, and he shall also receive his share of accrued profits at the time of withdrawal.

"ART. VIII. It is agreed that in case of the death of any member of this company, the survivors shall forward to his legal representatives his share of the profits at the time of his decease, with a full and complete statement of the affairs of the company, attested by the officers thereof.

"ART. IX. It is agreed that the company shall pursue such business in California, or elsewhere, as shall be agreed upon by a majority of its members, and that the expenses of the company shall be mutually borne and the profits equally divided among them.

"ART. X. It is agreed, and we hereby pledge ourselves, to support and protect each other in case of emergency and sickness, and in all cases to stand by each other as a band of brothers.

"ART. XI. Inasmuch as the evil tendency of the use of intoxicating beverages in promoting disturbances, and in rendering persons unfit for business, and their liability to injure health, being well understood, it is hereby agreed that from and after our arrival in California, no member of this company shall use intoxicating liquors of any kind, except in case of urgent necessity.

"ART. XII. It is agreed that in case any member shall intentionally violate either of the foregoing articles, or hereafter refuse to be governed by them, he shall, after receiving his share of the joint stock and profits of the company, be expelled therefrom.

"ART. XIII. It is agreed that this company shall not be increased beyond the number of seven, unless such addition be sanctioned by a unanimous vote.

"ART. XIV. It is also agreed that all vacancies that shall occur by death, expulsion or resignation, shall be filled by persons receiving the unanimous vote of the company.

"ART. XV. It is furthermore agreed that in all matters relating to the company, the voice of its members shall be ascertained by ballot.

"JOHN HEYBERGER, "SAMUEL C. UPHAM,
"WILLIAM FETTER, "AMOS S. KELLY,
"CHARLES S. KELLY, "GEORGE WILSON,
"THOMAS S. BERGER."

The officers of "THE PERSEVERANCE MINING COMPANY" are:

JOHN HEYBERGER, *Pres't.* WM. FETTER, *Treas.*
SAMUEL C. UPHAM, *Secretary.*

Distance sailed, 112 miles. Lat. 43° 17'. Therm. at M. 59°.

["The Perseverance Mining Company," like many others formed *en route* to the new *El Dorado* by sea and land, "vanished into thin air" soon after the arrival of its members in California. George Wilson, of San Francisco, Charles S. Kelly and S. C. Upham, both residents of Philadelphia, are the only members of the above company known to be living at this time.]

CHAPTER VI.

Another gale—Salt-water coffee—Cabin stove broken—Another hail-storm—Terra del Fuego—Staten Land by moonlight—Double Staten Land—Death of Jocko, the sailors' pet—Furious gale off Cape Horn—The cook's galley capsized—Cabin passengers on a jamboree—Another gale—Drifting about in the region of icebergs—Raw pork and hard-tack—Fresh provisions all gone—Novel method of obtaining fresh grub at sea—Double Cape Horn—Boxing the compass—Passengers volunteer to stand watch—Capture of an albatross.

Tuesday, April 3.—Throughout to-day the brig has been skimming along at the rate of seven knots an hour.

We are within 600 miles of Cape Horn, and if we are blessed with a fair wind during the next five days, the *Osceola* will in all probability be pointing her head toward the north pole. This afternoon a school of porpoises played around us for several hours. The harpoon was made ready, and after several ineffectual attempts, one was finally struck, but in endeavoring to hoist him on board, the harpoon drew out and he was soon run down and devoured by his fishmates. Distance sailed, 168 miles. Lat. 45° 32'. Therm. at M. 61°.

Wednesday, April 4.—At sundown last night the wind commenced blowing very fresh, and before midnight it increased to a gale, which raged with such fury that the brig was hove to, and remained in that position until daylight this morning. Heavy head-seas have been running during the day, and the brig has been constantly plunging her head under water and shipping seas, which have completely deluged the forecastle and turned everything in that quarter topsy-turvy. The slush-barrel broke loose and jumped out of the bow-port, and a barrel of pork and the grindstone were about to follow suit, when they were secured by the cook and second mate.

This morning, the cook not having the fear of a rope's end before his eyes, treated the cabin passengers to a pot of *salt-water coffee*. The circumstance being reported to the Captain, he ordered the knight of the frying-pan and ladle and his assistant aft, and administered to each a quart of salt-water, which they drank with a bad relish, judging from the contortions of their physiognomies.

We are to-day about 40 miles distant from the eastern point of Cape Blanco, on the coast of Patagonia. During the past twenty-four hours the weather has been gradually growing colder, the thermometer having fallen ten degrees. Distance sailed, 115 miles. Lat. 47° 24'. Therm. at M. 51°.

Thursday, April 5.—Last night the wind headed us off our course five or six points, but this forenoon it hauled around fair again and since meridian we have been steering our course with studding-sails set below and aloft. The heavy seas of yesterday have strained the brig and caused a slight leak forward. The sea has been quite smooth to-day and the weather cool but pleasant. A land-bird, very closely resembling a sparrow, flew on board this morning, and after fluttering about the deck and rigging a few moments took his departure over the lee-bow and was soon out of sight. A mast floated past us this afternoon. It had probably been lost by some vessel off Cape Horn. Distance sailed, 134 miles. Lat. 49° 17'. Therm. at M. 50°.

Friday, April 6.—During last night and the greater part of to-day we have been heading our course, but owing to cross-seas have made but little progress. The weather is so cold that I have remained in my bunk nearly all the afternoon. Through the negligence of the Captain the cabin stoves have been broken, consequently the passengers have no fires to warm themselves by, which has caused unpleasant feelings. The steerage is at present the most comfortable part of the brig, and it is filled during the day with cabin passengers, some remaining during the night, preferring to sleep on chests rather than occupy their berths in the cabin.

We are to-day passing between the Falkland Islands and the coast of Patagonia, the former being about 40 miles distant. Distance sailed, 96 miles. Lat. 51° 39'. Therm. at M. 47°.

Saturday, April 7.—In the early part of last night we were treated to a specimen of Cape Horn weather in the shape of a hail-storm, which lasted about thirty minutes, during which time hail-stones, from the size of a pea to that of a marble, fell in abundance. After the storm had ceased, the wind freshened, and before ten o'clock it blew a

furious gale, before which we were compelled to
scud all night. The brig shipped seas constantly
during the night, some of which covered the deck
to the depth of three feet, carrying into the lee
scuppers everything movable. The deck over my
berth leaked like a sieve, and every time the brig
shipped a sea I received a shower-bath gratis.
Owing to head-winds and cross-seas, the brig has
been laboring heavily all day—not making more
than three knots an hour, and continually shipping
seas. The moon changes to-day, and I hope the
wind will follow suit and enable us to pass around
Staten Land and double Cape Horn. At sundown
we made Cape St. Diego, the south-eastern point
of Terra del Fuego, distant about 25 miles. Distance sailed, 143 miles. Lat. 53° 46'. Therm.
at M. 44°.

Sunday, April 8.—Last night at midnight I went
on deck for the purpose of seeing Staten Land. By
the aid of the moon, which was somewhat obscured
by clouds, I could discern the mountains about 6
miles distant towering to the clouds, their tops
covered with perpetual snow. Staten Land—rock
would be the better word—is a mass of barren
rocks 60 miles long by 15 miles wide. The highest
peaks rise several thousand feet above the level of
the ocean, and are continually covered with snow,
presenting to the mariner a prospect as cheerless as
they are barren and frigid.

It was the Captain's intention to have passed
through the Straits of Le Maire, thereby avoiding
the passage around Staten Land, but as we were

about to enter them, the wind chopped around and headed us off.

At three o'clock this morning, we passed around the eastern point of Staten Land, and at daylight were off Easter Harbor, distant 10 miles, and heading our course toward Cape Horn, which we hope to double to-morrow evening; but all human calculations are uncertain, particularly in this latitude. Before nine o'clock, A. M., we were in the midst of a furious gale, accompanied by rain and hail, which has driven us off our course and compelled us to steer toward the region of icebergs during the remainder of the day. A fair wind for twenty-four hours would place us in the Pacific to the northward of Cape Horn, but a head-wind will prevent us from reaching that point until doomsday. Several of the passengers have amused themselves to-day by catching gulls and Cape pigeons with a hook and line.

The cold weather of the past week has been too severe for the delicate constitution of our monkey. He had a chill last night, which was succeeded by a violent fever, and this morning at daylight he was so far gone that neither hot drops, quinine nor burnt brandy could save him. At ten o'clock, A.M., he bade farewell to all things sublunary, and at meridian was sewed up in a duff-bag and cast overboard. *Sic transit gloria Jocko!* Distance sailed, 85 miles. Lat. 54° 56'. Therm. at M. 43°.

Monday, April 9.—During last night the wind gradually died away, and this morning at daylight we were in a dead calm, an unusual occurrence in this latitude. At seven o'clock, A. M., a fresh breeze sprang up from the south-east, which enabled us to steer our course with all drawing sails set, and glide along at the rate of eight knots an hour.

All hands on board have been agreeably disappointed in regard to the weather which we have encountered in the vicinity of Cape Horn. Thus far it has been quite as pleasant as on the coast of North America during the month of October, and there is every prospect of a continuation of fine weather for several days. At this writing, five o'clock, P. M., we are steering our course, and the brig is bowling along at the rate of nine knots. If we can only manage to hold this breeze until meridian to-morrow, we shall most likely be to the westward of Cape Horn. Distance sailed, 94 miles. Lat. 55° 44'. Therm. at M. 44°.

Tuesday, April 10.—The wind of yesterday increased toward night, and at ten o'clock, P. M., it blew a furious gale. The brig shipped several heavy seas during the night, one of which capsized the steerage galley and broke it in several places. At midnight a huge wave broke over the forward cabin with such force as to cause several of the passengers to jump out of their berths and commence making preparations for a speedy departure for " Davy Jones's locker."

The fair wind of yesterday impressed all hands with the belief that we would pass Cape Horn before midnight last night, and upon the strength of this supposition several of the after-cabin passengers had a jollification which lasted all night and a part

THE "OSCEOLA" IN A GALE OFF CAPE HORN.

of this forenoon. The participants were as drunk as Bacchus and as merry as lords. About the time they had gotten fairly under way with a full head of steam on, the gale commenced, and, with the roaring of the elements and the carousing of the revelers, the night was rendered hideous.

This morning at sunrise the gale had somewhat subsided, but in consequence of strong head-seas we have made very little progress to-day. We are still to the south-east of the Horn, distant about 40 miles, but hope to double it to-night.

This afternoon two vessels were discovered on our weather-bow, about 5 miles distant, heading the same course as we are. One of the vessels resembles the bark *Harriet Newell*, which accompanied us out of the port of Rio. The other vessel is probably the ship *Architect*. A cold, drizzling rain has been falling all day, rendering everything on deck, as well as below, very unpleasant. The sun being obscured by clouds to-day, no observation was taken. Distance sailed, by log, 50 miles. Therm. at M. 44°.

Wednesday, April 11.—A terrific south-west gale has been blowing all day. During the forenoon the brig lay to with her helm lashed, in which condition she behaved admirably, although the waves ran mountain-high and threatened to overwhelm her at every roll. At noon the storm-staysail was set, and at this time, six o'clock, P. M., we are laying to under that sail, with the wind blowing a perfect hurricane. There are persons on board the brig who have doubled Cape Horn several times, and at different seasons of the year, and they all say this is the severest gale they ever experienced in this vicinity. When the gale commenced we were so near the southern extremity of the Cape that the loom of land was visible, and, had we been favored with a fair wind eight hours longer, we would have been steering north-west over the waters of the Pacific. To-day there has been no fire in either galley, consequently all hands have been compelled to subsist on low diet—raw salt pork and hard-tack!

At meridian we were 60 miles due south of Cape Horn. This afternoon a brig was reported on our lee-bow, distant 4 miles, laying to under bare poles. Distance sailed, 148 miles. Lat. 57° 10′. Therm. at M. 46°.

Thursday, April 12.—During last night the wind subsided considerably, but owing to cross-seas and a strong head-wind, we have made but very little progress during the past twenty-four hours. The sun arose clear this morning, and has not been obscured by a single cloud. The brig is rolling heavily, occasionally dipping her lower yards.

The steerage galley was rigged up this morning, and although in a sadly-demoralized condition, has, with attentive watching, performed its usual office quite satisfactorily.

The fresh provisions laid in at Rio for the use of the cabin passengers, gave out yesterday, and all hands on board are now placed on the same diet— salt beef, pork and hard-tack, with an occasional plum-pudding boiled in salt water for dessert!

Yesterday morning, being impressed with a desire to have something fresh for the inner man, either in the way of fish, flesh or fowl, I suggested to a friend the idea of catching a mess of Cape pigeons, which are hovering around the brig in abundance. A fishing-line was accordingly rigged by my friend, and with the hook baited with pork, he caught a half-dozen pigeons before noon. The birds were handed to me for the purpose of being cooked, which operation I performed as well as my limited knowledge of the culinary art would admit of, and at six o'clock, P. M., we sat down to a supper of roast pigeons, stuffed with pork and onions. We ate the pork and onions—*the pigeons were thrown overboard!* Distance sailed, 50 miles. Lat. 57° 59'. Therm. at M. 42°.

Friday, April 13.—Throughout last night and the greater part of to-day the weather has been cold, with frequent squalls accompanied by rain, snow and hail—genuine Cape Horn weather. Since the commencement of the stormy weather, the brig has been driven back to the eastward as far as Staten Land, and so long as this head-wind continues we shall drift still further eastward. We are further south this morning than at any time since we rounded Staten Land, and judging from the coldness of the wind, I presume we are in the vicinity of icebergs and fields of floating ice. The thermometer has fallen seven degrees in the past twenty-four hours, and being without stoves or fires brings forcibly to mind scenes in the Antarctic, related to me by an officer of the U. S. Exploring Expedition

8

who visited that icy region in the year 1839. While becalmed on the equator, a majority of the passengers were wishing for a gale—anything rather than a calm; but since we have been headed off so frequently, and driven about in these latitudes by adverse winds, the same individuals would gladly exchange positions with a vessel becalmed in the tropics, and also willingly submit to the *shaving operation* as performed by Neptune and his associates. Distance sailed, 84 miles. Lat. 58° 08'. Therm. at M. 35°.

Saturday, April 14.—Early last night the wind hauled around to the north-east, and since that time the brig has been heading her course with all drawing sails set. The wind has been fair all day and the sea quite smooth, which has enabled us to leave the frozen regions of the south pole for those of a more genial temperature, at the rate of eight knots an hour.

During the past ten days we have twice been off the pitch of Cape Horn, and have as often been driven back or headed off by adverse winds, but as there is luck in odd numbers, I hope that we shall be permitted to pass this time with flying colors. Should we be favored with a fair wind during the next twenty-four hours, we shall at the expiration of that time be so far to the northward and westward of the Horn that it will be a difficult matter for old Boreas to head us off and drive us toward the icebergs again. Distance sailed, 106 miles. Lat. 57° 34'. Therm. at M. 38°.

Sunday, April 15.—Throughout last night wind

W. N. W., with frequent squalls accompanied by hail and snow, and to-day it has been cloudy with strong indications of more snow. At meridian, Cape Horn bore north-east, distant 125 miles; therefore *we are at last in the Pacific!* Three cheers and a "tiger" for the *Osceola!*

This morning the Captain and second mate had an altercation in relation to the duties of the latter, which resulted in his being "broken" and ordered in the forecastle to do duty before the mast during the remainder of the voyage. It now remains to be seen whether the Captain will keep the "broken" mate's watch on deck or request the passengers to perform that duty, as was the case previous to our arrival at Rio de Janeiro. Distance sailed, 112 miles. Lat. 58° 11'. Therm. at M. 42°.

Monday, April 16.—During last night and the greater part of to-day it has been squally with frequent showers, which has kept the crew busily engaged shortening and making sail. We are still steering to the westward, which keeps us in cold weather, but shall probably commence running northward to-morrow, which will soon bring us into warmer weather.

Now that we are safely around Cape Horn, all hands are more anxious than ever to reach San Francisco, and in order to induce the Captain to carry a little more canvas on the brig, eight or ten of the passengers have volunteered their services to assist the crew in working her during the balance of the voyage. Two vessels were reported on our weather-bow this morning, standing to the

westward. A large school of porpoises paid us a
visit this afternoon, and when they bade us adieu
they were minus one of their number pierced with
a harpoon, but in our efforts to get him on board,
the iron drew out and he floated to the leeward.
Distance sailed, 80 miles. Lat. 58° 14′. Therm.
at M. 40°.

Tuesday, April 17.—Throughout last night
and to-day weather squally and a Scotch mist
has been falling, rendering the atmosphere chilly
and unpleasant. During the past twenty-four
hours, the brig has completely boxed the compass. Last night she headed west; this morning,
at seven o'clock, north-west; at meridian, north;
at two o'clock, P. M., south-east; at five o'clock,
P. M., south, and at this writing, seven o'clock,
P. M., she is heading south-west by west, which
course the Captain desires to run until to-morrow
noon, when, the wind permitting, he will steer
northward.

Our volunteers performed their duty last night
to the entire satisfaction of the Captain, but the
damp and chilly weather of to-day has completely
disheartened them. Three of the volunteers have
made up their minds not to stand watch to-night,
and have already turned into their berths. Distance sailed, 148 miles, by log. No observation.
Therm. at M. 43°.

Wednesday, April 18.—Last night and to-day
the rain has poured down in torrents, and the wind
has been blowing very fresh, causing the brig to
roll heavily and occasionally to ship a sea. We

steered a west course to-day, up to six o'clock, P. M., when the Captain wore the brig, and since that time we have been heading north-west, which will soon place us in mild and pleasant weather.

During the past two days, in consequence of the cloudy state of the atmosphere, the Captain has not been able to take an observation by the sun, therefore our position is not definitely known; but I am of the opinion that we are in the neighborhood of 75° west longitude, and latitude 58° south. If the Captain ascertains to-morrow that we are in 75° west longitude, we will steer our present course during the next two weeks, wind permitting. This afternoon and evening, several of the passengers have been trying to drive away dull care by playing chess, cards and dominoes. Distance sailed, 102 miles, by log. No observation. Therm. at M. 44°.

Thursday, April 19.—At midnight last night the brig was headed off her course by adverse winds, and during the remainder of the night and all day we have been heading south-west by west. Thus far, all our efforts to get to the northward have been futile. If by chance we get a slant of wind that enables us to run to the northward four or five hours, a head-wind invariably drives us back to Cape Horn. We certainly have a Jonah on board! During the day it has been squally, with occasional showers accompanied by hail.

This afternoon one of the passengers caught an albatross measuring across the wings from tip to tip, seven feet and two inches. It was captured with a hook baited with pork. Having been inspected by all hands, it was placed in the chicken-coop for safe-keeping. Distance sailed, 94 miles, by log. No observation. Therm. at M. 42°.

Friday, April 20.—At eight o'clock, A. M., we were struck by a squall which carried our foresail completely out of the bolt-rope, and the yards and masts would have gone by the board had not the passengers jumped on deck and assisted the crew in taking in sail and making things secure. The first mate had charge of the deck at the commencement of the squall, but in consequence of his tardiness in the management of the brig, he was relieved by the Captain, who immediately clewed up and furled every sail with the exception of the foretop-mast-stay sail, under which we have been laying to during the forenoon. The squall has increased to a gale, and at this time, three o'clock, P. M., the wind is blowing a hurricane, which is drifting the brig toward Cape Horn at the rate of six knots an hour. After the gale had partially subsided, the Captain called the mate aft and read him a lecture on the management of a vessel in a storm, every sentence of which was rounded off with an oath, which drove the subject home and clinched it effectually. Distance sailed, 80 miles. Lat. 57° 33'. Therm. at M. 42°.

CHAPTER VII.

Saturday, April 21.—The gale of yesterday continued throughout last night, during which time I did not close my eyes, for fear of being thrown out of my berth by the continual rolling of the brig. This storm is the severest we have encountered during the passage—the barometer at one time being as low as 29°.

Early this morning the mainsail, top-sail, spanker and jib were set, a new foresail broke out of the sail-room and bent on. Throughout the day we have been steering north-west by west, but owing to a light wind and heavy cross-seas, have made very little headway. During yesterday we must have drifted at least 75 miles to the southward and eastward, which places us in about the same locality that we were this day week. This morning a brig was reported directly astern of us, distant about 6 miles, heading north-east. Distance sailed, 64 miles. Lat. 58° 15′. Therm. at M. 42°.

Sunday, April 22.—The breeze of yesterday continued throughout last night, which has enabled us to regain what we lost during the gale of last Friday. This morning the wind chopped around to the north-west, which has compelled us to head south-west by west all day. Last night our amateur sailors again volunteered their services, and worked like Trojans, pulling and hauling at the ropes.

My feet have been very sore the past week, and to-day they are so badly swollen that it is with great difficulty I can draw on my boots. One-third of the passengers are similarly afflicted. Whether this swelling of the feet is occasioned by chilblains or the scurvy, I am unable to state, but am inclined to the belief that it is the incipient symptoms of the latter disease. Distance sailed, 130 miles. Lat. 56° 53′. Therm. at M. 42°.

Monday, April 23.—Fair wind all last night and to-day, which has enabled us to steer our course over the Southern Ocean at the rate of six knots an hour. Should this wind continue until to-morrow evening, we will have made sufficient longitude to warrant our steering a northwardly course. The weather is as coquettish as a maiden in her teens. At sunrise the mercury in the thermometer was down to 41°; at two o'clock, P. M., it stood at 50°; at three o'clock, P. M., 52°, and in two hours thereafter it was down to 45°.

Two vessels were in sight this afternoon; one a

bark, on our starboard-bow, distant about 8 miles, and the other a brig, on our larboard quarter, 10 miles off, both standing to the westward. They are, no doubt, California passenger vessels. Distance sailed, 118 miles. Lat. 57° 14'. Therm. at M. 48°.

Tuesday, April 24.—The breeze which we carried throughout yesterday died away in the evening, and during the remainder of the night it was squally, causing the watch on deck to be constantly exercising the sails. To-day we have been steering a northerly course, but owing to frequent squalls and a strong head-sea, have made but very little progress. The squalls have been accompanied by rain, hail and snow—gentle reminders of Cape Horn.

The *Osceola* seems to have fallen desperately in love with Cape Horn, and appears loath to leave, judging from the manner in which she is dodging around in this region. We are no farther from Cape Horn than we were ten days ago, and God only knows when we shall be permitted to leave this locality. A strange fatality seems to hang over us! Who is the Jonah? Distance sailed, 114 miles. Lat. 57° 04'. Therm. at M. 40°.

Wednesday, April 25.—To-day we have been steering north by west with a light wind, consequently have made very little headway. A strong head-sea has been setting down from the north all the past week, which has retarded our progress.

The Captain and mate had a growl yesterday concerning their relative positions on shipboard.

The Captain swore that his views were correct, but the mate begged leave to differ with him, which at once aroused the old man's ire, and seizing a belaying-pin from the rail, he handed it to the mate, and in language more forcible than polite, requested him to knock his (the Captain's) brains out! The mate declined to perform the sanguinary operation, and the old skipper is still left to growl whenever he feels disposed to indulge in his favorite pastime.

A homeward-bound vessel passed us this afternoon to the windward, distant about 10 miles. This evening one of the passengers shot an albatross which fell on deck. The wings were given to the steerage steward; the skin and feathers were retained by the person who killed the bird, and the carcass will be served up to-day at two o'clock, P. M., for the especial benefit of steerage mess No. 1. Thank God, I don't belong to that mess! *I can eat albatross, but I don't hanker after it.* Distance sailed, 110 miles. Lat. 55° 48'. Therm. at M. 41°.

Thursday, April 26.—Last night at eight o'clock, the Captain wore ship and stood to the westward until three o'clock this morning, when it commenced blowing a gale from the north-east which continued until noon, the brig scudding before it with canvas barely sufficient to keep her steady. At one o'clock, P. M., the wind lulled and the mainsail, foresail, jib and top-sails—the latter being close-reefed—were set, and during the remainder of the afternoon the brig has been heading a northerly course, which I hope will soon carry us into warmer weather.

One hundred days since we left Philadelphia, and we are not 30 miles to the northward of Cape Horn. Should the latter part of our voyage prove as tedious and unpleasant as the first, we shall all hail with joy the land of promise to which we are bound, whether we realize fortunes or not. If ever sixty-five individuals were more heartily disgusted with a sea voyage than are the passengers on board this brig, I have yet to make their acquaintance. Distance sailed, 144 miles. Lat. 55° 04′. Therm. at M. 46°.

Friday, April 27.—Last night at eight o'clock, the wind headed us off our course, and the Captain wore the brig and stood to the westward. At two o'clock this morning a gale crossed our path and the brig was hove to under foretop-mast-stay sail, in which position she remained until eight o'clock, A. M., when the foresail and top-sails were spread to the breeze, and since that time we have been heading northwardly and rolling over the water against a head-sea at the rate of three knots an hour. Last night it was showery, but the weather to-day has been delightfully pleasant.

An altercation occurred this morning between two of the cabin passengers, which caused a general rush toward the scene of action. During the affray one of the combatants drew a knife from his pocket, which was secured and thrown overboard before he had an opportunity of using it on his antagonist.

This afternoon a cabin passenger caught an albatross measuring ten feet four inches across the wings, from tip to tip. Distance sailed, 98 miles. Lat. 54° 46′. Therm. at M. 46°.

Saturday, April 28.—The brig has steered her course all day with all canvas set; the weather has been mild and pleasant.

Night before last, our amateur sailors declined to stand watch in consequence of the cook's having refused to serve them with their accustomed allowance of coffee during the morning watch. The circumstance was reported to Captain Fairfowl, who soon arranged matters to their entire satisfaction, and last night they were again on deck pulling and hauling the ropes as usual. The past week the gambling fever has again been raging fiercely on board, several of the cabin passengers having bucked away their last cent. Some of them have become so infatuated with this damnable vice that they have cut the buttons from their coats, vests and inexpressibles, for the purpose of playing button bluff. Distance sailed, 134 miles. Lat. 52° 50′. Therm. at M. 48°.

Sunday, April 29.—Last night the brig headed N. N. E., being two points to the eastward of her course. The weather during the night was squally with occasional showers. At eight o'clock, A. M., the Captain wore the brig, and since that time we have been making a due west course. The weather has been chilly, and this afternoon a cold, drizzling rain has been falling. Three weeks ago this morning we rounded Staten Land, and at this time we are only one degree north of the Straits of Magellan.

The old skipper turned out of his berth this morning in a very bad humor, and during the day has, to use a nautical phrase, been "working up" the sailors. They have been employed all day moving the larboard chain cable aft on the quarter deck, for the purpose of bringing the brig down more by the stern, thereby enabling her to sail faster and make less leeway. Sunday brings no rest for poor Jack.

> "Six days shalt thou labor,
>   And do all thou art able,
> On the seventh, wash decks
>   *And haul aft the cable!*"

Distance sailed, 101 miles. Lat. 51° 39'. Therm. at M. 46°.

Monday, April 30.—During the past twenty-four hours the brig has been wrestling with a head-wind and cross-seas. A cold rain has been falling since morning which has caused the passengers to remain in close quarters all day.

A faro-bank has been in operation in the after-cabin this afternoon, and several hundred dollars have changed hands. At sundown the bank was closed, but after supper it was again opened, and at this writing, eight o'clock, P. M., I hear the checks rattling on the table over my head.

The sun being obscured by clouds, no observation was taken. Distance sailed, by log, 114 miles. Therm. at M. 48°.

Tuesday, May 1.—Early last night the wind commenced blowing furiously from the north-west, and at midnight we were in the midst of a hurricane. At daylight this morning the brig was hove to, and she has been laying in that position, under the foretop-mast-stay sail, all day.

The after-cabin *blacklegs* opened their faro bank again this morning, and after gambling until noon, concluded to suspend operations until the storm subsided. Distance sailed, 35 miles. Lat. 50° 56'. Therm. at M. 48°.

Wednesday, May 2.—The gale continued to rage throughout last night with increased violence. During the night, the brig shipped several of the heaviest seas I ever saw break over the bow of a vessel. She shipped one in the early part of the evening that washed the steerage cook and a ship's boy out of the galley and carried them on an excursion down the lee scuppers as far as the companion-way, where they brought up hard and fast against a chicken-coop jambed between a water-cask and the bulwarks.

The brig rolled so heavily all night that several of the passengers on the weather-side were pitched out of their berths among the trunks and boxes. Fortunately no bones were broken.

At daylight this morning the gale subsided, the wind hauled to the south-west, and we have been heading our course with all drawing-sails set, but a strong head-sea has prevented us from making much headway. This morning all hands were put on an allowance of two quarts of water per man. This arrangement will answer very well so long as the weather continues cool, but in a warmer climate it will scarcely suffice for cooking purposes. Distance sailed, 28 miles. Lat. 50° 44′. Therm. at M. 46°.

Thursday, May 3.—Throughout last night the weather was squally with frequent showers. Since sunrise the wind has been on the increase, and strong indications of a gale before midnight are visible. A Scotch mist has been falling all day, and this afternoon the brig has been completely enveloped by a dense fog. One of the steerage passengers celebrated his birthday yesterday, and the result was that at least a dozen of his companions retired to their berths in a state of inebriation. The brig has been surrounded all day by gulls, goneys, albatross and other sea-birds. Distance sailed, 116 miles. Lat. 51° 01′. Therm. at M. 48°.

Friday, May 4.—My predictions yesterday in relation to a gale were verified. When the sun set last night the wind commenced blowing a severe gale, which continued until midnight, when it suddenly lulled and soon after we were becalmed. To-day the wind has been light and baffling, which has caused the Captain to wear the brig three times since sunrise. The weather during the forenoon has been foggy, damp and chilly.

Captain Fairfowl to-day issued a *pronunciamiento* to the blacklegs, and also gave the mate orders to furl all the sails and lay the brig to should he witness any more gambling on board during the voyage. This order created considerable excitement among the gamblers at first, but they soon cooled down and became as docile as lambs. The

Captain says, and he is in dead earnest, that there shall be no more *gambling* on board the *Osceola*, but all hands, including the cook, have permission to *pray* as long and as loud as they please. Tally one for Captain Fairfowl.

Now that gambling has been squelched, the Captain predicts a fair wind within the next twenty-four hours. We shall see. Distance sailed, 72 miles. Lat. 50° 30′. Therm. at M. 49°.

Saturday, May 5.—At eight o'clock last night the wind hauled around to the south-west, which has enabled us to steer our course, which we have been heading, with *square yards*, for the first time in thirty days, but the wind has been so light that we have made very little progress. The crew has been employed reeving studding-sail gear, and I hope that we shall have studding-sails set below and aloft to-morrow.

This morning I had a fine view of a finbacked whale, which I should judge would measure sixty feet in length. Distance sailed, 110 miles. Lat. 49° 34′. Therm. at M. 47°.

Sunday, May 6.—Throughout last night we were blessed with a fair wind, which has continued to-day, and wafted us along toward our port of destination at the rate of nine knots an hour. Several showers of rain, accompanied by hail, have fallen to-day, which have rendered the atmosphere chilly.

The weather foretop-mast studding-sail was set this morning, and it did good service until noon, when the wind hauled slightly ahead, and it was taken in. We have not carried studding-sails before in thirty days, in consequence of continued head-winds. The Captain hailed the setting of the studding-sails this morning as a good omen, and immediately ordered an additional pint of water to be served out with our daily allowance, which will hereafter be two quarts and one pint, and shocking bad water at that.

To-day the passengers have had their mattresses and blankets spread on deck for the purpose of giving them an airing, which they needed very much. Early yesterday morning a bark was reported on our lee-bow, distant about 10 miles, heading to the northward. We gained on her so fast during the day, that at sundown she was nearly hull down astern of us. Distance sailed, 140 miles. Lat. 47° 20′. Therm. at M. 46°.

Monday, May 7.—During the past twenty-four hours the brig has been steering her course at the rate of nine knots an hour. The weather is becoming more mild and pleasant, and "life on the ocean wave" seems more endurable. The passengers who have been shivering with the cold weather for the past twenty days, are skipping about the deck as lively as larks, enjoying a little sunshine. The mercury in the thermometer marked 53° to-day, being the first time it has reached that point in thirty days.

All hands were very much amused to-day by a novel punishment inflicted on one of the ship's boys. A pig, weighing twenty pounds, was slung under the right arm of the culprit by a lashing that passed over his right shoulder and around the body

of the porker.   Thus accoutred, he was ordered by
the Captain to march around the deck twelve times,
which command he obeyed to the infinite amusement of all hands, who lined the deck on either
side.   The scene reminded me of a Scotch piper.
At every step he jerked his elbow into the side of
poor piggy, at the same time pinching his ear,
which caused his porkship to discourse most shrill
and discordant music.   Distance sailed, 184 miles.
Lat. 43° 58'.   Therm. at M. 56°.

Tuesday, May 8.—We had a fair wind last night,
which has continued to-day, and the brig has been
gliding along at the rate of eight knots an hour.
The weather still continues showery, although it is
gradually growing warmer.

We have, in the last fifty hours, made nearly 500
miles on our course, which is very gratifying to
all on board.   Yesterday, when the latitude was
reported by the Captain, all hands gave three
cheers and a "tiger," which seemed to shake the
brig from stem to stern, and add fresh impetus to
her speed.

A diversity of opinion prevails among the passengers in regard to the port we shall next stop at
for provisions and water.   When we left Rio it was
generally believed that our next stopping-place
would be Valparaiso, but at present a rumor is rife
that the brig will put into the port of Talcahuana.
The old skipper is so obstinate that he will not
gratify the passengers by informing them in which
port he will drop anchor.   Distance sailed, 190
miles.   Lat. 41° 06'.   Therm. at M. 55°.

Wednesday, May 9.—Fair but light wind during the last twenty-four hours. The weather is delightfully pleasant, and all hands are on deck indulging in a sun-bath.

The agony is over. This morning the Captain altered the course of the brig, and since that time we have been steering direct for Talcahuana, where we hope to arrive day after to-morrow. This afternoon, at the request of the Captain, I made out a list of naval rations for eighty-two persons for seventy days. The provisions will be purchased at Talcahuana, and the probability is that we shall not stop again until we reach San Francisco. This evening one of the passengers had a severe attack of the cramp colic which came very near causing him to lose the number of his mess. Distance sailed, 180 miles. Lat. 38° 54'. Therm. at M. 57°.

Thursday, May 10.—We are still blessed with a fair wind, and are jogging along at the rate of six knots an hour. Royal yards were sent up this morning, and we have carried royals and studding-sails during the day. The anchors were gotten over the bow this afternoon, the chain cables hauled forward and shackled, and everything forward made ready for coming to anchor. During the afternoon the tops and yards have been crowded with passengers watching for land, but they have been disappointed, no land being visible at sundown.

Yesterday morning, the second mate was called aft by the Captain and restored to duty, and during the remainder of the voyage he will be *entitled* to the *privilege* of sleeping in the steerage and eating his meals in the cabin or galley. A school of sperm-whales made their appearance yesterday afternoon and accompanied us for several hours. Distance sailed, 143 miles. Lat. 37° 50′. Therm. at M. 59°.

Friday, May 11.—We steered our course all last night, but this morning the wind hauled around to the northward and headed us off three or four points. At meridian the Captain informed us that we were 40 miles to the leeward of Talcahuana, therefore there is little hope of reaching that port to-morrow unless the wind becomes more favorable.

This forenoon land was reported half a dozen times by different individuals, but like the Frenchman's flea, when they looked the second time it was not there. At sundown, however, *terra firma* was really discovered on our lee-bow, distant about 30 miles. Another school of whales visited us this afternoon, and after following in our wake for an hour turned flukes and disappeared. Several of the passengers have been busily engaged skinning and stuffing albatross and other sea-birds, but whether they will ever reach the United States, remains to be seen. Distance sailed, 112 miles. Lat. 37° 12′. Therm. at M. 59°.

Saturday, May 12.—The wind continued ahead all night, and in order to work the brig as far to the windward as possible, the Captain wore her at the commencement of each watch.

At daylight this morning, the Island of Santa Maria and the Paps of Talcahuana were distinctly in view; the latter on our weather bow, distant about 30 miles. We continued beating toward the harbor during the forenoon, and would probably have come to anchor ere this had we not encountered a norther, which compelled us to give the land a wide berth; therefore the Captain wore the brig and stood to the westward, which course we are steering at this time, eight o'clock, P. M. A cold, drizzling rain has been falling at intervals this afternoon, which has kept the passengers in their quarters.

The Captain and first mate had another growl in relation to the duty of the latter, and during the wrangle the lie direct was given on both sides. The old skipper swears that he will discharge the first mate on our arrival in Talcahuana, and the second mate says if the Captain does not serve him in like manner he will take the liberty of discharging himself. It is probable that both mates will be discharged at that place and other officers shipped to fill the vacancies. Distance sailed, 40 miles. In consequence of being in sight of land no observation was taken at meridian. Therm. at M. 68°.

Sunday, May 13.—The norther of yesterday continned blowing furiously until two o'clock this morning, when it suddenly abated. Two hours afterward, the wind hauled around to the northwest, and the Captain wore the brig and stood to the northward and eastward, which direction we have continued all day. During last night we were driven so far to the southward and westward that we did not make the land again until five o'clock this evening. At sundown we were about 15 miles

to the windward of the harbor of Talcahuana.
Owing to the darkness of the night the Captain
will not attempt to run in, but will lay off and on
until morning, when, if the wind remains fair, we
shall run into the harbor. The passengers have
been looking anxiously for land throughout the
entire day, and several have dressed themselves for
shore in order to be in readiness for the first boat
that leaves the brig after the anchor is down.
Distance sailed, 70 miles. Lat. 36° 35'. Therm.
at M. 62°.

CHAPTER VIII.

Put into the wrong harbor—Passengers go ashore—Reception by the natives of De Chatta—Deserters—Dine with the Alcalde—Ascertain our whereabouts, and start for Talcahuana—Scenery *en route*—Chilian peasantry—Their respect for the dead—Primitive wine-press and threshing-machine—Quarter of a century later—Henry Meiggs—His arrival in Chili—Brief sketch of his eventful life—Peace to his ashes.

Monday, May 14.—Last night about eight o'clock we came very near running aground on a reef off the harbor of Talcahuana, which caused a panic among the passengers. We hugged the land closely during the night, and at daylight this morning discovered through the fog an opening, into which we ran, the Captain supposing it to be the harbor of Talcahuana, but soon discovering his mistake, let go the anchor. When the sun had dispelled the fog, we found ourselves in a small bay, the name of which we could not determine. We could not put to sea, as a stiff breeze was blowing directly into the mouth of the bay; therefore the Captain concluded to go ashore and ascertain his whereabouts. The skipper gave the passengers permission to accompany him, and the boats were soon filled and pulling for the shore with willing hands. We landed near a mud hut with a thatched roof, which was occupied by an old man and woman, who received us with a hearty welcome, and set

(139)

before us wine, bread and apples, to all of which we did ample justice, and for which our host declined to receive any remuneration. We, however, prevailed on him to accept a cigar from each of us. We endeavored by signs and gestures to ascertain the name of the bay in which the brig was at anchor and its distance from Talcahuana. To the former question he shrugged his shoulders and shook his head, and to the latter he pointed to the southward. The old man soon started over the sand-hills to the northward and beckoned us to follow. From the top of the first hill we discovered a settlement about a half-mile distant, consisting of about twenty mud huts, for which we started at full run. On our arrival in the village the men met us with fear and trembling, and the women and children took refuge in the huts and looked cautiously at us through the cracks and holes in the walls, as we passed.

Among the first party that met us at the entrance to the village were a Yankee and an Englishman, who had deserted from a whale-ship at Talcahuana and were *en route* to Valparaiso, where they intended to ship for San Francisco. From the Yankee, we learned that the *Osceola* was at anchor in the Bay De Chatta, 9 miles to the northward of the harbor, and 27 miles from the town of Talcahuana. We also learned that there was a road leading to the village of Tome, distant about 7 miles and situated on the north-east side of the bay of Talcahuana, from which place we could embark in whale-boats and reach Talcahuana before night.

The Captain assented to our proposed adventure, and, after dining at the house of the alcalde, myself and thirteen other passengers started for Tome, where we arrived at five o'clock, P. M.

The road was very muddy and slippery, caused by the rain of the previous night, yet the scenery through which it wound, and the numerous picturesque views of the Bay De Chatta and harbor of Talcahuana, doubly repaid us for the fatigue endured while performing the journey. The peasantry of Chili are the most unsophisticated and hospitable people I have ever met. During our journey across the mountains we frequently stopped at their huts for *water*, and they invariably offered us *wine*, for which they declined to receive any compensation. At one hut at which I called for a drink of water, the *señora* was eating a quince, one-half of which she presented to me and insisted on my eating it. I complied without much persuasion, as fruit of any kind was a luxury after having been deprived of it for forty days. On the road we passed several apple-orchards, vineyards, strawberry patches and fields of wheat. At nearly all the road-crossings, I noticed rudely-constructed crosses, one of which, fashioned more smoothly than the others, was entwined with evergreens and fancifully decorated with flowers—the work, most likely, of some dark-eyed *señorita*, who delighted in performing this office of affection over the grave of a lover or brother.

Chilian wine possesses a peculiar flavor, which I could not account for until I had witnessed the pro-

9

cess of manufacture, which is decidedly primitive. A large tub is partly filled with grapes which are crushed by the naked feet of the natives, and after fermentation the juice is bottled and labeled wine. In justice to the grape-mashers, I will add, they always wash their feet—after leaving the tub.

A Chilian threshing-machine is also quite as primitive and novel as the wine-press. The thresh-ing is executed by mule-power, without the aid of machinery. A hard-beaten path or circle, very much resembling a circus-ring, is formed around the wheat-stack, and when ready for operation the sheaves are thickly strewn around the circle, and mules of all grades, good, bad and indifferent, are turned loose into the inclosure and kept moving lively to the music of the whip until the grain is thoroughly separated from the sheaves. A Chilian threshing-machine never requires oiling, but it sometimes becomes obstinate and kicks up behind.

[With the reader's permission, I desire to digress a moment from the thread of my narrative. A quarter of a century has wrought wonderful changes in the Republic of Chili. The wooden plough, primitive wine-press and threshing-machine have been supplanted by the introduction of modern and improved Yankee appliances. The world moves, and Chili now occupies a front seat in the car of progress!

To a single man, an American, is due in a large measure her wonderful progress during the past twenty-five years, and that man was the late HENRY MEIGGS, who died at Lima, Peru, on the 29th day

From a portrait, by the National Bank Note Co , N. Y.

of September, 1877, aged sixty-eight years. Harry Meiggs was, in many respects, one of the most remarkable men of the present century. The following brief history of his eventful life, gleaned from various sources, is believed to be correct:

Henry Meiggs was born in Greene County, N. Y., in the year 1811. He began life in Catskill as a lumber merchant, with the late James Milliard, who at that time was one of the most extensive lumber dealers between New York and Albany. Mr. Meiggs lived in Catskill until he was twenty-five years of age, going from there in 1835 or 1836 to Williamsburgh, L. I., where he again went into the lumber trade with Minor Keith, now living near Babylon, L. I., who married his sister, Clara Meiggs. Keith was formerly from Cairo, Greene County, and brother-in-law of General George Beach, ex-State Senator, who married his sister.

Mr. Meiggs remained with Milliard several years. He was the leader of the choir in St. Luke's Church. He was well versed in the lumber trade, highly respected, a man of tremendous energy, physically a perfect athlete, good-natured and gentlemanly. Speaking of his fists—you should have seen them! But perhaps you have seen those of the late Tom Hyer—Tom's manleys were not the smallest.

Several friends went down to the Hook with Meiggs when he sailed for California in 1849, on board the old Havre packet-ship *Albany*. A party of Catskill men accompanied him.

He arrived in San Francisco in July, 1849, where he sold his ship-load of lumber at twenty times its cost, making a clear profit of $50,000 on the venture. Then, with consummate discretion, he took a subordinate position in a lumber-yard, and studied all the phases and premises of the situation before he risked a dollar of his own capital. Foreseeing the future greatness of San Francisco and the inevitable demand for lumber, he quietly matured schemes for a grand success. When everything was ready, he hired five hundred men, sent them into the forests of Contra Costa County, felled the choicest trees in that then densely-wooded region, hauled them in saw-logs to the shore of the Bay of San Francisco, built them into huge rafts, floated them to a wharf which he had constructed, converted them into lumber by the agency of a steam saw-mill which he had erected, and made $500,000 in gold by the operation.

Thenceforth until he fell, Henry Meiggs was a foremost man in California in business, in municipal politics and in social life. He had three manias —land, lumber and music. His land and lumber operations were conducted on a scale of unprecedented magnitude; and he was popularly believed to be the richest man on the western coast of America. But, when the great financial pressure of 1854 seized California with its paralyzing grip, bankruptcy came upon him like an armed man. He rose to the contest with such enormous strength and such resourceful genius, that, had he sought only to save himself, he might have come off victorious; but, with the ill-judged generosity which was a pervading element of his character, he attempted to save all his friends, and was by them dragged down into bottomless ruin.

In the frenzy of that death-struggle Mr. Meiggs succumbed to the tempter. He was a restless, alert and enterprising man, having at the same time a great deal of good nature, frank, open, obliging, doing a good turn for others, and getting a great many favors in return. Among the pioneers he was a marked man. He was elected to the Board of Aldermen as early as 1851, and served very acceptably for two or three terms. He ranked among the better men who at that time were connected with the municipal government. During the latter part of his service as alderman he became interested in street contracts, while engaged largely in the lumber business. He built the long pier known as Meiggs's Wharf, and probably did more than any other man to develop the North Beach side of the town. He built Music Hall, on Bush Street, on a part of the site of the present Occidental Hotel. At that time Harry Meiggs was one of the most influential men of the city. His reputation was good, and although he was a venturesome man, yet he could command an almost unbounded credit.

Captain Jacob Cousins, who was master of the bark *America*, in which Meiggs made his exodus, says that on the 26th of September, 1854, he was in the cabin of the bark conversing with Captain Wiggins, who was then in command of the vessel, when Vickery Seaman, a warm personal friend of Meiggs, and connected with him in business, came aboard and announced that he had bought the vessel, and asked Captain Cousins if he would take charge of her. The Captain asked where the vessel was going, to which Seaman replied, " Probably to Australia with passengers, and I want you to ballast the vessel and get ready for sea as soon as possible."

The Captain knew that Meiggs was very much embarrassed financially, and suspected that he was to be the principal passenger, but said nothing of his suspicions, simply accepting the command. The vessel was fitted up just as any ordinary lumber coaster, as far as cabin accommodations were concerned, with very little furniture, and no carpet on the floor. The only extra expense incurred for the comfort of the expected passengers was in furnishing two small state-rooms forward for officers' quarters, and the purchase of a second-hand sofa for the cabin. On the 3d of October the Captain reported the vessel ready for sea, and about nine o'clock the same evening, Seaman came on board and told Captain Cousins that Henry Meiggs and his family were the passengers going in the ship. At midnight Seaman and the Captain went ashore in the ship's boat alone, landing at Broadway wharf, where they left the boat and went up to Mr. Meiggs's residence. They were met at the door by Mr. Meiggs, who took the Captain by the hand, saying, " Captain, this is hell, but I can't help it." In the house, besides Mrs. Meiggs and her three children, were Ned Seaman, a young man named Gilchrist, a clerk in Meiggs's employ, John G. Meiggs, David Thayer, a cousin of Meiggs, and two servant girls. The party sat and talked until three o'clock in the morning, during which time Meiggs spoke freely of his troubles. As the clock struck three, Captain Cousins announced that it was time they were going on board. Meiggs jumped up, put on his hat, and giving it a knock on the top, said, "I'm ready." John Meiggs then produced a sack containing $10,000 in gold, which was emptied out on a table and divided into two equal portions, Captain Cousins taking one-half and Henry Meiggs the other. This is all the money that went on board of the vessel. The entire party then walked down to the wharf, where Gilchrist and Ned Seaman took leave, and the rest getting into the boat, the Captain sculled them out to the bark. In the morning a thick fog hung over the bay, and there was not a breath of air stirring. A tug was engaged to tow them out to sea, but the fog was so dense that they could not find their way out through the Golden Gate, and the vessel was anchored off Fort Point.

About four o'clock in the afternoon they again got under way, and were towed out as far as the North Head. After making a few tacks, the Captain found that the tide was drifting them back into the bay, and he was again forced to come to anchor. At high water, the Captain hove up anchor and drifted out with the tide in a dense fog. Toward morning a light wind sprang up from the land, and by daylight they were half-way to the Farallones.

There they lay becalmed for two days, but the fog was so thick that they felt no uneasiness about being followed. During all this time, Mr. Meiggs was calm and cheerful, not showing the slightest sign of excitement. The story about the pistol in readiness to commit suicide the Captain pronounced absurd, as the only fire-arm on board was a revolver belonging to himself, which was never loaded. A breeze finally came, and the vessel was kept away to the southward. After getting clear of the land, Mr. Meiggs, in answer to an inquiry as to where he wished to go, said to the Captain that he might go where he pleased, but that he should like to see some of the South Sea Islands, and then go to Australia or Chili. They first went to Otahiti, where they remained thirteen days, leaving there just three days before the papers from San Francisco, with an account of Meiggs's flight, arrived. They then touched at Pitcairn Island, where they lay two days, and from there sailed for Talcahuana, Chili. Meiggs landed there and took his family up to the city of Concepcion for a short time.

He engaged as sub-contractor of bridges on a railroad then in process of construction in Chili. His remarkable executive ability drew attention to him. He was a driving man, and could get more work out of native laborers than any one else. The story of his sudden departure from San Francisco injured him in his early efforts. But soon after ex-Governor Bigler became Minister to Chili; a kind-hearted man, who was disposed to look on the better side of Meiggs's life. The fact that Bigler recognized him and was on friendly terms with him, produced a favorable impression upon the people. Meiggs could not be a very bad man, if the American Minister was disposed to overlook his irregularities. A short time afterward, he contracted with the Chilian government to complete the Santiago and Valparaiso Railroad in four years, for $12,000,000. He completed the work in about two years, making a clear profit of over $1,300,000. Then followed other gigantic railroad enterprises, chief among which was the railroad from Arequipa to Mollindo, in Peru, completed in 1871, from which he derived a very large profit. He celebrated the completion of this road by a lavish expenditure of money for a public dinner and for gold and silver medals, the outlay being not less than three-fourths of a million dollars. He afterward contracted for six railways in Peru, most of which he completed, the longest being that which extends from Callao to the summit of the Andes and beyond, and which was intended to tap the rich valleys near the head waters of the Amazon River. It was the most stupendous enterprise ever undertaken by one man. The engineering on this railroad is one of the marvels of the world. But the road did not pay, and for two or three years Meiggs fell into financial embarrassments. He seems at all times to have had the confidence of the government, and it is understood that the Peruvian government indorsed all his railroad paper, although this did not bring him out of his difficulties. He was the financial brains of Peru. His last project was to tap some famous silver mines and make the transportation of the ores to the coast a profitable business for his road. Had he lived, he would probably have developed a new era of silver-mining in Peru, in connection with his railroad enterprises. His financial troubles no doubt shortened his life by many years. He carried a load which finally crushed him. As a railroad builder, he stood in the front rank. He was a man, also, of considerable taste. His residence near the road, between Callao and Lima, was one of the grandest palaces occupied by any private individual in South America.

A few years ago, the friends of Meiggs in California sought to have his disabilities removed, so that he might return to that State. A bill to this effect became a law, but he never returned. He provided for the redemption of his outstanding paper in that State, and to a great extent *he redeemed the great error of his early life.* For that error nothing now need be said by way of palliation. It was the cloud on the life of a man whose after-career was an honorable record, and who was, in respect to great enterprises, the most conspicuous man of modern times.

Brave, noble, generous, chivalric Harry Meiggs! We all recollect the blazing cathedral at Santiago, and how he risked his own life to save the lives of others. That was Meiggs all over. As to his failings, let him that has none cast the first stone. Those who knew him, loved him. *They will drop a tear to his memory.*]

CHAPTER IX.

TOME contains about two hundred *adobe* huts
with thatched roofs and earth floors, and a population of about one thousand persons. Among its
residents are fifteen or twenty Americans and Eng-
lishmen connected with the flouring mills, and they
are literally coining money. Dogs are as plentiful
in Tome as negroes in Rio, and fleas are abundant
both in and out of doors. Bow-wow meat is considered as great a delicacy with the Chilians as is
rat flesh among the inhabitants of the Celestial Empire. I saw a dog on the stall of a butcher dressed
ready for market, which circumstance will prevent
me from eating mutton during my stay in Chili.
Whistling was strictly prohibited in that market.

At sundown we chartered a whale-boat for $10
to convey us across the bay to Talcahuana, distant
21 miles, and after shivering in the night-air for
four hours, arrived at our destination.

(153)

On our arrival, we repaired to the Red Lion Hotel, kept by a Yankee of the name of Keen, where we partook of a miserably-cooked supper for which we paid three *reals* each. After supper we informed the landlord that we wished to retire for the night, but imagine our surprise on being told that he had no beds. He informed us that lodging *was not on his bill of fare*, boarders not being lodged at any of the hotels in town. He very politely informed us that we could be accommodated with lodgings by the *señoritas* about town, they being the only persons authorized to take in strangers during the night. Several of the party followed the directions of the landlord, but myself and ten others obtained permission to make a field-bed on the dining-tables, where we slept soundly until morning, although the fleas punctured us severely.

Tuesday, May 15.—After breakfast, accompanied by a party of friends, I visited the market, a rudely-constructed one-story frame building, resembling very much a row of sheds, inclosing a hollow square. The area or court, about eighty feet square, at the time of our visit was occupied by a squad of half-naked natives pitching *reals*, a silver coin of about the value of one dime United States currency. The sheds inclosing the area were divided into stalls, in which were exposed for sale flesh, fish and fowl of various kinds, and fruit in great abundance. The pears and grapes were truly luscious.

From the market we strolled leisurely along the beach toward the southern part of the town for the purpose of visiting the coal mines. The bituminous coal taken from these mines is of a good quality and yields a fair profit to the owner, an Englishman, long a resident of the country.

On the beach to the southward of the coal mines we discovered the bones of a huge monster, which we conjectured to be a mastodon, but I have since learned that it was the skeleton of that leviathan of the deep—a *whale*.

Having heard the South American muscles very highly spoken of by epicures, I resolved upon testing their quality. I accordingly repaired to the boat of a fisherman and by gestures made known my wants to the owner. A fire was soon kindled on the beach, and a quantity of bivalves placed around it, and, as fast as roasted, I devoured them with a gusto that would have caused a blush on the face of a New York alderman.

In the afternoon I attended the funeral of a young man belonging to the whale-ship *Franklin* of New Bedford, who was poisoned by one of the cyprians of Talcahuana during a fit of jealousy. The poison was administered in wine, and he survived the fatal drug forty-eight hours. His remains were followed from the custom-house landing to the burial-ground by a procession of over five hundred Americans, a majority of whom belong to the California passenger vessels at anchor in this port. At the grave a chapter was read from the Bible and an impressive and appropriate prayer made by the doctor of the ship *Trescott* of Boston. At the conclusion of the prayer the coffin was lowered into the grave, and the "clods of the valley" soon hid from mortal ken the remains of one who, but a few months previously, had left the home of his boyhood with buoyant spirits and elated hopes to be cut down in a strange land, without father, mother, sister or brother to soothe his last moments or listen to his dying prayer; but he died surrounded by *friends*, and his remains were deposited in their last earthly resting-place by his *own countrymen*, who dropped many a tear on the grave of the young whaleman who had found a premature grave in a foreign land.

In the evening, accompanied by five or six friends, I strolled about the town for the purpose of "seeing the elephant" in Chili. We visited several *fandango* establishments, well filled with mixed audiences, who were

"Tripping the light fantastic toe,"

to the music of the castanets and guitar. The Chilian women—those whom I have seen—are not very prepossessing. They are low in stature and inclined to corpulency, which gives them a squatty appearance. Their hair and eyes are jet black, and complexion a light copper color. Their cheekbones are very prominent, and the general contour of their faces reminds one very much of the North American Indians. They paint highly, and, like their American sisters, are passionately fond of dress, invariably preferring bright and gaudy colors. The males are somewhat taller than the females, but in complexion and general features resemble them very much. They are generally an idle, indolent class of people, laboring only when necessity compels them to do so. The Chilians are blessed with a soil as fertile as any on which the sun shines, and their climate is a perpetual summer; yet, with all these natural advantages, they remain a poor, flea-bitten, priest-ridden people! In the cities and large towns native labor commands only one *real*, twelve and a half cents, per day, and in the country, scarcely half that amount. American and English mechanics receive from $3 to $10 per day, and clerks and accountants from $1,500 to $2,000 per annum.

At night, I occupied my former quarters on the dining-table at the Red Lion, with fleas here, there and everywhere, but not one could I catch.

Wednesday, May 16.—Early this morning I visited the slaughter-house, situated on a small stream in the northern suburb of the town. During the half-hour I remained there, some six or eight beeves were killed and dressed ready for the market. Beef in Talcahuana is remarkably cheap, selling on an average at three cents per pound. On my return to town I passed half a dozen dark-eyed *señoritas* seated on the ground around a spring of water making their toilets. As I approached them, they arose and saluted me in the language of the country, which I could not understand, but presume it was complimentary. I therefore raised my hat, made one of my best bows and passed on.

On reaching the town, I stopped at a ten-pin alley kept by a Yankee from New Bedford, where I met

eight or ten of my fellow-passengers just arrived
from De Chatta, where the *Osceola* lay wind-bound
when they left her at three o'clock yesterday afternoon. They left the brig at so late an hour that
they were benighted on the road and compelled to
remain over night at the *hacienda* of a farmer, who
treated them with great kindness and hospitality.
They were feasted on eggs, bread, apples, grapes and
wine during the first part of the night, and during
the latter part, by way of variety, were treated to a
little flea-botomy.

From the ten-pin alley we went down to the custom-house landing, and looking toward the mouth
of the harbor saw a brig beating in which proved
to be the *Osceola,* and in about two hours she came
to anchor off the town. After the brig had been
boarded by the Port Captain and Custom-house
Officer, we chartered a boat and went on board. As
soon as we reached the deck the Captain informed
us that the brig, by running into the Bay De
Chatta, had committed a breach of the marine
laws of Chili and, he feared, would be confiscated.
The Captain of the port informed Captain Fairfowl, that the *Osceola* with her cargo was liable to
confiscation, in consequence of the passengers having
landed before the vessel had been boarded by the
port officers. I think we shall be able to prove to
the entire satisfaction of the Chilian government
that we put into De Chatta by mistake, and that no
contraband goods have been landed from the brig.
I fear we shall be detained in port longer than may
prove agreeable, and perhaps compelled to pay a

fine; but I cannot believe that the brig and her cargo will be confiscated. If so, God help us passengers.

Having slept very little during the two previous nights, I stripped off my clothes, shook the fleas out of my pantaloons and turned into my berth with the hope of enjoying a good night's rest, and I was not disappointed.

Thursday, May 17.—I went on shore at eight o'clock this morning and joined a party of friends who were about to start on foot for the city of Concepcion, 9 miles distant. We set out, staff in hand, and after traveling three hours over a sandy road, arrived at the city of a thousand earthquakes very much fatigued and as hungry as half-famished wolves. On the road we met several Chilians armed to the teeth, but we passed unmolested, although those Job's comforters, the Talcahuanans, informed us that we would be lassoed and robbed *en route !* Passing through a thicket of *chaparral,* we saw several of the cut-throat gentry near the road mounted on ponies, with lassos hanging in coils over the horns of their saddles. As we passed them they cried out in broken English, " California !" and spurring their animals, soon disappeared in the bushes. On our arrival in the city, we ordered dinner at a hotel kept by a Yankee from the land of baked beans and pumpkin pies, of the name of Brooks. Our dinner consisted of boiled eggs, stewed chickens, beefsteak and potatoes, with a dessert of cheese, grapes and pears, which we quickly dispatched. After dinner I had a chat

10

with Brooks, who informed me that he deserted from a whale-ship on this coast six years ago, and in the meantime had worked at brickmaking, shoe-making, carpentering, butchering, and had during the past four months kept a hotel, which he informed me was the luckiest move of his life. He said he was coining money. At parting I shook him heartily by the hand—for he had given us a good dinner at a reasonable price—and wished him continued success in the hotel business. He thanked me, and added, when business got dull he would pull up stakes and squat in California.

After leaving the Yankee landlord, we strolled through the city for a short time, and toward night clambered to the top of a mountain near by for the purpose of viewing the city and surrounding country. From our elevated position we had a magnificent view of Concepcion, the surrounding country and the River Biobio, winding at the base of green hills and furrowed ravines, on its way to the Pacific.

The city of Concepcion is situated on the northern bank of the Biobio, about 10 miles above its entrance into the ocean, and is built on a plain, surrounded on three sides by high hills. Concepcion, at this time, contains about thirteen hundred one-story houses and mud huts and a population of fifteen thousand inhabitants, one-eighth of whom are foreigners. In the year 1836, the entire city, with the exception of three houses, was destroyed by an earthquake, and all the buildings erected since that time, with two exceptions, the cathedral and the residence of the governor, are one story high. Every attempt during the past hundred years to add an additional story to the former has proved abortive. Before the walls had become thoroughly dry, an earthquake shock would crack them so badly that life and limb required their removal. But hope on, hope ever, seems to be the prevailing motto with the Chilians, and I presume the process of shaking down and rebuilding will continue indefinitely. The habitations of the poorer classes are built of *adobes*, with thatched roofs and earth floors. The wealthier classes live in more substantial buildings, the walls being fully three feet in thickness, and in many instances constructed of kiln-burned bricks. The roofs are mostly covered with tiles composed of the same materials as the bricks, and the floors are also constructed of large oblong bricks or tiles, and in many cases covered with Brussels and Turkish carpets of rare and exquisite workmanship. The dwellings of the aristocracy are built in the form of a hollow square, the area or court in the centre answering the double purpose of house and stable-yard.

This being Ascension Day, and the inhabitants zealous Catholics, nearly all the shops and other places of business were closed; consequently, the city presented rather a sombre and gloomy appearance. In the evening we fell in with a Frenchman, for ten years a resident of Chili, who informed us that he would accommodate some of our party with lodgings. Three of us accepted his invitation and accompanied him home, where we found good beds and few fleas.

Friday, May 18.—We arose at eight o'clock, A. M., very much refreshed with a good night's rest, and while breakfast was being prepared, our host showed us around his premises, which would have done credit to a citizen of the land of steady habits. He carried on baking, shoemaking, tanning and last, though not least, "took in strangers" and sold *aguardiente* and *vino*. The different branches of business carried on under the same roof were all under the supervision of our host, who informed us that he was making *very mooch monish*, and judging from appearances he told the truth.

Breakfast was delayed until half-past ten o'clock, but what was lost in time was fully made up in variety, as the following bill of fare will attest: First course, chicken soup; second ditto, beefsteak and onions; third ditto, fried fish; fourth ditto, boiled fish, dressed with butter; fifth ditto, baked leg of mutton and celery; sixth ditto, cheese, fruit and wine. Each of us being blessed with a good appetite, the different courses disappeared rapidly, which, to use the little Frenchman's own words, pleased him very *mooch*. There were others present equally well pleased.

After breakfast we visited the store of a Philadelphian, of the name of Johns, who had just left for Talcahuana, therefore we did not have the pleasure of making his acquaintance. His clerk, however, introduced us to Mrs. Johns, a Chilian lady, rather above the medium size and very fleshy.

Her countenance was quite pleasing and her eyes and hair as dark as the wing of a raven. She regretted very much her husband's absence, and in broken English urged us very strongly to remain until his return, as he would be very much pleased to meet with Philadelphians. We were compelled to decline her kind invitation, but before leaving took the liberty of using for a few moments a Fairbank's scales standing in the store. I kicked the beam at one hundred and forty-five pounds, having added fifteen pounds to my avoirdupois since leaving Philadelphia. After sauntering about the city until three o'clock, P. M., we bade Concepcion adieu and started for Talcahuana, where we arrived at six o'clock.

We were overtaken on the road by two Chilians on horseback, who requested two of our party to ride behind them to Talcahuana. Mr. Butcher and I availed ourselves of their kind offer, and mounting were soon galloping over the road in advance of our companions. The horse on which my friend Butcher was astride, unfortunately for that gentleman, had a very prominent backbone, which caused the rider to sit as lightly thereon as possible. After riding about a mile, friend B. commenced screwing and turning like an eel undergoing the skinning process. He reminded me very much of a lad I once saw with a nettle in the seat of his trouserloons. At length his seat became so unpleasant that he resolved to leave it at the risk of his neck. All endeavors to induce the Chilian to stop his horse were unavailing; therefore he watched for a soft spot in the road and slid off stern foremost over the tail of the horse. Not wishing to leave my friend alone on the road, I dismounted and, giving the Chilian a *real*, walked back to assist B. in adjusting his apparel, a *certain portion* of which was sadly demoralized.

Friend Butcher and I being too much fatigued to go on board the brig, engaged a bunk in a *fandango* house, into which we both bundled and slept soundly until morning.

Saturday, May 19.—During the voyage I have grown so fleshy that it is with extreme difficulty I can wear my clothes. This morning I carried my coat to a tailor for the purpose of having the sleeves enlarged, and I hope hereafter to be able to wear it with more comfort. Afterward I went to the office of the agent of the English mail steamers, in order to ascertain the postage on a letter to the United States, *via* Panama, and was somewhat surprised to learn that it was $1. I went on board the brig, wrote a letter to my wife, returned to the office of the agent and mailed it for Philadelphia, where it will probably arrive in about fifty days.

During the past two weeks the following passenger vessels bound for California have put into this port for water and provisions:

From New York, ships *Albany* and *Panama*, and brig *Georgiana*. From Boston, ships *Trescott* and *Leonore*, bark *Oxford*, and brig *Mary Wilder*. Brig *Charlotte*, Newburyport, Mass.; ship *Hopewell*, Warren, R. I.; bark *Diamond*, New Bedford, Mass., and brig *John Petty*, Norfolk, Va.

On board of these vessels are nearly one thousand Americans bound for the gold-diggings of California. The Chilians have fitted out three vessels at this port for San Francisco; two of which have sailed and the third is on the eve of departure. Several foreigners, resident at this place, have engaged passage on board the American vessels lying in this port bound for the new El Dorado.

Saturday, May 20. — I went ashore at eight o'clock this morning and visited the market for the purpose of treating myself to grapes and apples, and while there a pretty *señorita* presented me with a bouquet of flowers. Soon after leaving the market I met a party of friends on their way to the Maiden's Paps, two very high hills overlooking the town, and at their request I accompanied them.

On our way we passed a procession of children bearing, on a rudely-constructed bier, a fancifully-ornamented coffin containing the remains of an infant which they were about to consign to mother-earth. The little mourners appeared very sorrow-ful, and to me the scene was deeply affecting and impressive. My thoughts wandered back to a little golden-haired darling I had left behind me, and as I turned away unbidden tears dimmed my eyes.

After a fatiguing walk of an hour, we reached the summit of the higher pap, from which we had a magnificent view of the town and Bay of Talca-huana, the city of Concepcion, the Biobio winding like a silver thread among the hills and ravines, the little village of Tome nestling at the foot of the mountains on the eastern shore of the bay, and the waters of the Pacific rolling and breaking over the reefs and dashing against the rock-bound shore. From our elevated position, every street and nearly every building in Talcahuana could be distinctly seen.

CHAPTER X.

THE town of Talcahuana contains about three hundred *adobe* houses and mud huts and, perhaps, three thousand inhabitants. The present town has been built within the last thirteen years, the old town having been thrown down in 1836 by the earthquake that destroyed Concepcion. The dwellings in Talcahuana, like those of Concepcion, are only one story high, and the walls are constructed of *adobes* or reeds plastered with mud. The *adobe* walls are of immense thickness, and the roofs are mostly thatched with a species of long sea-grass. In a majority of the houses and stores there are no plank or board floors. In the dwellings of the aristocracy the floors are of tile, but the poorer classes are always on the " ground floor." The streets are irregularly laid out, and the buildings erected without any regard to beauty or uniformity. The streets are unpaved, consequently they are very dusty

(167)

during the dry season, and in rainy weather are extremely muddy and filthy.

This afternoon the town seems to be overrun with *los Americanos.* There are at least five hundred California passengers on shore, and to use a nautical phrase, they are putting the town "in stays." Being foot-sore and weary, at five o'clock, P. M., I hired a boat and went on board the *Osceola.*

Monday, May 21.—After breakfast I went ashore and purchased a hamper of apples, a Chilian cheese, two dozen loaves of bread and twenty pounds of flour—private stores for the balance of the voyage. After carrying my provisions on board the brig, I returned with my rifle for target practice. Having obtained permission from the Captain of the port to use fire-arms on shore, I repaired to a ravine in the suburbs of the town and practiced until noon. I fired some twenty shots, at the distance of eighty yards, and, strange to say, the target was not injured in the least. On my return to the brig, I learned from one of our sailors at the ship's watering-place that one of the water-casks belonging to the *Osceola* had been stolen by a native and found secreted in his hut. The circumstance was reported to the Captain of the port, and in about an hour afterward the culprit was arrested and compelled to march before a guard of soldiers to the watering-place, with a rogue's cap on his head and a ladder on his shoulders. On arriving at the place where the theft was committed, he was lashed to the ladder and while in that position received on his bare back twenty-five lashes

with the end of a lasso, well laid on by a drummer.
He received the first dozen lashes without a mur-
mur, but as each remaining lash fell upon the
quivering flesh, he howled like a savage.   On being
released, he went among the crowd with his hat and
took up a collection amounting to upwards of $3.
He received the money with great delight, and I
have no doubt he would have willingly submitted
to another flogging for a like sum.   At sundown
I went on board the brig.

Tuesday, May 22.—After breakfast I went on
shore with my fowling-piece for the purpose of
shooting ducks.   I walked along the beach for several miles without seeing any game worth bagging.
I then struck off to the right, crossed over a hill
and entered a ravine where I found robins and
other small birds in abundance.   I soon killed a
dozen robins and returned to town.   From a fellow-
passenger I learned that it was currently reported
about town, that the Chilian government intended
to seize the *Osceola* for an infringement of their
marine laws in landing passengers at De Chatta before being boarded by the port officers.   The Captain and passengers are very much excited about
the matter.   This morning a hearing was had before the Captain of the port, witnesses examined,
etc., but no decision was reached, and the case will
most likely be sent to a higher tribunal at Concepcion.   Mr. Wainwright, our supercargo, was dispatched to headquarters this morning, for the purpose of setting matters in their true light before the
officials.   He returned at sundown without bringing

a decision, the judges having gotten matters so badly mixed that they are unable to decide definitely. They will dream over the matter to-night and wrestle with it again to-morrow.

The American consul at this port—Crosby, from Ohio—although appointed by a Democratic President, is a dyed-in-the-wool "*Know Nothing.*" Had he performed *his duty* promptly in this matter, nothing serious would have grown out of it. Either through ignorance, fear or connivance with the Chilian government, he has rendered us no assistance.

I went on board the brig at four o'clock, P. M., and had broiled robins for supper.

Wednesday, May 23.—I have resolved not to go ashore again while we lay in this port, unless compelled by the Chilian government to do so. Have been engaged during the forenoon mending my clothing. In the afternoon I repaired a gun-lock, cleaned and oiled my fire-arms and laid them aside ready for use on my arrival in California.

No decision in the *Osceola* case having been received by our Captain, Captain Finch, a merchant of this place, has volunteered his services to go up to Concepcion and urge a speedy settlement of the matter. He will return to-morrow morning, and should the decision be adverse, we have resolved to slip our cable and put to sea. The guns at the fort have been double-manned to-day, and should we attempt to take French leave we shall probably receive a few shots, but we are fully determined to make the attempt and abide the consequences.

Both of our mates have been discharged, and the Captain is again without officers. We have had four mates since we left Philadelphia, and God only knows how many more we shall have before we reach California. Two sailors came on board the *Osceola* to-day and volunteered to work their passage to San Francisco, and the offer has been accepted by Captain Fairfowl. Our provisions and water are now all on board, and if we had our clearance papers we should sail without mates.

Thursday, May 24.—Last night the wind blew very fresh from the north, and every indication of a norther was visible. In the early part of the evening the sailors went ashore, and the brig was left entirely to the care of the passengers. Chain was paid out several times during the night for the purpose of preventing the brig from dragging her anchor.

Yesterday afternoon Captain Fairfowl went ashore, and during his peregrinations about town took too much "wine for his stomach's sake." In his endeavors to get on board the brig, the boat swamped and he lost his hat and got thoroughly drenched with salt water. About eight o'clock, P. M., one of our passengers came across the old skipper pacing the beach in front of the custom-house, bareheaded. He was taken to a hotel and persuaded to remain there during the night. In the morning, dry clothes were sent on shore to him, and after making his toilet he came on board the brig looking rather crest-fallen. He says the wine he drank was drugged.

Captain Finch returned from Concepcion to-day with the news that we will be permitted to depart from Talcahuana in peace, provided we pay the expenses incurred in the case, amounting in the aggregate to fifty dollars. Our Captain will acquiesce in this decision, and we shall probably sail to-morrow.

The Captain shipped a first mate to-day, which means business. One of our passengers came on board this afternoon as tight as bricks and as noisy as a demon.

Friday, May 25.—Last night the wind commenced blowing from the north, and toward morning rain began to fall, and it has been blowing and raining throughout the day, causing a heavy swell in the harbor and a tremendous surf on the beach. Our new mate and the sailors took " French liberty" last night—not one remaining on board—and the Captain was compelled to call on the passengers to keep anchor-watch.

Captain Finch went up to Concepcion again to-day and made a final settlement of our case. We are promised our clearance papers this evening or to-morrow morning, and shall sail as soon as the wind will permit.

All hands are anxious to be on the wing again. Had the weather permitted, the Americans belonging to the California passenger vessels would have marched in procession through Talcahuana to-day. During the afternoon our passengers have been coming on board laden with fruit, nuts and bread, preparatory to sailing. The old skipper has been sampling drugged wine again. He came on board this evening as merry as a lark.

Saturday, May 26.—The rain is still pouring down, and a stiff breeze has been blowing into the harbor all day, which has prevented us from getting under way and putting to sea. Our new mate has already become dissatisfied with the Captain, and is just going over the side of the brig with his bag and baggage. Another first mate was shipped this evening, but I fear we shall lose him unless we sail soon. The Captain has been "working up" the sailors to-day, by causing them to scrub paint-work in the rain. We are now ready for sea, and are waiting for a fair wind to take our departure.

Sunday, May 27.—The rain poured down in torrents all last night, and early this morning we were completely enveloped by a dense fog. At sunrise the fog disappeared, and the day has been delightfully pleasant.

After breakfast the anchor was hove short, and at ten o'clock, A. M., we received our clearance papers from the Port Captain, got under way, and at meridian passed the Island of Quiriquina, at the entrance to the harbor, and were soon at sea, gliding merrily along over the swelling billows of the Pacific.

At the mouth of the harbor we spoke the California passenger ship *Christoval Colon*, of New York, bound in for a supply of provisions and water. The American brig *Mary Wilder*, bound for California, got under way about an hour before us, but we passed her in the harbor, and at this time, six o'clock, P. M., she is fully 10 miles astern of us. As we passed the *Christoval Colon*, cheers were exchanged, and our band, consisting of a bugle, cornet and trombone, struck up the "Star-Spangled Banner," which was cheered at intervals by the passengers of the *Colon* and *Mary Wilder*, until their voices were drowned by the dashing of the waves against the prow of the *Oseeola*.

As soon as we were outside the harbor, studding-sails were set below and aloft, and the coast of Chili rapidly disappeared in the distance.

Monday, May 28.—During last night and to-day the *Oseeola* has been gliding along before a delightful breeze with all studding-sails set. This morning at daylight the *Mary Wilder* was about 10 miles astern of us, and at sundown she was nearly hull down. The weather has been very pleasant, and I hope it will continue so during the remainder of the passage.

This morning angry words passed between the after-cabin and steerage passengers in relation to their rights on shipboard. One of the former intimated that the steerage passengers had no right to promenade the quarter-deck. This brought the steerage boys out in full force, and a long contro-versy ensued, in which both parties took an active part. The matter was finally referred to the Cap-tain, who decided that the steerage passengers had the same right to the use of the quarter-deck as their aristocratic neighbors of the cabin. The opinion among the steerage passengers *to-day is*, that Captain Fairfowl's head is perfectly level. Distance sailed, 147 miles. Lat. 34° 55'. Therm. at M. 58°.

Tuesday, May 29.—Throughout last night the wind continued fair, but this morning it hauled ahead, and the Captain wore the brig and stood to the westward. At eleven o'clock, A. M., the wind hauled around fair again, and since that time we have been running before a light breeze with the sea as smooth and placid as a mill-pond. At meridian we were off the Island of Juan Fernandez, once the abode of "poor old Robinson Crusoe."

This morning the Captain reprimanded the steerage cook for using too much salt pork in a lobscouse he was preparing for breakfast. From this time forward, the steerage passengers will insist on having their allowance of meat weighed out daily. This afternoon the weekly allowance of tea, sugar, butter, cheese, molasses and vinegar was served out by the mate for the use of the steerage passengers. Distance sailed, 91 miles. Lat. 33° 31'. Therm. at M. 64°.

Wednesday, May 30.—During last night and to-day the wind has been ahead, consequently we have made very little progress. We hope soon to fall in with the south-east "trades," which will waft us to the equator in a short time. The weather is daily becoming milder, which has brought the passengers on deck attired in their summer costumes. Flannel shirts and other woolen clothing have been stowed snugly away for future use.

Yesterday the after-cabin gamblers, not having

11

the fear of Captain Fairfowl's mandate before their eyes, commenced operations again. The game during the day was "*keno*," not before played on board. The game being new, the green ones bet heavily with the never-failing result—the more they put down the less they took up! Distance sailed, 94 miles. Lat. 32° 01'. Therm. at M. 65°.

Thursday, May 31.—Have been becalmed all day with the sails flapping lazily against the masts. We were not looking for a dead calm in this latitude; but during our pilgrimage in this world of woe, we must take things as they come and thank God they are no worse.

Steerage mess No. 1 furnished the cook with apples for dumplings which were served at dinner, but they were very unsavory in consequence of of having been *boiled in salt water*.

The blacklegs have been busily at work again to-day. Toward night they came to grief. One of the boys won $300, which bursted the bank! At sundown this evening, a passenger reported from the maintop-sail yard a sail on our lee-bow, distant about 20 miles. Distance sailed, 41 miles. Lat. 31° 13'. Therm. at M. 68°.

Friday, June 1.—The calm still continues, and during last night and to-day the brig has not made 10 miles on her course. The weather has been pleasant and the sea smooth. I have been perusing a file of Boston papers brought on board by our first mate. They contain several letters written by the passengers of the steamer *Crescent City* on her first trip to Chagres. The letters were written at Cruces, Gorgona and Panama, and the writers all state that the climate is unhealthy, provisions scarce and sickness very prevalent—three cases of Asiatic cholera having occurred at Cruces. They regret having taken the Isthmus route, and recommend their friends who are about to start for California to go by the way of Cape Horn. My opinion is, that those who go by the way of Cape Horn will wish they had taken the Isthmus route! Distance sailed, 24 miles. Lat. 37° 07'. Therm. at M. 64°.

Saturday, June 2.—We are still in the "horse latitudes," and the wind has been blowing a "Paddy's hurricane" during the past twenty-four hours. This is the first month of winter in this latitude, and the weather is as mild and balmy as midsummer in the United States. As we approach our port of destination, fire-arms and mining implements increase rapidly in value. Twenty-five dollars has been offered and refused for revolvers that cost $10 in Philadelphia. A gold-washer that cost $6 was sold to-day for $15, and I refused an offer of $3 for a hand-pick that cost me only fifty cents. I am waiting for an advance in the market before I unload. At meridian the sun was obscured by clouds, therefore no observation was taken. I imagine, however, that we are in the neighborhood of 30° south latitude. Distance sailed, by log, 23 miles. Therm. at M. 64°.

Sunday, June 3.—Head-wind and very little of that. Our expectations of reaching the equator in fifteen days from Talcahuana have already vanished like a dream. One week has elapsed since we left that port and we have made scarcely one-third of the distance. When the *Osceola* sailed from Philadelphia, we expected to reach San Francisco in five months at the farthest. That time has nearly expired, and we are still nearly 6,000 miles from the land of promise. It is now a fixed fact that our voyage will not be completed in less time than six months, with the chances in favor of its being prolonged beyond that time. Verily, the way of the California-bound passenger is hard. Distance sailed, 30 miles. Lat. 29° 46'. Therm. at M. 65°.

Monday, June 4.—Early last evening the wind died away, and during the remainder of the night and this forenoon we have been becalmed. At one o'clock this afternoon a fresh breeze sprang up from the south, which wafted us along at the rate of seven knots an hour until sundown, when we were again becalmed. The brig is rolling lazily; the sails are flapping against the masts and rigging, and the yards and booms are creaking and moaning fearfully. Distance sailed, 70 miles. Lat. 28° 41'. Therm. at M. 70°.

Tuesday, June 5.—The wind has been very light during the past twenty-four hours, barely sufficient to keep steerage-way on the brig. This forenoon I tried my hand at washing soiled unmentionables, socks and towels, and succeeded beyond my most sanguine expectations. I was less fortunate in the drying process, there being no clothes-line on which to hang my "wash."

A convoy of Cape pigeons has followed the brig

from Staten Land, but the hot weather of the past few days is rapidly decreasing their number and driving them back to the icy region of Cape Horn.

This afternoon the cabin passengers have amused themselves by playing monté and faro, and the steerage passengers have killed time by firing their rifles and pistols at porter and wine bottles suspended from the yards. Distance sailed, 55 miles. Lat. 27° 51'. Therm. at M. 70°.

Wednesday, June 6.—The weather to-day has been delightful, but the calm continues, and we are not happy. This morning I witnessed one of the grandest scenes of my life, and one that I shall probably never again behold. I beheld at the same moment the god of day lift his golden head above the waves of the ocean to resume his diurnal course, and the goddess of night, after having performed her wonted task, sink into the embrace of the great deep. It was a scene of great sublimity, and every soul on board gazed upon it with feelings of reverence mingled with admiration. During the forenoon the stern-boat was lowered and manned by the passengers for the purpose of towing the brig. A line was made fast to the bowsprit and attached to the stern of the boat, and the boatmen plied their oars merrily for a couple of hours, but the brig moved so slowly that they became disheartened, and, casting off the line, gave three hearty cheers, and started on a private pleasure excursion. In about two hours they returned and the boat was soon filled with another party, who started on an exploring expedition to the windward. In about an hour they returned

and informed us that during their voyage of discovery they had fallen in with the carcass of a sperm-
whale, surrounded by myriads of boobies, gulls and
Cape pigeons. The odors inhaled from his whale-
ship as he floated past us were not as pleasant and
odoriferous as those wafted from " Ceylon's Isle."
The carcass was escorted by a body-guard of sharks,
and a retinue of sea-birds screaming like devils in-
carnate. Distance sailed, 49 miles. Lat. 27° 13'.
Therm. at M. 69°.

Thursday, June 7.—Last night, at eight o'clock,
a light but fair breeze sprang up from the south,
which we have carried all day with studding-sails
set below and aloft.

Last evening the passengers mustered on the
quarter-deck for the purpose of having a dance.
The " El Dorado Band " played a variety of lively
airs, which were accompanied by the "light fantastic toes" of a majority of the passengers. At
nine o'clock, P. M., Captain Fairfowl spread a collation in the after-cabin, to which all hands were
invited. Distance sailed, 82 miles. Lat. 26° 03'.
Therm. at M. 64°.

Friday, June 8.—During last night and to-day
we have been favored with a fair wind, and the
brig at this time, six o'clock, P. M., is making five
knots an hour.

The weather has been cloudy all day, with
strong indications of rain. Last night the steerage
cook was ordered by the Captain to keep watch,
which so exasperated him that he did not turn out
this morning at the usual hour to commence his

culinary duties. The old skipper called him aft
and asked him why he had not kindled a fire in
the galley, as usual. He informed the Captain
that he would not perform the duties of both cook
and sailor—he shipped as cook, and would perform
that duty only. He was ordered by the Captain to
go forward and commence operations in the galley
at once, but being rather dilatory in his movements,
the old skipper seized a rope and commenced plying
it briskly over his back and shoulders, at the same
time ordering him to go forward, which command
he obeyed very reluctantly. In a few moments he
was again called aft by the Captain, who ordered
the mate to seize him up in the main rigging for
punishment. The cook informed the Captain that
he *was not on board a man-of-war*, and would not
submit to a flogging. The old skipper did not wait
upon the order of going, but went for the knight of
pots and kettles immediately, and for a few moments there was a lively time on board the *Osceola*,
with the following result: Captain knocked down
and the cook placed in irons. At eleven o'clock,
A. M., the Captain relented—hunger will tame a
crow—released the cook and ordered him to resume his duty, and in future to behave himself like
a man. The cook nodded assent, and will not
knock the old skipper down again until he makes
another attempt to flog him! Distance sailed 94
miles. Lat. 24° 01'. Therm. at M. 68°.

Saturday, June 9.—Throughout last night and
to-day the brig has been skimming over the water

at the rate of eight knots an hour, with square yards and all studding-sails set.

Our prospects of reaching California by the 20th of next month are now very promising. If we are not becalmed on the "line," we shall make an average run between Talcahuana and San Francisco. The weather to-day has been damp, with an occasional sprinkling of rain. We are now in the tropics, having crossed Capricorn this forenoon. This afternoon all the sugar on board the brig was taken aft and served out in equal portions to each individual on board. Each person received five and a half pounds—six weeks' allowance, according to the United States Naval ration. Since we left Talcahuana the cabin passengers have been using the sugar rather extravagantly, which caused the Captain to divide it *pro rata* to-day. Distance sailed, 90 miles. Lat. 23° 16'. Therm. at M. 65°.

CHAPTER XI.

Sunday at sea—Light and baffling winds—Man-of-war birds
shot—Fresh pork—Canchalagua pills—Passengers on their
muscle—Crossing the equator—Old Neptune initiates one
of the sailors—Bed-bugs and fleas—Our old skipper under
the weather—Fourth of July at sea—Jolly time and no
whisky—Ship ahoy!—Visit from the passengers of the ship
Pacific—We treat them to salt pork and hard-tack—Later
news from the land of gold—Captain Fairfowl has the
dumps.

Sunday, June 10.—During the last twenty-four
hours we have been gliding along over a smooth
sea, at the rate of nine knots an hour. A Scotch
mist has been falling at intervals throughout the
night and to-day.

The day has passed away very quietly—something unusual for Sunday. The sailors rigged
themselves out in their Sunday toggery, and most
of the passengers turned over a new leaf by putting
on a "biled" shirt. At dinner, the steerage passengers were treated by the cabin steward to mince-
pies for dessert, and I will do the old darkey the
justice to say they did him great credit. No observation. Distance sailed, by log, 168 miles.
Therm. at M. 68°.

Monday, June 11.—A ten-knot breeze during
the past twenty-four hours has rendered all hands

(183)

happy. The "trades" were light at first, but they have gradually increased to a ten-knot breeze, and should they continue ten days, we shall be north of the equator. The weather has been warm and hazy, reminding me of Indian Summer in Pennsylvania. This afternoon all the cheese on board the brig was served out in equal portions to the passengers, each receiving about two weeks' allowance. Distance sailed, 161 miles. Lat. 19° 59'. Therm. at M. 68°.

Tuesday, June 12.—Last night we made an unusually good run, but to-day the wind has been light and baffling. Strong indications of another calm are visible. This forenoon the members of the "Perseverance Mining Company" commenced work on a sail for their batteaux, which will save them many a tug at the oar.

At one o'clock this afternoon, one of the passengers in the maintop reported a sail on our weatherbow, distant about 15 miles. The stranger is heading the same direction we are, and is most likely a California passenger vessel. Distance sailed, 150 miles. Lat. 19° 05'. Therm. at M. 70°.

Wednesday, June 13.—All last night the wind was light and baffling, and before daylight the brig completely "boxed the compass." At eight o'clock, A. M., a light breeze sprang up from the south-west, which we have carried the balance of the day, but have made very little progress. For some unexplained cause, the south-east "trades" have left us in the lurch, which is a great disappointment. We expected they would waft us to the equator. Two vessels heading north have been in sight all day. Distance sailed, 40 miles. Lat. 18° 44'. Therm. at M. 70°.

Thursday, June 14.—Last night the wind continned light and baffling, and early this morning it died away to a dead calm. At nine o'clock, A. M., a rain-squall suddenly sprang up from the southwest, and we have carried a five-knot breeze during the remainder of the day. The weather has been hazy and showery. One of the sailors who had the wheel during the morning watch, thinking that the time passed away rather slowly, removed the watch from the binnacle and undertook to move the hands ahead, but being more accustomed to handling a marline-spike than a timepiece, he broke both hands. The watch was a gold lever belonging to one of the passengers, who read jack-tar a lecture in very forcible language. Distance sailed, 70 miles. Lat. 17° 38'. Therm. at M. 69°.

Friday, June 15.—Fair wind and plenty of it during last night and to-day. The brig has been flying over the water before a ten-knot breeze. The yards are square and every drawing sail set— a sight that a sailor's eye delights to dwell upon, and one that is not unpleasing to a landsman after having been five months at sea. The weather has been mild and pleasant. Distance sailed, 170 miles. Lat. 16° 03'. Therm. at M. 70°.

Saturday, June 16.—The continued fair wind has sent the *Osceola* jumping through the water at the rate of ten knots an hour. If we are fortunate enough to escape a calm on the equator, and are blessed with this wind for thirty consecutive days we shall be at anchor in the harbor of San Francisco.

The passengers are now organizing companies in order to be ready for action immediately upon their arrival in California. There are several professional gentlemen on board who, when they left Philadelphia, informed their friends that they were going to California to practice their professions; but they, too, have recently joined mining companies, believing that they can put more money in their purses by handling the spade and pick, than by perusing musty law books or serving out potions of jalap, calomel and quinine. Several "man-of-war" birds were shot this afternoon by one of the cabin passengers. Distance sailed, 191 miles. Lat. 14° 52'. Therm. at M. 74°.

Sunday, June 17.—We are still blessed with a fair wind and delightful weather, and are gliding rapidly along toward the land of promise.

This morning the Captain expressed his intention of crossing the equator between 112° and 115° west longitude. Should we cross the line as far west as 115° we shall not be to the northward of it before this day week. This has been one of the most quiet Sabbaths passed on board the *Osceola* since she left Philadelphia. During the first four months of the voyage a growl on Sunday between the Captain and passengers or crew was looked for regularly, and I regret to state that we were seldom disappointed. Captain Fairfowl is one of those old sea-dogs who cannot survive without an occasional growl. Distance sailed, 172 miles. Lat. 13° 36'. Therm. at M. 74°.

Monday, June 18.—We have carried an eight-knot breeze throughout last night and to-day, and the weather has been delightfully pleasant. All hands, including the cook, are in good humor. Now that we are on the last quarter of our voyage, the passengers are busily engaged overhauling their tents and mining utensils. One of our mining companies has been employed during the past two days making a tent of material purchased at Rio de Janeiro. Not being accustomed to the use of the palm and needle, they have made but very little progress. Distance sailed, 164 miles. Lat. 12° 01'. Therm. at M. 76°.

Tuesday, June 19.—A favorable wind during the past twenty-four hours has wafted us along at the rate of nine knots an hour. The weather is gradually becoming warmer—this being the hottest day experienced since we doubled Cape Horn. We shall in all probability soon have occasion to use the awnings and wind-sails, as the weather must necessarily be hot at this season of the year north of the equator.

This afternoon the Captain opened his heart and ordered a hog killed, a portion of which will be made into a sea-pie to-morrow for the steerage passengers. Distance sailed, 161 miles. Lat. 10° 21'. Therm. at M. 77°.

Wednesday, June 20.—The wind continues fair, but is gradually growing lighter as we approach the equator. This has been general washday with the

passengers. Lines stretched across the deck are
loaded with wet clothes, as also are the stays, rigging and spanker-boom. Salt-water soap is just
now in great demand among the *washermen*—some
exchanging shaving soap of a superior quality for
the same bulk or weight of salt-water soap. One
of the passengers, not being overstocked with dis-
cretion, offered to sell his traveling-bag for two bars
of salt-water soap, but he did not find a purchaser.

I have been engaged to-day making a knapsack,
which will no doubt be of great service to me in
the gold diggings. Distance sailed, 160 miles.
Lat. 8° 52′. Therm. at M. 79°.

Thursday, June 21.—During last night and to-
day the "trades" have wafted us along at the rate
of eight knots an hour. We have carried the trade-
winds for the last fifteen days, and hope to hold
them until we pass the equator. The sky has been
cloudless and the weather hot, but not oppressive.

Last night several of the passengers "took up
their beds and walked" on deck, where they slept
until morning, undisturbed by bugs or fleas. This
morning I treated myself to a dose of Captain Fairfowl's famous *Canchalagua* pills, but what effect
they will have remains to be seen. The Captain
believes them to be a sovereign balm for all the ills
that flesh is heir to. Distance sailed, 172 miles.
Lat. 7° 28′. Therm. at M. 80°.

Friday, June 22.—The wind throughout last
night and to-day has been very light, and I fear
that we shall be becalmed before we reach the
equator. The weather has been hot and sultry,

with strong indications of rain. This forenoon I did my week's washing, and this afternoon have been engaged mending my old clothes. At the commencement of the voyage I handled the needle very awkwardly, but practice and perseverance have enabled me to use it quite satisfactorily. Distance sailed, 152 miles. Lat. 5° 52'. Therm. at M. 81°.

Saturday, June 23.—For the last twenty-four hours the wind has been fair but light, yet, with the aid of all drawing sails, we have made a very fair run. The weather has been cloudy all day. This evening a shower of rain fell, which has cooled the atmosphere considerably, and rendered the early part of the night unusually pleasant. Distance sailed, 140 miles. Lat. 4° 38'. Therm. at M. 86°. Hot as blazes!

Sunday, June 24.—Throughout last night and to-day we have been skimming over the water before a seven-knot breeze, with studding-sails set below and aloft. The atmosphere has been rather cooler, which has rendered the day very pleasant. We have passed several schools of flying-fish, but none have been caught.

Now that the weather is growing warmer, the passengers are becoming as rabid as mad dogs. At breakfast, this morning, three altercations occurred —two in the after-cabin and one in the steerage. The steerage row commenced first, and passed off without any blows being struck. The first quarrel in the cabin resulted similarly; but in the second melee a rough-and-tumble fight ensued, in which a little bad blood was spilled.   Distance sailed, 135 miles.   Lat. 3° 02'.   Therm. at M. 81°.

Monday, June 25.—The "trades" still continue, and all last night and to-day we have been ploughing through the water at the rate of seven knots an hour.   The sky has been cloudless and the weather pleasant.   We are now near the equator, and hope to cross it before daylight to-morrow morning.   We are half-way between Talcahuana and San Francisco, with the prospect of reaching the latter place within twenty-five days.

I have been on board the *Osceola* so long that every plank in her deck looks like an old acquaintance; yet, as familiar as they appear, I am extremely anxious to bid them farewell forever. Distance sailed, 150 miles.   Lat. 0° 59'.   Therm. at M. 82°.

Tuesday, June 26.—We carried a seven-knot breeze throughout last night and to-day, which has placed us 160 miles nearer our port of destination.   The weather during the day has been delightful.   We crossed the equator at one o'clock this morning, in longitude 115° 40' west.

When we crossed the dominions of Neptune, the old salt visited us, and initiated one of the crew. The passengers refused to submit to the operation. The soap used by Neptune on this occasion was highly perfumed with a compound of "villainous smells," and his razor was as dull as a lecture on woman's rights.   Distance sailed, 152 miles.   Lat. 1° 06' north.   Therm. at M. 82°.

Wednesday, June 27.—All last night and to-day

the wind has been light and baffling, but the weather continues pleasant. We expected to meet with frequent showers on the equator, but thus far have been happily disappointed. During the day the passengers have been lounging about the deck in the shade of the sails endeavoring to keep cool. A few days since one of the steerage passengers resolved to dispense with the use of tobacco henceforth and forever, and this morning he disposed of his stock of pipes and tobacco at a raffle. Distance sailed, 139 miles. Lat. 3° 12'. Therm. at M. 83°.

Thursday, June 28.—Last night the wind hauled around to the southward and westward, and since that time we have been skimming along at the rate of seven knots an hour. The heat was very oppressive, but to-day we have been fanned by a delightful breeze, which has in a slight degree counteracted the effects of the heat. Since we left Talcahuana every berth in the brig has been over-run with bed-bugs and fleas, and the past two weeks our sufferings have been intolerable. To-day several of the passengers have been figuring out the date of our arrival in San Francisco. According to their ciphering we shall arrive there on the fifteenth of next month—if figures don't lie. Distance sailed, 162 miles. Lat. 5° 26'. Therm. at M. 82°.

Friday, June 29.—The wind has been blowing steadily from the south-west all day, and we have encountered several squalls accompanied by rain, thunder and lightning. The wind has blown so fresh this afternoon that the Captain has taken in the studding-sails, furled the mainroyal and recfed

12

the foretop-gallant-sail. This is the first squally weather we have encountered the past two weeks, and it has somewhat surprised us, as we did not count on meeting rough weather during the balance of the passage, but we know not what the morrow may bring forth, particularly in these latitudes. This afternoon in working the brig one of the sailors through mistake let go the wrong halyard, which caused the old skipper to go for him with a rope's end, and afterward to put him in irons. We are now in the latitude of Panama. Distance sailed, 179 miles. Lat. 8° 18'. Therm. at M. 79°.

Saturday, June 30.—Last night the wind hauled around to the northward, and to-day it has been light and baffling. Squalls, accompanied by rain, have been frequent during the day.

I fear the next settled wind will prevent us from heading our course. If so, we must be content, for it is an ill wind that blows no one good. To-day considerable rain-water has been caught by the passengers, which will prove quite a god-send, for to-morrow is washday. Captain Fairfowl has been quite unwell all day, and has remained in his berth most of the time. There is a rumor floating about the brig that he has been sampling drugged wine again. We are off Guatemala. The sun being obscured, no observation was taken. Distance sailed, by log, 130 miles. Therm. at M. 78°.

Sunday, July 1.—Our good luck is failing us. During last night and to-day the wind has been unfavorable, which has headed us off our course five or six points. The weather has been clear, and the wind bracing and invigorating. The morning and forenoon passed off quietly, but this afternoon the Captain cursed the cabin passengers for insinuating that he had sampled the brandy in the doctor's medicine-chest. Liquor is getting scarce and the Captain is convalescing rapidly. In consequence of the indisposition of the old skipper no observation was taken, but I presume that we are in the neighborhood of 13° north latitude. Distance sailed, as per log, 137 miles. Therm. at M. 81°.

Monday, July 2.—Last night the wind was light and baffling, and to-day we have been becalmed. The weather has been hot and oppressive. The next wind that crosses our track will probably be the north-east "trades," the prevailing wind in these latitudes, and the sooner we meet with them the better; for, of all things on earth or ocean, a calm in the tropics is the most annoying.

The old skipper is on his pins again, and to-day resumed his accustomed duty. One of his first acts was to release the sailor confined in irons on the 29th ult. Distance sailed, 97 miles. Lat. 13° 18'. Therm. at M. 82°.

Tuesday, July 3.—During last night and to-day the ocean has been as smooth as a mirror, and the weather hot and sultry.

Captain Fairfowl opened his heart this afternoon and presented to the steerage messes three turkeys, which will be served up for dinner to-morrow—the glorious Fourth! Distance sailed, 16 miles. No observation. Therm. at M. 83°.

Wednesday, July 4.—Fourth of July and a dead

calm in the tropics, with the thermometer at 83° in the shade! This day being the seventy-third anniversary of American independence, all hands concluded to celebrate the event in a becoming manner. Accordingly, at daylight, the ensign, union-jack and pennant were spread to the breeze, a salute of small arms fired, and at ten o'clock, A. M., a meeting was organized, Dr. George Guier, Jr., presiding, supported by six vice-presidents, myself being one of the number. A secretary was appointed, and a committee selected to prepare the regular toasts for the occasion. After the reading of the Declaration of Independence, by Col. James A. Banks, another salute was fired, and the meeting adjourned until three o'clock, P. M.

Having partaken of the best dinner the *Osceola* could spread, we met at the appointed hour to conclude the festivities of the day. Thirteen regular toasts appropriate to the occasion were read by the president, which were loudly cheered by the assemblage. The intervals between the toasts were enlivened by appropriate music by the El Dorado band and several patriotic songs by the "O Susannah Serenaders." The regular sentiments were succeeded by some fifty volunteer toasts, many of which were rich, rare and racy, and called down thunders of applause.

The regular and volunteer toasts having been read, Colonel Banks, in compliance with a request from the president, delivered an eloquent address, creditable alike to his head and heart. The colonel was followed by two other passengers, one of whom

recited an Ode to the American Flag, and the other
attempted to make a speech but, poor fellow, he got
stuck! and in order to relieve him from his awkward
predicament, a friend moved an adjournment *sine
die*, which was unanimously carried.

At sundown, when the colors were hauled down,
another salute was fired and three hearty cheers
given, which aroused the fishes and caused old Neptune to send back the echo; and thus ended the 4th
of July, 1849, at sea! Everything passed off
quietly and soberly. There was no liquor on board!
Distance sailed, 20 miles. Lat. 13° 41'. Therm.
at M. 83°.

Thursday, July 5.—The calm continued last
night, but this forenoon a light breeze sprang up
from the north-west, and although dead ahead, was
hailed with joy by all hands on board, as a breeze
from any quarter is preferable to a calm. Last
night I was so terribly annoyed by that lively and
ubiquitous little "animile," the flea, that I was
compelled to vacate my bunk and go on deck. The
rays of a tropical sun have been concentrated all
day on my mattress and blankets, and I have also
given the latter a salt-water douche. I hope that
the sun and salt-water combined have given the
fleas their eternal quietus.

This forenoon, a ship, supposed to be a homeward-
bound whaler, was reported on our lee-bow, distant
about 15 miles. This is the first vessel reported
during four weeks. For reasons best known to
the Captain no observation was taken to-day.
Distance sailed, per log, 9 miles. Therm. at M. 81°.

Friday, July 6.—During last night and to-day there has not been sufficient wind to fill the sails, consequently they have been flapping listlessly against the masts and rigging. The sky has been unclouded and the weather oppressive.

Early this morning we discovered on our lee-quarter a full-rigged ship, distant about 15 miles. About two o'clock, P. M., a small sail, in the direction of the stranger, was seen approaching us, and when distant about 4 miles, our stern-boat was lowered and manned by passengers, who pulled merrily away toward the boat, which could now be distinctly made out without the aid of a glass. In about forty minutes our boat returned, accompanied by the metallic life-boat *Crusoe*, belonging to and manned by seven of the passengers of the California passenger ship *Pacific*, which sailed from New York on the 23d of January last. We left the *Pacific* in Rio de Janeiro, whence she sailed on the 3d of April, touching at Callao for water and provisions, sailing thence on the 8th of June.

At the latter place intelligence from California down to the 1st of May had been received, which confirmed all previous reports in regard to the richness of the gold mines in that country.

Our guests partook of a collation of salt pork and hard-tack, lubricated with a little brandy from the doctor's medicine-chest, and at five o'clock, P. M., bade us adieu, and entering their boat, were soon gliding over the water toward their vessel, which was now distant about 10 miles. When our friends shoved off three hearty cheers were given by us, which were returned with a will. At sundown our visitors were within a mile of their ship, which they probably reached before dark. They are a jolly, whole-souled set of fellows, and deserve success. Distance sailed, 12 miles. Lat. 14° 06'. Therm. at M. 82°.

Saturday, July 7.—Some time during last night a breeze sprang up from the north, which we have carried throughout the day. We have been looking for the north-east "trades" during the past eight days, but have not yet found them. "Hope deferred maketh the heart sick." Either a head-wind or a dead-calm has been the order of the day the past week, and how long this will continue remains to be seen.

The news received from California by the visitors from the *Pacific* has renewed the gold fever, and all hands on board are more or less affected by it. One of the sailors went aloft this morning and scanned the horizon with a glass, but not a solitary sail could be seen. Distance sailed, 47 miles. Lat. 13° 55'. Therm. at M. 80°.

Sunday, July 8.—Last night the wind commenced hauling to the westward, and during the day we have been heading the course laid down by the Captain, and running before a strong south-west wind at the rate of six knots an hour. A strong head-sea has been running during the day, which has somewhat impeded our progress.

We are now about 1,300 miles distant from the Golden Gate, with a fair wind that would waft us there in eight days, if the brig were allowed to head the proper course; but our Captain is afflicted with the dumps, and is as obstinate as a mule. He will steer any course in preference to the correct one, which will probably prolong our voyage another month. He informed one of the passengers to-day that we would not reach San Francisco before the 10th of August. A cold, drizzling rain has been falling all day. Distance sailed, 100 miles. Lat. 15° 20'. Therm. at M. 78°.

CHAPTER XII.

Our last porker slaughtered—Cold weather in the tropics—
Off Lower California—The Captain predicts a fair wind—
Will wine vinegar inebriate?—Provisions and water scarce—
Head-winds—First mate ordered below—Encounter a
squall—The cook and cabin steward have a free fight—Fog
and Scotch mist—Drift-wood—Brig ahoy!—Visit from the
mate of the brig *Spencer*—Land ho!—Farallone Islands—
Come to anchor outside the Golden Gate.

Monday, July 9.—The wind continued fair last
night, and throughout to-day we have been steering
north-west by west with all studding-sails set. The
wind is gradually hauling around to the eastward,
and I should not be surprised if we were to fall in
with the north-east "trades" within forty-eight
hours. The weather has been clear and pleasant,
and the passengers have spent most of the day on
deck. We are to-day off the coast of Mexico.
Distance sailed, 110 miles. Lat. 17° 04'. Therm.
at M. 81°.

Tuesday, July 10.—Last night the wind hauled
around to the south-east, and during the day it has
changed to the north-east, from which quarter it is
still blowing quite fresh. We have been heading
north-west by west all day, and running at the rate
of eight knots an hour.

The weather up to three o'clock, P. M., has been
warm and pleasant, but from that time to the present

(199)

writing, eight o'clock, P. M., the mercury in the thermometer has fallen from 81° to 72°, and the atmosphere is damp and chilly.

The last two nights a heavy dew has fallen, which has thoroughly wet the deck and rigging. Our last porker was slaughtered to-day; therefore, we may expect a good dinner to-morrow.

> Our last pig is slaughtered
> For to-morrow's sea-stew,
> And we'll go for that porker
> Like Yankees, true blue!

Distance sailed, 139 miles. Lat. 19° 03′. Therm. at M. 72°.

Wednesday, July 11.—Throughout last night and to-day we have been wafted along by the north-east "trades" at the rate of eight knots an hour; but the brig is still heading north-west by west, although we are two degrees to the westward of our port of destination! The weather is damp and chilly, reminding one more of fall in the United States than midsummer in the tropics. The thermometer this evening is down to 70°, and overcoats are in demand among the passengers. The past two days the members of the "Perseverance Mining Company" have been employed painting their boats, in order to be in readiness for a start up the Sacramento immediately upon their arrival in San Francisco. Distance sailed, 172 miles. Lat. 20° 50′. Therm. at M. 78°.

Thursday, July 12.—We are still being driven to the north-west by the "trades" at the rate of seven knots an hour. The Captain regrets not having steered a northerly course at the commencement of this week, when he had the opportunity. Should the present wind continue until we reach the latitude of San Francisco, by steering our present course we shall be some 1,200 miles to the westward of that port. Although directly under the sun, the atmosphere is quite chilly. We are this evening off Cape St. Lucas, the southernmost point of Lower California. Yesterday we exchanged colors with a Chilian ship bound to the southward. Distance sailed, 148 miles. Lat. 22° 20'. Therm. at M. 70°.

Friday, July 13.—A head-wind to-day has prevented us from steering within six points of our course. There is a variation of the compass of about one point in our favor, but this is nearly, if not quite, overbalanced by the lee-way occasioned by a strong head-sea that has been running the past five days. The weather is so cold that the passengers have dressed themselves *cap-a-pie* in their Cape Horn clothes, in order to keep comfortable when on deck.

The month of October in Philadelphia is more mild and pleasant than have been the past five days in the tropics. This forenoon we crossed the Tropic of Cancer, and if we are permitted to steer our course during the next six days, we shall at the expiration of that time be at anchor in the Bay of San Francisco. Distance sailed, 134 miles. Lat. 23° 56'. Therm. at M. 68°.

Saturday, July 14.—The wind is still north-east,

but is gradually getting lighter, and I hope will soon die away or haul around to the westward. The Captain predicts a fair wind within the next forty-eight hours, but little faith can be placed in his opinion, in consequence of his having so often proven himself a false prophet.

The head-winds which have prevailed during the past week have given all hands the blues, and they move silently about the deck with elongated visages, reminding one very much of a disconsolate widow or a young married man with a strong-minded mother-in-law. Distance sailed, 118 miles. Lat. 25° 25'. Therm. at M. 68°.

Sunday, July 15.—Last night the wind veered a little to the northward, and to-day we have been heading nearly a due west course. The wind has been very light, and all on board are inclined to the belief that it will haul around to the westward very soon or die away entirely. The sun has been obscured by clouds nearly all day, and the weather has been chilly and unpleasant.

This Sabbath has passed off very quietly, neither a fight nor a growl having occurred—an unusual circumstance. One of the passengers of the Irish persuasion, however, not having the fear of Father Mathew before his eyes, managed this evening to get gloriously drunk on wine vinegar, but he is very docile. This morning at sunrise the mercury in the thermometer was down to 66°. Distance sailed, 126 miles. Lat. 26° 33'. Therm. at M. 68°.

Monday, July 16.—We are still wrestling with an adverse wind, and the weather is damp and chilly. We are now in longitude 130° west, and the Captain says he will put the brig on another tack to-morrow and run direct for the Golden Gate.

A box of clothing belonging to one of the passengers, stowed in the hold since we left Rio, was opened to-day and its contents found to be very much injured by mould and mildew. Distance sailed, 88 miles. Lat. 27° 12′. Therm. at M. 69°.

Tuesday, July 17.—Last night the wind hauled around to the northward and eastward, and since that time we have been heading north-west, but in consequence of being so close on the wind we have made very little progress. The wind is dead ahead, and so good-bye, San Francisco, until it changes. The sun has been obscured by clouds nearly all day, and the weather continues chilly and disagreeable. Provisions are getting scarce—some articles being entirely exhausted. The hold was broken out to-day for pork, but not a single barrel could be found. The sugar and cheese are also among the things that were but are not, and the water is nearly all gone. The truth of the matter is, we are in one of those predicaments sometimes narrated but not often experienced. Distance sailed, 87 miles. Lat. 27° 43′. Therm. at M. 68°.

Wednesday, July 18.—Last night the wind hauled back to the northward, and this forenoon it veered still further around and resumed its old position in the north-east. This afternoon we have been heading north-west, but owing to a head-sea have made very little progress. If the wind continues in the north-east during the next eight days, we shall be compelled to run as far westward as 140° before we tack the brig and run for our port of destination.

The weather this forenoon was quite winterish. At meridian the clouds that have shrouded the sky the past week broke away, and the sun shone brightly for about two hours. The latter part of the day has been squally, with occasional showers. The crew has been employed to-day painting the brig. Distance sailed, 84 miles. Lat. 28° 53′. Therm. at M. 68°.

Thursday, July 19.—During last night and to-day the wind has been blowing steadily from the north-east, and we have been sailing as close-hauled as possible. The weather has been cloudy, damp and chilly, and all hands have the dumps. How long we shall be knocked about by adverse winds, is one of those things that no "feller" can find out. At meridian San Francisco bore north-east by north, distant 800 miles. The crew has been reeving new signal-halyards, repairing the side-ladders, and doing other odd jobs, in order to get the brig "ship-shape" before reaching port. Distance sailed, 112 miles. Lat. 30° 15′. Therm. at M. 68°.

Friday, July 20.—The north-east trades still continue, which prevents us from heading higher than north-west by north. We did not expect to carry the trades farther north than latitude 28°, but in this, as well as in many other things, we have been sadly disappointed. I have now come to the conclusion that we are booked for a passage of *two hundred days!*

This morning Captain Fairfowl ordered his first

officer below. This is the fifth officer the old skipper has put off duty since we sailed from Philadelphia. Should he ever be fortunate enough to obtain command of another vessel, I would advise him to ship at least a gross of mates. He would find use for all of them before the expiration of a voyage of ninety days. Distance sailed, 100 miles. Lat. 31° 38′. Therm. at M. 68°.

Saturday, July 21.—Last night the wind hauled a point to the eastward, and to-day we have been steering N. N. W. We shall probably be in the latitude of San Francisco on Wednesday next. The Captain will then tack the brig and stand to the eastward, wind permitting.

Last night the moon dispersed the clouds, and to-day the atmosphere has been clear and the weather cool. Three large sea-birds have followed the brig for the past three weeks, and during that time at least fifty shots have been fired at them by the passengers without effect. They appear to bear charmed lives. At all events, they are shot and bullet-proof. Distance sailed, 108 miles. Lat. 33° 11′. Therm. at M. 67°.

Sunday, July 22.—All last night and up to six o'clock, P. M., to-day, the wind has blown steadily from the north-east, and the brig has been heading a north-by-west course. At seven o'clock this evening the wind hauled around to the south-east, which has enabled us to lay our course for the space of *fifteen minutes,* when it hauled back to its old quarter in the north-east, where it still remains.

The sun has been obscured by clouds nearly all

day, which has rendered the atmosphere chilly. We are now in the same latitude as San Luis Obispo, Upper California, and at meridian to-morrow we shall probably be off Monterey.

Early this morning the Captain reported a vessel on our weather-bow, distant about 15 miles, and in two hours afterward it could not be seen. It was probably a California-bound steamer. Distance sailed, 122 miles. Lat. 35° 01'. Therm. at M. 67°.

Monday, July 23.—Last night the wind was light and baffling, and to-day the face of the great deep has been unruffled by a breeze. We have lost the north-east trades, and I hope the next wind we fall in with will be a fair one, for things are getting rather monotonous. The weather has been warmer than on any previous day the past two weeks. I availed myself of the sunshine, and washed and dried sundry shirts and towels. Several turtles have been seen floating on the surface of the water at no great distance from the brig. As we shall not run much farther to the northward, I will, during the remainder of the voyage, record longitude, as well as the latitude. Distance sailed, 72 miles. Lat. 36° 11'; long. 139° 02' west. Therm. at M. 73°.

Tuesday, July 24.—Throughout last night and to-day the wind has been light and baffling, and a part of the time we have been becalmed. The entire day has been a succession of variable breezes and calms. This morning at eight o'clock the brig was put about three times in about the time it requires to record the fact, and on the last tack she headed her course *twenty minutes.* We find that we have only twenty-five days' water on board, which causes things to look rather squally. We are now on an allowance of two quarts of water per day, which allows us only one pint each for drinking, and if we do not soon get a fair wind this quantity will be reduced one-half. Distance sailed, 18 miles. Lat. 36° 29′; long. 139° 08′. Therm. at M. 68°.

Wednesday, July 25.—The calm of yesterday continued throughout last night. Early this morning the wind commenced hauling to the southward, and at this time, eight o'clock, A. M., it is blowing from the south-west. Although the wind has been light, by the aid of studding-sails we have managed to make about three knots an hour. Captain Fairfowl is of the opinion that the present wind will waft us into port. God grant that it may, for our water and provisions are getting very scarce, and much suffering will occur should the voyage be prolonged another month. Distance sailed, 42 miles. Lat. 37° 12′; long. 139° 10′. Therm. at M. 70°.

Thursday, July 26.—The wind increased gradually last night, and up to four o'clock this afternoon we have been heading our course at the rate of six knots an hour with studding-sails set below and aloft. This afternoon at five o'clock we encountered a squall accompanied by rain, during which the wind hauled around to the north, and is blowing an eight-knot breeze from that quarter.

This forenoon the cabin cook and steward had a rough-and-tumble fight about their relative positions, in which both parties were severely pummeled.

The cook gave the steward a whack on his *cabasa* with the potato-masher, and the latter returned the compliment with his fists so effectually that in a few moments the cook's figure-head was sadly disfigured—it is doubtful whether his mother would recognize him. Distance sailed, 70 miles. Lat. 37° 52′; long. 137° 57′. Therm. at M. 74°.

Friday, July 27.—All last night we headed our course and ran at the rate of six knots an hour. At ten o'clock this forenoon the wind hauled around to the north-east which headed us off, and the Captain put the brig about and ran to the north-west until three o'clock, P. M., when the wind hauled a little more to the northward, and the brig was again put about, but on this tack she could not lay within two points of her course, in consequence of the variations of the compass and the lee-way, which were both against her. The weather during the day has been damp and chilly, the mercury in the thermometer having fallen *ten degrees* within the past twenty-four hours.

Yesterday all hands were very much elated with the prospect of reaching San Francisco in the course of four or five days, but the sudden change in wind and weather to-day has saddened their hearts, and they look as crest-fallen as disappointed politicians. We are on an allowance of three pints of water each. Distance sailed, 142 miles. Lat. 37° 30′; long. 135° 30′. Therm. at M. 64°.

Saturday, July 28.—At midnight last night the brig was put about, and she ran north-west by west until ten o'clock this forenoon, when she was put on the other tack, and since that time has been heading east by north, within one point of our course. The wind is hauling slowly to the westward, and I am inclined to the belief that we will be heading our course before to-morrow morning. A fair wind would carry us into our port of destination in three days, but the wind in these latitudes is so fickle that very little reliance can be placed upon it. This afternoon a general search was made in the hold for water, and, to our great joy, we find that there are thirteen casks on board, being thirty days' allowance at the rate of two quarts for each person. Distance sailed, 87 miles. The sun was obscured at meridian, consequently no observation was taken. Therm. at M. 65°.

Sunday, July 29.—Early last night the wind hauled to the north-west, and since that time we have been running our course at the rate of six knots an hour. A heavy head-sea has been running all day, which has somewhat retarded our progress.

The cold weather and rough sea causes reminiscences of Cape Horn to flit through the mind. Owing to the favorable wind the Captain has added a pint of water to our daily allowance. Cloudy weather; no observation. Distance sailed, per log, 86 miles. Therm. at M. 62°.

Monday, July 30.—During last night and to-day we have been heading our course and jogging slowly along at the rate of four knots an hour.

Were it not for the strong head-sea constantly butting against the bow of the brig, our speed would be increased at least two knots an hour. We are also close-hauled on the wind, which somewhat retards our progress.

Our hearts were gladdened this forenoon by the appearance of the sun for the first time in two days. Toward the close of the afternoon the weather became thick and foggy, and at this time, eight o'clock, P. M., a Scotch mist is falling which will probably turn into rain before morning. At meridian to-day, San Francisco bore due east, distant 383 miles. Distance sailed, 87 miles. Lat. 37° 49′; long. 130° 01′. Therm. at M. 62°.

Tuesday, July 31.—Throughout last night and to-day the brig has been heading her course under a seven-knot breeze. The wind has gradually increased since noon, and at this time, seven o'clock, P. M., it is blowing a gale. If the atmosphere should be clear to-morrow we hope to sight land.

The weather during the day has been foggy and chilly—the thermometer at five o'clock this morning being 58°. The past two days, large quantities of drift-wood, sea-weed and kelp have floated past us—strong indications that land is not far distant. A great change in the color of the water has also been apparent within the past thirty hours; and this evening wild geese and a species of duck that does not venture far from land, flew past us. Distance sailed, 160 miles. Lat. 38° 30′; long. 127° 38′. Therm. at M. 59°.

Wednesday, August 1.—The wind blew so fresh all night that the brig was hove to, and remained in that position until daylight this morning, when

she was put before the wind and made good headway until ten o'clock, A. M., when the wind died
entirely away. This afternoon the wind has been
light and baffling, and a heavy ground-swell has
kept the brig rolling about like a saw-log in a mill-
pond.

During the day we have been enveloped by a
dense fog which has prevented us from seeing half
a mile in any direction. The anchors were got
over the bow ready to be let go should occasion
require. Land-birds have been hovering about
the brig all day. Distance sailed, 30 miles. Lat.
38° 28'; long. 125° 08'. Therm. at M. 58°.

Thursday, Aug. 2.—Light and baffling winds,
a dense fog and damp and chilly weather all day.
At sundown the fog partially lifted, which enabled
us to get a glimpse of the "land of promise,"
directly ahead and distant about 10 miles. Later
in the evening, the fog disappeared, and we could
define the bold outlines of the coast for many miles.
The Captain says we are some 15 miles to the northward of the harbor of San Francisco, therefore we
shall lay off and on during the night and run into
port to-morrow, wind permitting. Soon after
making the land we discovered a vessel close in
shore evidently bearing down toward us. When
distant about 3 miles, she lowered a boat, and in
three-quarters of an hour thereafter, we were
boarded by her first mate, accompanied by a cabin
passenger. The stranger proved to be the English
brig *Spencer*, from Sydney, New South Wales,
bound for San Francisco, with thirteen passengers

and a cargo consisting principally of provisions, spirits and clothing. The mate of the *Spencer* boarded us for the purpose of ascertaining his whereabouts, which Captain Fairfowl defined to his entire satisfaction. The *Spencer* had been becalmed and befogged since Monday last on this "blarsted" coast. Our Captain presented the mate, at parting, with a copy of the *New York Herald* containing a map of the harbor of San Francisco, which I hope will prove more reliable than did one of the "Gold Diggings" published in the same journal. No observation to-day. Distance sailed, per log, 60 miles. Therm. at M. 60°.

Friday, Aug. 3.—During last night the wind was very light, and to-day we have been in the midst of light breezes and calms.

The Captain took an observation at noon and found that we were 22 miles to the northward of the port of San Francisco. This afternoon we have been running slowly down the coast. Several of the passengers are so anxious to get on shore that they have been ahead in one of the boats nearly all the afternoon towing the brig.

When we tacked the brig this forenoon and stood down the coast, the brig *Spencer* followed us, but before two o'clock, P. M., we lost sight of her. The land was visible until eleven o'clock, A. M., when the fog hid it from our view. The fog the past week has been so dense that the sun has been obscured most of the time. During the day whales, porpoises, puffing-pigs, sea-lions, seals and sharks have been seen in all directions.

Distance sailed, 50 miles.   Lat. 38° 10′.   Therm. at M. 60°.

Saturday, Aug. 4.—The wind died away last night about ten o'clock, and up to four o'clock, P. M., we have not made ten miles. This forenoon the water has been as smooth as a mirror, but the fog is so dense that we cannot see twice the length of the brig.

At half-past four o'clock, P. M., the fog lifted a little, and we discovered a sail directly ahead, about 4 miles distant.   Soon after a boat left the stranger and was shortly alongside of us.   The vessel proved to be the schooner *John L. Day,* from New York, which port she left on the 4th of March last.   She is bound for San Francisco, and has twenty-two passengers on board.

At five o'clock, P. M., we made the Farallone Islands, bearing south by east, distant some 3 miles. The Farallones are a mass of barren rocks, projecting several hundred feet above the surface of the water, and are inhabited only by sea-fowl, sea-lions and seals. They bear west by south from San Francisco, and are about 25 miles distant from that port.   At half-past five o'clock a four-knot breeze sprang up, and at this writing, eight o'clock, P. M., we are within 12 miles of the Golden Gate.   We shall anchor to-night off the mouth of the harbor and run in to-morrow morning, wind permitting. Distance sailed, 31 miles. Lat. 37° 58′; long. 123° 42′. Therm. at M. 64°.

CHAPTER XIII.

Sunday, Aug. 5.—Last night we came to anchor
just outside the Golden Gate, in eighteen fathoms
of water, where we remained until six o'clock this
morning, when we stood into the harbor, and at
eleven o'clock, A. M., rounded Clark's Point and
dropped anchor off the town of San Francisco.

The cable had scarcely ceased rattling over the
bitts, before half a dozen shore-boats, manned by
piratical-looking beach-combers, were alongside of
us, which were soon filled with passengers at $2 per
head. Not being overstocked with the one thing
needful, I concluded to await a passage ashore in
one of the brig's boats, which the Captain informed
me would be ready in a few hours.

The first Philadelphian that came on board was a
man named Brown, formerly a dry-goods merchant
in Bank Street, in that city. Mr. Brown, like
a sensible man, availed himself of the Isthmus

(214)

ENTRANCE TO THE GOLDEN GATE.

route in preference to a passage around Cape Horn, and although he started at the same time we did, reached California some four months ahead of us. He had already made several thousand dollars by transporting goods from San Francisco to Sacramento City, and trafficking in provisions and mining implements.

Immediately after dinner the boat was got ready, and I went ashore for letters, but on reaching the post-office I found it closed, which caused me to turn away with a sad heart. I soon returned on board the brig and commenced arranging my baggage preparatory to transferring it on shore.

The following is a recapitulation of the voyage of the *Osceola* between Philadelphia and San Francisco:

Sailed from Philadelphia, January 16, 1849, and arrived at Rio de Janeiro on the 6th of March following; number of days at sea, 49; distance sailed, 6,088 miles. Remained in Rio, 12 days. Sailed from Rio de Janeiro March 18, and arrived at Talcahuana, Chili, May 14; number of days at sea, 57; distance sailed, 6,156 miles. Remained in Talcahuana, 13 days. Sailed from Talcahuana May 27, and arrived at San Francisco, August 5, 1849; number of days at sea, 70; distance sailed, 7,064 miles.

Total number of days at sea, ...	176
" " " in different ports, . .	25
" " " from Philadelphia to San Francisco, ...	201
Total number of miles sailed between Philadelphia and San Francisco, ...	19,308

At daylight on the morning of the 6th, I went ashore in the market-boat and again wended my way over the sand-hills to the post-office, where I found some two hundred individuals already formed in file at the delivery-window anxiously awaiting the opening of the office. I filed in at the rear of the line formed at the window; at seven o'clock, A. M., the shutters were unbarred and thrown open, and the delivery of mail-matter commenced. After remaining in the line upwards of two hours, I reached the window and received three letters and a *New York Herald*, containing my letter written for that paper at Rio. I clutched the letters with a nervous hand and with fear and trembling broke the seals and glanced hurriedly over their contents. They contained intelligence from the States up to the month of June, and, when I learned that the loved ones in their far-away home were all well, my heart leaped with joy. On my way down to the *Plaza* I met several of my fellow-passengers on their way to the post-office. When I informed them that it would require half a day to reach the delivery-window, a disconsolate Dutchman, from one of the interior counties of Pennsylvania, ejaculated, "Mine Got in himmel; vat a tyfel of a country dis ish!" I consoled him with the idea that the farther he went, the worse he would probably fare.

In the afternoon I visited the encampment of the gold-diggers in Happy Valley, for the purpose of selecting a site on which to pitch my tent. On the following day I moved my luggage ashore, and

BEACH OF YERBA BUENA COVE, 1849.

POST-OFFICE, 1849

located myself among the sojourners there. My provisions and mining implements were soon landed from the *Osceola*, and I made the necessary arrangements for spending a few weeks in San Francisco as comfortably as possible. I learned from the experienced in such matters, that the water in the tributaries of the Sacramento and San Joaquin was too high to admit of working in the wet diggings to advantage, and that the dry diggings could not be successfully worked until late in the fall, after the rainy season had set in. I therefore concluded to remain in San Francisco until the middle of September. The limited state of my finances—*six dollars and seventy-five cents, all told*—would not admit of my remaining idle during the interim, therefore I immediately set out in quest of employment. Passing down Pacific Street toward Clark's Point, I saw several of my fellow-passengers engaged shoveling and wheeling dirt, at $5 per day. I applied for a situation, but was informed there was no vacancy. I soon after obtained a situation in the lumber-yard of Palmer, Cook & Co., at $8 a day, which I held until I had raised the requisite funds to defray my expenses to the mines. Some old fossil has said or written, perhaps both, that "poverty is no disgrace;" but to a person with a diaphragm and an appetite, it is very unpleasant and depressing, with the following bill of fare staring him in the face : " Beefsteak, $1 ; coffee, 75 cents ; bread, with butter, 50 cents !"

San Francisco—formerly Yerba Buena—is a queer place. It contains at this time a dozen *adobe* structures and perhaps two hundred roughly-constructed frame buildings, mostly shipped around Cape Horn. The beach, Happy Valley, for the space of two miles, is covered with canvas and rubber tents, and the adjacent sand-hills are dotted to their summits with these frail but convenient tenements of the prospective miner. The population, numbering perhaps five thousand, is as heterogeneous as their habitations. It seems as though every nation on the face of the earth had sent a representative to this place, and that they had all arrived with their credentials. Such a medley of languages and jargon of tongues the world has seldom seen. It is a modern Babel. Yet, paradoxical as it may seem, it is nevertheless true, that life and property are as secure here as in the cities of New York, Boston or Philadelphia, and fire-arms are seldom carried as weapons of defense by either citizens or strangers. The commission of a theft is a rare occurrence, although millions of dollars' worth of merchandise is "lying around loose" and unguarded. The raid by the citizens on the "Hounds," a gang of cut-throats and thieves, and the incarceration of five of the ringleaders on board the U. S. sloop-of-war *Warren*, some four weeks previous to our arrival, has completely revolutionized affairs in San Francisco and placed a wholesome check on roguery. It is universally conceded in this country, that hanging *is not* one of the "Lost Arts," and, so long as Judge Lynch shall continue to occupy the bench, justice will be meted out with an impartial hand.

THE "HOUNDS" ON A RAMPAGE.

There are lying at anchor in the harbor of San Francisco at this time, four U. S. vessels of war and upwards of two hundred sail of merchantmen, most of the latter being without crews, the gold fever having *carried them off* to the mines. Rents are enormously high. The Parker House, the principal hotel in town, rents for *one hundred and seventy-five thousand dollars per annum !* The tenants are principally gamblers, who, in some instances, pay as high as $1,000 per month for the privilege of running a *monté* or *faro* table. The *roulette, keno, rattle-and-snap* and other small-fry gamblers pay less amounts, but I am inclined to the belief that they put as much money in their purses as do their more aristocratic neighbors. The gaming-tables are always crowded with those who have no better sense than to stake their last ounce of dust on the "hazard of a die." If the fickle goddess smiles on them, well and good; if she frowns, and they lose the last farthing in their possession, they immediately hie away to the mines, and after having filled their buckskin pouches with the "dust," return and buck against *faro* and *monté* until their purses are again depleted, and then once more to the mines to retrieve their lost fortunes. In ninety-nine cases out of every hundred, the *more* an individual puts down on a gaming-table the *less* he takes up. In the Parker House and El Dorado, full brass bands are engaged at a cost of several hundred dollars a night to draw victims into their toils—

"Step into my parlor, said the spider to the fly."

Pyramids of golden nuggets of various sizes, aggregating in value thousands of dollars, are displayed on the gambling-tables to excite the avarice and cupidity of the unwary.

Mrs. Grundy has not yet arrived here, consequently social and society lines have not been strictly drawn. One man is equally as good as another, and in some instances a little better. Every one seems fully impressed with the belief that it is either "root hog or die"—the majority root! All seem to be working harmoniously on the same plane. A graduate of Yale considers it no disgrace to sell peanuts on the *Plaza*, a disciple of Coke and Blackstone to drive a mule-team, nor a New York poet to sell the *New York Tribune* at 50 cents a copy. Mechanical labor commands from $12 to $16 per day, and common laborers receive from $6 to $8 per day. Provisions and building materials are exorbitantly high, but clothing and dry-goods are selling as low as in the States. An article in demand will sell at any price your conscience will allow you to ask for it. I sold a force-pump that cost $40 in Philadelphia to a Californian for $175, and he considered that he got it remarkably cheap, as he afterwards informed me. I assured him that I was perfectly satisfied, and that my *motto* in business was, quick sales and light profits.

The climate of San Francisco, though reputed healthy, is not agreeable to the unacclimated. The mornings and evenings during the spring and summer months are damp and chilly, and at meridian the thermometer is usually somewhere in the neighbor-

PARKER HOUSE AND DENNISON'S EXCHANGE, 1849.

INTERIOR OF EL DORADO SALOON, 1850.

hood of 80°. A heavy dew falls at night, which renders woolen clothing requisite during the summer months. Were it not for the heavy rains, the winter months would be the most delightful part of the year. Between the rains the atmosphere is as mild and balmy as June in the Atlantic States. I find that summer clothing is of no manner of use here. In the mines the dew, I am informed, is very light during the spring, summer and fall, and the climate approximates nearer to our own.

On the 4th of September I began to make the necessary arrangements for my departure to the mines. I exchanged my large sea-chest for a trunk, which I packed full of clothing and placed in a store-house, with the understanding that I should pay *three dollars per month* storage or forfeit the trunk and its contents at the expiration of six months. The only articles of clothing I selected to take to the mines were two red flannel shirts, a pair of pilot-cloth pants, a pair of long mining boots and a Mexican *sombrero*. I disposed of all my provisions, with the exception of a half-barrel of pork and a barrel of pilot-bread, which I concluded would serve for my subsistence until I could dig gold enough to replenish my stores. It was several days before I could determine whether to visit the northern or southern mines. I had heard nothing of the southern mines previous to my arrival in California, they having been discovered several months after the first gold was found by Marshall at Sutter's Mill. The southern mines are reported more healthy than the northern and equally rich, therefore I concluded to give them the first trial. Accordingly, on the morning of the 6th of September, I engaged passage on board the brigantine *Rambler*, Captain Dunham, bound for Stockton, on the San Joaquin River, distant from San Francisco 160 miles. The *Rambler* belonged to Palmer, Cook & Co., owners of the lumber-yard in which I had been employed most of the time since my arrival in San Francisco, consequently they charged me only $16 passage to Stockton.

During the forenoon I struck my tent and removed it, together with my provisions, on board the *Rambler*. At one o'clock, P. M., accompanied by two of the *Osceola's* passengers, I went on board the brig, where I found some thirty adventurers *en route* to the southern mines. We hove up anchor at two o'clock, and at sundown the wind died entirely away, and we came to anchor in San Pablo Bay, where we remained during the night. We got under way at an early hour on the following morning, and during the forenoon passed Benicia, Boston and New York of the Pacific. The latter place was surveyed and laid out in blocks, with streets crossing each other at right-angles, by its original proprietor, Colonel J. Stevenson, of the New York Regiment of California Volunteers. It contains a solitary frame building, and I fear it will never rival its Atlantic namesake, either in population or wealth.

At two o'clock, P. M., we left Suisun Bay and entered the San Joaquin River. The wind and tide being favorable, we made a good run during

SUTTER'S SAW-MILL, COLOMA, 1849.

the afternoon, and when the tide turned came to anchor for the night.

When the sun went down behind the *tulés* that night the mosquitoes rose up. They swooped down upon us like the locusts of Egypt, with a determination to devour every *green* thing. There were several on board the brig, and the mosquitoes seemed to know it. They didn't wait upon the order of coming, but they came in platoons, regiments and brigades, and their music made night hideous. We stood up manfully against fearful odds, and. fought with a desperation worthy of a better cause. We proposed an armistice, then a treaty of peace with indemnity—anything to stop the flow of blood; but our adversaries presented their bills so often that we found it impossible to liquidate their claims, and as a last resort beat a hasty retreat into the hold of the brig and fastened down the hatches.

Either side of the San Joaquin, from its entrance into Suisun Bay to within a few miles of Stockton, is bordered by a continuous *tulé* marsh, and during the summer and fall all the mosquitoes in California hold high carnival here. Early on the morning of the 8th we proceeded up the river with a fair wind and favorable tide. Before night we came to the conclusion that our brig was either too large for the river, or the river too small for the brig. Our Captain knew very little about seamanship, and less about the channel, therefore the brig ran aground several times during the day. Whenever she grounded on a sand-bar or a mud-

14

flat, a rope was made fast to the taffrail and all hands went ashore among the *tulés* and mosquitoes and pulled her off. Captain Dunham being of an irritable disposition, and never having experienced religion in the natural way, nor taken any stock in early piety, made things on board the *Rambler* extremely lively for all hands. The exercise of pulling the brig off of mud-flats became monotonous before night, and the passengers rebelled. The Captain's remarks being more forcible than polite or convincing, we refused to obey his commands, and he tied up the brig for the night within 15 miles of Stockton. In nearly every bend of the river, which is as crooked as a Virginia fence, we started a flock of ducks. I shot several during the day. At five o'clock next morning we got under way and proceeded up the river to the mouth of the slough on which Stockton is situated, where we again grounded, but got off without much difficulty, and at four o'clock, P. M., reached Stockton.

On my departure from San Francisco, I had received from Mr. George W. Wright, the junior partner of the firm of Palmer, Cook & Co., a letter of introduction to a merchant in Stockton, of the name of Leland, whose acquaintance I made immediately upon landing, and was invited by him to remove my baggage on board his store-ship, tied up at the bank of the slough, and consider it my home as long as I remained in that place. I gladly availed myself of his kind invitation, which was also extended to my two companions, the brothers Kelly,

CITY OF STOCKTON, FALL OF 1849.

nent business men several Philadelphians, among whom are Messrs. Gillingham and Henry Hugg.

During my brief sojourn in Stockton, miners were constantly arriving from the different diggings, some in quest of provisions, and others *en route* to San Francisco for the purpose of returning to the States by the first conveyance. Those who had gone to the mines with the determination to give them a thorough trial before crying *peccavi* were generally successful; but those who had expected to realize fortunes immediately upon reaching the *placers* were invariably disappointed, and becoming disheartened returned to San Francisco with their hands in their breeches' pockets, and their hearts very nearly in the same place. I made it a rule to inquire of every miner I met about his success in the mines, and the best location for a green-hand to visit. Some answered my interrogatories in a satisfactory manner, and others, not being overstocked with the milk of human kindness, intimated that I had better learn from experience. I soon came to the latter conclusion, and commenced making the necessary preparations for my departure. I packed my provisions in raw-hide sacks, engaged transportation mules, and on the morning of the 13th, accompanied by the brothers Kelly, set out for the *placers* on the river Calaveras, distant about 40 miles.

CHAPTER XIV.

OUR first day's journey was over a level and sparsely-timbered country, thickly covered with wild oats and mustard. Owing to the excessive heat of the weather and the proverbial stubbornness of our mules, we encamped the first night 12 miles from Stockton. After the mules had been relieved of their loads and pack-saddles and securely tethered, we kindled a fire at the roots of a large oak, and, having eaten a hastily-prepared meal of broiled pork, pilot-bread and coffee, spread our blankets on the ground and turned in for the night. When I awoke next morning, the muleteers had the animals packed ready for a start, and my companions were seated around the camp-fire discussing a pot of coffee which I helped them to dispatch, then shouldering our fire-arms we resumed our journey. The heat and dust during the day were almost insupportable. The dust in our trail was as hot as the ashes

(239)

of a volcano, and curled and crisped our boots until it was with great difficulty we could travel. We bivouacked the second night under the wide-spreading branches of an oak on the north bank of the Calaveras, 20 miles from our previous night's encampment. We killed several quail and squirrels during the day, which, with the addition of hardtack and coffee, served for our supper.

In the evening we visited the lodge of a party of Digger Indians *en route* to Stockton, who were encamped a few hundred yards below us. They treated us with great civility, and at parting presented us with a quarter of dried venison, which was very acceptable. I presented the chief—who, by-the-by, was one of the ugliest-looking red-skins I ever beheld—with a plug of tobacco. The Digger eats very little animal food. Like his brother, the gorilla, he is a vegetarian and subsists principally on wild berries and acorns, occasionally luxuriating on snails and grasshoppers. He cuts his hair with a sharp stone, and boils water in a basket. In the winter he burrows in the earth like a prairie dog, and emerges from his den in the spring as fat as a grizzly. His costume is decidedly primitive and airy, consisting of a breech-clout and a pair of moccasins. Since civilization has overtaken him, he occasionally dons a paper collar and a pair of Mexican spurs.

On our return to camp we placed the muleteers on guard, and wrapping ourselves in our blankets, were soon fast in the embrace of Morpheus. Just before daylight I was startled by the sharp report

ON THE ROAD TO THE MINES.

of a rifle and a tremendous clattering of tin pans, pots and kettles. I grasped my rifle, which was lying alongside of me, and sprang behind the nearest tree, where I found my two companions dodging about like lizards around a cabbage-tree, expecting every moment to be skewered by the arrow of an Indian. I am not easily frightened, but I will confess that I felt a little nervous. Our fears were soon relieved by one of the muleteers, who informed us that he had discharged his gun at a *coyote*. The "*varmint*," not having the fear of powder and lead before his eyes, had commenced depredations on one of our provision sacks. He escaped unscathed, but, in his sudden departure, had upset our coffee-pot and other tinware, which impressed us with the belief that the Diggers had made an attack on our camp.

After rolling up our blankets, we set about preparing our morning repast, which being completed at sunrise, we assisted the muleteers to pack the animals and again resumed our journey. Charley Kelly and myself started ahead of the train, and being in a musical mood, I struck up the following song, to the air of "O Susannah," and my companion joined in the chorus:

SONG OF THE GOLD-DIGGER.

I.

I came from Quakerdelphia
  With my wash-bowl on my knee,
I'm going to California,
  The gold-dust for to see.

It rained all night the day I left,
 The weather it was dry,
The sun so hot I froze to death,
 O Anna, don't you cry!

Chorus—O California!
  That's the land for me,
 I'm going to Calaveras,
  With my wash-bowl on my knee.

II.

The *Osceola* I did board,
 And traveled on the sea;
And every time I thought of home,
 I wished it wasn't me!
The brig she reared like any horse
 That had of oats a wealth—
But she found she couldn't throw me,
 So I thought I'd throw myself.

Chorus—O Ann Eliza!
  Don't you cry for me,
 I'm going to Calaveras,
  With my wash-bowl on my knee.

III.

I thought of all the pleasant times
 We'd had together, dear;
I thought I ought to cry a bit,
 But couldn't find a tear;
The pilot-bread was in my mouth,
 The gold-dust in my eye,
And though from you I'm far away,
 Dear Anna, don't you cry.

Chorus—O Ann Eliza!
  Don't you cry for me,
 I'm going to Calaveras,
  With my wash-bowl on my knee.

IV.

I soon shall be in mining camp,
  And then I'll look around,
And when I see the gold-dust there,
  I'll pick it off the ground.
I'll scrape the mountains clean, old girl,
  I'll drain the rivers dry,
A pocketful of rocks bring home,
  So, Anna, don't you cry.
Chorus—O California!
      That's the land for me,
    I'm going to Calaveras,
      With my wash-bowl on my knee.

During the morning we killed a hare and several quail. We also saw in the trail the fresh footprint of a grizzly, and congratulated ourselves that the foot was not in it, for we had no desire to meet one of those animals, even under the most favorable circumstances. We stopped on the bank of a small stream, 12 miles from our last encampment, and awaited the arrival of our companions and baggage. After dinner, I again set out ahead of the train, and at four o'clock, P. M., arrived at *Dos Agua*— "double springs"—where I learned from a Sonorian that I had traveled some 4 miles beyond the trail that led to the Calaveras diggings. After partaking of a cup of coffee, for which I paid fifty cents, I retraced my steps to the Calaveras trail, and though weary and footsore, pushed on as rapidly as possible after my companions, whom I overtook at sundown, as they were entering the Calaveras cañon. I was completely exhausted, and spreading my blanket on the bank of the river, retired supperless for the night. I awoke at an early hour next morning, and after partaking of a hearty breakfast, discharged the muleteers and commenced making preparations for pitching my tent.

I suggested to my companions the propriety of messing together, to which they readily assented. We accordingly pitched our tents under a large oak near the bank of the river, and spent the remainder of the day unpacking and arranging our stores and cooking utensils. Although our provisions were joint stock, we agreed to dig for the *oro* separately— each man for himself.

On the morning of the 17th, I arose at five o'clock, and dressing myself *a la California*, shouldered my pick, crow-bar and spade, and started, tin pan in hand, for the bar of the river, where I commenced my initiatory labors at gold-digging. I was engaged all the forenoon removing the large rocks from my claim. In the afternoon I commenced washing the earth, and at sundown I weighed my " dust " and found I had panned out a quarter of an ounce—$4 worth. On the following day I washed out $10 worth of the precious metal. Learning from a Mexican that rich diggings had been discovered by a party of Digger Indians, on a bar several miles lower down the river, I reported the circumstance to my companions, and a party was forthwith formed to visit the Indian diggings on the following day.

On the morning of the 20th of September, accompanied by a party of miners of various nationalities and colors, I started on a prospecting

MINERS AT WORK IN 1849.

tour to the reported rich Indian diggings. On our arrival at the encampment of the Indians, we were somewhat surprised at meeting only half a dozen squaws and papooses. We inquired for the bucks, but could obtain no satisfactory answer to our interrogatories. Being somewhat fatigued by a march of three hours over hills and through gulches and cañons, exposed to the broiling rays of the sun, we placed our fire-arms against a tree, and sat down to rest our weary limbs and chat with the squaws. We had been seated only a few moments, when the Indians commenced making their appearance from all points of the compass. Every rock in the cañon seemed to send forth a red-skin. We secured our fire-arms and again sat down. The Indians were rather shy at first, but after a little persuasion seated themselves around us, and those who could speak Spanish entered into conversation with us. After a few preliminary remarks, we informed them of the object of our visit, and asked if there was plenty of *oro* in the cañon. They shrugged their shoulders and informed us that the cañon was *much a malo;* but we placed very little reliance on what they said, and in order fully to satisfy ourselves in regard to the richness of the locality, commenced prospecting. After traveling over the cañon and bed of the river several hours, looking for gold, we came to the conclusion that the Indians had told the truth, and, bidding them good-bye, commenced retracing our steps.

Midway between the Indian encampment and our own, we discovered a bar richer than the one we were working, and concluded to remove to it on the following day. Accordingly, at an early hour next morning, we bundled up our tents and provisions, packed them on mules, and started for the new diggings, which we reached at noon. The afternoon was spent in pitching our tents and arranging the provisions. At daylight next morning I selected what I considered a good location, and commenced operations. I labored hard two days in removing the boulders from my claim, but was amply rewarded for my labor. On the third day I reached a crevice in a rock, some four feet below the surface of the ground, and in two hours succeeded in extracting therefrom forty-five dollars' worth of gold in nuggets of the value of from one to five dollars. I did not report my good-luck to my companions, but toiled on, early and late, day after day, until I had extracted nearly four hundred dollars' worth of the precious metal from the claim. I then abandoned it, and reported progress to my fellow-diggers, all of whom had been less fortunate than myself. Some had not averaged one dollar per day; others had been more successful, yet none had met with the success they anticipated. Those who had expected to realize a fortune in a few days or weeks were sadly disappointed. I left San Francisco with the intention of remaining in the mines during the fall and winter, but I had not dug three weeks before I found my health and strength failing. On the 10th of October, I had an attack of rheumatism which doubled me up like a rainbow and put a veto on any further attempts at

MINING SCENE, 1849

gold-digging. My companions advised me to return to Stockton or San Francisco and recruit my health, but I declined doing so until I had become so crippled by disease that I could scarcely hobble out of my tent.

On the morning of the 12th, I sold my provisions and mining implements by auction at ruinous rates, and packing my wardrobe, consisting of an extra flannel shirt, a pair of linsey-woolsey pants, a six-shooter and a bowie-knife, I engaged passage in a trader's cart, and, bidding my companions adieu, started for Stockton, where I arrived the following evening.

On my arrival in Stockton, I was advised by my friend Leland to place myself under the charge of a physician for a few weeks, or until I had fully recovered my health. Accordingly, I visited the City Hospital, a large canvas tent, resembling very much a circus pavilion, and inquired the price of board with medical attendance. The attending physician informed me that the charge was two ounces—$32—per day; but if I preferred being visited at my own quarters, it would be somewhat less. After having learned that I was not overstocked with the "root of all evil," he very condescendingly informed me that he would charge me only $16 a visit, and the cost of the medicine prescribed. I left him with the promise that I would employ him if I did not get better in a day or two. On my way back to my lodgings, I recollected having purchased, before leaving Philadelphia, a bottle of opodeldoc, and I at once resolved upon testing its virtues before purchasing medicine at California prices. I accordingly applied it freely to my swollen limbs, and on the following day I felt very much relieved. I continued the application, and when the bottle was emptied of its contents, I was a well man. I consider the twenty-five cents paid for that bottle of opodeldoc the most judicious investment I ever made. Having recovered my health, I cast about for some employment whereby I might turn an honest penny. During my sojourn in Stockton, I mixed freely with the returning and disgusted miners, from whom I learned that they were selling their mining implements at ruinously low prices. An idea struck me one day, which I immediately acted upon, for fear that another might strike in the same place and cause an explosion. The heaven-born idea that had penetrated my cranium was this: start in the mercantile line, purchase the tents and implements of the returning miners at low figures, and sell to the greenhorns *en route* to the mines at California prices! I purchased a large tent in which to store my goods and commenced operations. Fortune smiled on me, and I was happy. But every rose has its thorn, and

"The best laid plans of mice and men gang aft aglee."

The first rain of the season dampened my ardor and disheartened me. My bowels yearned for the flesh-pots of San Francisco, so, early in November, I bade farewell to Stockton, engaged passage on

SAN FRANCISCO, WINTER OF 1849-'50.

board a schooner, and in due course of time reached the city of the Golden Gate.

San Francisco, during my absence of two months, had become so changed that I scarcely recognized it. Substantial frame buildings had superseded frail canvas tenements, and piers had been extended many hundred yards into the bay, at which vessels from the four quarters of the globe were discharging their cargoes. I visited the gold-diggers' encampment, Happy Valley, but that too was so changed, that I could hardly recognize a familiar spot or countenance. A three-story warehouse was being erected on the spot where I had pitched my tent two months previously. The saw and hammer of the carpenter could be heard in every square, and the voice of the crier and auctioneer at the corner of nearly every street. The *Plaza* was covered with booths, in which could be had the merchandise of all nations.

As hotel accommodations were limited as well as expensive, I purchased for $100 a ship's galley, size four by five feet, which I located in Happy Valley and commenced housekeeping. My furniture consisted of an empty flour-barrel and a nail-keg. The former served for a table and the latter as a chair, minus a back. My cooking utensils were as inexpensive as my furniture. A second-hand frying-pan, a dilapidated coffee-pot, and a rheumatic jack-knife comprised the catalogue. My bed consisted of two blankets and a soft block of wood for a pillow. Unfortunately, I was, by actual measurement, eight inches longer than my shebang; there-

fore, when "I lay me down to sleep," I was compelled to lie bias, and I couldn't turn over without
going out-of-doors.

"Man wants but little here below,"

but he wants that little long enough to turn over in.
With no disrespect to Happy Valley, there is one
thing which, as a truthful historian, I am compelled,
more in sorrow than in anger, to relate. The flea,
that festive and lively little "animile," was quite
prevalent. He annoyed me sorely, yea, prodig-
iously! The sojourners in Happy Valley and surrounding sand-hills never required cupping or
leeching, as both operations were performed by the
fleas, *nolens volens.*

Being the owner of a house, I commenced looking about for some employment whereby I could
raise the needful to keep the pot boiling. My first
business venture was in the pickle line, and the
following extract from my journal will illustrate
the *modus operandi:*

"Pickles are scarce and sell at fabulous prices. The
beach of Happy Valley for miles is lined with dis-
carded pickle-jars and bottles, and I have conceived
the happy idea of utilizing them. I have gathered
up, cleansed and stored around my shebang, several
hundred bottles ready for use. This afternoon, I
boarded a vessel just arrived from Boston, and persuaded the Captain to sell me a barrel of salted
cucumbers and half a barrel of cider-vinegar, to be
delivered to-morrow morning."

After supper I wrapped myself in my blankets

and laid down to pleasant dreams; but toward morning, I had a vision, and in that vision I saw—pickles. Captain Perkins delivered the cucumbers and vinegar, according to agreement, received his pay, and I immediately commenced bottling them. Before night, I had the largest stock of bottled pickles in San Francisco, and at the close of the week I struck a balance-sheet, and found that I had cleared $300 by the speculation. My next mercantile venture was a "corner" in tobacco pipes, by which I realized $150 in twenty-four hours.

Having abiding faith in the old aphorism, "change makes change," I concluded to abandon mercantile pursuits and try my luck at the newspaper business. I resolved to commence at the lower round of the ladder, and gradually work my way upward. Suiting the action to the thought, I at once applied to the proprietors of the *Pacific News*, a tri-weekly, printed on a foolscap sheet, then in its infancy, for permission to canvass for a carrier's route on their journal. After a long interview, during which the project was discussed *pro* and *con*, I obtained the sole and exclusive right to canvass for subscribers, and serve the *News* in San Francisco and suburbs, which latter included Happy Valley and adjacent sand-hills.

Messrs. Falkner & Leland, proprietors of the *Pacific News*, were both Eastern men. Falkner formerly published a paper in Norwich, Conn., and Leland was one of the proprietors of the Clinton Hotel, New York. The first number of the *News* was issued on the 25th of August, with Falkner

15

as editor, and Leland, business manager. A few weeks subsequently, Charles Eames, of Washington, D. C., appointed by President Polk consul to the Hawaiian Islands, arrived in San Francisco, *en route*, but was prevailed upon by Falkner & Leland to forego his mission, locate in San Francisco, and assume editorial charge of their journal, at a salary of $500 per month. As the election and inauguration of Zachary Taylor, as President of the United States, had rendered the recall of Mr. Eames a foregone conclusion, that gentleman considered discretion the better part of valor, and accepted the editorship of the *News*.

Simultaneously with the engagement of Mr. Eames as editor-in-chief, a tall, lank, hirsute Yankee, of the name of Ames *alias* "Boston" *alias* "Big Ames," was engaged as local reporter. A few weeks subsequently Mr. Ferdinand C. Ewer, a recent graduate of old Harvard, and a gentleman of fine literary attainments, was added to the staff of the *News* as assistant editor.

I experienced little difficulty in getting up a paying list of subscribers for the *News*. Nearly every one on whom I called gladly subscribed for it, and paid me promptly at the end of each week. I had scarcely become accustomed to my new vocation, when the situation of book-keeper was tendered to me by the proprietors of the *News*, with a salary of $100 a week. I sold my carrier's route for $200, my shebang in Happy Valley for $125, and accepted the situation, with the proffer of a sleeping-bunk in the office. Soon after I was installed in my new quarters, Mr. Leland sold his half-interest in the *News* to Major Allen, U. S. A., for $50,000, returned to New York and resumed his former occupation, hotel-keeping.

The *Pacific News* was the *first* tri-weekly, and the *third* newspaper then published in California, its cotemporaries being the *Alta California*, published by Gilbert & Kemble, in San Francisco, and the *Placer Times*, published by E. Gilbert & Co., Sacramento City, and edited by Jesse Giles—both weekly sheets, and small patterns at that, the latter being foolscap size. Printing-paper was very scarce in California, but the market was overstocked with unruled foolscap, which was substituted for the former. The size of the *News* was a foolscap sheet, and as enlargement was a matter of impossibility, supplementary sheets were added to accommodate advertisers. The price of the *News* was 12½ cents a copy. Steamer edition, printed on wrapping-paper of various colors and qualities, 50 cents a copy. Advertisements were inserted at $5 a square, each insertion.

CHAPTER XV.

First State election—The winning candidates—"Fire! fire! fire!"—A million dollars' worth of property destroyed—"Big Ames's" report of the conflagration—An eccentric judge—Muddy streets—First vocal entertainment in San Francisco—Early theatricals—"Them literary fellers"—Terrence McVerdant—"A rallying song for the gold-diggers."

THE State Constitution, framed and signed by the delegates at Monterey, in October, was submitted to a vote of the people on November 13th. State officers were also voted for at the same time; and the election passed off in an orderly manner. Out of the two thousand votes polled in San Francisco only five were opposed to the Constitution, and in the whole country less than a thousand votes were cast against it, and upwards of twelve thousand for it. The following State officers, U. S. Senators and Representatives were elected:

Governor, Peter H. Burnett; *Lieutenant-Governor*, John McDougal; *U. S. Senators*, John C. Fremont, Wm. M. Gwin; *Representatives in Congress*, George W. Wright, Edward Gilbert; *Secretary of State*, Wm. Van Voorhies; *Treasurer*, Richard Roman; *Comptroller*, J. S. Houston; *Attorney-General*, Edward J. C. Kewen; *Surveyor-General*, Charles J. Whiting; *Chief Justice*, S. C.

(262)

"OLD ADOBE" CUSTOM-HOUSE, 1849.

Hastings; *Associate Justices*, J. A. Lyon, Nathaniel Bennett; *State Senators*, Gabriel B. Post, Nathaniel Bennett; *Assembly*, Wm. Van Voorhies, Edward Randolph, Levi Stowell, J. H. Watson, J. A. Patterson.

Late in October a Democratic meeting, the first in California, was held in the *Plaza*, in front of the "old *adobe*," at which the following officers were chosen: *President*, Colonel John W. Geary;* *Vice-Presidents*, Dr. McMillan, Thomas J. Agnew, John McVickar, W. H. Jones, O. P. Sutton, Annis Merrill, E. V. Joyce and W. H. Jones; *Secretaries*, J. Ross Browne, John A. McGlynn, Joseph T. Downey and Daniel Cronin. A series of resolutions were adopted, a red-hot Democratic speech delivered by the Hon. Wm. Van Voorhies, and the meeting adjourned.

Early on the morning of the 24th of December, San Francisco was aroused by the startling cry of "*fire! fire!*" and the citizens rushed pell-mell to the scene of conflagration. The fire originated in Dennison's Exchange, adjoining the Parker House, situated on Kearney Street, opposite the *Plaza*, and in a few hours property valued at more than a million dollars was destroyed. The Parker House, one of the most imposing buildings in San Francisco, with its *faro* and *monté* tables and other gambling paraphernalia, was totally destroyed, as was also the El Dorado, at the corner of Washington and Kearney Streets. The blowing up of several buildings in Washington Street, near Montgomery,

---

* Afterward Governor of Pennsylvania.

by order of Alcalde Geary, arrested the progress of
the fire in that direction.   Nearly every building
in the square bounded by Washington, Clay, Montgomery and Kearney Streets was destroyed.   The
controlling spirit during the progress of the fire
was David C. Broderick,* a New York fireman,
who worked like a Trojan, and whose stentorian
voice, shrill as a trumpet, could be heard above the
crashing of the falling buildings and the din of the
excited crowd.   Before the ground in the burnt
district had become cold, the *debris* was removed,
canvas tenements erected, and the "gay gamboliers"
were again plying their vocation as unconcernedly
as if nothing had occurred to interfere with their
business.

That fire was a "big thing" for "big Ames,"
local editor of the *News*.   He wrote out a spread-
eagle report as long as the Declaration of Independence, but when it appeared in print on the following morning, "curtailed of its fair proportions,"
cut down to less than a foolscap column, he was
completely demoralized.   He lost his temper and
swore like a trooper.   All efforts to soothe his
wounded feelings only added fresh fuel to the pent-
up volcano raging within his breast, which erupted
iron-clad oaths at every breath.   He said "the
News was a contemptible one-horse sheet; its proprietors might possibly run a hotel, but they didn't
understand the first principles of newspaper publishing, and he'd be darned if he'd write another
line for the d——d paper"—and he didn't.

---

* Subsequently U. S. Senator from California.

During the fall the business of the Alcalde had increased to such a degree, that the establishment of another court, with civil jurisdiction only, and in cases of sums exceeding $100, was authorized by the Governor, and William B. Almond was appointed judge. His court was called the "Court of First Instance." Almond was no paper-shell, but a decidedly hard nut to crack, as the legal fraternity who practiced in his court soon learned. He was a man of few words, and, to economize time, generally decided a case on the testimony of the first witness, without listening to the arguments of counsel. During the trial of a trivial case before his Honor, the counsel for the plaintiff called his opponent an oscillating Tarquin. The judge, in a stentorian voice, roared out: "A what?"

"An oscillating Tarquin, your Honor."

The judge removed his feet from the table in front of him, leaned forward, and pointing his index finger toward the offending disciple of Blackstone, ejaculated, in a voice of thunder: "If this honorable court knows herself, and she thinks she do, that remark is an insult to this honorable court, and you are fined two ounces, and stand committed till you down with the dust."

"But, your Honor," replied the trembling pettifogger.

"Silence, sir; this honorable court won't tolerate *cussing*, and never goes back on her decisions!"

It is needless to add that the fine was paid, and the trial proceeded.

"Old Tarquin," as the judge was afterward called,

was a decided character.   On a subsequent occasion
he adjourned court ten minutes in order to take a
drink with one of the jurors.   On another occasion
he insisted on trying two separate cases with the
same jury.   He said the jurors understood the
rulings of the court, and rendered a square verdict!

The rainy season was now at its height—that
ever-to-be-remembered fall and winter of 1849–'50
—and the streets were simply awful!   Awful is a
mild term, but I can't just now call to mind a more
expressive adjective.   They ran rivers of mud, and
swallowed up every living thing that attempted to
cross them.   Water-proof suits and cavalry or long
boots were in great demand, and commanded Mun-
chausenistic prices.   It was no uncommon occurrence to see at the same time a mule stalled in the
middle of the street with only his head above
the mud, and an unfortunate pedestrian who had
slipped off the plank sidewalk, being fished out by
a companion.   Some good Samaritan, with a heart
overflowing with the milk of human kindness,
erected at the corner of Clay and Kearney Streets
the following warning to the unwary :

> THIS STREET IS IMPASSABLE,
> NOT EVEN JACKASSABLE!

On January 8th, the anniversary of the Battle of
New Orleans, another election, the second in San
Francisco, was held for members of the Legislature,

OLD SCHOOL-HOUSE, OPPOSITE THE PLAZA

MUDDY STREETS, WINTER OF 1849-'50.

Alcalde and *Ayuntamiento*. Despite the rain, which poured down in torrents during the day, the unterrified voters turned out in full strength, and elected the following gentlemen to the offices named: *State Senator*, David C. Broderick; *Member of Assembly*, Samuel J. Clarke; *First Alcalde*, John W. Geary; *Second Alcalde*, Frank Turk; *Ayuntamiento*, Hugh C. Murray, A. M. Van Nostrand, M. Crooks, J. Hagan, F. C. Gray, Frank Tilford, A. J. Ellis, Talbot H. Green, Wm. M. Stewart, Samuel Brannan, W. H. Davis and James S. Graham.

Man is naturally a social being; he likes rational enjoyment, and is fond of amusement. The first vocal entertainment in San Francisco was given by Mr. Stephen C. Massett, in the school-house, fronting the *Plaza*, on the evening of June 22d, 1849. It was a one-man entertainment—Mr. Massett being the only performer. Front seats were reserved for the ladies, of whom there were four present. Tickets were $3 each, and the house was crowded to overflowing. During the year 1849, and the early part of 1850, circuses were established in San Francisco, first by Rowe and soon after by Foley. The following were the prices of admission: Pit, $3; box, $5; private boxes, $50. The first theatrical performance in San Francisco was given in January, 1850, by a company under the management of Atwater & Madison, in the second story of Washington Hall, on Washington Street, opposite the *Plaza*. The plays produced were *Charles II* and *The Wife*. Subsequently, Mr. Rowe added a stage to his circus for theatrical performances, and the following artistes were engaged: Mr. and Mrs. Hambleton, Mr. and Mrs. Battuss, and Mr. and Mrs. McCron. Mesdames Ray and Kirby soon after joined the company.

About this time the editor of the *News* was sorely worried by "them literary fellers," who abound in all communities, with their contributions on all conceivable subjects, which in most cases were consigned to the waste-basket, that receptacle of the outcroppings of unappreciated genius.

The following epistle, however, found its way into print. It was written by a disconsolate son of the Emerald Isle to his sweetheart in New York, and shows the status of matters viewed from a Hibernian stand-point:

SAN FRANSISKY, Dec. 1, 1849.

BIDDY DARLIN':—I've been to the mines, bad luck to 'em. For sivin long weeks, Biddy, acushla, I sarched the bowels of *terry firmer* for goold, and all I got was the dissinterry, by rasin of workin' on an empty stomick. The divil a thing to ate for brekfist, and the same for dinner, and ditto repated for supper; an' all the time throwing up mud an' wather, is mighty wakening for the insides. Pitaytees was a $1 a pound, and no mate to be had but gristly bares, which is tough customers. In cowld wether the craythurs—I mane gristly bares—comes down from the mountains, with their arums extended, as if they wanted to bid ye welkim; but the moment they're fornenst ye, they grab ye, the craythers, and squaze the breth o' life out ov ye. Some ov the byes that wint out in the same ship wid me found goold galore, but the divil as much as the vally of a weddin'-ring, Biddy, did Terry git for his thrubble. The black luck was on me, darlin', for lavin ye, a dacent, modest colleen, as ye are, to come to a kunthry where the wimin are the color of a dirthy copper-kittle, and have no more dry-goods on their backs, savin' your prisence, Biddy, than mother Ave had before she turned manty-maker an' interduced the fashun of the vegetabul apruns.

I got back from the mines a fortnit ago, and a most unfortnit go it was for me that I ever wint there. Here I am in San Fransisky knockin' about without a rap. What's to become of me, Biddy, mavourneen, the saints only know. Only to think that I should lave the comfortable berth I had swaping the . strates of New Yorick, to come to this haythen kunthry, where the strate-claning is done by the burds, and drinkin', gamblin', speckalatin' an' shooiside is the only fashionable amusements. Ye'll see it statid in the papers, Biddy, that the diggers are findin' goold in "quartz." Biddy, it's a lie!—a base, disateful, onchristian lie! I niver seen a lump of goold yit that would fill a gill measure.

Couldn't ye raise a subskripshun, Biddy, among the strateswapers, to pay me passidge back. If I was only back in New Yorick, dead or alive, I'd niver lave it while grass grows and wather runs. Your loving,

TERRENCE McVERDANT.

The following poem, the earliest written and published in California, appeared in the *Pacific News*, with the following editorial comments:

We cannot refrain from publishing the following vigorous stanzas, trusting that they will impart as much pleasure in the perusal, to our readers, as they have to ourselves. We should be happy to give the author's name, as we deem them to possess no ordinary merit:

A RALLYING SONG FOR THE GOLD-DIGGERS.

To the mines! to the mines! away to the mines!
Where the virgin gold in the crevice shines!
Where the shale and the slate and the quartz enfold,
In their stony arms, the glittering gold.

'Tis in vain that ye seek any longer to hide
Your treasures of gold in your rivers so wide,
In your gulches so deep, or your wild cañon home,
For the Anglo-American race is come.

And the noise that ye hear is the sound of the spade,
The pick, the bar, and the bright shining blade,
Of the knife and the shovel, the cradle and pan,
Brave adjuncts of toil to the laboring man!

Far up in the mountain, all rugged and steep,
Far down in the cañon, all foaming and deep,
In the bars of the rivers—the small mountain plains,
Lies the wealth that ye seek for, in numberless grains.

Turn the stream from its bed—search the bottom with care,
The largest, the richest, the finest is there;
Dig deep in the gulches, nor stop till the stone
Reveals thee its treasure, or tells thee there's none.

Nor be thou disheartened, dismayed nor cast down,
If success should decline thy first efforts to crown;
Go ahead! Go ahead! Since creation began,
"No wealth without toil," is the record to man.

Old Mammon the sound of your coming hears,
And, aroused from his sleep of a million years,
He gazes around him, in wild surprise,
As Mexican rule from the region flies.

Now hie thee, old Mammon, far over the sea!
Thy long-hidden treasure all scattered shall be;
For the hands that now grasp it, free, ardent and bold,
Will give to the world its lost millions of gold.

Then away to the mines! away to the mines!
Where the virgin gold in the crevice shines;
Where the shale and the slate and the quartz enfold,
In their stony arms, the glittering gold!

A. R. K.

San Francisco, *March* 22, 1850.

CHAPTER XVI.

Locate in Sacramento City—The *Sacramento Transcript*—
First election in Sacramento—Three tickets in the field—
Names of the city and county officers elected—Meeting of
the Council-elect—Demas Strong chosen President—He
makes a speech—Adjourned meeting of Council—Mayor
Bigelow's message read and accepted—First message of the
first Mayor of Sacramento City.

DURING the winter of 1849–'50, I made the
acquaintance of Mr. George Kenyon Fitch, a practical printer, from New Orleans, who arrived in
San Francisco *via* Isthmus of Panama, in the
month of September. Before leaving New Orleans,
Mr. Fitch shipped, in a sailing vessel around Cape
Horn, two presses, (a hand and card press,) types,
ink, and some thirty reams of printing-paper, with
the view of publishing a newspaper in California,
on the arrival of the material. The invoice price
of the paper, types and presses was $950, but when
they arrived in San Francisco, in the early part of
March, 1850, they were valued at $15,000, and
could have been sold for that amount in coin, as
printing material was very scarce, and "sorts"
were worth their weight in gold! Mr. Fitch proposed to five of the *attachés* of the *Pacific News*—
F. C. Ewer, H. S. Warren, J. M. Julian, Theodore
Russell—and S. C. Upham—the formation of a co-

partnership, with a view to the publication of a newspaper in Sacramento City. The proposition was accepted, articles of agreement executed, and we started at once for that place.

We arrived in Sacramento immediately after the great flood, which had inundated the town, and it was in a sadly demoralized condition. We rented the second floor of a frame building, on Second Street, between J and K Streets, and on the *first day of April*, 1850, the initial number of the tri-weekly *Sacramento Transcript* was issued by Fitch, Upham & Co. It was printed on a folio sheet, in Brevier and Nonpareil type. A steamer edition, for circulation in the Atlantic States, was printed on the first of each month. The tri-weekly sold at 12½ cents a copy, and the steamer edition at 50 cents a copy. Advertisements were inserted at $4 per square, each insertion. The six copartners occupied the following positions on the paper: G. K. Fitch, heavy and fighting editor; F. C. Ewer, literary editor; H. S. Warren, foreman; J. M. Julian, compositor; Theodore Russell, pressman, and S. C. Upham, local reporter, printer's devil, business manager, "dead-head," etc.

Sacramento City being in its infancy, in a chrysalis or state of transition, just emerging from its shell, hotel accommodations were limited. We lodged in the office, and obtained our meals at different places. I paid $16 a week for two meals a day at a French restaurant, on the levee, and slept on the soft side of the office counter, with a roll of paper for a pillow.

The object and aims of the *Transcript* were fully set forth in the following " Introductory :"

The opening of a new paper is like the planting of a tree. The hopes of many hearts cluster around it. The anxious mind labors over it by night and by day, and the watchful eye guards it, as, in its youth, it struggles into life. Encouraging words and the helping hand of its friends fall like raindrops around it, and the approving smile of the public steals in, like the sunshine, to open its buds. In the covert of its leaves all pure principles and high aims should find a home; and from it invisible voices should rise forth from the nests of those pure principles, to delight, to warm and to instruct the world. Its shade should be free to all. It should reach forth its branches to shield the innocent from the pelting storm; and, conscious of its fearless might, men should come to it for protection, and find refreshment in its shade. It should be nurtured by no unhealthy influences; it should be propped up by no interested motives; its growth should be free and unrestrained. Perchance it may wither in its youth, and no longer be the home of healthy influences. Perhaps it may be stricken in its manhood by the storm of adversity. Perchance it may flourish through the years and grow green; but, of all dangers that assail it from without, the insidious influence of those who may cluster around it for their own private ends is the most withering, and the most to be feared. A newspaper should never be *used*. It is too tremendous a lever to be brought to bear for any purpose, save the good of the public.

Such is our ideal; and with such an ideal before us, do we present ourselves before the public of Sacramento City. In politics, the *Transcript* will sedulously maintain an independent course, endeavoring to do justice to both parties. In religion, it will be neutral. We shall earnestly advocate such measures as we deem to be for the best interests of our city. We shall urge the introduction of every class of improvements—shoot error as it flies, and watch for every injury that is stealing in upon us. We shall endeavor to present to our readers in Sacramento City and the mines, the news from the

Pacific Coast, from the States, from Europe, from China and the Islands of the Pacific. For our friends in San Francisco and abroad, we shall collect the earliest intelligence from the mines. We shall inform them of the condition of things in California during the successive stages of its rapid growth, and shall spare no labor or expense to give our sheet that variety and interest which an intelligent community demands. Every facility will be extended to our advertising friends. So soon as the want of Sacramento will warrant it, we shall enlarge our sheet and issue our paper daily.

A part of our columns will be devoted to literature, to criticism, poetry, and anything of the *belles-lettres* cast. We have procured not only correspondents who will keep us advised of the latest intelligence from the mines, but several from San Francisco and the States, whose papers will be of a lighter and more literary character. We shall endeavor to give the *Transcript* an extensive circulation in the *placers*. It will thus be a connecting link between the business and mining community; furnishing merchants in San Francisco and Sacramento a convenient means for communication with the mines.

Such are our aims, and to attain them we shall use our highest endeavors; trusting, as we embark in the enterprise, that our well-meant efforts will meet with support from the known liberality of the inhabitants of the city of our adoption.

The day on which the first number of the *Transcript* was published, in addition to being "*All-fools' Day*," was election day in Sacramento. It was the first election under the City Charter, and there were three tickets in the field. Canvassing had been going on for several weeks previously, both in the city and throughout the county, and an immense number of ballots and handbills had been circulated. The polls remained open until late in the evening, and there were lively times around the ballot-boxes. There was no rioting, but a great deal of superfluous gas was ventilated and considerable whisky drunk. The following political advertisements, published in the *Transcript* on the morning of the election, will serve to show the complexion of affairs:

DEMOCRATIC NOMINATIONS. — In pursuance of a public call, a meeting of Democratic citizens was convened at the City Hotel, in Sacramento City, on Monday evening, March 25, 1850, for the purpose of organizing the Democratic Party, and nominating a Ticket for City and County Officers, to be supported at the ensuing election. John S Fowler was called to the chair; J. P. Rogers, H. A. Shelden and Lorin Pickering were chosen Vice Presidents, and John K. Brown and Orlando McKnight appointed Secretaries.

On motion, a committee of three was appointed by the chair to draft resolutions, whereupon L Pickering, James McClatchy, and J. K. Brown, were appointed such committee:

On motion, a committee of fifteen was appointed by the chair to report a Ticket to be supported at the coming election for City and County Officers, and the following gentlemen constituted such committee:

Wm. C. Kibbe, John Ayres, Alex. Boyd, C. H. Cummings, James McClatchy, James Orchard, D. B Milne, —— McCalla, —— Noulton, J. Sherwood, J. F. Thorp, Levi Hermance, J. R. Riggs, Wm. S. Jackson, J. Deming.

The committee appointed to report a Ticket, having retired, reported the following—

CITY TICKET.

For Mayor—Thomas J. Henley.
For City Recorder—Charles A Johnson.
For Marshal—N. C. Cunningham.
For City Attorney—A C Monson.
For Assessor—B F. Moore.
For Treasurer—Barton Lee.
For City Council—John S. Fowler, J. Sherwood, R. W. Vansickle, Wm Baker, Wm C. Kibbe, J Hardenbergh, Orlando McKnight, E L Brown, P. M. Dorsey.

COUNTY TICKET.

For Clerk Supreme Court—E. H Tharp.
District Attorney—John K. Brown.
County Judge—Ansel J. McCall.
County Clerk—Leander Warren.
County Attorney—Lewis Aldrich.
County Surveyor—J. H. Dickerson.
Sheriff—
County Recorder—Lewis A. Birdsall.
Coroner—P. F. Ewer.
County Treasurer—Eugene F. Gillespie.
County Assessor—L. P. Stafford

The Committee on Resolutions reported the following preamble and resolutions:

Whereas, a Government has been organized; a Constitution adopted; and a new State already, or about to be admitted into the Union: and, whereas, through the proper authorities, a City Charter has been obtained for this city, it becomes all true Republicans to exert themselves in procuring wholesome laws, and the success of sound democratic principles—the only principles that can secure a proper administration of

16

government and equal rights and privileges among
the governed—therefore, be it

Resolved, That the organization of government creates a necessity for the organization of party.

Resolved, That the republican principles laid down by Jefferson, the Father of Democracy, and the measures that have characterized all democratic administrations, meet with our hearty approval and unqualified support.

Resolved, That in Municipal, as well as State and National Governments, the laws should be so framed as to secure equal rights to all, and special privileges to none.

Resolved, That honest and honorable competition is the life of trade, and that we are opposed to fostering one branch of business at the expense of another, or building up one enterprise by taxing another, but that we stand on the broad platform of "Free Trade and Sailors' Rights."

Resolved, That the practice heretofore adopted, of taxing business instead of property, *and which is still authorized by section 5th of the City Charter*, is neither wise nor democratic, but that all revenue necessary to defray the expenses of government should be collected by a direct tax, levied upon property.

Resolved, That a fair and liberal compensation *only*, be awarded to office holders for their services, and *not such emoluments as may induce all to become office seekers*.

Resolved, That as it is *never too soon* to advocate Democratic principles, so it is *never too early* to exercise our united efforts in securing their triumph.

Resolved, That we now launch the good old ship of Democracy—spread her canvas to the breeze—nail her colors to the mast—and pledge our united efforts to secure the triumphant election of the regularly nominated Democratic candidates.

On motion, Levi Hermance Barton Lee, E. W. Crowell, S. W. Gregg, and J. F. Thorp, were constituted a Town Committee.

On motion, The Town Committee were instructed to confer with Democrats throughout the county for the purpose of holding a County Convention and organizing the Democratic party throughout the county.

On motion, the meeting adjourned

          JOHN S. FOWLER, Chairman.

J. K. BROWN,   } Secretaries.
ORLANDO McKNIGHT, }   1t

CITIZENS' MEETING.—At a spontaneous assemblage of the citizens of Sacramento City, held at the City Hotel, on Monday evening, the 25th inst., immediately upon the adjournment of the self-constituted Democratic meeting, whereat an attempt was made to organize a Democratic party, Demas Strong was called to the chair, and Jos. W. Winans appointed Secretary.

After some able and eloquent addresses, in explanation of the object of the meeting, the following resolutions were unanimously adopted:

Resolved, That a committee of five be appointed to draft a series of resolutions, for presentation at a subsequent public meeting of the citizens of Sacramento City, of the time and place of holding which, public notice shall be given by the chairman

Resolved, That Messrs Nickerson, Nolan, Bullock, Winans, and Warbass, constitute such committee

Resolved, That the Chair be added to such committee as the chairman thereof

Resolved, That in the view of this meeting, any attempt at this time to effect a political organization, on party grounds, is TOTALLY UNCALLED FOR, and that the meeting held this evening, prior to the present meeting, *did not*, and *does not* represent the Democratic Party of Sacramento City.

Resolved, That the Democratic Republicans here assembled, protest against the very partial proceedings of said meeting, as being contrary to Democratic principles and usages, and recommend the electors of Sacramento City to give their franchise to such men as they may deem most suitable to fill the various offices in their gift

Reso.ved, That the proceedings of this meeting be published in the "Placer Times" and "Sacramento Transcript"

On motion, the meeting was thereupon adjourned.

DEMAS STRONG, Chairman.

Jos. W. WINANS, Secretary. 1t

RANCHEROS, TO THE RESCUE!—The enemy is in the field—our bills have been mutilated, and in some instances destroyed; but let not your "angry passions rise" in consequence of the indignity. Imitate as far as in your power lies the example of your leader. Keep cool, work hard and vote early. Remember that abuse and curses, like young chickens, "will come home to roost." When once the votes are in the ballot boxes, no appeal can be taken. HOMBRES.

RANCHO TICKET.

THROUGH BY DAYLIGHT!

For Mayor—JOSEPH GRANT.

For City Recorder—B. F. Washington

For Councilmen—T. McDowell, C A. Tweed, Z. Hubbard, Charles O. Brewster, E. J Fcency, D Strong, Dr. J. F. Morse, Dr. James S. Martin, Charles H. Miller.

For City Marshal—M. D. Eyre.

For City Attorney—A. C. Monson.

For City Assessor—Wm. F. Prettyman.

For City Treasurer—Barton Lee.

RANCHO TICKET—FOR THE COUNTY.

"*All's well that ends well.*"

For Clerk of the Supreme Court—E H. Tharp.

For District Attorney—William C. Wallace.

For County Judge—Edward J. Willis.

For County Clerk—Presley Dunlap.

For County Attorney—John H. McKune.

For County Surveyor—Andrew J. Binney.

For Sheriff—Joseph D. Magee, (better known as Johnny Rancho)

For County Recorder—Thomas A Warbass.

For County Assessor—D. W Thorpe.

For Coroner—Henry F. Beadle

For County Treasurer—Wm Glaskin. 1t

☞ Capt. W. G. MARCY authorizes us to announce the withdrawal of his name as candidate for the office of Clerk of the Supreme Court, in favor of E. H. THARP, Esq , the present Clerk.

☞ TO THE PUBLIC. I am authorized to say to the friends of EUGENE F. GILLESPIE, that his business makes it impossible for him to run for or accept any office; at the same time he is grateful to his friends for their confidence manifested by the nomination of him for Councilman and County Treasurer.

A. M. WINN.

Sacramento City, March 29, 1850. ap 1 1t

The whole number of votes polled for Mayor was 2,493, and Hardin Bigelow, the peoples' candidate, had a majority over all others of 323. The following is a list of the city and county officers elected, with the number of votes received by each candidate:

Mayor, Hardin Bigelow,	1,521
City Recorder, B. F. Washington,	885
" *Marshal*, N. C. Cunningham,	1,323
" *Attorney*, J. Neely Johnson,	1,697
" *Assessor*, J. W. Woodland,	792
" *Treasurer*, Barton Lee,	2,310
" *Council*, C. A. Tweed,	1,629
' " V. Spalding,	1,621
" Demas Strong,	1,420
" T. McDowell,	1,462
" " J. McKenzie,	1,182
" C. H. Miller,	887
" J. R. Hardenbergh,	862
" Jesse Moore,	869
" " A. P. Petit,	804
County Treasurer, William Glaskin,	1,104
District Attorney, Wm. C. Wallace,	2,011
County " J. H. McKune,	2,021
" *Judge*, E. J. Willis,	1,818
" *Clerk*, Presley Dunlap,	1,567
" *Recorder*, L. A. Birdsall,	714
" *Sheriff*, J. McKinney,	619
" *Surveyor*, J. G. Cleal,	1,152
" *Assessor*, D. W. Thorp,	1,224
" *Coroner*, P. F. Ewer,	579
Clerk Supreme Court, E. H. Tharp,	1,313

A meeting of the Council elect was held at the Court-house, on the morning of the 4th of April, and, on motion of Jesse Moore, C. A. Tweed was called to the chair, as President *pro tem.*, and on motion of Volney Spaulding, Chas. H. Miller was requested to act as Secretary *pro tem.* On motion of Demas Strong, the members of the Council proceeded to the election of President of that body. Mr. Demas Strong having received a majority of the votes was declared duly elected President of the Council, and, after being conducted to the chair by a committee, returned thanks for the honor conferred on him in a brief but appropriate address. A committee was also appointed to wait upon the Hon. Hardin Bigelow, Mayor-elect, and inform him that the Council was duly organized, and ready to receive any communication he might think proper to make. The Mayor appeared before the Council and delivered a short and pertinent address. The Council then adjourned to meet on the following day at ten o'clock, A. M. The Council met the next day pursuant to adjournment, and a message from his Honor, the Mayor, was read, accepted and referred to a select committee. The regular meetings of the board were ordered to be held on Tuesday evening of each week, at seven o'clock, at the Court-house; and the board then adjourned. The following is the *first* message of the *first* Mayor of Sacramento City:

To the Honorable the President and Council of Sacramento City:

Gentlemen:—In compliance with a duty imposed upon me by our City Charter, I respectfully submit the following for your consideration.

The first great and paramount object to be accomplished the present year, and one which involves the deepest interest of the citizens of Sacramento City, is the immediate construction of a levee, to protect permanently the city from future inundation by water. By the 7th section of the Charter, the city is restrained from raising a revenue to exceed $100,000 for the current expenses of the year, without direct authority from the people.

I, therefore, respectfully recommend the immediate passage of an order in Council directing an election at an early date to raise the necessary revenue for the completion of the work. The estimated amount of material required for the entire work, ascertained by the late survey of the City Engineer, is about 160,000 cubic yards, and the estimated cost $250,000. This sum, I believe, will exceed the actual cost of the work, but it is far safer to raise more than is required than not enough.

I would further recommend that a cheap railway track be laid along the levee or bank of the river, and the material brought from more distant points where it can be obtained of a better quality and at a cheaper rate. Such a track along the levee, of not over two miles in length, will not interfere with the business on the levee, and will afford the most ready and cheap conveyance of material to fill up the low places in the city.

I would recommend also that the present banks of the river be not disturbed, as they are bold and easy of access, and form a far more permanent barrier to the action of the water than the finances of the city will allow to be made the present year without rendering taxation at once onerous and oppressive. The grading and paving of the levee is a work that can be accomplished at a later period, when our population and taxable property shall have greatly increased, and as the necessity may arise.

Few, if any, of the commercial points along the margins of our great and navigable rivers present less obstacles to the complete success of a city than that of Sacramento, occupying, as it does, the most elevated position upon the banks of the Sacramento River above Suisun Bay, being at the immediate head of ship-navigation, and controlling nearly three-fourths of all the gold region of California—with no evident marks of periodical inundation, but subject only to those occasional and violent convulsions of water that occur in all countries, and which have been more destructive upon the north-western Pacific Coast the present year than ever before known. But an embankment averaging two and a half feet in height along the bank of the river, or a levee, with a fifty-foot base, and a dike or embankment from the levee or high ground in the southern part of the city of about one mile in length, and the filling of two or three inlets from the American River, would have completely protected the city from the late unusual high water, and the consequent loss to the citizens. The necessity of an early commencement of the work is apparent from the fact that the material becomes very hard and compact in the extreme drought of the latter part of the season.

The three small lakes that will be included within the limits of the levee are of the utmost importance to the city, as they form natural depositories for the surplus water that may accumulate within the city limits during the winter or rainy season, or that may find its way through any porous strata during the high water.

The whole limit of the present corporation should be included within the levee, for there cannot be a doubt but the whole area will soon be covered with buildings, in view of the commanding position of Sacramento, and its relation to a constantly-increasing mining region, capable of sustaining a population of five millions by its mining and agricultural resources.

I would recommend that the fund raised for this object be raised as a separate and distinct fund from the other expenses of the city.

I would further recommend the establishment of such regulations upon the present levee as will best promote the interest of the business community and yield the greatest revenue to the city. The regulations as adopted upon the levee in the different municipalities of New Orleans, would, I think, be very applicable to this city. It will be necessary to have some wharf-ships, anchored at convenient places, for steamboat and passenger landings, under suitable rates of wharfage.

The practice of keeping powder and loaded guns in stores

and tents, generally, is one that requires immediate remedy. The accident that occurred at the late fire by the discharge of a loaded gun, and the constant explosions of powder that occur at every fire, will soon drive the citizens from saving the property of their neighbors during a fire, as their own lives are in danger.

I would, therefore, recommend the licensing of certain establishments, in safe locations, for the sale of powder, and the restraining of others.

And I especially recommend liberal appropriations for the establishment of fire companies; and that every aid and encouragement consistent be given said companies, as the only security to property in a city without insurance is in a well-organized fire department.

I would further recommend to the early attention of the Council the adoption of immediate measures for the removal of the deposit of animal matter and other nuisances within the limits of the city proper, and that a sum of $5,000 be loaned for this and other purposes so essential to the health and credit of the city.

The necessity will arise in due time, or as soon as the finances of the city will permit, for the erection of a City Hospital, to be supported by the city. Such institutions are the just pride of Americans in all our cities. Any regulations which may now be in existence for the care of the poor, should receive liberal support from the city.

The necessity for establishing a City Prison will soon arise, unless one should be established by the county which will answer both purposes. One can be obtained at very small expense, as a foreign vessel can be purchased below very cheap, which the Collector will permit to come up to this place for that purpose.

In regard to the various offices within your gift, I would recommend the appointment of honest and capable men, and hold them to the strictest accountabilities, and that the most rigid economy be practiced in all the departments of the city government.

I would also recommend that just and uniform assessments

be made upon real and personal property as the basis of taxation, with such incidental taxation as the circumstances and wants of the city may require; and that such assessments and levy of taxes be made quarterly during the current year, in order to make the burden of the people as light as possible, meet the rapid increase of real and personal property, and more justly equalize taxation. The stranger that may arrive six months hence with his capital is as much to be benefited by the improvements of the city as the present citizen. When the assessment-roll is once made out, it will require but little additional expense to correct it once in three months.

I am unable to ascertain the exact liabilities of the city; but, from the best information I am able to obtain, they will amount to $60,000, and no accruing revenue whatever. This sum, together with the current expenses of the year, cannot be less than one hundred and sixty thousand (160,000) dollars. All just liabilities of the city should, by all means, be paid, and at as early a date as the city finances will allow. I have no doubt that the sum authorized by the Charter, with such incidental revenue as can be created, will be ample and sufficient for the current expenses of the year and the payment of present liabilities. The only sum necessary to be raised by a vote of the people will be for the levee.

It will require much patriotism and forbearance on the part of the people to meet the accruing wants of the city the coming year. I believe, however, the sum can be raised so as not to be oppressive.

I would especially recommend to the Council that every aid, consistent with their authority and the finances of the city, be given to public schools.

There are other very necessary and important improvements to be made in the city, such as the grubbing and grading of the streets, the building of bridges and sidewalks, and the erection of a market-house; all of which will claim your attention in due time; but our present embarrassments and limited authority for raising money admonish us not to undertake too much.

I believe, however, that a just, energetic and economical course on our part, which will command the confidence and respect of the people, will insure a sufficient revenue for all practical and beneficial purposes.

HARDIN BIGELOW,

Mayor of the City.

SACRAMENTO CITY, April 6th, 1850.

CHAPTER XVII.

First conflagration in Sacramento City—Amount of property
destroyed—Collation given to the fire department by Mayor
Bigelow—Henri Herz, the French composer and pianist—
His concerts in Sacramento City—First negro minstrel per-
formance in Sacramento—Rowe's Olympic Circus—Grand
soiree—Rival politicians—First meeting of the I. O. of
O. F. in Sacramento City—The Masons and Odd Fellows
establish a hospital—Sutter Lodge of Ancient York Masons
—Private hospitals—First public marriage in Sacramento—
The *Placer Times*—Colonel Joseph E. Lawrence.

At one o'clock, on the morning of the 4th of
April, the citizens of Sacramento City were aroused
from their slumbers by the appalling cry of "fire!"
The fire commenced in the store of Messrs. Hoope &
L'Amoreux, and spread rapidly north and south.
The buildings consumed fronted on the levee, between J and K Streets. The El Dorado, adjoining
the store of Hoope & L'Amoreux on the north,
soon caught and was enveloped in a sheet of flame.
At the same time, the next store to the south, in
which was the Express Office of Brown & Knowl-
ton, caught and was speedily consumed. The wind
was blowing from the north at the time, and
Fowler & Co.'s store next became a prey to the
conflagration. The fire also spread in a northerly
direction from the El Dorado to the general merchandise store of Bailey, Morrison & Co.; nor was

(289)

its course stayed in this direction until the next building, occupied by Thomas Bannister as a general grocery and eating-house, had been consumed; while at the same time, at the south from Messrs. Fowler & Co.'s store, the fire passed to the General Jackson House, which was entirely destroyed. Here the progress of the flames was arrested; the drug store of Dr. Crane, the next building toward the south, having been torn down. Messrs. Jackson & Adams occupied a canvas house in the rear of Hoope & L'Amoreux's building, which was also consumed.

The loss sustained by Thomas Bannister was $2,000; Bailey, Morrison & Co., $5,000; El Dorado, owned by Geo. H. Pettybone, $14,000; James Hyslop, $3,000; Hoope & L'Amoreux, $20,000, together with the loss of books and papers; Mr. Yates Ferguson had also in this store $2,000 worth of goods and $1,000 in gold-dust; the books, drugs and instruments of Dr. Chas. Burrell burned were valued at $1,000; stock of provisions in Jackson & Adams's canvas house, $2,000; Messrs. Fowler & Co., $10,000; Frank Green, $600. A large amount of property was saved by Mr. Demas Strong, aided by the fire department. Both the engine and hook and ladder company were upon the field early and worked manfully. The hook and ladder company did good service in hauling away buildings that must have otherwise been the cause of spreading the conflagration, and the engine company spared no pains or labor to make their engine as effective as possible. There were several explosions of powder during the fire. A loaded gun in one of the burning houses exploded, wounding Jos. M. Hancock in the hand.

After the fire, the members of the fire department were invited, with their friends, by Mayor Bigelow, to repair to the City Hotel, where a collation was spread for them on the long table, which reached from one end of the dining-room to the other. After having fortified the inner man, toasts were offered and brief speeches made by Messrs. Bigelow, Strong, Fowler, McNulty, Bailey and others, and the company adjourned in much better spirits than when fighting the fire.

On the day of the fire, before the ashes were cold on the site of the General Jackson House, Frank Green cleaned away the rubbish and erected a frame 22 by 23 feet, which he covered with canvas, and before night had his bar fully supplied with liquors, which he dispensed to the thirsty crowd at 50 cents a drink!

Henri Herz, the celebrated composer and pianist, who arrived in San Francisco on the 1st of April, gave the first of a series of three concerts in Sacramento City, on the evening of the 16th of the same month, at the New Hall, corner of M and Front Streets. The following announcement of the affair appeared in the *Transcript :*

THE Composer and Pianist, H. HERZ will give his first Grand Concert, vocal and instrumental, at the New Hall, corner of M and Front street, on
THIS EVENING, April 16,
On which occasion Henri Herz will play several of his most celebrated pieces, and conclude the Concert with an extemporaneous performance on several American, French, Italian and German popular songs
Mr. REED will sing several of his favorite ballads.

Mr. S. BROWN will perform two solos on the Cornet-a-Piston.

G PETINOS will preside at the Piano Forte.

Mr HERZ, at the earnest solicitation of many of our citizens, has agreed to give three concerts in Sacramento City, previous to his departure by the next steamer.

For further particulars, see small bills

Tickets for the course, (three concerts,) $10; single tickets, $4 each;—to be procured at the bars of the Sutter and City Hotels; at the office of the "Transcript," and at the door.

Doors open at 7—concert to commence at 8 o'clock.

ap16-1t

The concert came off on the evening announced, but owing to the absence of Mr. Brown, who was engaged to perform two solos on the cornet-a-piston, the programme was somewhat curtailed. The piano used on the occasion, the only one in the city, contained only six octaves, which somewhat cramped the genius of the great master, but he gave an admirable entertainment, nevertheless, and the audience was delighted. As tickets of admission were $4 each, and no one was admitted without a "biled shirt," the audience was not large, but very *select.* At the conclusion of the concert, Mr. Herz and several of the audience repaired, by invitation, to the cottage of Mr. P. B. Cornwall, where they "tripped the light fantastic toe" until a late hour. Mr. Cornwall, during a residence of eighteen months in California, had amassed a fortune of half a million dollars, and was on the eve of his departure for the States. During the evening, Mr. Cornwall presented to Mr. Herz a magnificent gold watch-chain, composed entirely of specimens artistically linked together. At the remaining two concerts, Mr. Herz was assisted by Mr. S. C. Massett, who was announced on the programme as follows: "The celebrated vocalist, S. C. Massett, will sing several songs and ballads, and give comic recitations, together with imitations illustrative of the peculiarities of Yankee character."

I will here state, that the first regular theatrical entertainment in California was given in Sacramento City, on October 18th, 1849, at the *Eagle Theatre*, on Front Street, between I and J Streets, by the following company: Messrs. J. B. Atwater, J. H. McCabe, T. Fairchild, Chas. B. Price, H. F. Daley, Henry Ray, A. W. Wright, J. Haines and Mrs. Ray. The *Eagle Theatre*, a frail structure, closed never to open again on the 4th of January, 1850, and was succeeded by the *Tehama Theatre*, under the management of Mrs. J. C. Kirby, an accomplished and talented actress, and widow of "wake me up when Kirby dies" Kirby. Attached to the *Tehama* company were Mesdames Hambleton, Mestayer and Bingham, and Messrs. Atwater, Fairchild, McCloskey, Bingham, Byers and Downie. Mr. and Mrs. Hambleton were both accomplished artistes; Mr. Hambleton was a fine comedian, "a fellow of infinite jest," and he could also play tragic characters in an acceptable manner.

On the 23d of April, 1850, "*Donnelly's Ethiopian Serenders*" gave their first entertainment at the New Hall, corner of Front and M Streets, being the *first* exhibition of Ethiopian Minstrelsy given in Sacramento City. The price of admission was $2, and the house was crowded. The following announcement was published in the *Transcript* of April 20:

On the evening of May 2d, Mr. J. A. Rowe opened his *Olympic Circus,* the *first* circus in Sacramento City, at the new *Pacific Theatre* on M Street, with the following programme:

Rowe's Olympic Circus,
At the New Pacific Theatre, on M street.

J. A. ROWE, Proprietor and Manager, has the honor to announce to the citizens of Sacramento City, that his arrangements are at length completed for the opening of a new and elegant building devoted to feats of Horsemanship He relies with confidence on the liberal support of the admirers of the Equestrian art, assuring the public that nothing shall be wanting on his part to win their approbation.

Equestrian Director, Mr J. Rowe; Ring Master, Mr. Westcott; Clown, Mr. Moor; Leader of the Orchestra, Mr. Smithsnyder.

PROGRAMME FOR THIS EVENING, May 2d —The performance will commence with an Overture from William Tell, performed by the Orchestra; followed by a Grand Star and Waltz Entree, on six horses, led by Mr. and Mrs. Rowe, embracing a variety of rapid evolutions. After which, Mr Rowe will dance his celebrated Dancing Horse "Adonis," to the favorite tune of Yankee Doodle. To be followed by an act of horsemanship by the Little Rising Star, Master Rafael, a pupil of Mr Rowe's, who will execute his daring Equestrian Feats, Leaping Whip, Garters, Hoops, riding upon his head, with the horse at full speed. Mr Rowe will then introduce his celebrated domestic Horse Adonis, in the beautiful scene of the Indian Hunter, and his Wild Charger. Mr. Burke will sing an Irish Comic Song, "You may travel the wide world over." Mr. Rowe will appear in the circle and go through his principal Leaping Act, on his favorite charger, leaping a variety of difficult objects held over the circle, displaying many classical attitudes, with his horse at full speed At this period of the performance there will be an intermission of ten minutes, giving the audience an opportunity of refreshing themselves at the adjoining saloons. Part II —Dr. Downs will introduce the laughable scene of the Peasant's Frolic, in which the Clown will take an active part on the noble horse Napoleon. Mr. Burke will dance a Sailor's Hornpipe. Mr. Rowe will represent on horseback the much admired scene of the American Tar. Intermission of fifteen minutes in order to give time for the preparation of the Afterpiece. The whole to conclude with the very laughable pantomime of *The Cobbler's Daughter.* Clown to the whole performance, Mr. Moor.

The Assistant Manager, Mr. Kirbey, with sufficient officers, will be in attendance to keep order and decorum.

Price of Admission.—Private boxes $5; dress circle and parquette, $3; second tier, $2.

Doors open at half past seven, and performance to commence precisely at 8 o'clock.

Tickets and private boxes can be obtained by applying at the box office from 10 A. M. to 12 M , and from 3 to 5 P. M.; also during the performance.   m2

The completion of the new *Pacific Theatre* was celebrated by a grand ball, which came off at the theatre on the evening of the 25th of April, and was the grandest affair of its kind that had ever taken place in California. In order to make the event more attractive, invitations were extended to ladies residing in San Francisco and Stockton, several of whom were present. The following announcement of the *Grand Soiree* appeared in the advertising columns of the *Transcript:*

☞ At a meeting of a number of citizens of Sacramento City, the following gentlemen were constituted Managers of a Grand Soiree to be given in honor of the erection and opening of the Pacific Theatre:

Hon. Hardin Bigelow,	Capt. Sackett,
" T. J. White, M. D.,	Job H. Watson,
" P. B. Cornwall,	S. Brannan,
Barton Lee,	Almarin B. Paul,
Judge Schoolcraft,	J. F. Morse,
Judge Thomas,	Thomas A. Warbass,
Eugene F. Gillespie,	J. A. Blossom,
C. D. Cleveland, M. D.,	A. Lee,
Col. Winn,	B. F. Washington,
S. P. Dewey,	D. Strong,
A. P. Petit,	P. Brunell,
J. H. Giles,	G. B. Freeland,
F. C. Ewer,	J. Nicholas,
Col. H. A. Baker,	T. McDowell,
R. P. Pearis, M. D.,	E R. Pratt,
James Queen,	W. F. Prettyman,
Murray Morrison,	I. B. Marshall,
J. S. Fowler,	R. D. Tory.

☞ At a meeting of the Managers of the Grand Soiree, held at the counting room of Messrs. Paul, White & Co., Dr. THOMAS J. WHITE was called to the

17

chair, and ALMARIN B. PAUL appointed Secretary. The meeting being duly organized the following resolutions were offered and adopted:

1st. *Resolved*, That this party shall be given on the 25th of April.

2d. *Resolved*, That the President shall appoint such persons as he may deem suitable to act on the following committees:

    1st. Reception and Invitation.
    2d. Floor.
    3d. On Refreshments.
    4th. On Finance.

Judge Schoolcraft being called upon to perform this duty, reported the following:

Committee of Invitation and Reception.

Hon. Hardin Bigelow,	Murray Morrison,
" T. J. White,	R. P. Pearis, M. D.,
F. C Ewer,	Col. H. A. Baker,
John S. Fowler,	C. D. Cleveland, M. D.,
J. H. Giles,	R. D. Tory.

Floor Committee.

Judge Thomas,	Almarin B. Paul,
G. B. Freeland,	Thomas A Warbass,
F. C. Ewer,	G. P. Dewey,
A. P. Petit,	W. F. Prettyman.

Refreshment Committee.

D Strong,	James Queen,
B. F. Washington,	Capt. Sackett,
J. Nicholas,	E. R. Pratt,
	J A Blossom.

Committee on Finance.

Eugene Gillespie,	Barton Lee,
J. F. Morse,	Col Winn,
B. Brunell,	Judge Schoolcraft,
	A. Lee.

3d. *Resolved*, That the duties of each committee be defined, and that the Secretary shall notify them of the same.

4th *Resolved*, That the Secretary be empowered to fill all vacancies

5th. *Resolved*, That the various committees be under the control of the managers, as a Committee of the Whole.

6th. *Resolved*, That the managers meet at the Saloon of the Theatre, to receive the reports of the various committees on Monday Evening, 22d inst., at half past 7 o'clock.

7th. *Resolved*, That the proceedings be published in the several city papers, and that the meeting now adjourn. T. J. WHITE, President.

ALMARIN B. PAUL, Secretary. 1t

Grand Soiree.

☞ At a meeting of the Managers of the Grand Souee, holden at the Saloon of the Pacific Theatre, on the afternoon of the 19th inst., the following resolutions were adopted:

1st *Resolved*, That tickets of admission be issued to ladies as well as to gentlemen, and that the gentlemen be required to present them as well as their own, at the door on the evening of the Soiree.

2d. *Resolved*, That gentlemen desiring tickets will apply for them to the Committee of Invitation, through the secretary

3d *Resolved*, That the price of admission tickets be $25. ALMARIN B PAUL, Sec'y.

Committee of Invitation and Reception

For the Grand Soiree to be given on the evening of the 25th April, at the Pacific Theatre

HON. HARDIN BIGELOW,	MURRAY MORRISON,
" T. J WHITE,	R. A. PEARIS, M D,
F. C. EWER,	COL. W. A BAKER,
JOHN S. FOWLER,	G. B CLEVELAND M. D,
J. H. GILES,	ALMARIN B. PAUL.

ap20-3t

Sacramento City put on her best bib and tucker in honor of this affair. The parquette of the theatre was floored over, a fine band of music engaged, and a magnificent supper was served for the occasion under the supervision of Mr. John S. Fowler, proprietor of the City Hotel. Dancing was continued until the "wee small hours," and many of the participants "didn't go home till morning, till daylight did appear." Mr. E. C. Kemble, one of the editors of the *Alta California*, came up from San Francisco to attend the soiree, but on examining his apparel, found that his pantaloons were a little too seedy to pass regulation muster. His "biled shirt" and swallow-tail coat were unexceptionable, and to complete his *tout ensemble*, I loaned him my best black cassimeres, which had been laid away in lavender since leaving Philadelphia. The fit was a tight one; so tight in fact, that a sudden attempt to sit down would have caused an irreparable collapse of the fabric in a very undesirable and embarrassing quarter; but luck favored him, and he passed the ordeal without accident to the pants.

Mr. Charles H. Miller, one of the city fathers elected on the 1st of April, upon "sober second thought," declined the honor conferred upon him, and an election to fill the vacancy was ordered by the President of Common Council, to take place on the 21st of May. The following patriots, anxious to serve their country, announced themselves as candidates for the office. The cards of the two *Aeronauts*, and that of A. D. Bell, are decidedly unique:

☞ We are authorized to announce Dr. T. J WHITE
as a candidate for a seat in the Common Council, in
the place of C H. Miller, resigned   m11-5t

☞ CANDIDATE FOR THE COMMON COUNCIL—The
many friends of JAMES QUEEN, Esq , propose his
name to the voters of Sacramento as a candidate for a
seat in the Common Council to fill the vacancy of Chas.
H Miller, Esq , resigned

☞ NOTICE —The undersigned having been presented to the public as a candidate to fill the vacancy
in the City Council, respectfully solicits the consideration of those of his friends who think him worthy of
their support   JAMES QUEEN
Election on Tuesday, May 21st.   4t

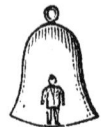
At the solicitation of individuals who have
the good of Sacramento City at heart, Doct.
CHARLES H. MORRILL, formerly Eronaut in the
States, (a permanent resident here,) is a can-
didate to fill the vacancy in the Council, oc-
casioned by the resignation of C. H. Miller,
Esq. Election to take place on the 21st instant.
            m14 4t

At the solicitation of my wife Nancy,
who has the good of herself at heart, and
deeply interested in the successful cultivation of mutton-heads, A D. BELL, who has
made several descents in a diving bell,
and late one of the *floating* population of
this *aquatic* city, is a candidate for the City
Council at the election to take place on the 21st inst.
            1t*

At the earnest solicitation of numerous friends who
cherish a lively interest in the welfare of Sacramento
City, J. F. LUKEN, formerly Eronaut of Cincinnati in
the United States, (and now permanently located here,)
announces himself as a candidate for a seat in the
Council Election to take place on Tuesday, (this
day) the 21st inst.

The election came off as announced with the following result:

James Queen,	1,008
W. N. Doughty,	571
T. J. White,	337
C. H. Morrill,	36
A. D. Bell,	1
Rejected as illegal, ,	4
Whole number of votes polled,	1,957
Queen's plurality,	437
" majority,	59

Queen was triumphant, and the *Aeronauts* went up in a balloon!

On the evening of April 4th, the members of the Independent Order of Odd Fellows, in Sacramento City, met in the Court-house, A. M. Winn, President of the Odd Fellows Association, in the chair. The chairman having explained the object of the meeting, a committee of five, with proper credentials, was appointed to apply to Lieutenant Fraser, D. D. Grand Sire for the State of California, requesting him to visit Sacramento and formally establish a lodge. About the same time, the Odd Fellows, in connection with the Masons, established a hospital, the board of trustees being elected by both orders. A series of concerts were given for the benefit of the hospital, which were liberally patronized. The managers of the *Tehama Theatre* and Rowe's *Olmypic Circus* also gave benefits for the same object. The following card of thanks to Mr. and Mrs. Rowe and the opening address delivered on the night of the benefit, by its author, Francis N. McCron, were published in the *Transcript:*

To the Editors of the Transcript:

GENTLEMEN:—Will you have the kindness to give publication to our acknowledgment of the liberal and humane conduct of Mr. Rowe, as manifested in the benefit which he recently gave to the Masons' and Odd Fellows' Hospital. It is due to that gentlemen and the persons composing his company to say, that they all refused to deduct anything from the proceeds of the evening, for their own services; and the interest that this gentleman exhibited in making the house a good one gives him a strong claim upon the members of these orders for a liberal reciprocal patronage and support.

We return Mr. and Mrs. Rowe, and all the individuals composing the Olympic Circus, our sincere thanks for the benefit we have received, through the efficient proceeds of their house on the 16th inst. We also reiterate our thanks to the gentlemen of the two papers for gratuitous advertisements.

Truly, yours,

J. F. MORSE,
Secretary of Board of Trustees.

SACRAMENTO CITY, May 19th, 1850.

MR. McCRON, *Dear Sir:*—The Board of Trustees of the Masons' and Odd Fellows' Hospital, having been highly gratified with the very appropriate and interesting address which you prepared and delivered with so much felicity at their recent benefit given them by Mr. and Mrs. Rowe, beg the favor of a copy of the same for publication.

Yours, truly,

J. F. MORSE,
Secretary of Board of Trustees.

JOHN F. MORSE, ESQ., *Dear Sir:*—Your kind note, in the name of the Board of Trustees of the Masonic and Odd Fellows' Hospital, requesting a copy of my poor address prepared and delivered by me at the Pacific Theatre, on the occasion of benefit in aid of the funds of above-named establishment, is truly flattering. Enclosed, I send a copy. And allow me to remain, my dear sir, yours respectfully,

FRANCIS N. McCRON.

Sacramento City, May 18th.

OPENING ADDRESS.

Can the striped banner, or the stars of State,
That on the brave, or on the vicious wait,
Such emblems with such emphasis impart,
As an insignium near the Mason's heart!
Hail, Sacred Masonry! of source Divine,
Unerring mistress of the faultless Line:
Whose Plumb of Truth, with never-failing sway,
Makes the joined parts of symmetry obey.

Hail to the craft, at whose serene command
The gentle arts in glad obedience stand ;
Whose magic stroke bids fell confusion cease,
And to the finished orders yield its place—
Who calls creation from the womb of earth,
And gives imperial cities glorious birth!
To works of art her merits not confined,
She regulates the morals, squares the mind—
Corrects with care the tempest-working soul,
And points the tide of passions where to roll.
On Virtue's tablets marks each sacred rule,
And forms her Lodge an universal school,
Where Nature's mystic laws unfolded stand,
And sense and science joined, go hand in hand.
Oh, may her social rules instructive spread,
Till Truth erects her long-neglected head—
Till through deceitful night she darts her ray,
And beams full glorious in the blaze of day—
Till man by virtuous maxim learns to move,
Till all the peopled world her laws approve,
And the whole human race be bound in Brother's Love.

On the evening of April 30th, "Sutter Lodge, Ancient York Masons," was organized by Deputy G. M. John A. Tutt, under a dispensation from the Grand Lodge of California. The lodge commenced with eighteen members; among whom were the following officers: E. J. Willis, W. M.; C. E. Thorn, S. W.; Addison Martin, J. W.

In addition to the Masons' and Odd Fellows' Hospital, there were several private hospitals in Sacramento City. Their location, the names of the proprietors and tariff of prices, are fully set forth in the following advertisements, published in the *Transcript:*

Besides the foregoing, Drs. Morse and Stillman ran a hospital at the corner of K and Third Streets, but either professional etiquette or excessive modesty prevented them from advertising.

About the middle of May, the *élite* of Sacramento City were thrown into spasms by the following marriage in high life:

Married,
On Wednesday evening, the 15th inst., by the Rev. Mr. Moorhouse, WM. C. YOUNG, Esq., of this city, to Miss LUCY A. BARNES, daughter of Henry Barnes, Esq., of Philadelphia.

The following editorial notice of the event appeared in the *Transcript* of May 18th:

The most genteel affair that we have as yet witnessed in California, came off in this city night before last. We have heretofore been inclined to yield to the ball given at San Francisco, in the Hall of the California Guards, the precedence over all other fashionable assemblages; but the affair night before last stands pre-eminently the first. There was nothing like effort apparent, but all was ease and gentility. The bride was dressed in white satin, trimmed with flowers. Her dark hair was braided in the most elegant style, and a beautiful white veil added its airy grace to her person. The bridegroom was tastefully dressed in black, with white satin vest and neckerchief. The bridesmaid attracted scarcely less attention than the bride. A splendid specimen bracelet, a present from the bridegroom, graced her arm, and lace caught up with flowers added to the beauty of her rich satin dress. The ceremony was the most impressive of the kind that it has ever been our good fortune to witness. The parties were married according to the Episcopal ritual. They were impressed with the spirit of the solemn act, and every response was clear, distinct and heartfelt. May the Goddess of Happiness strew their pathway with flowers.

The beautiful cottage, which has been an enigma for many weeks to some of our citizens, is tastefully and elegantly furnished. The music was excellent, and the merry hours sped swiftly and silently away. Our sincerest wish is, that

> "——adown life's valley, hand in hand,
> With grateful change of grave and merry speech,
> Or song, their hearts unlocking each to each,
> They'll journey onward to the silent land!"

On the 22d of April, our cotemporary, the *Placer Times*, published by E. Gilbert & Co., and edited by Colonel Joseph E. Lawrence, commenced its tri-weekly publication on Mondays, Wednesdays and Saturdays, alternating with the *Transcript;* therefore, the citizens had a newspaper on every morning of the week, Sunday excepted. Colonel Joseph E. Lawrence, Mr. Jesse Giles's successor in the editorial management of the *Times,* was born on Long Island, but was a resident of New Orleans when the gold fever broke out in the States, and emigrated from that city to California, on mule back, *via* Mexico and Lower California.

ENCAMPMENT AT THE "EMBARCADERO," SACRAMENTO, 1849.

CHAPTER XVIII

Commercial advantages of Sacramento City—New buildings
—First daily issue of the *Transcript*—The *Placer Times*
follows suit—Sell my interest in the *Transcript* to Mr. G. C.
Weld—Death of Mr. Weld—Tribute to his memory—Captain John A. Sutter—Sutter's Fort—Attack on the Fort by
the Indians—They are repulsed—Hock Farm.

SACRAMENTO CITY is, at this time, in point of
commercial advantages and population, the second
city in California. Its population is variously estimated at from five to seven thousand, including
floating population. A year ago it contained
scarcely half a dozen tents and shanties, and a
bridle-path led from the bank of the Sacramento
River to Sutter's Fort.

Its growth during the past ten months has been
almost magical. Here labor asks its own price, and
its beck commands capital. No chartered institutions have monopolized the great avenues to wealth;
no aristocracy, grown proud from the long possession of exclusive privileges, can obtain a foothold or
assert supremacy. Circumstances have established
a level, in which it is honorable to be, from which
every one has an equal chance to rise, and where
merit is the only sure guarantee of success. Neither
business nor capital can oppress labor in California.
Whenever its rights are invaded, the gulches and
cañons that lead down the western slope of the
Sierra Nevada will furnish a safe retreat, where

(307)

labor will obtain a rich reward, until its end is gained and the powers that oppress it yield to necessity and consent to do justice.

A general independence is observable in the people here, which is the inevitable result of their mutual relation. All classes are alike dependent upon each other, and obligations are mutually incurred. The rich men of to-day were adventurers yesterday. How natural, then, that they should respect labor, by which they have accomplished their success. Few can be found who have secured a competency by their own exertions who do not feel a conscious pride in acknowledging it. Labor will continue to hold the first position in California. Rich and exhaustless as are her natural resources, they have slumbered in the bowels of the earth since creation, and the world could never be benefited by them, without the judicious application of bone and muscle—*the real capital of the world.*

The consciousness once spread throughout the people, that they can depend upon themselves with safety, has forcibly acquainted them with the tremendous strength that lies latent among them, which increases in them still more the feeling of self-reliance. Their opinions are heard at the corners of the streets; they stand, in all their vigor, in public assemblages; and every tone of their voices speaks of independence, of calm determination, and of self-reliance. Those who have immigrated here are, in most cases, the cream of the populace. A manly, vigorous, intelligent race of freemen, capable of meeting any emergency, have seized upon the hills and valleys, and California will, in less than five years' time, make herself felt among the nations of the world, either directly as a free land, or indirectly by her stern independence of feeling. Her voice will be respected, her decision will be looked for. She is the most practical of communities; and yet there is genius here. The pale-faced poet has stolen in upon us, and now and then, amid the din of building towns, his fine strain is heard. The painter, the musician, the artist—all are here. Stern life brings them down to the practical, but they are here, and will, in time, make themselves felt. Female society will be here soon, and then what more can be asked for? It is not strange, then, that this feeling of self-reliance should be so strong and broadcast in the land. With a country so rich in resources; so blest in a people to manage it, the future destiny of California is one of the sublimest subjects for contemplation that can be presented to the mind.

The rapidly-increasing commerce of Sacramento City presents the strongest reasons for making it a port of entry. It is situated at the head of ship-navigation on the Sacramento River. A few miles above the city a bar stretches across the river, and the water from that point up is so shoal as to be navigable only by steamboats and vessels of light draft. From Sacramento City down to the Bay of San Francisco, navigation is unobstructed. At the very lowest stages of the water last summer and fall, vessels came up to Sacramento drawing ten feet and a half of water. The bark *Undine* came up late in

August last drawing ten feet. The bark *Ann Welsh*, 390 tons, came up last October, drawing ten feet, and the bark *Strafford*, lying at the Levee as a prison-ship for the city, came up in September last, drawing ten feet and seven inches of water. The latter is 314 tons, custom-house measurement, and has a capacity of 5,000 barrels. Sacramento has an excellent Levee, alongside of which ships can lie with safety, and upon which they can discharge their cargoes without the expense of lightering. When the rivers are at their very lowest point, the water immediately alongside of Front Street and the Levee of the American River is from two and one-half to three fathoms deep. The river in front of the city is a quarter of a mile wide, giving ample room for the working of vessels. The Levee for a mile along Front Street is lined with vessels, and in some places they are two deep. They number upwards of twenty ships and barks, and thirty brigs. There are also a large number of schooners and other small craft. The distance from San Francisco is 104 miles. Vessels have come up from the bay in twenty-four hours, and the passage, at the longest, seldom exceeds four days. In a short time steam-tugs will ply on the river.

Sacramento is not only at the head of ship-navigation, but it is the natural metropolis for the rich and extensive mines of the north, south and middle forks, Yuba, Feather and Bear Rivers, Deer Creek, Cosumne, Dry Creek and the Upper Sacramento, together with all the dry-diggings contiguous. From this extensive section of the mining country, excellent

SACRAMENTO CITY. 1850

roads, in the dry season, converge to Sacramento City as the nearest and by far the greatest entrepot and depot. Along these roads hundreds of teams toil daily, supplying this vast mining region with provisions, clothing and other necessary articles of consumption. To supply the Sacramento market, which is thus continually drained, steamers and vessels of heavy burden arrive daily from San Francisco, in which merchandise, after having been discharged there, is reshipped to Sacramento City. Already have two hundred vessels cleared from the States for Sacramento City direct; and the advantages of this move are apparent from the fact that the cost of reshipment from San Francisco to Sacramento exceeds, to a considerable amount, that of shipment from New York to San Francisco.

While the work on the Levee was progressing, improvements were going on rapidly on Second and J Streets. The former street has undergone an almost complete metamorphosis. A number of large and well-constructed buildings are completed, or rapidly approaching that point—buildings, tasty and handsome in their outward appearance, and well calculated to ornament the city. Above J Street, there are four buildings of this description. A new building on the corner above the theatre, owned by Lee & Cornwall, designed for the post-office, is nearly finished, and stands in agreeable contrast to the ruin of the old *adobe* opposite; showing how rapidly the customs of our own race are doing away with those of the former occupants of the soil. The *Tehama Theatre* needs only a little outside polish to give it an imposing appearance. A little nearer J Street, two other two-story houses, also owned by Lee & Cornwall, have arisen within a few days. Crossing J Street, between the office of the *Transcript* and the fine brick building, corner of J and Second Streets, a splendid three-story structure, fronting forty-five feet on Second Street, is nearly completed. A few steps further down, on the opposite side of the street, two large two-story buildings will be completed in a few days. A little further down the street, is the cottage of Mr. William C. Young, nearly ready for occupancy.

J Street is also making rapid strides in improvements of various kinds. Through its whole length may be seen the most gratifying evidences of the energy and enterprise of its merchants. Besides the general improvements going on, in putting up new fronts, awnings and sidewalks, twelve new buildings are being constructed. Ten of these buildings are two and a half stories high, fronting from twenty to thirty-five feet on J Street, and running back from forty to sixty feet. It is now a settled fact, that the day for doing successful business in the open air or in canvas tents, has gone by, and consequently no one thinks of putting up a new building that is not of a character to confer credit on the city. One of the finest buildings in California, in respect to dimensions and architecture, is going up between Second and Third Streets, adjoining the Humboldt. It is forty feet front by one hundred and twenty-five feet deep, and two stories high. The whole lower story will constitute a single saloon, through the centre of which, at short intervals, are massive pillars to support the ceiling.   The entire second story is designed for a dancing hall, and it will surpass anything of the kind in California. K Street is also beginning to show signs of improvement.   The proprietors of the *Transcript* have purchased a lot on this street, above Second, on which they are erecting a fire-proof brick building, two stories high, to which they will remove their office on the 1st of July.

On the first day of June, the *Transcript* began its daily publication, with the following editorial announcement:

Such is the size of Sacramento City, and such has become its importance as a commercial mart, that we feel it to be due to the public, due to our patrons, due to ourselves, as the conductors of a public enterprise, no longer to remain stationary, while all else around us is improving in a truly liberal and energetic manner.   Newspapers are looked to as an index by which the importance of the localities they represent may be judged.   Since we could no longer do justice to the public as chroniclers of passing events, we have decided to commence with this number the issue of the " *Daily Sacramento Transcript,*" *the first daily newspaper in California out of San Francisco.*   When we remember that it is not yet five months since the first daily paper was established in California, it will be seen that Sacramento City is not far behind, if she did start after the race was well begun elsewhere.

Ten days later, June 10th, the *Transcript's* cotemporary, the *Placer Times*, came out daily in a new typographical dress.

On the first day of July, I sold my interest in

18

the *Transcript* to Mr. Gilbert C. Weld, California correspondent of the New York *Journal of Commerce;* and on the same day the proprietors of that journal moved into their new fire-proof brick building on K Street above Second. Although having no pecuniary interest in the *Transcript*, I remained in charge of the business department of the paper until the latter part of August. Soon after purchasing my interest in the *Transcript*, Mr. Weld was prostrated by an attack of typhoid fever. He was for a few days an inmate of Drs. Morse & Stillman's hospital, but was subsequently removed to a private boarding-house, kept by a Mr. and Mrs. Aldrich, on K Street near Fifth, where, despite the best medical treatment that could be procured and careful nursing, he passed from earth to that bourn whence no traveler returns, on the evening of the 9th of August. Mr. Weld was a ready and graceful writer and a man of decided genius. Had he lived, he would have made a shining mark in California journalism. The *Transcript* of August 10th was published with inverted column-rules, draped in mourning, with the following obituary of the deceased, written by Mr. F. C. Ewer:

This morning a melancholy duty devolves upon us. Death has snatched from our midst one who, though newly come among us, had endeared himself to our hearts as a brother. It is the fairest flower of our garden that is plucked. A voice that we listened to for instruction, that cheered us through the trying hours, that joined with us in our mirth, that was full of wisdom and of love, and consolation and hope, is hushed forever. · Oh, how will kindred hearts, in a land that is far away, be wrung with anguish! By our side are the miniatures of his beautiful wife and three lovely children, whose hearts must soon feel the keen pangs known only to the widow and the orphan. A lovely daughter passed away but a few months since, and nearly broke the heart of the solitary father. Now he has gone to meet her. The intelligence of his bereavement cast a gloom over his silent moments which it was impossible to shake off. It was in one of these spells that his soul burst forth, as if by inspiration, in the following gush of feeling:

"Thy last sweet letter, treasured as a prize,
  I daily read, and think of thee, dear Mary;
Of all thy beauties, all thy virtues rare,
Thy lustrous, bright blue eyes, thy golden tresses,
Thy matchless features, and thy seraph voice,
Thy tender, loving, sympathizing heart—
I think of these, and thousand other graces,
And then my stubborn *will*, prone to *rebel*,
Curses the hand which laid thee low in death,
And robbed thy father of his choicest blessing!
But thou art gone! Why should I wish thee back?
Thy sufferings are ended—thou art saved!
Saved from the sins, the sufferings of earth,
The woes, the griefs which rack thy father's heart;
Freed from temptation, trouble, care and pain!
Saved with a *full* salvation, rich and free;
Boundless as God's benevolence can give,
And lasting as the Giver.
                "O my soul!
Cease thy rebellings! God has taken my child
From ills to come. What seems to thee a curse
Is blessing in disguise. Assuage thy grief,
For He who caused the stroke 'doeth all things well!'

"'Tis done! The bitterness of woe is past—
My grief is o'er—my tears shall cease to flow!
And when my spirit sinks, in days to come,

And gloom, like winter, settles o'er my soul,
Thy mem'ry, Mary, and the blessed thought
That thou art happier far than him bereaved,
Will light the gloom, dispel the gathering storm,
And leave the fountain in my troubled breast
As peaceful as the hill-girt lake in summer.
Oh! I will live, my child, as one who hopes
To meet thee in a brighter, better world!"

For versatility of talent, for brilliancy of thought, for serenity of disposition, for genial, social feeling, Mr. Weld was rarely equaled. He was a man who won upon the affections mysteriously, and he had not an acquaintance that was not his friend. The career before him was brilliant. His writings were graceful, filled with the play of lively fancy, and illumined by the light of a brilliant imagination. They had gained for him an enviable fame; but the withering blast of disease came o'er him, and the high anticipations of his friends were blighted. His death was as his life, serene and hopeful. He sank as sinks the star, silent, uncomplaining, beautiful. The hearts of his many friends will be touched with grief; the spirit of his beloved wife will be bowed under the heavy bereavement; the tears of his sweet little children will flow as they remember his parting kiss. But the star, though set, is shining still in the heavens. He was a devoted Christian, and unaffectedly pious. He breathed his last at about nine o'clock last evening, "at peace with God and the world."

Captain John A. Sutter, the first white man who settled at New Helvetia, now Sacramento City, came overland from Jackson County, Missouri, in 1838–9. At that time the country was the abode of savages and wild beasts. Here, in this distant and secluded dependency of imbecile Mexico, he determined to rear the standard of American freedom. Such was the intention and feeling of this

veteran soldier, when he conceived the idea of uniting this land of gold, the link between Asia and America, completing a commercial chain, now encompassing the whole world. The privations, hardships, mental anxiety and peril, necessarily encountered by Captain Sutter, during this long period, cannot be adequately depicted. Repeatedly the savage foe, under various pretexts, sought his life; and to good judgment, promptness and energy, does he owe his continued existence. At one time, while conversing with a friend in the fort, at a late hour of the night, a sudden noise burst upon their ears. The savages had entered the walls of the fort. The Captain and his friends were saved by a faithful dog, that suddenly sprang at the throats of the intruders and felled them, one by one, to the ground, until several were dangerously wounded and the rest fled. The wounded Indians confessed the plot.

Captain Sutter has vacated the fort at Sacramento, removed to Hock Farm and turned his attention to farming. This farm is situated on a high and beautiful plain, on the Feather River, about 8 miles below Yuba City, and comprises about six hundred acres, around which a deep ditch has been dug. Near the bank of the river, and close to the steamboat landing, stand the residence and outbuildings of Captain Sutter. Above and below these are large gardens, which, in their appearance, give the best possible evidence that California is not altogether the barren, unproductive region it is sometimes reported. The hardy pioneer who owns this place has heard the unfavorable report, concerning his adopted home, and he is laboring to show all who are open to conviction that the earth, even in California, will reward the husbandman for his toil. He is sanguine of success, and has good reasons for his expectations. A large variety of vegetables are in a flourishing state, while of radishes, lettuce, onions and beets, he has enough and to spare. Nearly every steamboat that touches at Hock Farm brings away a choice variety of the products of his gardens to regale his friends at a distance. Back of these gardens are large fields of wheat, and to see them is all that is necessary to convince the beholder of the adaptation of the soil and climate to the production of this important article of consumption. Here, in one field, are eighty acres, and in the best grain sections of the States it would be difficult to find a more even and healthy-looking crop. Indian corn is also receiving attention here, but thus far its appearance is not very flattering. A space of about half an acre has been thickly planted with a choice variety of the grape, and the shoots appear from almost every scion, giving the most encouraging hopes of a successful cultivation of the vine.

CHAPTER XIX.

Grand entertainment given at Hock Farm by Captain Sutter—
Full report of the affair—Letter from Thomas O. Larkin—
Mr. Francis D. Clark and others *resolve* that one man is as
good as another, provided he behaves himself—The glorious
Fourth—Its first celebration in Sacramento City—"The
Ancient Order of Bricks" and the Sons of Temperance
publish their programmes of exercises—A jolly Fourth of
July.

On June 2d, Captain Sutter gave a grand entertainment at Hock Farm, to which about one hundred ladies and gentlemen from Sacramento City
were invited. The following report of the affair
appeared in the *Transcript* two days afterward:

Day before yesterday we found ourselves in the midst of a
delightful party of about one hundred ladies and gentlemen on
board of the *Governor Dana*. The steamer left the foot of K
Street about half-past eight, A. M. Hundreds of spectators
stood upon the Levee and on the neighboring vessels watching
her departure. The band was playing on the upper deck; the
ladies and gentlemen were collected under the awnings; her
flags were flying; the sun was shining brightly, while at the
same time a cool breeze was blowing; in short, everything
augured a pleasant time. There were two things that could be
depended upon: No rough weather was to be looked for, to
discompose the placidity of a hundred breakfasts and cause
"noise, confusion," etc., and no fears were to be entertained
that a rain-storm would come up to mar the pleasure of the
occasion. The crowd on board were congenial to each other,
and commenced forthwith to enjoy themselves by taking the

(323)

proper preparatory steps. The steamer darted swiftly up the river, leaving Sacramento behind, and carrying away from it a hundred happy hearts. The usual amusing small-talk on those highly important subjects, "charming day," "exquisite weather," etc., passed between certain of the ladies and gentlemen, leaving behind a strikingly apparent and a semi-serio-comic dearth of other matter, while the ladies looked at the opposite bank of the river in the interim, and the gentlemen stood with smiling countenances and glistening eyes all ready to listen to any subject that any one in the vicinity might suggest. Meanwhile others, the older and more sedate, were exhausting the weightier topics of "invigorating breezes" and the distant Sierra Nevada. Editors were asked the latest news; physicians answered learnedly interrogatories as to the state of health in the Sacramento Valley; the squatter question was discussed, and the wrongs suffered by California were not forgotten. The crowd soon become acquainted with each other, and these merry meetings warm the heart and draw the mind away from the sternness of business and expand the social feeling.

The *Governor Dana* is an excellent boat. The river was placid and she steamed swiftly up, now grazing one bank of the winding stream and now passing under the shade of the trees upon the other. Fremont was soon reached. The towns-people were down to see the landing. The American flag was flying from the pole on the Levee, and the music of the band was heard in the interval between the cheers which, as we touched the Levee, arose from those who had come out to welcome us to their town. After a reinforcement of ladies and gentlemen from Fremont had stepped on board, we left and touched at the opposite town of Vernon. Then striking from Sacramento into the Feather, we wended our rapid way to Nicholaus. Eberhardt was ready to receive the guests, who dined at his excellent hotel.

The next place we stopped at was Plumas. This town flourishes finely, having grown up since our last trip to Marysville, some two months ago.

After passing the steamers *Martha Jane* and *Linda* on their way from Marysville to Sacramento, both of which we saluted, we reached Hock Farm, where the great pioneer of California stood upon the bank to receive us.

The arrival at this place was one of the most interesting parts of the trip. As we rounded into sight, our coming was announced by the blowing of the whistle. This was responded to by the firing of cannon on the bank of the river in front of Captain Sutter's house. Amid the echoes, our band struck up "Hail Columbia," and as we neared, another report from the cannon was responded to by the crowd upon our deck, who raised nine hearty cheers for the inmates of Hock Farm. Captain Sutter and his family came forth from the house and down to the edge of the bank. One more report from the cannon and the plank was thrown to the shore, and the crowd poured out of the boat, as this was their place of destination. Captain Sutter, after recognizing his old acquaintances in his usual cordial manner, stepped back into the spacious inclosure in front of his house, where he received his friends and was introduced to his other guests.

The Indians who stood in crowds upon the bank were thunderstruck, not less with the whole scene than with the music from the band. Captain Sutter informed us that this was the first time they had heard anything of the kind. A long table was set in the shade in front of the house, loaded with the delicacies of the season. The company seated themselves under the direction of General Winn, the agent of Captain Sutter, who had previously been appointed by the company Master of Ceremonies. Captain Sutter and family took seats at the centre of the long table; the ladies sat at his right and left; General Winn sat at one end, and the rest of the company seated themselves promiscuously at the table. The time was passed very sociably and at last the regular toasts came off. The first was drunk by the whole company, standing, it was—

1. To Mrs. Sutter. Captain Sutter responded on behalf of his lady and gave—

2. A hearty welcome to the ladies and gentlemen at Hock Farm.

Music, "Hail Columbia."

After a pleasant little talk by which the Master of Ceremonies brought the company to order, the following toasts, which have been handed to us by the Secretary, were then given:

3. By Mr. Stephens—Captain Sutter first, Captain Sutter last.

4. By Mr. Morrill—To the ladies of California! God bless them.

5. By Mr. Johnson—Miss Sutter.

6. By Mr. Fendrick—To the welfare of California and Hock Farm.

7. By Mr. Hamilton—John A. Sutter, the Pioneer of California.

8. By Mr. L. E. Boren—May the despots of all nations be dethroned and Republicanism be triumphant.

9. By Mr. Gore—Captain Sutter; his hospitality will always be imprinted on our hearts and never forgotten.

10. By Mr. W. E. Moody—Hock Farm, the remembrance of which will always cause our hearts to be warm.

11. By General Winn—The World, may it all be Republican.

Two toasts were then given—one to our host and hostess and the other to the Captain of the *Governor Dana*.

C. H. Pierson then rose and gave—To our absent mothers and fathers, wives and children.

Bachelors and maidens all arose and drank heartily to this toast.

Mr. Sweezy then gave a toast which he read from a piece of paper. We were unable to procure it subsequently. We regret this as it was an excellent one.

A gentleman then arose in behalf of Miss F., of Yuba City, and gave—May all proprietors be as agreeable toward the ladies as the proprietors of Veazie City.

General Winn then gave a toast, which, if the Secretary understood correctly, was—May the charity of Californians equal the charitable feelings of Captain Sutter.

17. By a lady—Captain Sutter: the man who taught the Digger Indians how to dig!

18. Mr. Wilder proposed Sacramento.

19. By General Winn—California, may it be settled by those who have daughters and sons willing to enjoy themselves in this country!

This was a toast which breathed the spirit of a true Californian, who has set the example of his precept.

20. His eldest daughter then gave—To absent friends!

21. Mr. Buscara of China—The friends of Captain Sutter!

22. By George W. Tyler—Captain Sutter and California— the fame of the former is world-wide and inseparably connected with the latter!

The following was given by a gentleman, name unknown— The Beauties of California, the wild flowers and the tame ladies.

Colonel Grant was called upon and gave—Brigadier-General Winn, a brave and good soldier; may he, in his march through life, never be in want of good pay and plenty of rations.

Mr. Rust gave—The reunion of the family of Captain Sutter.

Mrs. Winn gave, through her husband—To the ladies now on their way to California.

Mr. Latson gave—To Peter H. Burnett, the first American Governor of California.

After it had been moved and carried by acclamation, "that the thanks of the company be given to Captain Sutter for his princely hospitality," the party adjourned. About half-past six the company took their leave, delighted with the hospitable treatment they had received; and, after giving nine cheers for Hock Farm, the boat pushed from the shore. The band struck up "Yankee Doodle," and we wended our way back to Sacramento.

The distance up and back was about 130 miles. The speed of the *Governor Dana* can be judged somewhat by this.

We are confident that we echo the feelings of every one present when we say that it will be long before the pleasure-trip to Hock Farm will be effaced from our memories.

In the month of July the proprietors of the *Transcript* received the following letter from Mr. Thomas

O. Larkin, for many years American Consul at Monterey. Mr. Larkin's letter is copied in order to show how a Californian feels when he visits the States, after becoming fairly attached to the country of his adoption:

IRVING HOUSE, NEW YORK, May 27th, 1850.

MESSRS. FITCH, UPHAM & Co., Sacramento, California, *Gentlemen:*—By favor of Mr. Cornwall, I am in possession of your *Sacramento Transcript.* There is no improvement in California that pleases me more than the issuing of another newspaper in that young and advancing State. I owe much to California, and my last breath shall be spent in that acknowledgment. That myself and wife might visit the land of our birth, after eighteen years' absence, caused me to leave that country; and the education of the *first children* born there of United States' parents—rather of United States mother*—causes us to remain here for the present.

Please put me down on your list as a subscriber—direct to New York. I am, with much respect,

THOMAS O. LARKIN.

A strong prejudice against foreign miners existed throughout the northern and southern mines. Most Americans seemed to think that a foreigner had no rights which they were bound to respect. The inhabitants of Georgetown seemed to think differently, as will be seen by the following resolutions unanimously adopted at a public meeting, and signed by Francis D. Clark, Chairman, and others:

1. *Resolved,* That *all men shall have permission to live in this camp, without being in any way molested.*

---

* There were many of foreign fathers and California mothers.

2. *Resolved,* That the civil law shall be sustained, and that all those under the civil law shall be supported.

3. *Resolved,* That two hundred and fifty copies of these resolutions be printed in English and Spanish, and distributed through the various diggings.

FRANCIS D. CLARK, *Chairman.*

JOHN POWERS,	E. MONTGOMERY,
WILLIAM TURNER,	T. JEFFERSON WELLS,
WILLIAM B. McELVOY,	JOHN F. WORTH,
P. COURTRELL,	A. TURNER,

Georgetown, Tuolumne County.

During the month of June, the citizens of Sacramento City became very patriotic and set about devising means to celebrate the "Glorious Fourth" in a becoming manner. The "Ancient and Honorable Order of Bricks" held a meeting and promulgated the following order of exercises:

At a meeting of the Ancient and Independent Order of "Bricks," held at the City Hotel, in Sacramento City, June 12th, 1850, officers present: A. M. Winn, Brigadier-General, President; Frank Bates, Esq., Vice-President; George McKinstry and J. Bawden, Secretaries. The officers being seated, and the meeting organized, on motion,

1st. It was Resolved, That we will celebrate the 4th day of July next in an appropriate manner; and for this purpose Captain J. A. Sutter and all other "Bricks" be requested to attend.

2d. It was Resolved, That one gun for each State be fired from Sacramento City, Sutter and Sutter's Fort, at sunrise, and that the American flag be hoisted at each place.

3d. It was Resolved, That Captain Sutter and his old California friends be invited to attend, and head the procession.

4th. It was Resolved, That the celebration of the 4th of July should be public and free to all, and that the ladies be invited to attend.

5th. It was Resolved, That a Barbecue and Bear Dance be provided for the occasion.

6th. It was Resolved, That forty managers be nominated to superintend the celebration of the 4th of July.

7th. It was Resolved, That the Ancient Order of Free Masons, the Order of Odd Fellows, the Municipal Authorities of San Francisco and Sacramento City, and the Military and Fire Companies, the Sons of Temperance, and other benevolent institutions of Sacramento City, be invited to attend.

8th. It was Resolved, That the Attorney-General be requested to deliver the oration, and that Geo. McKinstry, Esq., read the Declaration of Independence.

9th. It was Resolved, That the Governor and his staff, the Major-General and Brigadier-Generals and their staffs of this division, be also requested to attend.

10th. It was Resolved, That Captain Sutter be added to the list of Managers, and that his name be placed at the head of the list.

11th. It was Resolved, That the captains of vessels in port be requested to hoist their flags at sunrise, and that they and their crews be invited to attend the procession in a body.

And then, according to the resolutions adopted, the following gentlemen were appointed Managers: Captain J. A. Sutter, Hock Farm; His Excellency, P. H. Burnett, Governor; J. McDougall, Lt. Governor; Maj. Gen. T. J. Green, Brig. Gen. Eastland, Brig. Gen. A. M. Winn, Col. H. E. Robinson, J. P. Rodgers, Maj. J. S. Fowler, Maj. Murray Morrison, Maj. N. E. Latson, Maj. J. P. Hughes, Maj. W. Bryarley, Maj. T. Emory, Col. G. A. Grant, Capt. W. E. Shannon, Lt. A. H. Barber, Capt. Hammersley, Maj. Justus McKinstry, Maj. P. B. Reading, Maj. Snowden, Hon. S. C. Hastings, Hon. H. Bigelow, Hon. J. Bigler, Hon. E. O. Crosby, Dr. T. J. White, Mr. D. Strong, Mr. J. McDowell, Hon. J. L. Thomas, Hon. B. F. Washington, Hon. C. E. Lackland, Hon. E. J. Willis, Dr. Frank Bates, Mr. Geo. McKinstry, Mr. Saml. Norris, Mr. J. W. Hastings, Mr. Wm. Dowlin, Mr. J. Bowden, Mr. Samuel Brannan, Hon. T. J. Henley, Mr. Barton Lee.

On motion, it was Resolved, That the Managers be requested to meet at the City Hotel, on Wednesday next, the 19th inst., at seven P. M.

Resolved, That the Editors of the *Placer Times* and *Sacramento Transcript* be requested to publish these proceedings.

Signed: A. M. WINN, *President.*

FRANK BATES, *Vice Pres.*

Signed:

GEO. McKINSTRY, ⎫
JOSEPH BAWDEN, ⎬ *Secretaries.*

For some unexplained reason, the adjourned meeting of the " Bricks" did not take place, and only two of the schemes for celebrating the Fourth of July were carried out—that of the Sons of Temperance and the celebration at Brighton, on the south bank of the American River, about five miles from Sacramento City. The first Fourth of July celebration in Sacramento City passed off in a blaze of glory, in accordance with the following programmes, and the participants were happy:

Fourth of July Celebration,
AT THE PAVILION, BRIGHTON.
ORDER OF EXERCISES.

☞ Under the direction of Major A. C. Latson, one gun for each state will be fired, commencing at sunrise.

On the arrival of the procession from Sacramento, the Declaration of Independence will be read by George McKinstry, Esq , and an oration by Col. E. J. C Kewen; after which a splendid Dinner will be served at the Pavilion for as many as desire to partake. In the evening a splendid *Ball Souee* and supper will be given in the spacious saloon.

The Pavilion is unsurpassed by any public house in this country, furnishing ample accommodations for all; private rooms for families, newly furnished, and the whole house fitted for the comfort of regular or transient visitors.

A band of music will be in attendance during the day and evening.

The ball soiree will be under the direction of the following gentlemen:

Honorary Managers.	*Acting Managers.*
Capt. J. A. Sutter,	Col. E. J. C Kewen,
Hon Hardin Bigelow,	F. C Ewer, Esq.,
Gen. A M. Winn,	Dr. W. Bryarly,
Col. J B Starr,	J E. Lawrence, Esq.,
D. G. Whitney, Esq.,	Hon. C. C. Sackett,
Geo. McKinstry, "	J. Sherwood, Esq ,
R. D. Merrill, "	A. C. Monson, "
Barker Burnell, "	Col. T. A. Warbass,
J R. Hardenbergh, Esq ,	Maj. J P. Hughes,
J. A. Haines, Esq ,	Col. John S Fowler,
J W Winans, "	Col H. E Robinson.

☞ Omnibuses will run from Sacramento to the Pavilion at all hours of the day.　　　　　　　　　　　　　　　　　　　jy2-3t

Fourth of July.

☞ At a meeting of the Pacific Star Division No. 1, of the Order of the Sons of Temperance, held at their Hall on J street, June 20th. 1850, it was unanimously agreed to celebrate the coming Anniversary of our Nation's Independence, as an "Order," in connection with the citizens of Sacramento City generally.

PROGRAMME.

The exercises will open at 10, A. M., in a suitable room—due notice will be given hereafter.

1st. Music—a National Air
2d. Reading the Declaration of Independence—Hon. E. J. Willis, reader.
3d. Music.
4th. Oration—J C. Zabriskie, Esq , orator.
5th. Music—Hail Columbia.

At 12, M., the procession, under the direction of Benj. B. Nickerson, Esq , Marshal, and two assistants, will move to the river, and, after a short excursion thereon, will proceed to the house of Capt. Coon, where a collation will be served up expressly for the occasion. After the cloth is removed, there will be addresses, toasts, &c.

The Mayor, Common Council, and citizens generally, are respectfully invited to participate in the exercises.

A good band of music will be secured for the occasion.

By order of the   COMMITTEE OF ARRANGEMENTS.

N. B. Col. Zabriskie has consented at this late hour to prepare an Oration for the occasion, in consequence of the decease of the Rev. Mr. Kalloch, who had previously been engaged.   je25 tt

BRIGADE HEAD QUARTERS, ⎫
2d Brig. 1st Div C M. ⎬
Sacramento City, June 29th, 1850. ⎭

ORDERS NO. 2.

Our Nation's birthday will be celebrated throughout this Brigade on next Thursday, the 4th day of July.

One gun for each State will be fired.

From Sutter's Fort, by Maj. W. Bryarly.
"   Brighton, by Maj. A C Latson.
"   Norristown, by Capt. Sam'l Norris.
"   Sutter, by Maj. L. W. Hastings
"   Sac. City, by Maj. John P Rodgers.

The first gun will be fired at sunrise, when the flags at each of these points, as well as the flags of the shipping in port, will be hoisted. Music—"Hail Columbia "

Immediately after each regular round and simultaneous with each gun at Sacramento City, the shipping will fire their guns.

A salute of thirteen guns will be fired for Capt. John A. Sutter, from Sutter's Fort, at 12 o'clock, under the superintendence of Maj John S. Fowler.

The members of the staff, and those intending to take part in the morning celebration, will meet at the City Hotel at 8 o'clock, on the evening of the 3d of July.

Capt. Sutter, his old California friends, and the Brigadier General and staff will join the general procession at half past 11 o'clock.

By order of Brig. General A M. WINN,

jy2   JOHN S. FOWLER, Aid.

Fourth of July.

☞ An Oration will be delivered and a cold collation served up at Washington, opposite Sacramento City, on the Fourth of July, at the spacious Hall of Capt. M. T. Coon

The Pacific Star Division Sons of Temperance, No. 1, will be present. The citizens of Sacramento, Fremont, Marysville, Yuba City, Eliza and Nicholaus, are particularly invited. A steamer will leave Marysville at an early hour on the morning of the 4th, to arrive at Washington in time for the festivities of the day.

Programme: 1st A salute of thirteen guns will be fired at sunrise, when the stars and stripes will be unfurled to the breeze.

2d. At 12 o'clock, M , a salute of thirteen guns, when the Sons of Temperance will embark from Sacramento City, and on their arrival will be escorted to the dining hall, by the citizens of Washington and visitors.

3d. The exercises will commence at 3 o'clock, P. M., with

1st. Music
2d. Reading of the Declaration of Independence, by Dr. H. A. Weeks, of Fremont.
3d Oration by Wm. M. Zabriskie, Esq.
4th. Music: Hail Columbia.
5th. Salute of thirteen guns at sunset.

The hall will be illuminated in the evening, and the whole will conclude with a ball. A band of music will be in attendance.

jy1-2t   MAHLON T. COON.

CHAPTER XX.

DURING the summer the squatter element portended trouble. The titles to real estate in Sacramento were somewhat mixed, and the squatters contended that they had as much right to the land as those holding titles under Sutter. A squatters' organization was formed, which held frequent meetings, and its members made violent and incendiary speeches, which, at first, were considered by the Mayor and more conservative citizens, as mere vaporings; but they soon learned that the squatters were in dead earnest and meant business.

· On the 21st of June, four or five persons, holding property under Sutter's title, demolished a squatter's house erected on a lot belonging to one of the party. On the following day, twenty-five or thirty persons made a raid on certain other lots of land which had been seized and appropriated by the squatters. They repaired with the proper implements to the Levee just above J Street, partially

19   (333)

destroyed a house belonging to a squatter, and then shoved it over on to a large tent, also owned by a squatter, which was standing on the adjoining lot. The next lot visited had been seized by a squatter and inclosed by a fence, which was soon demolished. They next commenced the work of devastation upon a house belonging to a squatter, erected on another man's land, which they completely destroyed. Quite a number of citizens witnessed the demolition of the buildings, but no opposition was offered. As the party were about dispersing, one of the gentlemen stated that he owned two lots on J Street, over the slough, upon which the squatters had seized, and that he would like to gain possession of his property. The party promptly accompanied him to his lots, and found that they had been fenced in, but no houses had been erected. The fences were torn down and thrown into the street. The object of the party having been gained, they left for the town. Several of the squatters followed them, and attracted quite a crowd by their vociferous shouting. Much excitement existed in the city.

A few days afterward, a squatter who had taken possession of a lot in the outskirts of the city, was asked by a gentleman by what authority he expected to hold the property on which he had squatted.

"By preemption, *of course*," was the reply.

"Look here," said the gentleman, "what causes the ground here to be so uneven?"

"Why, it has been ploughed," was the answer.

" Well," continued the former, " don't you think
the man who ploughed this land has got the start
of you; is he not the oldest settler?"

When the squatter learned that Captain Sutter
had actually *settled* on the land a number of years
previously, and had all the title he required to
make his property secure until another government
assumed jurisdiction, the squatter concluded the
preemption law would not reach his case, and
immediately pulled up stakes and *vamosed* to the
mines.

On the evening of the 1st of July, the squatters
held a meeting at the Herkimer House, on Fourth
Street. Dr. Robinson was appointed Chairman,
and Mr. Milligan, Secretary. The Secretary stated
the object of the meeting, which was to make arrangements to meet the suits against them, *en masse;*
each man was now defending himself, on his own
hook; the poor could ill afford it; the meeting had
been called to form a contract, raise a requisite
subscription, and employ the *right kind of counsel.* Mr. Milligan enforced his remarks with an
eloquent appeal about the sacred right of the homestead—a right which every man was bound to protect in justice to himself, etc. After he had concluded, Mr. McClatchy offered the following resolution:

"*Resolved,* That a committee of two be appointed
to confer with the counsel, and inquire as to the
terms, etc."

Mr. Edwards thought Mr. Milligan's remarks
cast reflection upon the counsel who had already

been employed ; he thought their counsel were *the best*, and they deserved great credit.

The resolution was amended by increasing the number from two to five.

Dr. Robinson said the Common Council had undertaken to legislate in regard to public property—property on which no action can be taken except by the Legislature. He would ask "has the Mayor any right to say what is *my* property and what is not?" He scouted the idea of landholders making land for themselves. He would disregard the Council, notwithstanding their assumed dignity; they were destitute of common sense, and should be regarded accordingly. It has been said, "answer a fool according to his folly;" he would say "treat a fool as a fool;" and if a man showed himself too low to be respected, don't respect him. For his part he looked down on the Council—way down—down so low that he could not see them. They were far out of sight of decent men. For his part, he meant to imitate the Mayor, meant to be a big squatter! It was just as easy to squat on one hundred and sixty acres as on one acre, and what he didn't need he would give to the poor squatters who are coming along by and by. It was as easy to defend a big piece as a small piece, and far better to take it themselves than to let the big landholders get it and sell it. After Dr. Robinson had concluded his remarks, the meeting adjourned to give way for a spontaneous meeting of the whole body of squatters, and for a short time they made things lively.

In about half an hour the meeting reorganized. Dr. Robinson was again placed in the chair, and Mr. Edwards was appointed Secretary. Mr. McClatchy requested the reading of an article from the *Pacific News*, which was frequently interrupted with applause and stamping of feet. It was now

"*Resolved*, that a committee of five be chosen, whose duty it shall be to confer with counsel on the subject of land-claims on the part of the settlers, and that all persons in the County of Sacramento who have taken, and may take up land-claims, and will share in the expense, shall reap the benefits."

Mr. Burt thought going to law unnecessary, for the whole thing was illegal and could not be sustained. Mr. Milligan said the object was to keep their enemies at bay until the question could be brought before a legal tribunal, where justice would be done. He asked nothing but what was right. Squatters were only aiming at justice; *satisfy them* that Sutter's title was good, and they would leave the land *as quick as a flea would jump off a hot griddle!* The resolution was again read and adopted, and the following committee appointed: Messrs. Wenner, Milligan, Mayhall, Plumbe and Canfield. An additional committee of five was then appointed to solicit subscriptions, and as a remuneration for their services, they were allowed to *retain five per cent. of the amount collected.* The committee consisted of Messrs. Milligan, Wadden, Wenner, Hays and Washington. The meeting again adjourned to meet on the following evening.

Pursuant to adjournment, the squatters met on

the following evening. Dr. Robinson occupied the chair, and Mr. Edwards acted as Secretary. The committee appointed at the previous meeting was called upon to report. Mr. Milligan, of the subscription committee, stated that the committee was not yet prepared to report, and asked for time; but in answer to several questions as to the progress of the committee, replied that he had been in the county, but had unfortunately not succeeded in finding the persons at home whom he went to see. He had understood that the members of the committee who had canvassed the city had done better than they expected. For his part, he had his hopes and his fears, but he believed they would succeed. He would do the best he could, but if they thought some one else would do better, he would willingly resign; he had not craved the office; it was no pleasant task; he had been sent to a man who he was told was a brother-squatter; he went to see him and asked his assistance, and all he got from the man was the reply, "that he had known people to make money by minding their own business!" and with this saying, the worthy squatter jumped on his load and moved off. As he said before, he craved no office, and if the meeting thought another would fill his place better, he was willing to stay at home and sit in the shade, and if a fly lit on his nose he would quietly knock it off!

The Secretary asked, "How much money has your committee obtained already?" Mr. Milligan replied, "We are not prepared to answer definitely, but think the subscriptions and cash in the city amount to $1,200. His friend, Mr. Allen, had told him he knew fifteen men who would give liberally, probably $100 each." Mr. Milligan thought if they got that amount it would be a good beginning; not much had been done; all that part of *Squatter-row* beyond where he lived had not been canvassed.

The chairman, Dr. Robinson, said that lawyers always like to know where their bread and butter is, and if the money could not all come, they would no doubt ask good security. Now suppose they ask $2,000 down and $2,000 secured, where are your bondsmen? That must be arranged; and if the immigrants are expected to pay a part, some plan must be adopted to let them into the benefits when they come, by paying a fee. If this is not done, the immigrants, when asked to subscribe for what has been done, may say the lawyers are a villainous set of scoundrels, and we will cheat them out of all we can anyhow. So some one ought to be responsible, that the counsel might feel secure. Mr. Milligan thought the committee themselves ought to be the bondsmen. Mr. McClatchy thought it best to leave the matter open until next meeting. He desired to go into the country on Sunday if he could *steal a horse* or borrow one. Sunday was a good day, and collecting squatter subscriptions a good deed. Dr. Robinson tendered his horse, and said that the animal had once made $300 on a similar excursion. Mr. McClatchy accepted the offer. After some further desultory remarks, a committee of three was appointed to draft a proper

heading for subscriptions, which would make it a
joint-stock matter, and if any surplus should be
subscribed over and above expenses, *it should be
divided.*   Mr. Mayhall was appointed one of said
committee.   Mr. Washington was nominated by a
gentleman, who said he did not mean Mr. Recorder
Washington, but Colonel Crawford Washington;
therefore Messrs. Mayhall, Washington, and John
W. Carter were the committee.   Mr. McClatchy
had learned that the committee had refused to take
a subscription of less than $25 from any individual.
Mr. Edwards knew a lady who had given $25.
Mr. Milligan thought a lady *ought to be worth* $25
in California! if she was worth anything.   Mr.
Edwards thought this a slur, and there was some
cross-firing.   After a few remarks by Mr. Plumbe,
and a detailed history of the squatter movement by
Mr. Edwards, the meeting adjourned.

On the evening of July 24th, another squatter
meeting was held at the Herkimer House.   The
meeting organized by appointing Dr. Merrick,
Chairman, and James McClatchy, Secretary.   Dr.
Robinson stated the object of the meeting was to
take into consideration the matter of lawsuits.   He
stated that the committee had employed Messrs.
Tweed, Aldrich, Mayhall and McKune on equal
terms—$1,000 each.   These gentlemen had con-
sented to do the settlers justice, if they would in
turn do their part, and pay them *a sum* of money—
which Dr. R. did not name—in advance.   If the
issue was successful, the settlers were expected to do
what they could afford to in addition to the $4,000.

Of the subscriptions, all over $4,000 to be common stock for the subscribers for their benefit as an association—collector to receive five per cent., and Mr. James McClatchy to be collector. The speaker said he was willing to trust Mr. McClatchy in town, but he wouldn't be responsible for him when he got out of town! Mr. McClatchy said he was a law-abiding citizen, but if these speculators were ready to fight, so was he. He would rather fight than collect subscriptions, any day; and if they showed fight, give them battle, and the devil take the hind-most. Let us put up all the fences pulled down, *and put up the men who pulled them down!* [Great applause and stamping.] After further remarks by Messrs. Robinson, Burke, Malony and Edwards, the meeting adjourned.

On the morning of August 14th the culminating point was reached, and the impending conflict commenced. On the previous day, James McClatchy and Michael Moran were arrested and taken before Justice Fake, charged with being parties in a contemplated attempt to resist the Sheriff, should he enforce the law in accordance with a decision given by Judge Willis against the squatters. The testimony was against the prisoners, and in default of bail of $2,000 each, they were both confined in the prison-ship.

On the morning of the 14th, a house on Second Street having been seized by the Sheriff, in accordance with the law, the squatters assembled in armed force of about thirty, under a leader by the name of Malony. They proceeded to the house which was in possession of the authorities and retook it. Their leader then harangued them, and they proceeded down L Street to the Levee. The party were armed with guns and pistols; their leader was on horseback, armed with pistols and a sword. They marched along the Levee toward the prison-ship, a crowd of citizens gradually collecting behind them. The report soon spread that their intention was to release the prisoners confined in the prison-ship.

Mayor Bigelow, who was on horseback, issued his orders at Warbass's corner, calling upon the citizens to take up their arms for the defense of the laws of the city and of California He then made the same proclamation on the opposite corner, and subsequently further up on J Street, opposite the Southern Hotel. Numbers at each place rushed for their arms, and began to assemble at the prison-ship. It seems, however, that the squatters, when they reached the outlet of Sutter's Lake, just above J Street, stopped and commenced moving lumber from a certain lot of land. Soon, however, Malony, their leader, addressed them briefly, stating that the lumber belonged to a friend, and that he would have it removed soon. This was satisfactory to them, and they marched in regular order, headed by their captain with drawn sword, up J Street. They were followed by a crowd of unarmed citizens, who were hooting and laughing at them. When the crowd of citizens reached the corner of Second and I Streets, one of their number stated that the Mayor was approaching, and that they had better await his orders. The crowd stopped and the squatters marched on, turned into Third Street and entered J. As the Mayor rode up to the citizens on the corner of Second and I Streets, he was asked what his orders were. He promptly replied, that he wished those men who were in arms against the authorities to be arrested. Three cheers were then given for the Mayor. Mayor Bigelow said he would lead the party himself, and they immediately proceeded after the squatters. The squatters, meanwhile, had turned into J Street and were marching out. When on the corner of Fourth Street, Malony, their captain, turned around, and seeing the Mayor, Sheriff and several armed citizens after them, commanded his men to halt.

They drew up in line across Fourth Street, facing on J Street, with their leader on the right. The Mayor and Sheriff rode up and commanded the squatters to lay down their arms and deliver themselves up as prisoners. As the citizens were approaching, Malony commanded his men to fire, and said distinctly : "*Shoot the Mayor; shoot the Mayor !*" The squatters leveled their guns and fired. Some of their guns, however, were pointed several feet over the heads of the citizens; while others were aimed lower and took more deadly effect. A general free fight ensued, in which there was firing on both sides. After the squatters had fired their guns, they drew their pistols; but the citizens rushed upon them, when they broke and dispersed.

At the first fire, Mayor Bigelow, who, throughout

the whole affair, showed himself a brave and determined man, was wounded very dangerously.   One
ball glanced his cheek; another passed into his
thigh; one tore his thumb badly and shattered the
bones of his hand, and the fourth produced the
most serious wound of all.   The ball passed through
his body, in the region of the liver.   After he was
shot, he fell upon the neck of his horse.   The
horse started, and he was enabled to hold himself
upon his back a short time, when he fell to the
ground.   He arose, however, walked a few steps
and dropped on the ground.   He then said that the
citizens must protect their city themselves, for he
was disabled and could do no more.   He was borne
to the Columbia Hotel, where he received the best
medical attendance.

Mr. J. M. Woodland, City Assessor, was also shot.
He did not speak after he fell, and survived but a
few moments.   The ball passed through his body,
on the left side.   No citizen was more respected
than Mr. Woodland, and few were more useful.

Malony, captain of the squatters, was also shot
dead.   He received three wounds; one in the arm,
one in the back and one through the head, which
caused almost instantaneous death.   A man by the
name of Jesse Morgan was also killed by a shot
through the neck.   He was from Holmes County,
Ohio, and had but recently arrived with his wife
and one child.   He was proprietor of the Oak
Grove House.   One other person was killed on the
side of the squatters, name unknown.   In addition
to Mayor Bigelow, the wounded were Dr. Charles

Robinson, a leading squatter, from Fitchburg, Massachusetts. He was badly though not mortally wounded in the left side, the ball passing through his body. He was placed on a cot and taken to the prison-ship. Mr. J. H. Harper, of Independence, Missouri, was also wounded. He exhibited great bravery, facing the squatters, and after firing off the barrels of his revolver, he threw it at them, whereupon they fired on him. He was wounded in both hands while they were placed across his breast to protect it from the shots of the squatters. A ball which passed through one hand, glanced against his side and produced a slight wound. Mr. Harper, though severely hurt, was not mortally wounded. Mr. Hale, of the firm of Crowell, Hale & Co., on J Street, was wounded slightly in the leg by a musket-ball. A child of Mr. Rogers, of the firm of Burnett & Rogers, was also slightly wounded in the leg.

During the fight there were four persons killed, and five wounded. Of those killed, three were squatters, and one of the citizens party. Of the wounded, four were of the citizens party, and one was a squatter.

Sheriff McKinney showed himself, through the whole affray, every inch a man. A squatter who was armed with a revolver, deliberately aimed at the Sheriff and discharged six balls at him, none of which, fortunately, took effect. Dr. White, Recorder Washington, Mr. Ruth and Dr. Pearis also acquitted themselves nobly.

Assessor Woodland was buried on the following

day, and after the funeral, Sheriff McKinney and about twenty others, proceeded out toward Sutter's Fort. When the party arrived at the Fort, the Sheriff stated that he intended to go out to the Five-Mile House, and arrest any squatters that he could find, either there or further on, if it should be to Mormon Island. Some of the party, not knowing the Sheriff's object when they started, were entirely unarmed, and one man left and rode back to town. The others armed themselves. The Sheriff then drew up the party in rank of four, and in this order they proceeded in a quick gallop out to the Five-Mile House. The Sheriff, however, learned nothing there. The party proceeded on toward the Pavilion, but, before arriving there, they were met by a man who informed the Sheriff that a party of squatters were located at "Allen's," two or three houses beyond the Pavilion.

The Sheriff thereupon commanded a halt, and sent two men forward to the house. While these men were absent, the Sheriff drew up his small force in line, and divided them into three squads of six men each. One squad was under the command of General Winn and another under Mr. Robinson. The Sheriff's orders were that one party should approach the house from the left, Mr. Robinson's party were to approach it from the right and General Winn's in front. Thus the parties proceeded, Sheriff McKinney taking charge of General Winn's division. When they reached the front of the house, the Sheriff called upon the men, in a jocose manner, to dismount and take a drink. He, with several others, entered the house, while the balance of the squad were hitching their horses. Upon finding men in an adjoining room, armed and ready to receive him, he commanded them to lay down their arms. The squatters replied with a volley. There were eight or ten squatters in the house. A general melee then ensued, and brisk firing was kept up by both parties for a few minutes. Shots passed in and out of the windows and the door, and constant firing was going on in the house. In the confusion, Sheriff McKinney had gotten out of the house, and as he was standing near the front door, a tall man fired at him from the inner room. He had a long gun loaded with buck-shot. The aim was too sure, and Sheriff McKinney was shot. He raised both hands and said three times, *"I'm dead, I'm dead, I'm dead."* While he was repeating the foregoing, he walked about ten steps and then fell dead.

Just after the tall man shot the Sheriff, Dr. Bryarly, who was near, aimed his pistol at him and fired. The ball probably took effect, for the man dropped his gun and fell over. In the melee, two squatters named Kelly and Henshaw, who fired from behind the bar, were shot dead. Captain Radford was severely wounded in the forearm, the bones being broken. Four prisoners were captured and taken to the Pavilion. During the firing, Captain Hamersley was thrown from his horse and injured in the back. One of the prisoners was then taken to town under guard, and parties proceeded to the city to inform the citizens of the state of affairs.

The first reinforcement that reached the Pavilion from the city, was a party of ten men led by Mr. Lundy. The second was a party of twelve men led by Mr. Tracy. General Winn formed them in line and made a brief address. The three remaining prisoners were placed in an omnibus, together with Captain Radford and the remains of Sheriff McKinney, and a guard of horsemen accompanied the omnibus to the city. The names of the prisoners in the omnibus were John Hughes, James R. Coffman and William B. Cornogg. The body of the Sheriff was left at Sutter's Fort, and the prisoners were conveyed down J Street, along Front, to the prison-ship.

On the part of the authorities, Sheriff McKinney was killed and Captain Radford wounded, not mortally. On the part of the squatters, two were killed and two wounded, and four were taken prisoners.

Dr. Bryarly, Mr. Hamilton, Mr. Milne, Mr. Creal, Mr. Bruce and an unknown German gave evidence of great bravery during the affray.

In a few hours after the outbreak of the 14th, Company A was formed and reported ready for duty. The following is the muster-roll of the Company: *Captain,* Jeremiah Sherwood; *First Lieutenant,* Lewis Smith; *Senior Second Lieutenant,* J. Weatherspoon; *Junior Second Lieutenant,* Lyman B. Munson; *Orderly Sergeant,* George Lattie; *Second Sergeant,* B. Phinney; *Third Sergeant,* Geo. H. Buckley; *Fourth Sergeant,* John Mason; *First Corporal,* George King; *Second Corporal,* Edward Corigan; *Third Corporal,* John Mattin;

Fourth Corporal, Lyman Bates; *Musician,* James Lattie; *Privates,* Thomas Kinney, George Graham, Andrew Bell, Jr., John Smith, E. Seymour, John R. Dickenson, James Burns, John Tinson, M. Henderson, John H. Underhill, Henry M. Jewett, Henry F. Beadle, Charles L. H. Long, Henry Coverdale, Charles Gordon, James Northrop, T. G. Hewlett, James Evans, J. W. Honrer, T. Wilson, John Wilson, E. McGinnis, William Shifmire, C.W. Coats, F. N. McCron, James Funston, James Henman, Albert Morgan, Jesse Toby, Edward Bestwick, Lewis A. Barnes, S. B. Elwell, Martin Metzger, Henry Rosenbaum, Robert Clark, J. S. Applegate, John Duncan, M. G. Whitlock, Richard Clark, Isaac M. Yearley.

On the evening of the same day, another company was organized under the name of "*The Sacramento Guard,*" and the following officers were elected: *Captain,* David McDowell; *First Lieutenant,* Henry Hale; *Second Lieutenants,* W. H. Crowell, James Queen; *Sergeants, First,* H. G. Langley; *Second,* B. B. Gore; *Third,* C. C. Flagg; *Fourth,* W. H. Talmage; *Corporals, First,* L. J. Wilder; *Second,* G. L. Hewitt; *Third,* T. H. Borden; *Fourth,* W. E. Moody; *Clerk,* W. R. McCracken; *Privates,* sixty-five.

After Mayor Bigelow had fallen, the Common Council assembled and placed Recorder Washington at the head of the police of the city. The Council then granted him authority to raise any number of men not to exceed five hundred. It was also voted that Mr. Demas Strong, President of Council, should

20

assume the duties of Mayor, and that the rest of the
Council should arm and place themselves under
Recorder Washington. Coroner P. F. Ewer as-
sumed the duties of Sheriff.

On examination of the wounds of Mayor Bigelow,
it was deemed advisable to amputate his thumb, and
the operation was performed by Dr. Birdsall. Subsequently mortification set in, and the Mayor was
removed to San Francisco, where his arm was
amputated. For nursing, etc., after the operation
had been performed, the following *modest* bill was
presented to the Common Council of Sacramento
City—female labor in California being at a pre-
mium, as will be seen by the last item of the bill:

SAN FRANCISCO, Nov. 29th, 1850.

HON. H. BIGELOW, *Mayor of Sacramento City,*

To J. W. STILLMAN, Dr.

For Cash advanced for sundries during his illness at
     my house, ... $480.00

" Cash paid *for washing clothes soiled* by his wounds,   165.00

" Five weeks' use of best and largest room in house,
     @ $100 per week, ... 500.00

" One carpet, ruined by chloride of lime, used in
     sick-room, ... 77.00

" Cash paid for pair of boots, ... 16.00

" Sundries, bandages, extra candles, extra refresh-
     ments, wines, etc., for self and attendants at
     night, etc., five weeks, ... 500.00

" *Five weeks' attendance of Mrs. Stillman, night and
     day,* 500.00

Total, . . $2,238.00

Sheriff McKinney was buried on the 16th, and

the obsequies were very impressive. His funeral, although it took place from Sutter's Fort, was very largely attended, not only by friends on horseback and in carriages, but by large numbers on foot. The Common Council had the general charge of the obsequies, but the body was buried with Masonic honors, and was under the immediate charge of the brethren of the Order. They preceded the hearse, which was followed by a long file of carriages. The militia, under Captain Sherwood, came next, and then about a hundred citizens on horseback. The ceremonies at the grave were conducted in an eloquent and feeling manner by Judge Willis, and after the coffin was deposited in its final resting-place, many were the sprigs of evergreen that were thrown into the grave—silent, eloquent tokens of the fellowship of numerous brethren. His afflicted wife and bereaved relatives stood at the edge of the grave; their grief and the solemn ceremonial hushed the crowd to breathless silence and brought tears to many eyes. Silently the body was deposited; the prayer was offered; the responses rose from hearts touched with sympathy, and the crowd departed, leaving behind them the remains of one whose name will ever live in the memory of every true lover of the common weal of California.

Late in the summer, intelligence reached Sacramento City, that great suffering existed among the overland immigrants. Public meetings were held, a relief committee organized, money subscribed, provisions purchased, and trains dispatched for the relief of the sufferers. The first meeting, started almost impromptu by Colonel John Bigler, without previous notice or regular organization, was largely attended, and the following amounts subscribed for their relief:

Captain Wm. Waldo, ...	$1,000
B. Jennings, ...	1,000
Thos. J. Henley, ...	100
M. Walthall, ...	100
R. J. Watson & Co., ...	250
S. P. Dewey, ...	100
W. W. Warner, ...	50
Cash paid on the spot, ...	200

William Rightmire, one good mule.

Several smaller sums were also subscribed, amounting in the aggregate to several hundred dollars.

Late in the month of August, with the following "Character"—from the editorial columns of the *Transcript*—in my pocket, I bade farewell to Sacramento City and turned my face homeward:

DEPARTURE OF MR. UPHAM.—The next steamer for the States will bear from us one who was with us in the commencement of our enterprise, and whose judgment and business talent have been to us of incalculable benefit. We allude to Mr. Upham. Our acquaintance with him was accidental. We became partners almost at first sight, but never did we find occasion to regret for a moment the unbounded confidence we always reposed in him. He leaves us while we are mourning the death, in our midst, of one of the noblest of men—thus adding to our sorrow and depriving us of another member of our family. Verily, the friendship which springs up between business men in this country is unlike the general acquaintanceship of other lands, which is laid aside without any apparent regret, and resumed only when politic or convenient.

Here, our partners in business form our social circles, and when one of a business firm retires, it is like dismembering a family.

Mr. Upham came to California prepared to commence at the bottom of the ladder, and climb slowly but surely up. Like most new-comers, he went to the mines and dug. His health failed him, and he returned to San Francisco late in the fall of last year. After a few days of unsuccessful effort to get into business, he finally secured the situation of carrier of the *Pacific News*. His fine capacity soon attracted the attention of his employers, who selected him to keep the books and transact the business of the establishment. It was there we found him. After living with us four months, he leaves us in our new home, and possibly we shall not see him again for years, if ever. But wherever he is, we shall not forget the qualities that have so conduced to our enjoyment and forwarded our business. We sincerely wish him a speedy return to his family and success in the business in which he may hereafter engage.

CHAPTER XXI.

I ENGAGED passage on board the steamer *Senator*. She made a fine run down the Sacramento, crossed Suisun Bay, and after exchanging passengers at Benicia, threaded her way through the Straits of Carquinez and entered San Pablo Bay. I retired early, and at daylight on the following morning, found myself alongside the steamboat wharf at Clark's Point. After removing my baggage to the City Hotel, I took a stroll about the city; but old things had passed away, and all things, comparatively speaking, had become new. During an absence of four months from San Francisco, a wonderful change had taken place.

The most populous part of the city had, within that time, twice fallen a prey to that devouring element—fire. New and tasteful brick structures had superseded the frail *adobe* and wooden tenements; the streets and sidewalks had been planked; piers and wharves, extending across the mud-flats far into the bay, had been constructed; in fact, the city had

(354)

EAST SIDE PLAZA. 1850.

put on an entirely new dress. Happy Valley, which, four months previously, contained scarcely half a dozen frame buildings, now boasted as many hundreds. Verily, this *El Dorado* is a wonderful country; and San Francisco, despite clouds of dust and chilly afternoons, is destined to become the second city on this continent. Farewell, San Francisco!

"Thy beautiful harbor, proud golden-gemmed Queen,
Is rivalled by none the world has e'er seen!"

We will now step on board the steamship *Columbus*, commanded by that prince of captains, J. B. Peck. At six o'clock on an August afternoon, amid the adieus of friends who had assembled to see me off, the scramble among trunks, bags and other luggage, the *Columbus* cast off her bow and stern lines—the last physical tie that bound me to California—swung into the stream and was soon puffing out of the harbor under a full head of steam.

As the shipping in the harbor receded from my view, the little hamlet of Soucileto, nestling quietly among the hills on the opposite side of the bay, hove in sight, but was soon lost in the dim distance. As the *Columbus* approached the Golden Gate, she bounded gayly over the water, impatient to reach the broad bosom of the Pacific. I shall never forget the memories that crowded my brain as I passed through the Golden Gate homeward-bound. When I entered the harbor of San Francisco, on board the brig *Osceola*, thirteen months previously, feelings of a far different nature occupied my mind. The difference between an outward and a homeward-bound voyage can be appreciated only by those who have experienced both.

Early in the evening, I threaded my way between market-baskets, trunks and camp-stools to my state-room, cogitating, as I passed along, upon the glories of a night's rest between clean sheets, but

"This world is all a fleeting show,"

and all things sublunary are very uncertain, as the case in question will illustrate. On reaching. state-room F, I was taken all aback by finding it stowed with strange baggage. I could, in fact, find anything but my own goods and chattels. The cabin-maid soon made her appearance, and entered into an explanation of matters. Women generally carry their point, and it so happened in this case, although the justice of the matter seemed to me rather questionable. It appeared, upon investigation, that two individuals of the male persuasion, occupying state-room E had surrendered their quarters to a gentleman and his wife, and during the absence of myself and room-mate, had taken possession of state-room F. I endeavored to convince them of the injustice of their proceedings, but it was of no use, and as a lady was involved in the case, I accepted a berth in state-room B and dropped the subject. My room-mates were a Mr. Clarkson, of San José, and Mr. Tittle, ex-Postmaster of Sacramento City; both bound to the States for their better-halves and little ones.

There were forty-two cabin and one hundred and seventy-six steerage passengers on board the *Colum-*

DEPARTURE OF A STEAMSHIP, FALL OF 1850.

bus, and when all were congregated on deck, there was not much spare room.   At the commencement of the voyage, petty jealousies and bickerings existed between the cabin and steerage passengers in relation to their rights to the hurricane or promenade deck.   On the fourth day at sea a line was stretched across the deck abaft the mizzen-mast by the cabin passengers, and the steerage passengers were requested to keep forward of the line. This movement on the part of the cabin passengers was taken in high dudgeon by their brethren of the steerage, and a war of words ensued, interlarded with epithets more forcible than polite.   On the ensuing evening a meeting was convened in the cabin, and after a free discussion of grievances on both sides, it wound up to the entire satisfaction of all concerned, with champagne and cigars for the crowd.

We were favored with fine weather and a smooth sea until we reached the Gulf of California, where we encountered head-winds and cross-seas for seventy hours, during which time a majority of the passengers paid the requisite tribute to old Neptune by casting up their accounts.   Mr. Tittle was decidedly opposed to a nautical life.   He was of the opinion that life on the plains was far preferable to a

“ Life on the ocean wave.”

We ran down the coast of Mexico with the land close aboard.   The coast was bluff and abrupt, presenting in many places a highly picturesque appearance; and, in the distance, the Cordilleras raised their snow-capped heads majestically to the skies.

On the afternoon of August 26th, the *Columbus* dropped her anchor in the harbor of Acapulco, near the shore, and immediately in front of the Plaza. The port officer had scarcely left us before we were surrounded by a fleet of small boats of almost every conceivable style of architecture, from the rude Indian canoe or *bungo* to the clinker-built whale-boat. Several of the passengers availed themselves of the opportunity offered by the numerous water-craft alongside, and went on shore to spend the night. A majority, however, myself among the number, having the fear of cholera before their eyes, concluded to remain on board during the night, and visit the shore next morning. After supper I seated myself on the hurricane deck and chewed the cud of reflection over the end of a cheroot until the cathedral bell tolled the hour of midnight. I then went below and was soon locked hard and fast in the embrace of Morpheus.

At sunrise next morning, I went ashore, accompanied by a couple of friends, for the purpose of seeing the sights in Acapulco. The first object that met my eye on reaching the shore, was a group of Mexican children gamboling along the gravelly beach, in a state of perfect nudity, and as I passed through the city toward the Fort, I saw several "children of a larger growth" attired in the same airy costume. In the vicinity of the Fort, I saw several soldiers with no other uniform than a cotton shirt, glazed cap with a red bobbin, and a rusty musket. I once saw at Gibraltar a company of Highlanders with bare legs and broadswords, which I considered a breezy uniform, but the costume of the Acapulco soldiers caps the climax.

The city of Acapulco is situated on the north-east side of the bay, and is surrounded on three sides by a range of mountains towering to the skies, and clothed to their summits with cactus and *chaparral*. Along the beach and throughout the suburbs of the city, the symmetrical cocoanut tree, with its long sword-shaped leaves and clusters of fruit, rears its head in all its majesty, affording shade and shelter as well as food for the natives. The city is mostly built on two streets, each about three-fourths of a mile in length, and running parallel with the bay shore. The buildings, with the exception of the cathedral, are only one-story high and are mostly constructed of *adobes*, with tile or thatched roofs. The street leading from the Plaza to the Fort, is paved with blocks of granite and sandstone. The other streets are graveled, and a stream of pure water is continually running along the gutters, giving them a clean and cool appearance. The houses in most cases are whitewashed inside and out; and the city, taken all in all, presents a cleanly appearance. It contains about 3,500 inhabitants, mostly Mexicans. The Bay of Acapulco is easy of access, completely landlocked, and is considered one of the safest harbors on the Pacific coast.

After having viewed the Fort, an ancient *adobe* and sandstone structure, we visited the house of an old Scotchman, who had, some thirty years previously, married a native wife and became Mexicanized. Immediately on landing, we had ordered a breakfast of chickens, eggs, milk and chocolate. The sanitary committee had *tabooed* milk during the prevalence of the cholera in the city; but chickens and eggs in abundance were set before us, to all of which we did ample justice. Chickens and fresh eggs were most assuredly a great luxury to those who had been deprived of them for nearly fifteen months.

During the early part of the day, Captain Peck watered and coaled the *Columbus*, and at four o'clock, P. M., the sound of her signal-gun came booming over the bay, the summons for the passengers to repair on board. A general stampede was made for the boats on the beach, and several were filled and about to shove off, when a file of soldiers emerged from the guard-house close by and ordered the boatmen not to enter their boats. A pretty state of affairs now presented itself. The *Columbus* had fired her signal-gun and would most likely get under way within half an hour, whether the passengers were on board or not, and a *taboo* had been placed on all the boats. Some cursed the boatmen; others remonstrated with the soldiers, and endeavored to ascertain the cause of the detention; but they shook their heads and said they "*no sabe Americano.*" However, we were not kept long in suspense. The soldiers, headed by a nervous little citizen with a small black stick in his right hand, which he was constantly twirling about in a fidgety manner, approached two of the passengers, who had, during the passage, proven themselves to belong to the sporting fraternity, and requested them to accompany him to the office of the Alcalde; but as they were decidedly opposed to being escorted through the city by an armed guard, they peremptorily declined the honor and retreated toward the boats. The soldiers cocked their muskets and commanded them to stand. One of the gamblers drew his revolver and threatened to shoot the first *hombre* that approached to arrest either himself or partner. The pistol cooled the ardor of the soldiers to such a degree, that the gamblers were allowed to seize a boat and make their escape to the steamer.

It appeared, from subsequent investigation, that the cause of the attempt to arrest grew out of a *melee* which had occurred at a gambling-table in the American Hotel on the previous night. The gamblers said that the proprietors of the *monté* bank used waxed cards, and attempted to come the " draw game" on them ; and they, as a set-off, came the " grab game" on the funds of the bank, which caused an order to be issued for their arrest and trial before the Alcalde. The escape of the gamblers on board the *Columbus* was reported to the American consul, who immediately went on board and stated the circumstances of the case to Captain Peck, who, in his usual bland manner, informed the two " sporting gentlemen" that they could have the choice of either being confined in irons on board the steamer, or of going ashore in the custody of the consul. After a few moments' consultation, they concluded to go ashore and stand their trial before the Alcalde, Judge Pratt, of Oregon, a passenger on board the steamer *Caroline*, having volunteered to act as their counsel in the case. As soon as the prisoners were put upon their trial, my two friends and myself engaged a *bungo* and went on board the steamer. We had scarcely reached the deck before the anchor was hoisted and the *Columbus* was steaming out of the harbor, leaving the gamblers and three or four of the passengers, who had been detained as witnesses, to the tender mercies of the Mexican authorities. Poor fellows; they were caught in bad company, and will learn a lesson that will no doubt be of future service to them.

While in Acapulco, I made the acquaintance of a party of Georgians, bound for California, who came by the way of Vera Cruz and the City of Mexico. Two of the party were brought into the city by the natives, on litters, having been taken sick on the road. One had been attacked with cholera, and was in a critical state; the other was recovering from an attack of dysentery. When this party left Vera Cruz, on the last of July, the cholera was raging there to an alarming extent. The City of Mexico was quite healthy when they passed through it. They saw several guerrilla bands on the route, but they were peaceably disposed. They performed the journey between the City of Mexico and Acapulco, a distance of 100 leagues, in eleven days. They report the streams very much swollen and the road very rough.

The steamer *Tennessee* left Acapulco on the evening the *Columbus* arrived, bound for San Francisco, with only twenty passengers on board. The steamer *Caroline*, from San Francisco, arrived at Acapulco some ten hours ahead of the *Columbus*. We had a smooth sea and a delightful run between Acapulco and Panama, where we arrived on the evening of September 4th, eight days from the former place. The weather, with the exception of an occasional shower, was pleasant, and we had a very agreeable passage. The health of the passengers was remarkably good during the entire passage. The *Caroline* arrived in Panama fifteen minutes ahead of the *Columbus*.

At six o'clock, A. M., on September 5th, I tumbled myself and baggage into a boat, bade the *Columbus* adieu, and in about half an hour thereafter found myself on the shoulders of a native, who was propelling through the surf as fast as his powers of locomotion would admit of. He landed me on the beach, in front of the city-gate, high and dry, safe and sound; damages, $4, including boat-hire. My friend, Bowditch, formerly attached to the steamer *Governor Dana*, was less fortunate than myself. The *hombre*, whom he undertook to ride ashore pig-a-back, unhorsed him—perhaps, unmanned would be the better word—in three feet of water on a coral reef, and left him floundering in the surf. He succeeded, however, in reaching the shore, amid the shouts of the assembled darkies. Ex-Postmaster Tittle also received an immersion without the benefit of clergy, at the hands of a boatman. The *hombre* who carried me through the surf, seemed extremely anxious to treat me to a salt-water bath, but I caught him by the ears, determined to bring his head under water should he submerge me. I would advise all persons going ashore at Panama, to land at the Market-steps, thereby avoiding a ride through the surf on the back of a negro, and also the probability of wet inexpressibles.

At the solicitation of a friend, I accompanied him to the American Hotel, kept by an American sea-captain, but neither the house nor its proprietor realized my expectations, and, after having partaken of a miserably-served breakfast, I removed my baggage to the Louisiana Restaurant, near the gate on the Cruces road, where I remained during the three days I sojourned in Panama. I cannot recommend this house too highly to persons traveling either to or from California. During my stay in Panama, I visited the barracks and prison; viewed the crumbling wall, in all its meanderings, that surrounds the city; inspected the large dismantled guns on the battery fronting the bay; and last, though not least, visited several of the ancient and dilapidated churches, that at one time were the pride of the city.

The *Padres* of Panama possess a wonderful penchant for cock-fighting, at any and all times, Sundays not excepted, and what they don't know about game-cocks, gaffs and spurs, it would be useless to learn.

During my stay in Panama, two of the *Columbus's* passengers—Benj. F. Browne, of New York, and Randolph Scott, of Texas—died of cholera.

The best medical attendance was procured, and they received every attention at the hands of their fellow-passengers, but human aid was of no avail. They died in a foreign land, far away from home and kindred.

CHAPTER XXII.

Leave Panama—To Cruces on mule back—Down the Chagres River in a *bungo*—Deaths by cholera *en route*—Mr. and Mrs. Gillingham—Go on board the steamship *Falcon*—Deaths by cholera—Burial at sea—Arrival at Havana—An afternoon and night on shore—Take passage on the steamship *Ohio* for New York—Arrival at New York—Departure for Philadelphia—Home again.

HAVING learned from the agent in Panama, that the steamship *Falcon* would leave Chagres on the 13th of September, thirteen of the *Columbus's* passengers, including myself, formed a party to cross the Isthmus, and, on the morning of the 6th, held a meeting at the Louisiana Restaurant, appointed a committee to engage mules and caterers to provide provisions for the journey, and early on the morning of the 8th, we mounted our animals in front of the restaurant, and started for Cruces, distant 22 miles. The first six or eight miles of our journey was over what the natives termed a *mucha bueno* road, but the balance of the road was *mucha malo* in the strongest sense of the term. I hired two mules at $16 each. On one of the animals I packed my trunk and the other I rode.

Belonging to our party were Mr. and Mrs. R. P. Gillingham, of Philadelphia. Mrs. Gillingham

(370)

having neglected to provide herself with a Bloomer costume, had either to ride a mule attired in her usual dress and take the chances of being dumped into the first slough she attempted to cross, or submit to the novel mode of riding on the back of a nude native, lashed in a chair. She adopted the latter mode of conveyance, and arrived safely at Cruces. Mr. Gillingham had arrived in San Francisco early in August, and at the expiration of two weeks his courage had so completely oozed out that he engaged passage for himself and wife on the first homeward-bound steamer.

Our pack-mules were addicted to the annoying habit of turning their loads whenever it suited their inclination, which caused us to scold the muleteers in bad Spanish, and the muleteers to belabor and curse the mules in a manner that proved them to be no novices at the business. Any one who has heard an Isthmus muleteer swear must be thoroughly convinced that profanity is his chief stock in trade. One of our party had the misfortune to bestride a recreant mule, probably a lineal descendant of the donkey chastised by Balaam, which bolted into the woods, threw his rider, and bruised him quite severely. I had the good fortune to select a gentler, though a very small animal, somewhat larger than a Sacramento grandfather rat, and he carried me safely to Cruces. As we commenced ascending the mountains the road grew worse, and we made very slow progress.

Night overtook us at a ranch 8 miles from Cruces, where we tied up until morning. I drank two cups of a villainous compound called coffee, and turned into a grass hammock, which

"Swung loose at the sport of the wind;"

but, owing to the combined attacks of an army of mosquitoes and fleas, I slept very little during the night.

In the early part of the evening, one of the *Columbus's* passengers was attacked with cholera, but, owing to good nursing during the night, he was able to be transported on a litter to Cruces next day. At daylight we awoke the muleteers and sent them after the animals. They returned about eight o'clock with all the mules except three, which they said had *vamosed* to Panama during the night. The delinquents proved to be saddle animals; consequently three of the party had either to engage fresh mules, which was no easy matter, or walk to Cruces. They concluded to adopt the latter course; but after walking two miles they engaged mules at a ranch and overtook us as we were entering Cruces at eleven o'clock, A. M.

At a ranch, 6 miles from Cruces, we saw the corpse of Thomas Robinson, of Illinois. Mr. Robinson died of cholera two hours previous to our arrival. While we were at the ranch, a friend returned with medicine for the sick man, but it came too late. We buried him under a large tree near the roadside.

We spent the afternoon making arrangements for our passage to Chagres on the following day. Myself and four others chartered a large *bungo* for $50, to convey ourselves and baggage to Chagres. The owner of the *bungo* swore by all the saints in the Spanish calendar, that he would be ready to start down the river at daylight next morning; and with this assurance we retired for the night. Friend Tittle and myself spread our blankets on the ground-floor of a bamboo hut, and turned in for a night's rest; but owing to a carnival held by the fleas over our bodies, we slept very little. Next morning our party was at the *bungo* at the appointed hour, but the boatman had not arrived. We soon found him, however, and at six o'clock, A. M., we shoved into the stream, and the current in a few moments hurried us out of sight of Cruces. We passed Gorgona early in the morning, and at one o'clock, P. M., dined at the ranch of the "Two Brothers," situated about halfway between Cruces and Chagres. Soon after leaving this place, the rain descended in torrents. It appeared as though the flood-gates of heaven were open. Had not two of our party kept constantly bailing the *bungo* during the *shower*, it certainly would have been swamped. When the rain ceased, the sun shone forth in all its splendor, and during the remainder of the day we were as comfortable as the circumstances of our case would admit of. A wet jacket at any time is unpleasant, but as this was the first and only shower experienced during our journey across the Isthmus, we bore up under it manfully, and considered that we had been highly favored by the elements. We reached Chagres at

six o'clock, P. M., having made the run down the
river in twelve hours, including stoppages.

On the passage down the river, I saw several
alligators and iguanas without number. On the
boughs of the trees and on the banks of the river,
I saw parrots, paroquets, and other birds of beautiful plumage. In the forest, on both sides of the
river, monkeys were constantly chattering.

While shifting our baggage into a surf-boat, preparatory to going on board the steamship *Falcon*, a
canoe arrived with the remains of Colonel Prigmore, of Saline County, Missouri, who died of
cholera just before reaching Chagres. Colonel
Prigmore was the gentleman, before alluded to,
attacked with cholera at the ranch 8 miles from
Cruces, on the night of the 8th.

At half-past seven o'clock on the evening of September 10th, I stepped into a surf-boat and was
soon on board the steamer *Falcon*, commanded by
Captain Hartstein, U. S. Navy, lying in Chagres
Roads, distant from the town about a mile. There
was a heavy swell setting into the mouth of the
Chagres River and dashing against the battlements
of the old fort, but the surf-boat rode safely over the
rollers. I went at once to the office of the clerk for
the number of my state-room and berth, having
purchased a through-ticket in San Francisco with
the express understanding that I should have a
saloon or first-cabin state-room on board the *Falcon*.
I was informed by the clerk that all the first-class
state-rooms had been taken; and, moreover, that
the agent in San Francisco was not authorized to

sell through-tickets. After considerable parleying, a berth was assigned me in the "house on deck," where I found some half a dozen others of the through-ticket victims, similarly situated. Some consoled themselves with the idea that they would obtain satisfaction from the agent on their return to California; others, that they would probably never travel the route again, and, like true philosophers, they made the best of a bad bargain.

On the night of the 11th, Daniel Norcross, Special Mail Agent, arrived with the mail, and at half-past one o'clock on the following morning, the *Falcon* weighed anchor and started for Havana, where she arrived at eight o'clock, A. M., on the 17th. During the passage between Chagres and Havana, the following persons died of cholera:

Captain Barnabas Kirby, Mass.,	died Sept.	11th,
Robt. T. Lawrence, Brooklyn, N. Y., "	"	12th,
Elias Orton, Iowa, . . . "	"	12th,
William Beal, Michigan, . . "	"	12th,
Ismael Worthington, Ohio, . . "	"	13th,
—— McGowan, N. Y., . . "	"	13th,
James H. Frye, Missouri, . . "	"	13th,
Captain Elisha Clark, Maine, . "	"	13th,
Captain Augustus Norton, " . "	"	14th,
Sol. Joseph, Western Islands, . "	"	14th,
John Pinchatich, Trieste, Austria, "	"	15th,
Captain Richard Macy, Maine, . "	"	16th,
J. Spaulpaugh, N. Y., . . . "	"	16th,
William Maynard, Conn., . . "	"	16th,
Crawford Riddel, Philadelphia, Pa., "	"	16th,
James Campbell, Ireland, . . "	"	16th,
—— Downing, Missouri, . . "	"	16th,
—— Gates, Indiana, . . . "	"	17th.

Captain Kirby died while the *Falcon* was lying off Chagres, and his body was sent ashore and buried at that place. The others, who died during the passage, were buried at sea.

A burial at sea is a solemn scene. "All hands to bury the dead!" is piped by the boatswain, amid the tolling of the ship's bell, and with the flag at half-mast, the corpse, wrapped in a sheet or blanket and incased in a canvas sack with a heavy weight at its feet, is placed on a plank in the gangway. The Episcopal burial service is read by the Chaplain or Captain, and at its conclusion, a tilt of the plank, a thud, a splash in the water and all that is mortal of the deceased is ingulfed beneath the waves of the ocean, there to remain until the last great day, when this globe shall dissolve, and the grave and the sea shall give up their dead.

Out of the twenty cases of cholera on board the *Falcon* only three were saved; and two of these were treated by Dr. J. Hobart Birge, of Sacramento City, a passenger on the *Falcon*, to whom many thanks are due for his kindness and attention to his sick and dying fellow-passengers on the Isthmus as well as on board the *Falcon* and the *Ohio*. The surgeon of the *Falcon* treated eighteen cases of cholera, and saved only *one!*

The accommodations for the sick on board the *Falcon* were most miserable, and the treatment of the passengers, in cabin and steerage, did not meet their expectations. They expected to fare as well on the Atlantic as on the Pacific, but they were disappointed so far as the *Falcon* was concerned.

During those five memorable days passed on board the *Falcon*, my friend Tittle became sadly demoralized. Whenever a corpse was consigned to the deep, he imagined that his turn would come next, and it was with great difficulty that I could divert his mind from the gloomy surroundings. The pall of death seemed to enshroud all on board. He gave me the address of his wife, and requested me to take charge of his gold-dust and other effects in case of his death. By way of consolation I reminded him of the old adage about those born to be hanged, etc., and he finally came to the conclusion that he was not a subject for the cholera.

On our arrival in the harbor of Havana, we were informed that we would be quarantined and not permitted to visit the city. We had anticipated this. Imagine our surprise then, on being informed, a few hours later, that the *taboo* had been removed, and we could go ashore at twelve o'clock, M. This news was hailed with joy by all on board, and at one o'clock, P. M., nearly every passenger was on shore enjoying himself to his heart's content. Dan Norcross and myself chartered a *volanté* for two hours, and, seating ourselves in the vehicle, ordered the postillion to trot us through the principal thoroughfares of the city. Jehu, an African as black as the ace of spades, who, by-the-by, was incased to his hips in boots as black and shiny as his countenance, mounted the horse attached to the *volanté*, and cracking his whip, we started off at a brisk pace, up one street and down another; now threading a narrow lane, and now rattling over the pavement of a wide and beautiful street, lined on either side by shade and fruit trees, that perfumed the air with their fragrance.

We hurried through the city at John Gilpin speed, and from the expression of the countenances of the little urchins, who threw up their tiny hands and cheered us as we passed, I believe they wished us much joy, and also that they might be present when we rode again. Boots performed his duty faithfully; and at the expiration of two hours, set us down in Palace Square, the place from whence we had started, and received his fee—$1—the cheapest ride between New York and California, at least I thought so at the time.

Havana is a beautiful city, and its harbor and surrounding scenery, with the exception of Rio de Janeiro and Naples, the most romantic in the world. In the evening I sauntered about Palace Square, which was crowded with the beauty and fashion of the gay metropolis, listening to the sweet and soul-inspiring music of the military band. The Havana *señoritas* are perfect houris, and, had I been a bachelor, the steamship *Ohio* would probably have had one passenger less to New York. I remained on shore during the night, and at six o'clock next morning went on board the *Falcon* and transferred my baggage to the *Ohio*, Captain J. Finley Schenck, U. S. Navy. The *Ohio* left Havana at half-past nine o'clock on the morning of the 18th of September, and arrived in New York at eleven o'clock, P. M., on the 22d, performing the passage in four days and fourteen hours.

On the day we left Havana, the following passengers died of cholera and were buried at sea:

Captain Ira Gould, Huntington, L. I.
George Howell, Sag Harbor,   "
William Fields, Providence, R. I.
A. Spencer, East Greenwich, "

The passengers on board the *Ohio* had no cause of complaint. Captain Schenck and his officers did everything in their power to render all on board as comfortable as possible. The table was bountifully supplied, and the servants were attentive and obliging—a marked contrast to the treatment on board the *Falcon*. The following resolutions were adopted, and a copy presented to Captain Schenck:

ON BOARD STEAMSHIP OHIO,
At Sea, Sept. 21st, 1850.

At a meeting of the passengers held on board this ship, to express their feelings of regard for Captain Schenck and the officers under his command, Judge Woodrooff, of New Orleans, was called to the chair, and R. P. Gillingham, of Philadelphia, appointed Secretary. The following gentlemen were appointed a committee to draft suitable resolutions: Samuel C. Upham, Philadelphia; James H. Brown, Baltimore; W. H. Bowditch, Boston; Captain Thomas F. Knowles, Baltimore, and D. S. Hunt, of New York, who presented the following resolutions, which were unanimously adopted:

Resolved, That we tender to Captain J. Finley Schenck our sincere and heartfelt thanks for the courteous manner in which he has borne himself toward all on board, and more especially for his kindly treatment of our sick and dying fellow-passengers since our departure from Havana. His skill as a commander, and other commendable qualities, will ever entitle him to our warmest regards; and we trust that through the voyage of life he may ever be favored with fair winds, and at last let go his anchor in the haven of eternal rest.

Resolved, That, through Captain Schenck, we extend our warmest thanks to the other officers of the *Ohio,* for their gentlemanly and officer-like deportment during the present passage between Havana and New York.

Resolved, That the proceedings of this meeting be published in the New York *Herald,* Philadelphia *Ledger,* Baltimore *Sun,* and Boston *Post,* and that a manuscript copy of the same be presented to Captain Schenck by the Secretary.

C. WOODROOFF, President.

R. P. GILLINGHAM, *Secretary.*

I arrived in New York thirty-eight days after my departure from San Francisco, including stoppages. Six days' detention *en route* deducted, leave thirty-two days traveling time between the two places. On the afternoon of the 23d, I left for Philadelphia to join my better-half and little ones, and the re-union, after a separation of nearly two years, can be better imagined than described.

When I left California, it was my intention to return the following year with my family, but "man proposes and God disposes." Life's current has drifted me into other channels; the heyday of life has passed, and now, at the age of threescore I despair of again visiting the land where

> "The vine and the fig-tree are laden with fruit,
> And the breezes blow soft as the tones of the lute,
> The orange-tree blossoms and fruits in the vale,
> The date and pomegranate, 'mid sand and the shale,
> The filbert and almond, and manna of yore,
> All abound in the land that I love and adore."

The kaleidoscope of life is constantly changing. The life of man is but a span—here to-day and gone to-morrow. The Argonauts of 'Forty-nine are fast falling by the roadside and being gathered to their fathers. Reader, as you pass down the pathway of life, culling flowers by the wayside, should you chance to meet one of those wayworn Argonauts, one of those old grizzlies of the Sierras, who has never "builded a city nor founded an empire," but who did assist in adding to the constellation of States of our glorious Union one of its brightest and sunniest stars, the Eureka State, Queen of the Pacific, treat him kindly, and when he shall have passed from earth, place upon his grave a wreath of immortelles, and God will bless you.

APPENDIX.

PIONEER JOURNALISM IN CALIFORNIA.

———

The *Pacific News*—Its editors and proprietors—"Boston," *alias* "Big Ames"—First newspaper published in California—The *Alta California*—*Sacramento Transcript* and *Placer Times*—The *Golden Era*—Bret Harte, Mark Twain and Prentice Mulford—San Francisco *Picayune*, *Courier* and *Herald*—Marysville *Herald*—Stockton *Times*—Sonora *Herald*.

THE following sketch, published originally in Rowell's *Newspaper Reporter* and subsequently elaborated and published in N. W. Ayer & Son's *Advertiser's Guide*, has been corrected and still further elaborated, and, in its present form, is believed to be a correct and impartial history of Pioneer Journalism in California:

On my return to San Francisco from the Calaveras mines, in the month of October, 1849, I applied to the proprietors of the *Pacific News* for permission to canvass for a carrier's route on their journal. After a long interview, during which the project was thoroughly discussed, *pro* and *con*, I obtained the sole and exclusive right to canvass for subscribers and serve the *Pacific News* in the city of San Francisco and suburbs, which latter included Happy Valley and the adjacent sand-hills.

Mr. Falkner, the senior proprietor of the *News*, prior to emigrating to California, published a paper in Norwich, Connecticut. When the gold fever broke out in the New England States Mr. F. was one of its first victims. He packed up his printing-office, and engaging passage for himself and two sons on board a vessel, sailed for the modern *El Dorado, via* Cape Horn. At Valparaiso, he made the acquaintance of Warren Leland, one of the proprietors of the Clinton Hotel, New York, *en route* to the gold-diggings of California. Leland having an eye to business, proposed to enter into copartnership with Falkner upon their arrival at San Francisco. His proposition was accepted; and immediately upon reaching San Francisco, a frame building was hastily constructed on Kearney Street, and on the 25th of August, the first number of the *Pacific News* was published, with Falkner as editor, and Leland as business manager. A few weeks subsequently, Charles Eames, of Washington, D. C., appointed by President Polk consul to the Hawaiian Islands, arrived in San Francisco *en route*, but was prevailed upon by Falkner and Leland to forego his mission, locate in San Francisco, and assume editorial charge of the *News*, at a salary of $500 per month. As the election and inauguration of Zachary Taylor, as President of the United States, had rendered the recall of Mr. Eames a foregone conclusion, that gentleman considered discretion the better part of valor, and accepted the editorship of the *News*.

Simultaneously with the engagement of Mr. Eames as editor-in-chief, a tall, lank, hirsute Yankee of the name of Ames *alias* "Boston," was engaged as a local reporter of the *News*. Ames subsequently published in San Diego, California, a *weakly* paper, called the *Herald*, which for a single week was edited by "John Phœnix," the California humorist. During the temporary absence of Ames, Phœnix changed the politics of the *Herald* from red-hot Democratic to Whig, which so exasperated Ames that a free fight occurred in the composing-room. During the *melee*, the forms were knocked into pi, and the combatants became so thoroughly mixed, that t'other couldn't be distinguished from which. Phœnix, in his published account of the fight, claimed he won the victory *by insert-*

ing his nose between the teeth of Ames, and holding him down until he cried *peccavi!*

The *Pacific News* was the first tri-weekly, and at that time the third paper published in California, the other two being the *Alta California,* published in San Francisco by Gilbert & Kemble, and the *Placer Times,* published at Sacramento City by E. Gilbert & Co., and edited by Jesse Giles, both weekly sheets, and small patterns at that, the latter being foolscap size.

The Monterey *Californian* was the first newspaper issued in California. It was published and edited by Rev. Walter Colton, a Chaplain of the United States Navy, and Dr. Robert Semple. The type was principally Long Primer, an old Spanish fount, badly worn and battered. There being no "W" in the Spanish alphabet, two "V's" were substituted for that letter. The press was an old "Ramage," which had been used by the Mexican functionaries for printing their edicts and other public papers. The first number of the *Californian* was issued in the summer of 1846, and was printed on an inferior quality of paper, used for tobacco wrappers. Mr. John R. Gould, at present a resident of Baltimore, Maryland, and Secretary of the "Maryland Association of Veterans of the Mexican War," with the assistance of a boy, set the type, worked off the paper and kept the books of the office. Mr. B. P. Kooser, a corporal in the United States Army, was compositor and pressman on the *Californian* in 1847. Mr. Kooser subsequently for several years published and edited the *Sentinel* at Santa Cruz, California, and was a commissioner from that State at the Centennial Exhibition.

The second paper published in California was the *California Star,* the first number of which was issued at San Francisco, on the 9th day of January, 1847. It was a weekly sheet, a trifle larger than the *Californian,* and was published by Sam Brannan, and edited by E. P. Jones. The press on which the *Star* was printed was a tolerably good one, and was afterward used by the Sonora *Herald*. On the 17th of the following April, Mr. Jones retired from the *Star*, and Mr. E. C. Kemble assumed editorial charge. The *Star* was published regularly during the year 1847, the last number of the first volume being issued on the 1st day of January, 1848.

In the month of May, 1847, the *Californian* was removed from Monterey to San Francisco, and on the 1st of June of that year, the first number of its second volume appeared. The second volume continued on from that time until April, 1848, during which time the paper changed publishers and editors several times. The first number of the second volume of the *California Star* appeared on the 8th of January, 1848, in an enlarged form, and its publication was continued regularly until the 26th of the following May, when the printers *vamosed* to the mines, and its publication was discontinued. In the month of April, the *Californian* was discontinued for the same reason. From the last of May until the latter part of June, 1848, California was without a newspaper.

About the 1st of July, a few printers, who had returned disgusted with the mines, commenced the publication of the third volume of the *Californian*. It was issued every now and then, without any regard to regularity, until August, 1848, when it recommenced its regular weekly issues, under the editorial management of H. I. Sheldon. In September of the same year, Mr. Kemble returned from the mines, purchased the *Californian*, also the interests of his partners in the *Star*, and united the two papers under the name of the *Star and Californian*, and recommenced its publication where the *Star* had stopped, Vol. III, No. 24. The *Star and Californian* was the only paper then published in California, and was issued weekly until the last of December, 1848, when it was discontinued, and on the 1st of January, 1849, Mr. Kemble united with himself Messrs. Gilbert and Hubbard, and commenced the publication of the *Alta California*. The *Alta California* was published weekly, until the 10th of December, 1849, when it was issued tri-weekly, and after the 23d of January, 1850, came out daily, simultaneously with the *Journal of Commerce*, published by W. Bartlett. On the 4th of the ensuing March, the *Pacific News* also appeared daily.

The next paper, the fourth started, and the second then published in California was the *Placer Times* at New Helvetia, Sutter's Fort, afterward Sacramento City. The first number of the *Placer Times* appeared on the 28th day of April, 1849, and was printed weekly, on a cap sheet, as paper of a larger size could not be obtained. The publishers were E. C. Kemble & Co., the editor being Mr. Kemble. On the 19th of the following June, on account of ill health, Mr. Kemble vacated the editorial chair, and T. R. Per Lee* assumed charge. On the 25th of August, 1849, Mr. Per Lee resigned, and Jesse Giles continued the publication of the paper for E. Gilbert & Co.

In 1849, very little printing-paper was to be had in California; but the market was overstocked with unruled foolscap paper, which was substituted for the former. The size of the *Pacific News* was a foolscap sheet; and as enlargement was a matter of impossibility, supplementary sheets were added to accommodate advertisers. The price of the *News* was 12½ cents a copy, or 75 cents a week, payable to the carrier. Steamer editions, published on the first of each month, and printed on wrapping-paper of various colors and qualities, sold at 50 cents a copy. Advertisements were $5 a square, each insertion.

I experienced little difficulty in getting up a paying list of customers for the *News*. Nearly every one on whom I called gladly subscribed for the paper, and at the end of

* At this time (September, 1878,) a resident of Baltimore, Maryland.

each week paid me promptly. I had scarcely become accustomed to my new vocation, when the situation of book-keeper was tendered to me by the proprietors of the *News*, with a salary of $100 a week. I sold my carrier's route for $200, and accepted the situation, which I held until the following spring.

In the month of March, 1850, there arrived in the harbor of San Francisco a ship from New Orleans, with an assorted cargo, among which was a second-hand printing office, with some thirty reams of printing-paper. The type, presses (a card and hand press), paper, ink, etc., were invoiced in New Orleans at $950, but were valued in San Francisco at $15,000, and could have been sold for that amount in coin, as printing material was very scarce, and "sorts" were worth their weight in gold. Mr. G. K. Fitch, the owner of the printing material, proposed to five of the attaches of the *Pacific News*—F. C. Ewer, H. S. Warren, J. M. Julian, T. Russell and S. C. Upham—the formation of a copartnership, with a view to the publication of a paper in Sacramento City. The proposition was accepted, articles of agreement executed, and on the 1st day of April, 1850, the initial number of the *Sacramento Transcript* was issued by Fitch, Upham & Co. The *Transcript* was published tri-weekly during the months of April and May, and on the 1st of June it became a daily. It was printed on a folio sheet, in Brevier and Nonpareil type. A steamer edition, for circulation in the Atlantic States, was printed on the first of each month. The daily sold at 12½ cents a copy, and the steamer edition at 50 cents a copy. Advertisements were inserted at $4 per square, each insertion. The six copartners occupied the following positions on the paper: G. K. Fitch, heavy and fighting editor; F. C. Ewer, literary editor; H. S. Warren, foreman; J. M. Julian, compositor; T. Russell, pressman, and S. C. Upham, local reporter, printer's devil, business manager, "deadhead," etc.

The *Sacramento Transcript* was the fifth newspaper published on the Pacific coast, and the first daily out of San Francisco published in California. Ten days later, the 10th of June, the *Placer Times* came out daily. The *Transcript* was a financial success from the start, but as the gold rolled in, its proprietors rolled out. Mr. Julian retired before the expiration of the second month, and the business manager a ·month later, having sold his interest in the *Transcript* for $10,000 * to Mr. G. C. Weld, California correspondent of the New York *Journal of Commerce*. Mr. Weld was a model business man as well as a versatile and graceful writer. Had he lived, he would have made a shining mark in California journalism. Being of a delicate and fragile organization, his system was prostrated by the vicissitudes of pioneer life, and within six weeks from the time he became one of the proprietors of the *Transcript* he passed from earth to that bourn whence no traveler returns. The *Transcript*, after the death of Mr. Weld, being without a competent business manager, began to wane. It was afterward merged into the *Placer Times*, another sickly daily at that time; but after the consolidation, the new enterprise was a success. A year later the *Times and Transcript* was removed to San Francisco, and took a leading position as a Democratic organ. In June, 1853, Pickering & Fitch sold the paper for $30,000 to Geiger, Washington & Kerr. It died in 1856 of a Democratic controversy. Too much Tammany killed it!

On the 13th of April, two weeks after the advent of the *Transcript* in Sacramento City, the *Placer Times*, then under the editorial management of Colonel J. E. Lawrence, came out tri-weekly. Early in the following October, E. Gilbert & Co. disposed of the *Times* to Messrs. Pickering, Lawrence & Co., the former gentleman assuming the chair of senior editor. Colonel J. E. Lawrence, the junior

---

* Three thousand dollars cash, and the notes of the purchaser for the balance. The notes were not paid. Mr. Weld's death cancelled them.

editor and one of the most genial and companionable gentlemen it has ever been my good fortune to meet, arrived in California early in '49, overland, *via* Mexico and Lower California, by mule express. Soon after the collapse of the *Times and Transcript*, Colonel Lawrence either started or purchased an interest in the San Francisco *Golden Era*, the leading literary journal of the Pacific coast, and assumed its editorial management.

The *Golden Era* was the *alma mater*, and Colonel Joe Lawrence the godfather of Bret Harte, Prentice Mulford, Charles Warren Stoddart, Dinsmore, the dramatizer of Mark Twain's "*Gilded Age*," Minnie Myrtle, and a host of lesser lights, whose early lucubrations first appeared in that journal. Bret Harte was for a short time compositor in the office of the *Golden Era*, the situation having been obtained through the intercession of his sister, an occasional contributor, and his first two productions were published anonymously in that journal, while he was working at case. When the authorship of the sketches became known, the *Golden Era* lost an indifferent compositor, but added to its staff of *litterateurs* a rough diamond, which, with careful polishing, ere long became a gem of the first water.

Steve Massett, "Jeems Pipes of Pipesville," was one of the early birds, having arrived in San Francisco early in '49. Mark Twain, Bret Harte, Prentice Mulford and Dinsmore arrived later, although it is generally believed by archæologists that Mark Twain started for California immediately after the deluge, but owing to snags in the Mississippi River and scientific researches *en route*, did not actually arrive in California until A. D. 1852. The first opening that occurred after his arrival in San Francisco was caused by an earthquake. This event so exasperated Mark, that he immediately laid in a box of pipes, a barrel of smoking tobacco and a few kegs of lager as small stores, and sailed direct for the Sandwich Islands, where for several years he hobnobbed with King Kamehameha, and played "Jumping Frog of the Calaveras," for the amusement of Prince Kalakaua and other sprigs of Kanaka royalty.

Prentice Mulford, after wasting his sweetness fourteen years in California, during which time he was by turns prospector, miner, politician, pedagogue and *litterateur*, quietly folded his tent, and hied himself to "merrie England," where, like a sensible man, he took unto himself a better-half, and is now striving to fulfill the scriptural injunction, "Increase and multiply." Mr. Mulford's letters to the San Francisco *Evening Bulletin*, during his sojourn in England, France and Austria, gained for him an enviable reputation, and his "*Centennial Notes*" from Philadelphia, contributed to the same journal during the year 1876, place him in the front rank of his profession. Mr. Mulford is also a pleasing lecturer, and if he were to devote his attention to the rostrum, would excel either Bret Harte or Mark Twain.

On the 16th of March, 1850, Mr. J. White published the first number of the *Stockton Times*, in the city of Stockton, on the San Joaquin River. The *Times* was a weekly paper printed on a cap sheet, in Long Primer type. H. H. Radcliff soon afterward purchased an interest in the paper, enlarged it and changed its name to the *Stockton Times and Tuolumne City Intelligencer*.

On June 19th, Mr. J. S. Robb, a native of Philadelphia, and at one time connected with the St. Louis *Reveille*, issued in Stockton the first number of the semi-weekly *Stockton Journal*.

On June 1st, Foy, Nugent & Co. issued the first number of the San Francisco *Daily Herald*. The *Herald* was edited by John Nugent, formerly connected with the *New York Herald*.

On the 1st of July, the first number of the San Francisco *Courier* (daily) appeared. It was published and edited by Messrs. Crane & Rice, and was Whig in polities, being the second political paper in California, the *Pacific News*, then edited by Mr. F. C. Ewer, having, in the preceding January, espoused the Democratic cause. On August 3d, John H. Gihon & Co. commenced the publication of the San Francisco *Evening Picayune*, edited by P. A. Brinsmade. The *Picayune* was the first evening paper published in California; and its senior proprietor was a native of Philadelphia.

The first number of the *Sonora Herald* (weekly) was published on July 4th, by J. White & J. G. Marvin. It was printed on a cap sheet, and in Long Primer type. The semi-weekly *Marysville Herald* made its first appearance on the 6th of August. It was published and edited by R. H. Taylor. The size of the paper was a cross between cap and folio post.

I will here state that to Mr. Edward Connor, formerly of the *New York Herald*, is due the credit of having brought the first steam-power printing-press to California. It was a Napier press, made by R. Hoe & Co., and arrived in May, 1850. The first paper printed by steam-power in California was the *Alta California*. When the writer left California, in the month of August, 1850, the *Alta California, Pacific News, Journal of Commerce, California Courier, Herald* and *Evening Picayune*, of San Francisco, the *Transcript and Placer Times*, of Sacramento City, the *Times* and *Journal*, of Stockton, and the *Sonora Herald* and *Marysville Herald* were the only newspapers published in that State, and with a single exception—the *Oregonian*, at Portland, Oregon—the only journals published on the Pacific coast north of Mazatlan.

The *Pacific News* had changed proprietors, and in August, 1850, was edited by General Jonas Winchester, a former associate of Horace Greeley in the *New-Yorker*. The *Evening Picayune* was at that time edited by Dr. John H. Gihon, private secretary to Colonel John W. Geary, then Mayor of San Francisco. The late General John W.

Geary was the last *Alcalde* and the first Mayor of San Francisco, and I am quite certain that city has never since been governed more ably or satisfactorily. As a brother-pioneer and .'Forty-niner, I feel an honest pride in the brilliant record achieved during the war of the rebellion by the first Mayor of San Francisco. May his laurels ever remain green in the hearts of his countrymen.

Twenty-six years have wrought wonderful changes in California, as well as along the entire northern Pacific coast. Old landmarks have become almost entirely obliterated. San Francisco, with her few dozens of *adobe* and frame structures in 1849, and a population of less than 1,500 souls, at the present time contains a population of 300,000, and is the second commercial city on the western continent. When the agricultural resources of the Pacific slope shall have become as fully and thoroughly developed as its mineral, New York must look to her laurels. The press has fully kept pace with other improvements. I have before me a list of 283 newspapers and periodicals published at this time in the States of California and Oregon. At present there are published in San Francisco 16 dailies, 43 weeklies, 1 semi-weekly, 15 monthlies and semi-monthlies. In the State there are published 239 journals and periodicals, of which 47 are daily papers. The average circulation is 2,035. Taking the last census as a basis, the ratio of newspapers and periodicals published in California is larger, according to population, than any other State of the Union, being 90 copies yearly to each inhabitant. The State of New York is second on the list, with 89 yearly copies to each inhabitant.

The San Francisco *Evening Bulletin* and the *Morning Call,* partly owned and controlled by Mr. G. K. Fitch, my former associate in the *Sacramento Transcript,* are ably-conducted journals and are said to be the best paying newspaper properties in California. Mr. Fitch's associates in the *Bulletin* and *Call* are Mr. L. Pickering, formerly one of the editors and proprietors of the *Placer Times*, and Mr. J. W. Simonton, agent of the New York "Associated Press," both experienced and able journalists. The *Bulletin* has always been a terror to evil-doers, and Mr. Fitch, the head and front of that journal, has, by his honest, able and judicious management, earned the deserved title of the Horace Greeley of the Pacific Coast—but will never *run for President*. Few of the journalists connected with the California press in 1849–'50 now reside in the State of their early labors; Fitch and Pickering being the only ones now in working harness. B. P. Kooser,* veteran pioneer printer, has recently vacated the sanctum of the Santa Cruz *Sentinel*, and now sits under his own vine and fig-tree in that beautiful semi-tropical city by the sea, surrounded by the idols of his heart—wife and children. Mr. F. C. Ewer has given the flesh and the devil the cold shoulder, donned sacerdotal robes, and is at present rector of St. Ignatius Church, New York City. Messrs. Kemble and Russell are also residents of the latter city. Some twenty years since, Mr. Gilbert was killed by General Denver, in a duel at Oak Grove, near Sacramento City.

Colonel Joe Lawrence has retired to the classic shades of Bay City, Long Island, where he presides with dignity over the Society for the "*Prevention of Cruelty to Animals*," nurses that same old meerschaum and luxuriates on cold tea with a stick in it.† Charles Eames returned to Washington, D. C.,

---

* Deceased since the above was written.

† DEATH OF COLONEL JOSEPH E. LAWRENCE —The telegraph announces the death at Tom's River, N. J., of Colonel Joseph E. Lawrence, of Flushing, Long Island, one of the old newspaper men of this coast. Colonel Lawrence came to this State in 1849. In the following year he was employed by E. Gilbert & Co. to edit the *Placer Times*, at Sacramento. Subsequently he became a partner of Loring Pickering in the publication of the same journal. In 1851 the *Times* and the *Transcript*, another Sacramento paper, were merged into one, and during the following year the paper was moved to this city. Colonel Lawrence continued his connection with the *Times and Transcript* till 1854. After that he was one of the proprietors of the *Golden Era* for a long time. He filled a position in the Custom-house during the administration of B. F. Washington. His latter years were spent between this city and

practiced law there, was subsequently appointed minister to Ecuador, and died seven or eight years ago. Dr. John H. Gihon is also dead. Warren Leland returned to California a few years since and managed the "Grand Palace Hotel," in San Francisco, until quite recently, when he returned to New York city, where he now resides. General Jonas Winchester, the veteran journalist, is at this time a resident of Grass Valley, California.

New York, where he was highly connected. For a considerable period he also had a lucrative place in the Custom-house of the latter city. Colonel Lawrence was one of those genial men who never make an enemy. In his more youthful days he was remarkable for the neatness of his dress and his personal beauty. As a newspaper man he took fair rank, though his writings as a general thing were more suited for the literary weekly than the daily newspaper. They were, for the most part, of the easy-chair, sunshiny sort, which one wishes to read in dressing-gown and slippers. For the last three or four years of his life Colonel Lawrence had undergone a great change, supposed to have been the result of sunstroke in New York. He had become careless in his dress and inert, but he never lost his good nature and pleasant manners. He will long hold a place in the memory of the old members of the profession. One of his most remarkable traits was his open-handedness. He was willing to share almost all he had with his friends. If he had not been so generous he might have been a rich man. As it was, the residue of a reasonable fortune—some $12,000 or $13,000—he took East for the purchase of an old homestead, for which he always manifested the greatest attachment.--*San Francisco Bulletin, July 15th,* 1878.

"CALIFORNIA DAY" AT THE CENTENNIAL EXHIBITION.

Preliminary meeting in New York—Committee appointed—Rev. Albert Williams addresses the meeting—Programme of exercises—'Forty-niners and other Californians present—Distinguished guests —Addresses by Hon. Rodman M. Price, Generals H. G. Gibson and Joe Hooker, Governor Curtin, General Sutter, Governor Hartranft and Colin M. Boyd—"Song of the Argonauts"—The banquet—Fire! fire!—Telegrams sent to San Francisco.

AT a special meeting of "THE ASSOCIATED PIONEERS OF THE TERRITORIAL DAYS OF CALIFORNIA," held at the *Sturtevant House*, New York, on the evening of May 15th, 1876, General H. Gates Gibson, U. S. A., President, in the chair, the following resolutions were unanimously adopted:

Resolved, That the members of this Society assemble at the PACIFIC COAST CENTENNIAL HALL, Centennial Grounds, Philadelphia, on the 9th day of September next, the twenty-sixth anniversary of the admission of California into the Union, and that all Californians throughout the country be requested, without further notice, to join with us upon that occasion, in *one grand re-union* of Californians.

Resolved, That the Secretary be instructed to furnish copies of the minutes of this meeting to the press of this and other cities, and also to all Californians whose names are registered in the book kept for that purpose by the Society, requesting their co-operation in the movement for a re-union of Californians at Philadelphia, on the 9th day of September next.

(398)

In compliance with a resolution, the President appointed the following committee to make the necessary arrangements in Philadelphia, for the visit of the Society in September: Messrs. E. F. Burton, Thomas D. Johns, S. L. Merchant, John Gault and W. M. Walton.

The President appointed the following committee to confer with non-member Californians, and ask their co-operation in the re-union at Philadelphia: Messrs. O. H. Pierson, H. B. Hawkins and John A. Godfrey.

During the evening, the Rev. Albert Williams, of San Francisco, Secretary of the Pacific Coast Centennial Committee, addressed the Society, on invitation of the Chair, and gave the details of the building in course of erection at Philadelphia, and stated that it would be ready for occupancy June 1st, and extended the use of the hall to the members of this Society, and all other Californians visiting the Exhibition.

Upon the conclusion of the remarks of Mr. Williams, the President returned to that gentleman the thanks of the Society.

At a subsequent meeting of the Society, the programme on the following page was adopted:

RE-UNION OF CALIFORNIANS

Under the auspices of

The Associated Pioneers of the Territorial Days of California,

(HEAD-QUARTERS IN NEW YORK CITY,)

AT THE

PACIFIC COAST CENTENNIAL HALL,

EXHIBITION GROUNDS, PHILADELPHIA,

On Saturday, September 9th, 1876,

AT ONE O'CLOCK, P. M.

(*Twenty-Sixth Anniversary of the Admission of California into the Union.*)

PROGRAMME OF EXERCISES.

1. INTRODUCTION OF Gen. JOHN A. SUTTER, *by Pres't Gibson.*
2. MUSIC—"Hail to the Chief."
3. PRAYER, *by Rev. Dr. Allen.*
4. ADDRESS OF WELCOME, *by General H. G. Gibson, U. S. A.,*
   President of the Associated Pioneers.
5. MUSIC—"Centennial Ode.".. . ... *Geibel.*
6 READING OF LETTERS, *by the Secretary of the Society.*
7. MUSIC –" O California !"
8. ADDRESS, *by Hon. Rodman M Price, ex-Governor of New Jersey,*
   And a participant with Commodore Sloat in the raising of the American Flag at Monterey, California, July 7th, 1846.
9. MUSIC—"Star Spangled Banner."
10. "SONG OF THE ARGONAUTS; OR. DAYS OF '49."
    Composed expressly for this occasion by S C Upham, Esq , of Philadelphia. Solo by Mr George A. Conly, Basso of the Kellogg Opera Troupe. The audience will please join in the chorus.
11. MUSIC—"Potpourri. Operatic Airs."
    BANQUET, *at Globe Hotel.*

Music by McClurg's Cornet Band. Selections of Music by the Band from 12 o'clock, noon, until the commencement of the exercises Also, appropriate Music on the " Centennial Chimes," by Professor Widdows.

Saturday, September 9th, was a charming autumn day, and at one o'clock, P. M., an audience of seven hundred persons had assembled in the " PACIFIC COAST CENTENNIAL HALL." The assemblage was composed mainly of

PACIFIC COAST CENTENNIAL HALL.

Gordon P. Cummings, Architect.

former residents of the Pacific slope; many of the number being ladies, who heartily enjoyed the festive occasion. Two large and beautiful American flags of California silk, belonging to Mr. Neuman, of that State, arched the space behind the speakers' platform, and strips of bunting around the entire walls and pillars decorated the hall, while McClurg's Cornet Band enlivened the intervals between the speeches, with choice selections of music. Placards with appropriate mottoes also adorned the walls. A large and artistically-executed seal of the Eureka State, composed entirely of native woods, and loaned for the occasion by Mr. J. R. Scupham, occupied a prominent position on the speakers' stand. On the platform were seated some half-dozen gentlemen, whose personal history had been more or less identified with the exciting days of the early gold discoveries in the modern *El Dorado*. Prominent among these was the veteran pioneer, General John A. Sutter, in his seventy-fourth year. Among other representatives of the first settlers of the Golden State, who occupied seats either on the platform or in the audience, were the following:

Hon. Rodman M. Price, ex-Governor of New Jersey, who was a participant with Commodore Sloat in the raising of the American flag at Monterey, California, on July 7th, 1846; Colin M. Boyd, President of the "Territorial Pioneers of California;" B. P. Kooser, of Santa Cruz, California, one of the Centennial Commissioners from that State, who, in 1847, was engaged as pressman and printer on the *Californian*, at Monterey, the *first* newspaper printed in California; Major-General Joseph Hooker, U. S. A., General H. Gates Gibson, U. S. A., John Sickels, Francis D. Clark and wife, General Thomas D. Johns, D. M. Chauncey, S. L. Merchant, William M. Walton, O. H. Pierson, H. M. Newhall, E. F. Burton, John H. Gardiner and wife, Mrs. Dr. Chas. Blake, William J. Curtis, James E. Nuttmann, Gordon P. Cummings, John H. Trowbridge,

John A. Godfrey and wife, Prentice Mulford and wife, Joaquin Miller, Samuel C. Upham, A. B. Duncan, T. Conklin, J. T. Fisher, James S. Wethered, and W. Lynch, of Los Angeles, California.   There were also present, Governor John F. Hartranft, ex-Governor Andrew G. Curtin, ex-Governor William Bigler and General Jos. R. Hawley, President of the Centennial Commission.

The exercises commenced at one o'clock, P. M., with a fervent and appropriate prayer, by the Rev. Dr. Allen, of the Old Pine Street Church, who had recently returned from a trip to California.   General Sutter was then introduced to the audience by President Gibson, in the following appropriate speech:

FELLOW-CALIFORNIANS, LADIES AND GENTLEMEN:—In accordance with the announcement just made by the Chairman of the Committee of Arrangements for this re-union, I have the pleasure and honor of introducing to you, as President of the day, General John A. Sutter, our grand old patriarch and noble chieftain, whom we all delight to honor; whose noble deeds and golden virtues, amid the stirring incidents and enchanting scenes of his pastoral life in the Golden Land, and in the exciting events of his discovery and development of her rich *placers*, have made his name as illustrious in history as it is grateful in our hearts.   You will rejoice with me that God has given him length of days, and that he is enabled to join with us to-day, in the full communion of body and spirit, in the commemoration of his proud achievements, and the brilliant results—as wonderful as those from the touch of the magical lamp of Aladdin—that sprang from his grand discovery.   You will join with me in the fervent prayer, that God will give him still greater length of days, and that the sunset of his life may be as serene and beautiful, as its meridian was glorious with full-orbed splendor, whose

> "Light *still* lingers 'round us yet,
>   Bright, radiant, blest."

You will also unite with me to-day in the earnest hope that

the justly-merited and long-deferred reward for his inestimable services to the whole country, may soon cease to be a reproach upon the justice, gratitude and magnanimity of the Republic; that it may yet be said, to the honor of our country, as of the warrior, renowned in Spanish history and song:

> " After high deeds not left untold
> In the stern warfare, which of old
>   'Twas his to share,
> Such noble leagues he made, that more
> And fairer regions than before,
>   His guerdon were."

And now, General Sutter, veteran pioneer and noblest of men,

> " Let *not* thy noble spirit grieve,
> Its life of glorious fame to leave
>   On earth below ;"

for, though the official and substantial recognition of thy grand services and grander life may be withheld, through the proverbial ingratitude of republics, we, thy clansmen and thy children, will never withhold from thee the just meed and loyal tribute of our grateful affection and honor ; and, better still,

> " In Heaven thou shalt receive, at length,
> The guerdon of thine early strength
> And *generous* hand."

On taking the chair, General Sutter made a few remarks, during which he said he felt proud of the honor conferred on him, and was glad his life had been spared him to meet his early California associates on the occasion of the twenty-sixth anniversary of the admission of California into the Union, and particularly at the Centennial Celebration of the Independence of the United States.

General H. Gates Gibson, President of the " Associated Pioneers," then delivered the following eloquent address of welcome, which was rapturously applauded :

FELLOW-CALIFORNIANS, LADIES AND GENTLEMEN :—Under the auspices of "The Associated Pioneers of the Territorial Days of California," this re-union has been initiated and inaugurated, and it now becomes my pleasing duty to extend to each and all of you, a cordial, hearty welcome. It was said of old, that "when Greek meets Greek, then comes the tug of war," but may it ever be said of us, the Argonauts of the nineteenth century, that when Californian meets Californian, then comes the warm clasp of the hand, the bright kindling of the eye, and the kindly, earnest greeting that springs from the heart. As with the pilgrims of the Holy Land, "palm to palm was holy palmer's kiss;" so we, pilgrims of the Golden Land, bestow on each other to-day the "palmer's kiss" of golden peace, affection and welcome.

On this natal day of California, we have come with proud and grateful hearts to exultingly sing with you our pæans of praise and honor to the Golden State, and to join in the patriotic rejoicings of our countrymen over this grand Centennial Jubilee of the Republic, on this historic spot whence the glad tidings went forth: "Proclaim liberty throughout the land to all the inhabitants thereof."

The distinguished orator, who will address you to-day will, no doubt, do full justice to the mighty thoughts inspired by the occasion and your presence; and, though they may not

> " suggest
> Life's endless toil and endeavor,"

yet they teach an invaluable lesson to those who may come after us, demonstrating by example, as rich and beautiful as "apples of gold in pictures of silver," the truth of the grand apothegm, that

> " In the lexicon of youth, which Fate reserves
> For a bright manhood, there is no such word
> As—*fail !*"

But, enticing as may be the theme of California, and the story of her sterling Pioneers, I must not encroach upon the province of your orator, or trespass upon your indulgence beyond the duty incumbent upon me as President of the Society; and, if tempted beyond it, your own hearts will plead for me:

> "The love he bore to *California* was at fault ;"

for our hearts go out to her to-day with an earnest longing, in some degree akin to that of the fond mother for the child of whom God has bereft her.

The scenes and incidents of our California life

"When fond recollection presents them to view,"

and the associations blended with our California experience, are replete with golden reminiscences of rare charm and rich felicity; appreciated by us at least, if not by the Gentiles, who never trod her soil or bathed in the waters of her Jordan, or reveled in the delights of her delectable climate and scenery. The skeptic and scoffer may, in the spirit of Naaman of old, exclaim: "Are not Abana and Pharpar, rivers of Damascus, better than all the waters of Israel?" but we who have seen the beauties and virtues of the waters, soil and clime of California, and felt the magical influence of her rich and novel experiences and associations, know whereof we speak, and know that we accord to her only the just meed of praise and honor. For "the gold of that land is good"—"a land of corn and wine, of oil, olive and of honey;" with crystal golden streams, and "broad-armed ports whereon rich navies ride;" with scenes of exquisite pastoral beauty, and landscapes of grandest sublimity; all, golden scenes, incidents, associations and experiences, aye, golden virtues, too, that "smell sweet and blossom in the dust" of our remembrance. Imbued with the spirit of the revived freshness and fragrance of these delightful memories, we bid you a glad and feeling welcome.

But in the gladness of our welcome to the coming guest from her golden shores, and in our grateful tribute of affection to our beautiful Golden Land, we must not forget that "the place whereon thou standest is holy ground"—sacred to the birth of a nation, and hallowed as the sanctuary of the tabernacle of the ark of the covenant—our matchless Constitution of government; the Mecca of Freedom to which we have, this day, made our pilgrimage to draw, at the altars our fathers built, fresh and pure inspirations of loyalty and devotion to our whole country. One hundred years ago, the Continental Congress here uttered the bold Declaration which severed our

connection with the mother country and made us a nation;
and, building better than they knew, left us a goodly heritage
of "Virtue, Liberty and Independence;" bequeathed us a noble
legacy of the most perfect league and covenant of union, that
the wisdom of man ever devised. If we fail to guard, with
jealous care, the security and purity of the one, or to protect
from the hands of the spoiler the majestic fabric of the other,
the blame will lie with us, not with the fathers of the Republic.
Then

> "Guard we but our own hearts; with constant view
>   To ancient morals, ancient manners true,
>   True to the manlier virtues such as nerved
>   Our fathers' breasts: then this proud land preserved
>   For many a rugged age."

> "Land of the brave, athwart whose gloomy night
>   Breaks the bright dawn and harbinger of light,
>   May glory now efface each blot of shame,
>   May freedom's torch e'er light thy path to fame;
>   May Christian truth *in this thy sacred birth*
>   Add strength to empire, give to wisdom worth,
>   And with the rich-fraught hopes of coming years
>   Inspire thy triumphs while it dries thy tears."

The age of California as a State, is but one-fourth of that of
the Republic as a nation, and when the English colonies of
the Atlantic were thriving settlements, not even the bold rover
of the Spanish main and of seas unknown had "spied out the
land and found that it was good;" yet she has "fretted her
brief hour upon the stage" of history to the grand purpose
and effect of the advancement of the greatness and richness of
the whole country. And her pioneers are here to-day to offer,
in the true Californian spirit of old, their devout and filial
homage to the fathers of the Union, whose precious inherit-
ance was borne by them, with the glorious ensign of the Republic, to the far distant shores of the Pacific. And, in grateful return, and in triumphant pride, it has been the mission
and glory of California

> "To scatter plenty o'er a smiling land
>   And read her history in a nation's eyes."

For out of her opulence and abundance from soil, and rock, and stream, "wealth gilded our cities, commerce crowded our shores," and but for our late suicidal strife, the world would have witnessed, as predicted by President Polk, the permanent transfer of the control of its monetary concerns from London to New York. And if the treasures and products which California poured with bounteous hand into the coffers and granaries of the nation have been wasted through misrule, passion and folly, you, Pioneers of the Golden Land, have the proud satisfaction of knowing that in all you have done to promote the progress and prosperity of your country, you have nobly illustrated the force and spirit of the words of the poet:

"Act *well* your part, for there all *honor* lies."

At the conclusion of General Gibson's address of welcome, Mr. Francis D. Clark, Secretary of the "Associated Pioneers," followed with the reading of letters from invited guests unable to be present. These were from President Grant, General Sherman, and from Emory L. Willard and Colonel A. C. Bradford, Secretaries respectively of "The Territorial Pioneers of California," at San Francisco, and the parent organization known as the "Society of California Pioneers," and Major-General Joseph W. Revere, of Morristown, N. J., who raised the first American flag on the Bay of San Francisco, at Sonoma, and took possession of that district in the name of the United States, on July 9th, 1846. Letters were also read from Major-General James A. Hardie, who went to California as major of Colonel Stevenson's regiment; Hon. Philip A. Roach, ex-President of the "California Pioneers," and Bayard Taylor. The last-named gentleman, referring to General Sutter, stated that he had not seen him since he saw him in Monterey, in 1849, when he waltzed with him at the ball given at the close of the Constitutional Convention.

After the playing of "O California" by the band, the orator of the day, ex-Governor Rodman M. Price, of New

Jersey, was introduced to the assemblage and delivered the following interesting and eloquent oration:

FELLOW-CALIFORNIANS, LADIES AND GENTLEMEN :—I greet you with the love and memories of our early associations. The retrospect of the occupation, settlement and progress of California for the past thirty years is so wonderful a history that it would seem to verify the poet's aphorism: "'Tis strange—but true; for truth is always strange—stranger than fiction."

The growth of California in so short a period of time has been truly marvelous. It is eminently proper that so important an event in the development of our country, to which California and our territory on the Pacific slope of the continent has contributed so abundantly, should be commemorated on these grounds dedicated to the exhibition of our national advancement for the past century in resources and power.

The re-union of those associated in the early events of the acquisition, settlement and sudden development of the wealth of California on this the twenty-sixth anniversary of its admission into the Union as the thirty-first State of the Republic, is to us most gratifying and auspicious.

In looking back and contrasting the condition of the Territory when first acquired by the United States, and its present condition, it seems as if the voice of the Creator, as in the beginning, again called darkness into light, and is an event cherished alike in its proud significance by the citizens of the Atlantic and Pacific States.

Scarcely had the echo of our victorious guns at Palo Alto and Resaca de la Palma, on the Rio Grande, reached the silent shores of the Pacific Ocean, when a small squadron of our naval vessels, under the command of Commodore John D. Sloat, anchored before Monterey, the Mexican capital of Upper California, and demanded a surrender of the place, which being refused, a force was landed on the 7th of July, 1846, which took possession, raised the American flag, and proclaimed the occupation of California by the United States, just in time to prevent its falling into the lap of England, whose ambition greatly coveted its possession.

It was a bold act for the American commodore, with so

small a naval force, to declare the occupation of so large a territory, so remote from supplies or reinforcements.

It was held, but not without a severe struggle, with the assistance of that gallant, hardy and brave battalion of the early settlers of California, commanded by General John C. Fremont, whose early exploration and military services under the indomitable Commodore Stockton, the successor of Sloat, contributed largely toward sustaining our flag during the war.

Immediately after the announcement had gone forth to the world, in 1848, that a treaty of peace had been made between the United States and Mexico, by which Upper California was ceded to our Government, James W. Marshall, a laboring man, discovered gold on the lands of Captain Sutter, on the American River. The news of this discovery spread rapidly, and the immense immigration in 1849 at once followed. A rush to California from all parts of the world soon changed that pastoral country into a broad scene of active commercial and mining life.

The mountain gulches in the wild Sierra Nevada, where the white man had never been, was soon teeming with ardent seekers for the golden treasure. The country whose currency had been hides was soon overflowing with gold-dust. The first discoveries were in placer diggings, but soon thereafter the auriferous veins of quartz were uncovered, and the skilled work of practical miners and the application of machinery followed. The indolent *ranchero* was supplanted by the active, intelligent and enlightened argonauts, enterprising, fearless, self-reliant men.

The production of gold was large during 1849, and the prices paid for provisions were enormous, flour selling as high as $60 a barrel at San Francisco, and $100 at the mines. The emigrants had to depend entirely upon a foreign supply of breadstuffs, nor was it then believed it would ever be otherwise.

It seems strange, indeed, that the soil supposed to be barren has proved the richest and most fertile of all the States, so that to-day, although its production of gold and silver is large, the value of its grain productions is much larger. Another mistake was the under-estimate of arable land, and the supposed necessity for irrigation to produce crops. A much larger fleet than was engaged in bringing subsistence to California is now employed in carrying away her productions.

The liberal character of the Constitution made for the State has had great influence upon its prosperity. Especially the rejection of slavery and involuntary servitude, which was carried by Southern men in the convention, though labor commanded higher wages than ever known before. The giving to women the right to hold separate property, both real and personal, which they had acquired either before or after marriage, by gift, devise or descent, was also a marked instance of progress. The prohibition of moneyed corporations from receiving special chartered rights was an important feature.

It seems a dream, looking back through the vista of thirty years, and contrasting that rude and unsettled country with the present condition of the rich and thriving State of California. We may almost claim a miracle has been performed, so great is the transformation. When I remember to have shot wild game in that early day on the site of the present business portion of the city of San Francisco, and on the very spot where the magnificent Palace Hotel has arisen in its grand proportions, I am deeply impressed by the rapid march of civilization, wealth and refinement; and when we reflect that San Francisco now ranks as the third commercial city of the Union, with a population of more than a quarter of a million, while the State is estimated at a million, and the Pacific slope at a million and a half of people, it is difficult to realize the change. The importance and value of its acquisition cannot be fully estimated. Its influence has been by far the greatest since the birth of the nation, not even excepting the purchase of Louisiana from France. Imagination could not have foreseen its importance, nor can we now foretell its future.

The climate of California, extending with its 10° of latitude along the Pacific coast between 114° and 124° west longitude, is much milder, even at high elevations, than that of the same latitude on the Atlantic. In climate, California is as favored as in gold, excluding the extremes of the torrid and frigid zones. The physical character of her climate no one can describe. The influence of location or topography or latitude puts all rules, as applied elsewhere, at defiance. Its infinite variety, both as to time and place, is not only charming, but exceedingly useful.

In localities, not more than five miles distant from each other, the varieties of fruit, with the same care and culture, will vary from fifteen to twenty days in ripening.

There is no fruit, grain or vegetable, native to any clime, save a few tropical plants, that California does not produce in the highest state of excellence and in the greatest abundance. Some of its valleys are said to be, by those of extensive travel and thorough observation, for their extent, beauty and fertility, unsurpassed on the globe. The sheltered valleys along the coast enjoy a delicious climate. In any other country ranging through 10° of latitude, the difference of temperature would be considerable, but in California this difference is greatly increased by the peculiarities of its surface.

The climate of California has thus been dwelt upon as having a great influence upon the marvelous fertility of the soil, both as to variety, quantity and size of its products. Figs, dates, oranges, olives and bananas flourish with the peach, pear, apple and apricot. Wheat, barley and oats yield largely. Tobacco, cotton, rice, tea and coffee are all cultivated successfully, and no one can doubt for a moment, who has any intelligence upon the subject, that California is destined in the early future to produce more and better grapes, raisins and wine than any other district of equal extent on which the sun ever shone. Indeed, all the productions of the earth seem to flourish within her boundary. It is a curious contemplation to speculate what influence her temperature, so uniform, and climate, so salubrious, are to have upon the mental and physical growth of man in the future. One-quarter more time can be given to labor and study, with less mental or bodily fatigue, than on the Atlantic, so we may reasonably look there for the highest mental and physical development. There are no real vicissitudes of climate, nothing enervating in temperature, and it is a land supplying every want and furnishing every luxury.

Twenty-five years ago a stream of gold went out in payment for breadstuffs and manufactured goods. To-day it is reversed—her production and export of wheat in value is greater annually than the product of her gold, in which, however, she still holds the first rank. She is now manufacturing her articles of necessity, and is self-sustaining, with all the elements of a great empire. There is not a want, there is not a luxury, there is not a creature comfort that cannot be supplied within her borders. There is not an element of national power, wealth or greatness, but what her hills and valleys produce.

If we may be permitted to look perspectively into the future, and take the growth of California for the past thirty years as a base for her future growth, what, we may ask, is to be the population and wealth on her Centennial anniversary? Even now, it is believed by many, that California offers larger inducements for settlement, and promises greater reward for labor and capital than at any time during her history.

We must not forget in tracing the events of her progress that she has constructed and completed 2,000 miles of railroad, which, in connection with her steamship line to Japan and China, will open up for her a great future in trade and commerce.

It is a singular reflection to the early pioneers, to know that the products of China are arriving almost daily at the Atlantic sea-ports, by the way of San Francisco and the Pacific railroad. Who of us could have ever expected that a passenger car carrying the mail could pass from New York to San Francisco in the incredibly short time of eighty-eight hours?

Year after year a continual stream of the precious metals, having its source in the hills and mountains of that coast, has been poured abroad into the channels of trade and commerce. In all, no less a sum than $1,763,000,000. Added to this, wheat has been produced worth $360,000,000; wool, worth $63,000,000; quicksilver, $20,000,000; wine, $20,000,000; coal, $23,000,000; lumber, 70,000,000, with other items a grand total of $2,336,000,000.

Her sister State, Nevada, will take the first rank in the production of the precious metals this year, in giving to the world $55,000,000 of gold and silver, but California still retains the pre-eminence in gold.

We are glad to say that in the rapid progress and growth of California, the church, the school and the press have advanced as rapidly in their various spheres of usefulness as the most enlightened Christian people could desire.

When we look over the list of our early associates in California, we can point to men eminent and distinguished in all the walks of life. The very air of California seems to stimulate an ambition to excel, quicken and enlarge the mind and to make it more comprehensive, clear and tenacious of its purpose. Generals Grant, Sherman, Hooker, Kearney, Fremont, Gibson, Mason, Riley and many others are graduates of California; as also are Sloat, Stockton, Mervine, Montgomery, DuPont, Shubrick, Jones, Revere, Beale and Paterson, of the navy.

Mercantile life was represented by men of the strictest integrity, sound business principles, enterprising, liberal and conservative, inspiring confidence and maintaining honest dealing at a time when men trusted each other implicitly; individual honor was at stake, and there was no breach of trust. The legal and medical professions were distinguished for their attainments, ability and thorough, sound professional acquirements.

Associates, we will not separate without paying a fitting tribute of respect to the parent society of pioneers, organized "to cultivate the social virtues of its members, to collect and preserve information connected with the early settlement and conquest of California, and to perpetuate the memory of those whose sagacity, enterprise and love of independence induced them to settle in the wilderness and become the germ of a new State." For thirty years we have cherished, almost as brothers, the ties of regard and friendship that have bound us together as pioneers of the west coast; and now, after a brief re-union, we are about to part. Undoubtedly to some of us this friendly meeting will be our last, but I am sure I express the common sentiment of all when I say that life has had for me no more grateful retrospect, and memory no more treasured recollections than the associations and friendships of those early days.

For you, Californians, who now enjoy the privilege and the blessings of a residence in the Golden State, let me say in your behalf:

> "Great God, we thank thee for this home—
>   This bounteous birth-land of the free;
> Where wanderers from afar may come
>   And breathe the air of liberty.
> Still may her flowers untrampled spring,
>   Her harvests wave, her cities rise;
> And yet till Time shall fold his wing,
>   Remain Earth's loveliest paradise."

The conclusion of the oration was followed by the "SONG OF THE ARGONAUTS, OR, THE DAYS OF 'FORTY-NINE," written expressly for the occasion by Samuel C. Upham, and sung by Mr. George A. Conly, *basso* of the Kellogg Opera Troupe. The song was rendered in fine style, the large audience rapturously applauding the sentiment, and joining in the chorus.

AIR—*Auld Lang Syne.*

> We are assembled here to-day—
>   A band of Pioneers,
> To celebrate with grateful hearts,
>   Events of by-gone years:
> We come from hill and valley fair,
>   Sierras capped with snow—
> With kindly words we greet you now,
>   Dear friends of long ago.
>
> *Chorus*—Oh, cherished be for evermore,
>   .   The days of auld lang syne,
>   Those golden days—remembered days—
>   The days of 'Forty-nine.
>
> Fresh laurel-wreaths we bring to-day,
>   To crown the Patriarch,*

---

* General John A. Sutter, aged 74 years.

Whose hand unlocked the golden ore,
　　In gulch and cañon dark.
Old Pioneer! thy name we still
　　In all our hearts enshrine;
God's blessing rest upon thy head,
　　Dear friend of auld lang syne!
Chorus—Oh, cherished be for evermore, etc.

We are a band of Argonauts,
　　Erst from Eureka State,
By some the golden fleece was found,
　　Whilst others mourned their fate.
We digged in gulch and delved in mine,
　　From morn till setting sun,
With aching limbs and moistened brows—
　　But perseverance won.
Chorus—Oh, cherished be for evermore, etc.

No maiden's voice, with cheering words,
　　Was heard in mine or camp—
The miner's food was grizzly meat,
　　And knot of pine his lamp.
But changes great have taken place,
　　Since days of 'Forty-nine,
The miner now in comfort dwells,
　　And kneels at woman's shrine.
Chorus—Oh, cherished be for evermore, etc.

Hillside, ravine and tulé marsh
　　Now blossom as the rose,
And 'round Diablo's verdant base,
　　The crystal streamlet flows.
Now glory be to God on high!
　　Let this our pæan be—
And peace on earth, good-will to man,
　　Our prayer, O God, to Thee!
Chorus—Oh, cherished be for evermore, etc.

After the rendering of a *Potpourri* of Operatic airs by the band, Major-General Joseph Hooker, who occupied a seat in the audience, was called upon by the Chairman, General Gibson, and introduced to the audience. When the enthusiasm which greeted his presence by the side of the Chairman had abated, the gallant General, amid repeated bursts of merriment, spoke as follows:

LADIES AND GENTLEMEN :—If you can tell me why I am on this platform, I wish you would. [Laughter.] I don't want to be placed in a ridiculous position, as I always am when I attempt to make a speech. I am not going to make the attempt, however. You have heard talking, and good talking; and if you want anybody to talk, here is ex-Governor Curtin— he will talk to you by the yard, and he will talk well, too.

A series of cheers, loud calls for " Curtin," and the introduction of ex-Governor Curtin by the Chairman as "the great War Governor of Pennsylvania," prepared the audience for another extempore speech.

Expressing his obligations to General Hooker for the complimentary reference to himself, and adding that his speech was not on the programme, the Governor said he had come as a spectator to look into the faces of the men who settled California and conquered the Pacific coast; but if anything could inspire a man to speak, it was the present occasion. In heathen mythology, Jason went to hunt the *golden fleece*, and this had been celebrated in song and classic poetry, and handed down through mysterious and uncertain history. Whether it was fact or fable, is not known, but a fact which is well known, is that an enterprising man left his free home in the Alps, and passing out to the Pacific coast, found in the tail-race of a saw-mill the glittering metal which has made California what it is to-day. The discovery has created new States, made marvelous changes in the commerce of the world and enabled the

American people to take a forward leap of fifty years. It is pleasant for a Pennsylvanian to be surrounded by the men who made a new empire and brought it into the great Commonwealth of States. The Pioneers of California before me have taken from the Eastern States the best blood of those States, their youth, integrity, energy and enterprise. With the traditions of the past in their minds, the glory of their great country in their hearts, they needed no school-masters, but brought California into the Union without probation, full-fledged in all that makes a Commonwealth great. Alluding to the Centennial and the patriotic memories of the Mecca of American liberty, he said that above all achievements of art, science and manufactures, the crowning glory of the Exhibition was its demonstration of what one hundred years of liberty could do for a people—nay, more, of how a free people, after discord, death and carnage, could come together in fraternity. The Governor's remarks were liberally applauded; and at their close three rousing cheers were given for him.

Mr. Colin M. Boyd, of San Francisco, President of the "TERRITORIAL PIONEERS OF CALIFORNIA," closed the oratory with an expression to the audience of the greetings of their associates in California, whom he had left a week before. He said the day was being generally celebrated by the Pioneer Societies in California, and that its members felt that, though separated from them by a continent, the Pioneers of the East were to-day identified with them as thoroughly as they were in 'Forty-nine.

At four o'clock, P. M., some four hundred ladies and gentlemen, with many guests of the Society, partook of a banquet at the Globe Hotel, under the management of that prince of caterers, Mr. John Rice. A sudden alarm, caused by a destructive conflagration in the immediate neighborhood, at half-past four o'clock, and which for a short time threatened the destruction of the hotel, caused a stampede among the guests and occasioned an interrup-

24

tion of the feast, which was finally resumed without serious inconvenience to the participants. When justice had been done to the substantials of the tables, Governor Hartranft welcomed the company to the State and commended the purpose of the organization. General H. G. Gibson, President of the "ASSOCIATED PIONEERS," then delivered the following address :

FELLOW-CALIFORNIANS, LADIES AND GENTLEMEN:—In the fullness of our joy at the success of the day, and after refreshing the inner man from the abundance provided for our delectation and sustenance by our goodly Boniface in this goodly city of Philadelphia, let us with merry hearts making cheerful countenances, hold sweet converse together about our beautiful and beloved California. We have been delighted today by the glowing recital of her glories and her triumphs, and by the well-told story of the proud achievements of her sturdy Pioneers, reminding us, if we needed any reminder, that in the acquisition and development of her opulent regions, and in the foundation of a noble State—*quorum pars magna fui*—each one of us contributed according to his opportunity, whether the widow's mite, or the largest measure of effort, influence and ability. Our hearts have been gladdened, too, to-day, by the presence of so many of the sons of the Golden State—her Pioneers of ancient days, and citizens of later years, as well as her exiles in the East, but still her children; for, she claims that " no divorce can separate a mother from her son." And, above all, while

> " Memory blends with the twilight charm,
>   And bears us back to other days,"

and.

> " Hand in hand as friends we wander
>   Down the golden aisles of the long-ago,"

we thank God that He has blessed to us the golden richness of her associations, and the diamond roughness of her experiences. We have not "gathered grapes of thorns, or figs of thistles," for the fruits of our experience have come from no barren soil or unnatural growth. And amid the richest and

best of God's gifts to man in her lovely clime, we have found
no fruit to "turn like Dead-sea fruit to ashes on the lip," but
only that which is delicious and fragrant in remembrance.
The magic glass of memory casts only "rare and roseate
shadows" from her varied scenes of the past, and the same
rich hue, the same *couleur de rose*, the same halo of enchantment which led us far away from home and kindred and
friends in years gone by, still lingers around the *El Dorado* of
our youth. And strong, vivid and charming as the scenes of
our childhood, when recalled, as

> "the musical clink
> Of the ice on your wine-goblet's brink
> A chord of my memory awoke.

> "And I stood in the pasture-field where,
> Many summers ago, I had stood,
> And I heard in that sound, I declare,
> The clinking of bells on the air
> Of the cows coming home from the wood.

> "Then the apple-blossoms shook on the hill;
> And the mullein-stalks tilted each lance;
> And the sun behind Rapalve's mill
> Was my uttermost west, and could thrill,
> Like the *Ultima Thule* of romance."

With so many pleasing memories and richly-instructive
experiences of the Golden Land, then our

> —"uttermost west that could thrill,
> Like the *Ultima Thule* of Romance,"

in which "our youth was nurtured and sustained," though
perhaps not always with a kindly hand, is it any wonder that
our pulses quicken and our hearts throb with pleasurable emotion on these occasions, and that "when two or three are gathered together in *her* name," then we feel her benign spirit is
"in the midst of them." Until the muffled drum within us
shall cease to beat, we can never become cold or callous to
these inspiring feelings and impressions, keenly felt alike by
the ancient Pioneer, whose name is a synonym for all that is

noble, "lovely, and of good report;" by "the toilers of the
sea" to her golden shores, who

> "Each took a horn in homage to the Horn;"

by the imperiled and delayed voyager by the Isthmus route,
or the way-worn traveler of the dreary plains and forbidding
mountains; by the seekers for the rich ore reposing in her
bosom; by those who "tickled her soil with a hoe and made
it laugh with a harvest," or quaffed the nectar of the rich
juices of her vintage,

> "Whose sweet perfume fills all the room
> With a benison on the Giver;"

by those who, standing awe-struck in the presence of the
mighty monarchs of her mighty forests, no longer wondered
at the peculiar idolatry of our Druid ancestors, but were impressed with a feeling of genuine "worship of that Divine
something, which blossoms in the weed and whose highest
phase is manifest in the beauty of holiness."

I will not detain you by repeating the story of her glory
and success, or of the blessings and benefits flowing in richest
streams of ever-widening channels throughout the whole
Union—resulting from the annexation of California, for it is
more than a thrice-told tale—and of which, I trust, you will
never weary. But in the radiant light of the past, it requires no

> "sunset of life—giving mystical lore,"

or vision of the prophet to predict that yet

> "High on his rock shall California's genius stand,
> Scatter the crowded hosts and vindicate the land;"

scatter the crowded hosts that imperil the safety and prosperity of the Republic, and vindicate the land by yet more
glorious triumphs and successes—still pointing as in the past
from her bold promontories, stretching far out toward "the
sunny regions of Cathay," and saying to the nation: "There
is the East! There is India!"

Brief remarks were also made by General Hooker, Joaquin Miller, poet of the Sierras, and Colonel Charles N. Pine, editor of the Philadelphia *Day*. The audience having tendered their thanks to **Mr. S. C. Upham**, for his contribution of "*The Song of the Argonauts*," that gentleman acknowledged the compliment in a brief speech. The festivities then closed with the singing of the above song, the entire audience joining in the chorus.

Major John S. Stevenson, manager of the "PACIFIC COAST CENTENNIAL HALL," and his assistant, Mr. A. D. Smith, rendered efficient aid during the day. Thus ended "*California Day*," one of the most agreeable re-unions and notable events of the Centennial Exhibition.

Before the close of the exercises at the Centennial Grounds, the following telegrams were sent to California:

PHILADELPHIA, Sept. 9th, 1876.

To JOHN C. BURCH, First Vice-President, *Platt's Hall*, San Francisco:—Your President, Colin M. Boyd, is our honored guest to-day. We greet you as brothers. May we ever remain true to our early California experiences.

FRANCIS D. CLARK,
Sec'y Associated Pioneers.

PHILADELPHIA, PA., Sept. 9th, 1876.

To THE TERRITORIAL PIONEERS OF CALIFORNIA, *Platt's Hall*:—The day was celebrated with great success here. Sutter, Price, Hooker, Gibson, Clark and four hundred others did honor to the Golden State.

COLIN M. BOYD,
President.

SECOND ANNUAL RE-UNION AND BANQUET OF "THE ASSOCIATED PIONEERS OF THE TERRITORIAL DAYS OF CALIFORNIA."

Committee of Arrangements—Report of Secretary and Treasurer Clark—Election of officers—The banquet—President Gibson's address—Addresses by General Thomas D. Johns, Joseph S. Spinney, Clark Bell, Colonel James M. Turner, Samuel C. Upham and Colonel John A. Godfrey.

THE Second Annual Re-union and Banquet of "THE ASSOCIATED PIONEERS OF THE TERRITORIAL DAYS OF CALIFORNIA," was held at the Sturtevant House, New York, on the evening of the 18th of January, 1877, being the twenty-ninth anniversary of the discovery of gold at Sutter's saw-mill, at Coloma, California. The different committees were composed of the following gentlemen, members of the Society:

COMMITTEE OF ARRANGEMENTS.

GEN. H. G. GIBSON, U. S. A.,	HON C. K. GARRISON,
GEN. C. S. MERCHANT, U. S. A.,	GEORGE HOWES,
GEN. JOSEPH HOOKER, U. S. A.,	GEORGE F. SNIFFEN,
COMMANDER RICH'D W. MEADE, U. S. N.,	JAMES A. SPERRY,
JOHN LAIMBEER,	JEREMIAH SHERWOOD,
EDWARD F. BURTON,	JOHN GAULT,

GEN. THOS. D. JOHNS, *Chairman.*

COMMITTEE ON INVITATION.

JOHN SICKELS,	JOSEPH S. SPINNEY,
GILMOR MEREDITH,	CHARLES R. THOMPSON,
EDWIN C. KEMBLE,	CORNELIUS LYDECKER,
JOHN G. HODGE,	GEN. JOHN S. ELLIS.

(424)

RECEPTION COMMITTEE.

GEN. JAMES F. CURTIS,	GEN. F. E. PINTO,
EDGAR W. CROWELL,	WM. C. ANNAN,
H. B. HAWKINS,	JAMES H. BUTLER,
WILLIAM M. WALTON,	S. L. MERCHANT,
CHAS. W. SCHUMANN,	EDWARD R. ANTHONY.

COMMITTEE ON TOASTS AND MUSIC.

COL. JOHN A. GODFREY,	R. R. GRIFFITH, JR.,
HON. R. II. McKUNE,	JOHN J. HAGER,
JOSEPH M. PRAY,	A. T. GOODELL.

COMMITTEE ON DECORATIONS

OLIVER H. PIERSON,	COL. JAMES E. NUTTMAN,
BENJ. W. JENNESS,	MAJOR RUSSELL MYERS,
WILLIAM II. ROGERS,	JOHN WOLFE.

GEN. II. G. GIBSON, U. S. A., *President.*
JOHN SICKELS, *Vice-President.*
FRANCIS D. CLARK, *Secretary and Treasurer.*

Previous to the banquet, Mr. Francis D. Clark, Secretary and Treasurer, read his report of the work of both offices for the year just closed. An election for officers for the year 1877 then took place, when the following gentlemen were re-elected :

GENERAL H. G. GIBSON, *President.*
COLONEL JOHN SICKELS, *Vice-President.*
MR. FRANCIS D. CLARK, *Secretary and Treasurer.*

At the close of the meeting, the Pioneers and their guests repaired to the banquet-room, which was handsomely decorated with flags and streamers, prominent among which was the " Pioneer Bear Flag." Among the mottoes and devices on the walls were: "Monterey, July 7th, 1846;" "The Bear Flagmen of 1846;" "The Horn, around in 180 Days;" "Sloat, Stockton, Shubrick;" "The Exchanges of '49—El Dorado, Bella Union, Parker House;" "The Fastest Ship, Young America—The Largest Ship, Three Brothers;" "The Isthmus, across, by Bungo and Mule;" "The First American Newspaper in California—The *Californian.*" The banquet was gotten up by the Messrs. Leland, in their inimitable style, and among the characteristic dishes were: "Lobster Salad, *a la* San Francisco;" "Pork and Beans, *a la* '49," and "Roast California Quail, *a la* Pacific Slope." The ornaments on the table included a "California Hunting Scene," and "Corn d'Abundance." Among those who sat down to the banquet were Generals Joseph Hooker, Innis N. Palmer, H. G. Gibson, U. S. A; Generals Thos. D. Johns, John S. Ellis, James F. Curtis; S. L. Merchant, Esq.; Commander R. W. Meade, U. S. N.; Colonels John A. Godfrey, James E. Nuttman, James M. Turner, T. B. Thorpe and Edward F. Burton; Francis D. Clark, Clark Bell, Prentice Mulford, S. C. Upham and Prof. Jules Lombard. After the removal of the cloth, the following eloquent address was delivered by General H. G. Gibson, President of the Society:

FELLOW-CALIFORNIANS:—This greeting of mine to-night comes with mingled feelings of pleasure and surprise, inasmuch as I had abandoned all hope of participating with you in this Annual Re-union and Banquet of the Society. Though, perhaps, among you I ought to feel like Macgregor on his native heath, full of the spirit aroused by familiar scenes and faces, yet I must confess, from the effect of various cares and duties, to some degree of unfitness for the occasion. "Though crowding thoughts distract the lab'ring brain," and filled though the heart may be with inspiring and delightful memories, even of the scenes and associations of our California life, "the thoughts that breathe and words that burn," do not always readily re-

spond to the promptings of the brain, or to the feelings or
emotions of the heart. But feeble as may be my expression of
them, I greet you none the less cordially, welcome you none
the less heartily, to the social board. I pray as the golden
light of other days illumines the rich clusters of incidents, "of
moving accidents by flood and field," recalled by each of us
to-night, that we may each enjoy in retrospect the delicious
happiness which we experienced when, in the heyday of youth,
we "listened with credulity to the whispers of fancy, pursued
with eagerness the phantoms of hope," and inspired by
"the voice of the charmer," toiled on, hoped on toward the
golden goal of our individual ambition. Whatever may have
been our fortune in seeking the "bright jewels of the mine,"
sought by us afar, in the wilds of California, we at least
learned the golden virtues of patience, fortitude and self-reliance. And proudly, too, of the Pioneers of California, it may
be said: Out of the wilderness at their touch came forth
plenty; out of the brain of the modern Jupiter—the American
Pioneer—leaped the full-armed, matured State; out of the lion
slain by this modern Samson came forth the sweetness of the
vine—"of oil, olive and of honey." But as the story of California and her Pioneers will be told you over and over again
to-night, to your gladly listening ears, I feel that I must refrain
from its repetition, in deference to others who may wish the
story to relate.

A few words before I close, and I utter them in no
spirit of party feeling or prejudice, but as "the words of truth
and soberness;" I have come to you to-night from the sorely-
stricken State of South Carolina, many of whose citizens were
and are of our near or full brotherhood, who, either as sons
of the soil of the Southern Palmetto stood shoulder to shoulder
with the sons of the soil of the Northern Oak, in the brilliant
war, which gave to the Union the treasures of California; or
with us

> "Digged in gulch and delved in mine,
> From morn till setting sun,"

in that land of beauty and of gold; whose hearts are yet warm with the sunny memories of their California life and experiences, and whose hands ever meet in manly, cordial grasp, the friends and comrades of the

> "Golden days, remembered days,
> The days of 'Forty-nine."

In the evil days which have come upon them, in their sore trial, and in their fiery furnace of affliction—be it from their sins or be it from ours—we may not be able to give them aid and comfort beyond the expression of our sympathy, but we can plead for them—act toward them in the spirit of the Golden Rule, and as sons of the Golden Land, cherishing the fond memories of the past, greet them from here to-night, as we greet each other around the festive circle:

> "And here's a hand, my trusty fier,
> And gie's a hand o' thine ;
> And we'll tak' a right guid willie-waught,
> For auld lang syne."

At the conclusion of General Gibson's address, Secretary Clark read letters of regret at their inability to attend the re-union, from President Grant, Generals Sherman, Sheridan and John A. Sutter, Mark Twain, Bayard Taylor and Peter Donahue, ex-President of the "Society of California Pioneers," of San Francisco.

In reply to the first toast—"*The President of the United States*"—Colonel T. B. Thorpe said he never saw such a Centennial. We couldn't tell who was our President, and three of our States had each two Governors, and nobody could tell who was who. The two Houses of Congress had got into a snarl, and the lower House (and by-the-way, it was very low), didn't seem to know what it was about, and had, apparently, lost its wits.

"*The Day we Celebrate, the Anniversary of the Discovery of Gold in California*," was responded to by General Thomas D. Johns, as follows:

Mr. President and Gentlemen :—Although the day we celebrate is not marked down in the Calendar of Saints as officially set apart as a close holiday; nor is it, perhaps, even noticed, except by this Society, it is one that may well be remembered as the commencement, the starting-point or moving cause of great events that followed.

Twenty-nine years ago to-day, near the Indian *Rancheria*, at Coloma, in what is now El Dorado County, the first gold was discovered in California. With the incidents of that discovery you are all familiar; they have been repeated many a time and oft, and have now passed into history. The bearing of that discovery on the future who can tell, or even imagine? We know what the results have been during the past twenty-five years, in which has been founded a grand and prosperous empire on the Pacific coast—and this is but the beginning.

Toiling through long years, the early settlements at Plymouth, New Amsterdam and in Virginia progressed slowly. True, they were builded on a firm foundation, but the advancement in a century of their existence did not equal that of a single decade in the more favored land of the farther West!

The little "nugget" that first saw the light of day at Sutter's Mill, was the talisman that wrought a wondrous change. Its pure ring sounded and vibrated almost to the uttermost bounds of the earth, and attracted a wave of emigration that rushed, with all the speed of wind and tide, from both hemispheres and, on our own continent, traversed the inhospitable plains, scaled the rugged peaks of our western mountains, and thus peopled the slumbering valleys and fertile plains from the Sierras to the sea.

When the unpretending Marshall raised that little "nugget" from its rest of centuries, wondering what manner of metal it might be, little did he dream that his accidental discovery would lead to such scenes as those in which we have participated, and to such results as the world now beholds! Even the keen intelligence and education of Sutter, recognizing at first sight the glittering gold, could not foresee the wonderful and rapid transformation to be wrought from the incidents of that day, whose recurring anniversary we have met to celebrate.

A certain class of moralists are wont to inveigh roundly against gold-hunting and gold-mining as demoralizing, revolutionary and semi-barbarous; as giving scope and activity to the lower passions, encouraging men to waste, to habits of idleness and improvidence, and causing them to neglect the higher duties of life in the search for what they term "filthy lucre;" while the lucre itself they value highly, and sometimes worship, after it is taken from mother earth and stamped as current coin of the realm. We know that the idea thus sought to be impressed is erroneous. And, gentlemen, I would stoutly defend your early career in the "diggin's" from any such unjust aspersions. Whatever you are now, the great majority of those before me were once "honest miners"—the representative men, who with level heads, stout hearts and willing hands helped to unlock the treasure-house of California, and at whose bidding was poured forth the plenty that belongs to man. And these results represent labor, honorable labor, which is the foundation of all values; those millions, whatever may be the changes through which they have passed, and whatever may represent them now, originally represented the industry, intelligence and thrift of the gold-miners of California.

And just here I would say a good word in behalf of that great army of irrepressible "prospectors," who, as skirmishers, fringe the advancing line of our frontiers in search of "colors to the pan," or of "pay rock," thus lead the way for a new civilization, and for new and peaceful conquests. Thus has it been from the discovery of that "nugget" at Coloma down to the present day.

Following in quick succession, towns and cities were built, States organized, broad acres cultivated, and the varied industries of man were quickened into life and activity by the fructifying influence of the gold-fields of the new *El Dorado*.

Nor has California alone received all the benefits resulting from Marshall's discovery. They have been felt in almost every part of the world—nowhere more than in our own country. Particularly in this imperial city, large enterprises have been stimulated by the gold of the Pacific slope; and we can point to opulent bankers, enterprising railroad and shipping proprietors and substantial merchants, who raised their first "stake" in or through the California gold-mines, and without which they might not have had the success to which they were entitled.

As the mountain-springs and the modest rivulets are but the beginnings of the majestic river and the mighty cataract, so this apparently insignificant discovery by an humble laborer has led to the wonderful development of the material interests of that great West. The stillness of those primeval forests has been broken by the echo of the locomotive, the frowning Sierras have been subdued, and the wilderness made to blossom as the rose. Towers, domes and spires cast their shadows upon the sea, on whose shores sits enthroned the palatial city, whose rapid march to greatness has been the wonder of the age.

To you, gentlemen, and to such as you, that discovery of gold gave the well-improved opportunity of founding this new empire on the shore of the Pacific—surely, "Peace hath her victories no less renowned than war."

"CALIFORNIA"—was responded to by Colonel Edward F. Burton in a humorous speech, which was frequently applauded.

"GENERAL JOHN A. SUTTER"—was responded to by General H. G. Gibson, in his happiest style.

"PIONEER DAYS"—by Joseph S. Spinney.

"PACIFIC RAILROAD"—by Clark Bell.

"OUR HONORED DEAD"—by Colonel Jas. M. Turner.

"DAYS OF 'FORTY-NINE"—by Samuel C. Upham, of Philadelphia.

"WOMAN"—by Colonel John A. Godfrey.

In response to "Days of 'Forty-nine," Mr. Upham said:

MR. PRESIDENT AND BROTHER PIONEERS:—In response to your invitation, I am here to-night, the guest of "The Associated Pioneers of the Territorial Days of California," and I thank God that life and health have permitted me to be with you on this occasion, an occasion fraught with incidents of the past, in which we were all participants.

I was somewhat surprised, on Monday morning last, at receiving from the Secretary of this Society a postal card containing the following announcement:

"4th regular toast—The Days of '49; response by S. C. Upham."

Unfortunately, Mr. President, my tongue is not like the pen of a ready writer. Rude am I of speech, and little blessed with the accomplishments of the orator, yet I will, relying upon your indulgence,

> "A round, unvarnished tale deliver,
>   Nothing extenuate, nor set down aught in malice."

At the re-union of Californians at the Centennial Grounds, in Philadelphia, on the 9th of September last, I had the pleasure of meeting, for the first time, the officers and several of the members of this Society, and the kindly greeting and the hearty welcome I have received this evening at their and your hands, Mr. President, I shall ever cherish as one of the most pleasurable events of my life. We met on that occasion to do honor to the State, at whose birth—more than a quarter of a century ago—many of us officiated as god-fathers. Our bantling has long since cast off her swaddling-clothes, and to-day, in the fullness of her maturity and matchless beauty, crowned with the gems once hidden in her soil, she stands the brightest and sunniest star in the constellation of the States of our glorious Union. The wealth of the Occident, that is constantly pouring into her lap through the portals of the Golden Gate, together with her unbounded mineral and agricultural resources, have gained for her the honored and deserved title of Queen of the Pacific.

To the members of this Society, Mr. President, and especially to the *untiring efforts of your Secretary, Mr. Francis D. Clark,* was the success of the re-union of the 9th of September last chiefly due. That it was a success, in the fullest acceptation

From a Photo by J. Rennie Smith, Newark, N. J.

Yours truly
Francis D. Clark.
Sec'y —

of the term, no one who was present can gainsay. It was one of the most noticeable and agreeable State re-unions that had taken place at the Centennial Grounds up to that time, and only in numbers was it subsequently excelled by the re-unions of other States.

The citizens of California, Mr. President, who are interested in the welfare and prestige of their State, owe to this Society and its co-laborers their heartfelt thanks. Had they not put their shoulders to the wheel, the name of California would not have been inscribed on the roll of Centennial State re-unions. In rendering the full meed of praise to this Society, I have no desire to ignore the services of a few patriotic and liberal-minded citizens of California and Nevada, who subscribed the funds and caused the erection of the "Pacific Coast Centennial Hall," under whose roof the re-union to which I have just alluded took place. They also deserve the thanks of their fellow-citizens. Let us "render unto Cæsar the things that are Cæsar's."

When I look around me to-night, Mr. President, and scan the faces of my brother-Argonauts, memories of the past, incidents by "flood and field" of the days when we went gold-hunting, long, long ago, crowd as thickly upon the mind

"As leaves in Valambrosa!"

May those memories ever remain green in our hearts.

Days of 'Forty-nine! Three simple, yet to me significant words; words that cause memories of the past to arise before me. The long and tedious voyage around Cape Horn; life in the mines; scenes in camp and cañon; across the Isthmus by mule and bungo, are so indelibly photographed upon the retina of the mind, that nothing but death will efface them. Many of our comrades who went forth in the flush of manhood never returned, and their bones lie mouldering on the western plains, in the sands of the ocean, and in the gulches and cañons of the far-off Pacific slope. Occasionally, one of those modern Argonauts found the golden fleece and returned home a richer if not a wiser man; but those cases were exceptions to the general rule. A majority, after toiling months and years in the mines, were as impecunious as the traditional fowl belonging to the good man we read about who was afflicted with boils!

In "the days of '49," the miner with his rude implements—pick, spade, pan and rocker or cradle, minus the baby—toiled early and late. When success crowned his efforts, he was jubilant and built castles in the air, but the ill luck of the morrow demolished those visionary fabrics, and with a saddened heart he yearned for his far-away home and the loved ones around the old hearthstone. In those days every miner was his own cook and washerwoman, and I shall never forget my experiences with the frying-pan and soiled unmentionables. I wrestled long and ardently, but could never acquire that peculiar and indescribable twist of the wrist which would enable me to flop and turn a griddle-cake without landing it in the ashes. I thought then and I promulgate it now, not in anger but with sorrow, that as a cook and washist I was not a success!

Those pioneer experiences in the culinary and washing line have imbued me with an almost sacred reverence for cooks and washerwomen, including that copper-colored, pig-tailed, almond-eyed disciple of Confucius—

> "With ways that are dark,
> And tricks that are vain"—

the Heathen Chinee!

In conclusion, Mr. President, let us—survivors of the old guard—the forlorn hope—assembled here to-night, "eat, drink and be merry," and for the nonce forget our gray hairs and imagine ourselves young again!

The theme of the next speaker was "Woman," but his speech was mainly a philippic addressed to the gentleman, *an invited guest,* who had preceded him. His vaporings were allowed to pass unnoticed.

During the banquet, Charles Mollenhauer's Orchestra discoursed excellent music, and between the toasts the Union Glee Club sang concerted pieces, including the "Song of the Argonauts; or, The Days of '49." Professor

Lombard sang the bass solo of "The Dying Trooper," with telling effect. The wine and cigars furnished for the occasion were of California manufacture. The entertainment broke up at a late hour, and, taken all in all, was an enjoyable affair.

CELEBRATION OF "ADMISSION DAY" AT LONG BRANCH, N. J.

———

Programme of exercises—Pioneers present—The Banquet—General Gibson's address of welcome—Introduction of General Sutter—Letters of regret—Mayor McKune's address—General Sutter's response—Poem—"The Land We Adore"—Bayard Taylor speaks a piece—"Song of the Argonauts"—Hop in the evening in honor of General Sutter—Telegram sent to California—The reply.

THE Twenty-seventh Anniversary of the Admission of California into the Union, was celebrated by the Argonauts of 'Forty-nine, under the auspices of "THE ASSOCIATED PIONEERS OF THE TERRITORIAL DAYS OF CALIFORNIA," at the Ocean Hotel, Long Branch, N. J., on Saturday, September 8th, 1877. The day was rainy and windy, but the hardy Pioneers who had braved dangers by " flood and field " in the days of '49' turned out in goodly numbers—nearly two hundred strong—some of them accompanied by their wives. Among the ladies present, were Miss Sutter, daughter of the American consul at Acapulco, Mexico, and granddaughter of General John A. Sutter; Mrs. Francis D. Clark, Mrs. Prentice Mulford and Mrs. S. C. Upham. The following committees were composed of gentlemen belonging to " *The Associated Pioneers of the Territorial Days of California,*" whose head-quarters are in New York:

(438)

SEPTEMBER 9TH,

1850.

SEPTEMBER 9TH,

1877.

COMMITTEE OF ARRANGEMENTS.

GEN. THOS. D. JOHNS,

COM. C. K. GARRISON,	COL. E. F. BURTON,
GEN. JOSEPH HOOKER, U. S. A.,	CHARLES R. THOMPSON,
COM'R R. W. MEADE, U. S. N.,	S. L. MERCHANT,
GEN. JAMES F. CURTIS,	JOHN J. HAGER,
HON. JEREMIAH SHERWOOD,	JOHN GAULT.

COMMITTEE ON INVITATION.

JOHN SICKELS, *Vice-President.*

GEORGE HOWES,	HON. DEMAS STRONG,
E. W. CROWELL,	WM. M. WALTON,
HON. D. M. CHAUNCEY,	JOHN S. ELLIS.

RECEPTION COMMITTEE.

HON. R. H. McKUNE,

HON. R. M. PRICE,	JOHN G. HODGE,
CHAS. W. SCHUMANN,	E. R. ANTHONY,
C. LYDECKER,	A. T. GOODELL.

H. G. GIBSON,

FRANCIS D. CLARK,
Secretary and Treasurer.

Brevet Brig.-Gen. U. S. A.,
President.

The following programme of the exercises was carried out as announced:

RE-UNION OF CALIFORNIANS,

Under the Auspices of the

Associated Pioneers of the Territorial Days of California,

(HEAD-QUARTERS IN NEW YORK CITY,)

AT THE

Ocean Hotel, Long Branch, N. J.

ON SATURDAY, SEPTEMBER 8TH, 1877,

AT 2.30 O'CLOCK, P. M.

(Twenty-seventh Anniversary of the Admission of California Into the Union.)

Programme of Exercises,

In connection with the Dinner.

1. ADDRESS, *by General H. G. Gibson, U. S. A.,*
   President of the Associated Pioneers.

2. MUSIC—"Star Spangled Banner."

3. ANNOUNCEMENT OF LETTERS, *by the Secretary of the Society.*

4. MUSIC—"Golden Gate Quickstep."

5. INTRODUCTION OF GEN. JOHN A. SUTTER, *by Gen. H. G. Gibson.*

6. WELCOME, to Gen. John A. Sutter, Pioneer of 1838,
   by Hon. R. H. McKune, Mayor of Scranton, Pa.

7. MUSIC—"Hail to the Chief."

8. POEM—"The Land We Adore,"
   Composed (expressly for this occasion,) and read by the author,
   SAMUEL C. UPHAM, Esq , a "49er."

9. MUSIC—"Bonanza March."

10. A FEW REMARKS, *by Col. E. F. Burton, a "Veteran" Pioneer.*

11. "SONG OF THE ARGONAUTS; OR, DAYS OF '49"
    Composed by S C. UPHAM, Esq , of Philadelphia; and sung by WM. J. HILL, Esq The audience will please join in the chorus.

12. MUSIC.—"Traumeres,"—*Schumann.*

Orchestra under the Direction of Mr. Charles Mollenhauer.

☞ The Complimentary Hop tendered by Messrs. CHARLES and WARREN LELAND, Jr., in honor of Gen. JOHN A. SUTTER, will take place at 9 P. M.

Conspicuous among the "Old Boys" was General John A. Sutter, the veteran Pioneer, aged seventy-five years, but who looked as hale and hearty as many of his comrades a score of years younger. The morning was spent in conversation, in the parlors, and at half-past two o'clock, P. M., the Pioneers and their guests sat down to a sumptuous dinner. General H. G. Gibson, President of the Associated Pioneers, occupied the central seat, and behind him, on the wall, hung the "Old Bear Flag." On either side of the flag were placards bearing the names of places and events famous in the early history of California. By the side of General Gibson sat General Sutter, and at his side was seated Bayard Taylor. Near by was Hon. R. H. McKune, Mayor of Scranton, Pa., just recovering from wounds received at the hands of the railroad rioters, because he knew his duty, and dared to do it, despite mob violence. There were also present ex-Governor Rodman M. Price, of New Jersey, who assisted in raising the first American flag in California, at Monterey, on July 7th, 1846; ex-Mayor Vance, of New York; Hon. Demas Strong, President of the first Common Council of Sacramento City, in 1850; General Thomas D. Johns, E. W. Crowell, Colonel Fritz, General McComb, Colonel T. B. Thorpe, A. T. Goodell, General James E. Curtis, Commander R. W. Meade, U. S. N., John Gault, Dr. Thos. A. Bailey, Chas. R. Thompson, Chas. W. Schumann, John G. Hodge, Colonel A. C. Ferris, who, in 1849, took the first party, two hundred men, by way of Vera Cruz, to San Blas, and thence to San Francisco, arriving on the 14th of May, ahead of all the parties that rounded Cape Horn or went overland; Colonel John Sickels, J. H. Butler, H. K. Cummings, J. C. Curry, J. J. McCloskey, the California actor of '49; Francis D. Clark, Colonel Jos. E. Lawrence and S. C. Upham, early newspaper men of Sacramento City, and Prentice Mulford, formerly of the *Overland Monthly*. After the dinner had been discussed, order was called by General Gibson, who delivered the following eloquent address of welcome to the Society and to General Sutter:

FELLOW-PIONEERS, LADIES AND GENTLEMEN :—In accordance with a custom, long observed by the parent Societies of the Pacific Coast, "THE ASSOCIATED PIONEERS OF THE TERRITORIAL DAYS OF CALIFORNIA," residing in the East, have assembled here to-day to celebrate the anniversary of the admission of California into the American Confederation of States. Twenty-seven years ago "the morrow morn," after a long and bitter political contest in the halls of Congress, the State which the Pioneers of California had founded and organized became "a bright particular star"—wedded to the Union. The Treaty of Guadalupe Hidalgo, terminating the war with Mexico, had extended our dominion on the remote Pacific over a vast region, to the south of

> "the continuous woods
> Where rolls the Oregon and hears no sound
> Save its own dashings"—

to us and the world at large a *terra incognita*. Beyond a narrow fringe of settlements—missions and *presidios*—on its line of coast from Cape Mendocino to Cape San Lucas, but little was known of the geography, character and resources of the territory of the Californias. To the commerce of the world, it was but a land of hides and tallow. The expeditions of the renowned Pioneer and Path-finder, JOHN C. FREMONT, opened to our people and to the world, a knowledge of its beauty, fertility and wealth. Though the mighty river, rising in the great Cordillerean chain, and cleaving, in its course to the ocean, the majestic Sierras that shut out California from the rest of the continent, and which the explorer's glowing fancy fondly pictured as freighted in the future with the argosies of a rich commerce—was never found; yet from the summit of the Sierras, the proud Pioneer gazed upon a region which, although in its native primeval wildness, gave a glorious promise of future opulence and greatness. Distance had not lent enchantment to the view, for on nearer approach it was found to be a land of wondrous fertility and surpassing loveliness.

But, Pioneers, I will not detain you by dwelling upon the material and physical beauty of the land with its delightful clime, the charming pastoral life with its serene repose and quiet felicity, before the modern Sassenach came with grim-visaged war, or the modern Argonaut seeking the golden ore; nor will I, in this greeting of mine, indulge in the rich-fraught retrospect of the past, or upon the real presence of to-day, or the glowing visions of the future—of the magical changes wrought, of the brilliant, substantial results accomplished, through much tribulation, toil and suffering; for you, who shared in the exciting scenes and trying incidents of early California days, know them well. In the bright glow of memory's light, you can look back and proudly say: "Out of the rocks of California *we* carved and shaped a noble State, beautiful in its every aspect of nature, rich in every product of art and culture, grand in its origin, grander in its career, grandest in the golden virtues of its people."

Impressed with all this, I bid you a cordial, gladsome welcome here to-day, and with the cherished memories of "auld lang syne," of "the joys that we've tasted," with the golden reminiscences of the fair Golden State, extend to each and all of you, the kindliest greeting of heart and hand. The mighty surf that rolls upon the grand old beach at our feet gives you a welcome, too, in its every tone, and sound, and roar, as it recalls to mind the booming of a mightier surf of a grander ocean, that beats on the rock-bound coast of California, and pours its tides and billows through the portals of the Golden Gate. As old ocean's spray mingles with the vintage in our cups that we drink to California; as its sounds blend with the notes of softer music, it welcomes you in the name of its sister ocean; and we need not ask, like little Paul Dombey, "what are the wild waves saying?" for they speak to us of joys and trials, dangers and delights, in the far-off Golden Land we love so well.

Ladies, I bid you welcome, welcome, too. Feeble though be the expression, I trust you will not find it lacking in that sweet courtesy, which "it is very meet, right, and our bounden duty" to render to the fairer, gentler portion of humanity. Though.

"bright eyes" may not "speak love to eyes which speak again," still whilst "soft music rises with a voluptuous swell" we may tell you "of the dangers we have passed," of the "most disastrous chances" of our California life—unshared, unsoothed by your sweet companionship, and some fair Desdemona may seriously incline to hear, to believe, to pity and to love. And we may tell you, too, on the faith of yᵉ truthful journalists of the day, that, in California, "in the desert a fountain is springing," from the virtues of whose waters, beauty ever retains its freshness and bloom, youth its grace, comeliness and strength, and "let thy loveliness fade as it will," the

> "endearing young charms
> We gaze on so fondly to-day,"

will return with a brighter glow and sweeter attraction.

> "Tourney and joust that charmed the eye,
> And scarf and gorgeous panoply,
> And nodding plume "—

have gone with the age and flower of chivalry. We no longer summon to the lists, or to the field of mortal combat, the rivals in our love; yet in this sober, practical age, the smiles and favors of fair woman are as sweet, as precious, as dear to us; we are as proud and ready to throw or accept the gauntlet in her cause, to make every sacrifice for our love, as

> "the gentle knights that came
> To kneel and breathe love's ardent flame
> Low at her feet."

"The smiles from partial beauty won "—

> "to know there is an eye will mark
> Our coming, and grow brighter when we come ;"

"dear woman's loving prattle," which "flows with sweet meanings for the heart alone"—are our proudest triumphs, our "empire of perfect bliss" in youth, our glory and delight in manhood, our joy and solace in declining years. Like the Pleiades that so "purely sparkle in Heaven," she "sheds her sweet influence over the earth," and man, who lords it over all the rest of creation, yields at once to beauty's charms and woman's loving wiles. The Paradise of Mahomet, with houris of exquisite form and feature, was but an unrefined expression of the power and influence wielded by woman, and with our knowledge of their potency in this enlightened age, do we wonder at the brilliant success and rapid spread of the Moslem faith, in a darker era, when the enjoyment of woman's lovingness and loveliness was the promised reward of every true believer, every faithful follower of the standard of the Prophet? And under the benign influence of a purer religion, we believe that those whose gentle hands and sweet, loving faces cheer and console us in this vale of tears, will be at our side in the realms of celestial light before the throne of God;

> "For love is Heaven, and Heaven is love."

In introducing General Sutter, General Gibson said:

The patriarchs of Israel, when they assembled their kindred and people in the land, which the God of Abraham, Isaac and Jacob had given them to possess it; the mighty conquerors of the world from Xenophon to Napoleon, when, at the momentous crisis of perilous conflict, there rallied around them the legions known "by the tried valor of their hands;" the proud chieftains of the Highlands, when they gathered their clans for counsel, battle, foray or raid, felt that exultant joy and grateful pride, which is inspired by the fealty and devotion of those bound to each other by the ties of blood, affection or association. The noble patriarch and world-famed Pioneer, at whose feet to-day we lay our tribute of love and honor, must be inspired by the same proud and grateful feelings, when he looks around upon the faces of his clansmen and his children—the Pioneers of California. For no patriarch of Israel, no warrior of ancient or modern renown, no chieftain of Highland clan, ever found kith or kin, liege-vassal or soldier, clansman or servitor more loyal and true than those who bid him welcome here to-day; than those who, on the distant Pacific recall with us the deeds and virtues of that great heart, that not only gave the *open sesame* to the treasures of California, but out of the riches of its bounty fed the hungry, clothed the naked, relieved the distress of every wayworn traveler, every weary pilgrim of the plains.   As the instrument under God of the discovery of gold, long lain hid in the recesses of California, and thus the conferrer of a glorious boon upon us, upon California, and upon our whole country, we do him all-grateful honor ; as our grand old patriarch and noble chieftain, we pay him leal and grateful reverence ; but for his golden deeds of charity and rich benefi- cence, we give him a wealth of love and gratitude from our inmost hearts.   To-day we look upon his kindly, noble face— the outward expression of a pure heart and a stainless life— and pray that God may bless him and give him length of days, with peace and health, happiness and abundance.   To Cali- fornians everywhere, his name is a household word ; and in after years, when our children's children shall gather by the winter's hearth, old gossips' tales shall tell of the noble deeds and golden virtues of John A. Sutter, the glorious Pio- neer !   The countryman of Tell !   The countryman of Wash- ington !   The beauty, purity and bravery of his life, the nobility of his nature, the kindliness of his heart, the generosity and benignity of his character, elevate him nigh unto their stature ; in all that ennobles man, the peer of the one, the peer of the other.

The nation, through cold or thoughtless selfishness, or want of appreciation of his " life of honor and of worth," may deny him the just guerdon of his great services, but long ere the muffled drum within us shall beat its last tattoo, history and song shall recount the story of that life in choicest diction and glowing rhythm, and " on the painter's canvas shall grow his life of beauty."   A life of virtue and of fame, worthy to be commemorated, not only in more modest bronze or marble, but in the richest metal from California's golden store.   I say that history, song and art will yet redeem in part the shame and reproach of the Republic for its neglect of its great bene- factor, but with you

"His signal deeds and virtues high
Demands no pompous eulogy ;
Ye saw his deeds!
Why should their praise in verse be sung?
The name that dwells on every tongue
No minstrel needs."

The

"Fresh laurel wreaths we bring to-day
To crown the patriarch,"

may wither, but for a life well spent " there is laid up for him a crown of glory which fadeth not away." With all due honor to the other illustrious Pioneers of Christendom, I now introduce to you the noblest Roman of them all, our renowned patriarch and honored chieftain, General John A. Sutter. [Great applause.]

Mayor McKune, of Scranton, then delivered the following address of welcome to General Sutter :

GENERAL SUTTER :—Having been selected by my associates to tender to you our hearty congratulations and join with you in earnest thanks to our Heavenly Father for His mercies who has protected you another year, and given you strength that has enabled you to join with us in celebrating the twenty-seventh anniversary of the admission of California to the Union of States, I am bidden by my associates to welcome you to our re-union, and to assure you that your presence fills our cup of gratification unto fullness. I have no language to express the pleasure your presence affords us. Your name, sir, is indissolubly joined to that of the Pioneer days of California. It was in the furtherance of your enterprises that the earth gave up her treasures, that had been hidden from the sight of man from creation. The development of those treasures changed the commerce of the world. The Golden Gate saluted, as they passed through, the ensigns of every maritime nation. In a word, " the world was turned upside down." But amid the disappointments and sufferings of hundreds of the pioneers and amid "man's inhumanity to man" there stood out one name bright over all ; one heart that beat in sympathy for the unfortunate ; one hand to relieve the distressed. That heart, that hand, dear General, was yours, and your name is remembered with the warmest emotions of gratitude by hundreds whom your princely generosity relieved in the hour of their distress. We remember with pleasure that every project for the advancement of the interests of California, found in you a hearty supporter. That amid the noble men who assembled at Monterey to form the first Constitution, your name led all the rest. In the long years of your residence in California, there was no honorable citizen but felt himself honored to be called your friend. You have lived to see California pass from petty Mexican rule and occupy a high position amid its sister States. And though you and I, in our declining days, have found a home amid the hills and valleys of the Keystone State, yet, I doubt not that our hearts go out in unison this day in earnest desires for the future welfare of California.

As I look around among my associates who are here to-day, I find the army and navy of our country well represented by associates whose names their country has placed high on the roll of fame. The civil professions and the various ranks of business here find worthy representatives. The incidents of our California days can never be effaced from our memories, and we beg to assure you that though the efforts we have hitherto made for an honorable settlement of your claims upon the general government have been unsuccessful, we hereby pledge ourselves, not only to use our individual, but to continue our united efforts until justice shall be done to you and yours.

Trusting, sir, that this day's re-union may bring to you sweet and pleasant memories of the past, and bind us together in closer fellowship, and as the shades of night gather around your pathway, you will be cheered by the assurance that you leave behind those who will always cherish your name with the warmest affection of their whole nature.

General Sutter arose in response to the hearty applause which followed Mayor McKune's address, and with a suppressed voice expressed his inability to respond adequately to the remarks which were so flattering to him, and which he so thoroughly appreciated. "It is not possible," he said—but here words failed him, and he sat down, when the assembled Argonauts rose up as one man, and waving their glasses in the air, gave three cheers that utterly drowned the music of the band.

Letters of regret were read by the Secretary, Mr. Francis D. Clark, from President Hayes, General Sherman, Governor Irwin, of California, Governor Robinson, General Hancock, Mayor Ely, Mr. Peter Dean, President of "The Society of California Pioneers," General F. J. Lippitt, General Joseph W. Revere, who, when a lieutenant in the navy, in 1846, raised the first American flag at Sonoma; Vice-Admiral S. C. Rowan and John W. Livingston, of the United States Navy, both of whom were lieutenants during the conquest of California, and served on that coast; General Edward F. Beale, Gilmor Meredith and R. R. Griffith, Jr. The regrets of Joaquin Miller, Poet of the Sierras, were conveyed in the following characteristic letter and poem :

GENERAL GIBSON, FRANCIS D. CLARK, AND OTHERS OF THE ASSOCIATED PIONEERS OF CALIFORNIA :—I thank you for your kind invitation to dinner at the gathering of your great and good brotherhood, but I am at work and cannot be with you. But do not imagine that I have forgotten you or the great gold shore by the vast west sea. A great land, a great people, and a great period in history—surely, they are worthy of all that can be said or sung, and my song is still of the Pacific :

> My brave world-builders of the West!
>   Why, who hath known ye? Who shall know
>   But I, who on thy peaks of snow
> Sang songs the first! I loved you best;
>   I hold you still of more stern worth
>   Than all proud peoples of the earth.

Yea, I, the rhymer of wild rhymes,
  Indifferent of blame or praise,
  Still sing of you as one who plays
The same wild air in all strange climes—
  The same wild, piercing, highland air,
  Because—because his heart is there.

JOAQUIN MILLER.

New York, August 30th, 1877.

The following poem, written for the occasion, was then read by its author:

THE LAND WE ADORE.

BY SAMUEL C. UPHAM, A "'FORTY-NINER."

Comrades and Brothers, we're assembled to-day,
But not as plumed warriors in battle array—
Assembled to honor the young Golden State,
Whose birth and whose grandeur we now celebrate.

The gleam of the camp-fires of emigrant trains,
Is seldom now seen on the far-away plains,
The screech of the engine, so loud and so shrill,
Comes echoing back from each cañon and hill.
The grizzly starts up with a snort and a growl,
The wolf and *coyote* chime in with a howl,
The buffalo tosses the earth in the air,
And the panther, aroused, springs up from his lair.

The antelope leaps o'er the plain in affright,
The prairie dog barks from morn until night,
From his eyrie the eagle looks down in disdain,
As the steam-whistle shrieks its startling refrain.
Our camp-fires no longer illume the ravine,
The Pan and the Rocker are rarely now seen,
Flap-jacks and *frijoles*, our diet of yore,
Have flown like a vision to return nevermore.

The Tom and the Sluice-box, once sparkling with gold,
No longer wash out the auriferous mould;
The Quartz Mill and Crusher have taken their place,
And steam's declared victor again in the race.
Our cabins now roofless and gone to decay,
Like their tenants of old, are passing away;
The grave on the hillside, with head-board decayed,
Marks the spot where a comrade we long ago laid.

O woman, dear woman! pure as gold without dross,
The first at the tomb and the last at the cross,
Thy presence ne'er cheered us in camp nor in mine,
In those long-ago days, the days of lang syne—
When the toils of the day had drawn to a close,
And wrapped in our blankets in silent repose,
Our thoughts wandered back to our sweethearts and wives,
The loved ones for whom we had periled our lives.

Famed *Yerba Buena*, old town by the sea,
Demolished long since by fate's stern decree,
Thy *adobes* all crumbled and razed to the ground,
Not a trace of thy walls is now to be found;
On thy site has been builded the Queen of the West,
Close by the portals, by the Golden Gate's crest,
Where church dome and steeple point up to the sky,
And the Stars and the Stripes wave proudly on high.

Thy city and harbor, proud golden-gemmed Queen,
Are rivalled by none the world has e'er seen;
Thy merchants and bankers, like Crœsus of old,
Have locked in their coffers their millions untold.
The school-house and college, like beacon-lights, stand
In vale and on hill-top, the pride of thy land;
Still, we in thy closet two skeletons see—
The vagabond "Hoodlum" and "Heathen Chinee."

Hamlets like magic to large cities have grown,
The *ranchero* has reaped the grain he has sown,

The vine and the fig-tree are laden with fruit,
And the breezes blow soft as the tones of the lute;
The orange-tree blossoms and fruits in the vale,
The date and pomegranate, 'mid sand and the shale,
The filbert and almond, and manna of yore,
All abound in the land that we love and adore.

The *Sequoias gigantea,* when the earth was quite young,
And birds in fair Eden their sweet music sung,
Then upward were towering in days far remote,
As the rings 'round their trunks unerringly note.
For thousands of years, as firmly as rocks,
These giants have braved the hurricanes' shocks—
Are older than Noah, the man without guile,
Older than Cheops in the vale of the Nile.

The Ship of the Desert,* long buried from view,
Once manned by Arch Masons—King Solomon's crew—
She sailed from the East bound for Ophir's gold shore,
But, shipwrecked and stranded, returned nevermore;
Her hull lies imbedded on the alkali plain,
And the desert simoon ever sings her refrain,
Sings the dirge of the sailors, those Masons of old,
Who never returned with their cargo of gold.

Fond recollections of the long-ago times,
Come echoing back like the music of chimes;
The Tuolumne rolls on as in ages of yore,
The Stanislaus laves its auriferous shore,
The Bear and the Yuba flow down to the sea,
Bright flowers are still blooming, and green is each tree;
The Sierras tower up in their helmets of snow,
And the wild rose and tulé still wave to and fro;
Diablo, proud monarch, all grizzled and gray,
Looms up in the distance his realm to survey.

---

* Some four or five years ago, the decayed hull of a ship was found imbedded in the sand of the great Western Desert. When and from what port did she sail, and to what nation did she belong?

But where are our comrades of long-ago days?
Some, grouped around me, crowned with laurels and bays,*
Others are present, with locks frosted by age,
Whose names add new lustre to history's page;†
And Stevenson's veterans‡ are with us to-day,
Erst from Sonoma, La Paz and old Monterey—
Heroes, who helped add to the red, white and blue,
A bright golden star, ever loyal and true.
Others lie mouldering on the plains of the West,
Their spirits have soared to the land of the blest,
Where soon we shall meet on that far-away shore,
Shall meet, and shall greet, and shall part nevermore.

At the conclusion of the poem, Mr. J. Berry, a "48er," delivered a humorous speech, which was frequently applauded.

Mr. Bayard Taylor, the next speaker, said he did not believe there was anything more wonderful in the march of Godfrey to Jerusalem than in the early argosy to California. It was a democracy of law and order, sustained merely by human nature. He had a kind of pity for those who did not have the pioneer's experience, and he recalled the time when he first saw San Francisco, in 1849, when there were more vessels in the harbor than canvas houses on the land; when Fremont was living there in a hut, and when the speaker had slept several nights under the same blanket with the Duke of Sonora. When he last saw General Sutter he was in Monterey, in 1849, after the Constitution had been adopted. There was a dance

---

* Generals Joe Hooker, Winfield S. Hancock, Horatio G. Gibson, Silas Casey, Thos. D. Johns, Francis J. Lippitt, Nelson Taylor and Colonel Geo W. Patten, U. S. Army; Vice-Admiral S. C. Rowan and Commander R. W. Meade, U. S. Navy.

† Generals John A. Sutter and John C. Fremont; Commodore C. K. Garrison, Hon. R. M. Price, Hon. R. H. McKune and General John S. Ellis.

‡ Lieutenant Jeremiah Sherwood, Privates Francis D. Clark, Russell Myers, Chas. J. McPherson, William C. Rogers, James Nuttman and Squire G. Merrill.

given in honor of the occasion, and as there were but eleven ladies to one hundred and twenty gentlemen, he had taken General Sutter for his lady, and been whirled about until he was breathless. He said that things had all changed since in California, that money was now sought for itself alone, and the miner no longer quoted Horace in the original and read Emerson in his tent.

After the singing, by Mr. Wm. J. Hill, of the "*Song of the Argonauts; or, the Days of 'Forty-nine.*" written by Mr. S. C. Upham, in the chorus of which the entire company joined; the reading of a resolution indorsing *The Pioneer*, a paper published at San Jose, Cal., and adopting it as the organ of the Society, the party broke up until evening.

At nine o'clock, P. M., the company gathered again in the large parlor of the hotel, and joined in a complimentary hop tendered to General Sutter, by Messrs. Charles and Warren Leland, Jr. The walls of the ball-room were decorated with banners bearing brief sentences in illuminated letters, recalling events and persons familiar to all the pioneers of California. The tripping of the "light fantastic toe" was kept up until a late hour. Everything passed off pleasantly, and the joyous event, with its pleasing associations, will never be forgotten by the participants.

Before the commencement of the exercises of the day, the following greeting was telegraphed to the Pioneers of the Pacific slope:

LONG BRANCH, N. J., September 8th, 1877.

To THE CALIFORNIA PIONEERS, assembled at San Jose, California:

To our friends in Eureka, the old Pioneers,
We send kindly greetings and three hearty cheers,
Three cheers and a tiger for the young Golden State,
Whose birth and whose grandeur we to-day celebrate.

General John A. Sutter, standing on the Atlantic beach, surrounded by his associates of early days, sends his greetings. God bless you all.

FRANCIS D. CLARK,
Sec'y Associated Pioneers.

The following response was received late in the afternoon:

SAN JOSE, CAL., September 8th, 1877.

FRANCIS D. CLARK, Long Branch, N. J.—"The Society of California Pioneers," and the "Santa Clara County Pioneers," greet their brothers of the Atlantic shore. May your lives be prolonged and prosperity ever yours.

A. C. BRADFORD,
Sec'y California Pioneers.
ALEX. P. MURGOTTEN,
Sec'y Santa Clara Co. Pioneers.

THIRD ANNUAL RE-UNION AND BANQUET OF "THE ASSOCIATED PIONEERS OF THE TERRITORIAL DAYS OF CALIFORNIA."

Secretary and Treasurer Clark's report—President Gibson's annual address—Election of officers for the current year—The banquet—Programme of exercises—General H. G. Gibson's address of welcome—Letters of regret—Prentice Mulford's address—Speeches by Judge Pratt, Colonel T. B. Thorpe, Colonel Edward F. Burton, Clark Bell, J. J. McCloskey, Colonel Joe Lawrence, Hon. Demas Strong, Joseph S. Spinney, Francis D. Clark and General Thomas D. Johns—"Ye Ancient Yuba Miner"—Notables present—"Song of the Argonauts"—Good-night.

On Friday evening, January 18th, 1878, "THE ASSO-CIATED PIONEERS OF THE TERRITORIAL DAYS OF CALI-FORNIA," held their third annual re-union and banquet, at the Sturtevant House, New York City, being the thirtieth anniversary of the discovery of gold at Sutter's saw-mill, at Coloma. Previous to the banquet, the annual meeting and election of officers took place, as follows:

President Gibson called the meeting to order, and Secretary Clark read the minutes of the annual meeting, following which the Secretary presented and read his report for the year ending that date, as also a review of the progress of the organization from the evening of its formation, February 11th, 1875, to date. Secretary Clark concluded with his report as Treasurer of the Society, the duties of which office had been performed by him in connection with those of Secretary. The minutes, reports and review were approved.

General Gibson presented and read his annual address,

(456)

which, in addition to a history of the Society for the past year, contained many valuable suggestions.

v General Johns moved that a committee of three be appointed by the President, to whom the address of that officer, and the reports and the review of the Secretary should be referred, with directions to take into consideration the suggestions therein offered, and report upon the same.

The President named Messrs. C. Lydecker, G. F. Sniffin and J. E. Curtis as said committee.

Hon. Demas Strong addressed the Society upon its very flattering progress during the three years of its existence, and urged upon each member the duty of using his influence to further its interests, and also paid a very high compliment to Secretary Clark for the zeal and energy displayed by that officer in promoting the welfare of the Society, and concluded by a motion that a committee of three be appointed by the President to prepare a suitable testimonial to be presented to Secretary Clark in recognition of his past services and the appreciation in which he is held by his associates.

The President named Hon. Demas Strong and Messrs. Joseph S. Spinney and W. M. Walton, as said committee.

On motion of Mr. Spinney, the sum of $150 was placed in the hands of the Secretary to meet the expense of stationery, printing and postage for the ensuing year.

On motion of Colonel Edward F. Burton, a fine copy of the "Group of '49 members," recently prepared for the Society, handsomely framed, was presented to the Secretary, the expense thereof to be defrayed out of the treasury.

The Secretary presented to the Society the names of General John C. Fremont, General Joseph W. Revere and Judge Theron Per Lee, and on motion these gentlemen were duly elected members of the Society. General Revere was the officer who hauled down the celebrated "Bear Flag" and hoisted the American flag in its stead at

Sonoma, July, 1846—and Judge Per Lee was a lieutenant in Stevenson's regiment; the former resides at Morristown, New Jersey, the latter at Baltimore, Md.

The Vice-President presented some proposed amendments to the present " Articles of Association," as also several new articles, and the Secretary read each with care, and no objection being offered, Mr. James A. Sperry moved their adoption, with the understanding that a committee should be appointed by the President further to examine the same and make such corrections as to the committee may seem proper, their action to be final.

The President named General Thos. D. Johns, Messrs. J. A. Sperry and J. Gault said committee.

Vice-President Sickels moved that the Society now proceed with the election of officers, in accordance with the adopted amendment, which provides for the election of one President, ten Vice-Presidents, one Secretary, one Treasurer and nine Trustees, which motion was adopted.

General Gibson, the President of the Society, named General John A. Sutter, the venerable and esteemed pioneer, as his successor, and upon a motion to that effect, the nominee was elected by acclamation. General Sutter was then conducted by General Gibson to the chair. General Sutter thanked his associates for the honor they had conferred upon him that evening, and wished he possessed the ability to fill the position as creditably as his predecessor. The election then proceeded, when the following gentlemen were chosen to the respective offices:

Vice-Presidents—General H. G. Gibson, U. S. A.; John Sickels, New York; George Howes, New York; Hon. Demas Strong, Brooklyn, N. Y.; J. J. Hager, Rhinebeck, N. Y.; Samuel C. Upham, Philadelphia, Pa.; Gilmor Meredith, Baltimore, Md.; General E. F. Beale, Washington, D. C.; Hon. R. H. McKune, Scranton, Pa.; William M. Walton, Newark, N. J.

Secretary—Francis D. Clark.

Treasurer—Hon. Jeremiah Sherwood.

Trustees—General Thomas W. Sweeny, U. S. A.; General Thos. D. Johns, Colonel E. F. Burton, Geo. F. Sniffin, E. K. Anthony, James A. Sperry, W. C. Annan, C. Lydecker and E. W. Crowell.

Vice-President Gibson presented the name of Reuben Lord for election to honorary membership, as provided in the amendments adopted this evening. Vice-President Sickels presented the name of Effingham B. Sutton, of New York, and on motion of Colonel Burton, these gentlemen were duly elected. (Honorary membership is only conferred upon those who are not otherwise eligible, having never been residents of California, but who were identified with the commercial interests of California prior to the 9th of September, 1850.)

Mr. Joseph Evans moved that the sum of $100 be appropriated and placed in the hands of the Secretary, to enable that officer to secure, for the proposed library of the Society, such works on California as are becoming scarce, and apply to its early history and the first stages of the gold discoveries, said fund to be accounted for at the next annual meeting. Carried.

General Johns moved that all expenditures made by the Treasurer during the past year in the interest of the Society be approved. Adopted.

Mr. Dowling moved that the meeting now adjourn, in order to attend the banquet, and that the President be requested to call a special meeting of the Society at the head-quarters, on Monday evening, Feb. 18th. Carried.

At the conclusion of the meeting, the Pioneers, with their guests, proceeded to the spacious dining-room, which was profusely and tastefully embellished with the national colors and picturesque mottoes, recalling vividly to mind Pioneer life in California. A sketch of Sutter's saw-mill, copied from an old photograph, was drawn with Castile soap on a large mirror at the upper end of the hall. On another mirror was sketched, with the same material, a grizzly bear, with the years "1848" and "1878" on either side.

The walls were embellished with placards bearing the following inscriptions: "The Flag-men of 1846—Sloat, Stockton and Shubrick;" "Stevenson's Regiment New York Volunteers, 1847;" "Gems of the Ocean—Ships *Three Brothers* and *Young America*, San Francisco;" "Sutter's Mill;" "September 9th, 1850;" "Marshall, January, 18th, 1848;" "Monterey, July 7th, 1846;" and "Sonoma." The table adornments included numerous designs, the most noticeable being a finely-executed hunting scene in a California cañon. At the foot of the main table was a chair slightly elevated, on which was fastened a card with a deep black border, with the name, "GODFREY." On the seat of the chair was a beautiful floral monument. This was in memory of a deceased member of the Society, Colonel John A. Godfrey, who died March 2d, 1877. The chair occupied the position always taken by Colonel Godfrey at the former banquets of the Society.

The Pioneers and their guests numbered about one hundred, and as they filed into the dining-room they assembled around the tables, and remained standing while the quartette, under the direction of Mr. Gilbert, accompanied by the orchestra, sang, "Praise God from whom all blessings flow." General H. G. Gibson, U. S. A., senior Vice-President, presided, and at his side sat General John A. Sutter, President of the Society. The *menu* was worthy of the world-renowned name, "LELAND," and upon this occasion the Messrs. Lewis and George S. Leland, of the "STURTEVANT," did full honor to the name, while the wines, which were of California vintage, in point of abundance and quality were unexceptionable. While the orchestra furnished choice and popular selections of music, the company proceeded to discuss the dinner, and in this agreeable duty fully two hours passed pleasantly away. In the meantime, the grizzled veterans were renewing acquaintances formed in the days of '49 and '50. At the conclusion of the dinner the "feast of reason and flow of soul" followed. The following programme was fully carried out:

An Address of Welcome, by Vice-President GENERAL H. G. GIBSON, U. S. A.

The Announcement of Letters from Absentees, by the Secretary.

Poem, "The Land We Adore," composed by SAMUEL C. UPHAM, Esq., a "49er," and read by Mr. J. BERRY.

A Few Remarks by PRENTICE MULFORD, Esq., on "The Old Guard Pioneers of the Diggings."

Song, "Y⁰ Ancient Yuba Miner of the Days of '49," composed, expressly for the occasion, by Mr. S. C. UPHAM, and sung by WM. J. HILL, Esq.

"Reminiscences of the Drama of '49," by Mr. J. J. McCLOSKEY, a Pioneer Actor.

Singing, by a Celebrated Quartette Club.

Popular Selections by the Orchestra.

General H. G. Gibson, the senior Vice-President, delivered the address of welcome to his associates and guests in the following eloquent language:

FELLOW-CALIFORNIANS:—I bid you welcome again tonight on this anniversary of one of the most eventful discoveries—alike advantageous and adventitious—in the history of a nation; an occurrence fraught with blessings and benefits to our whole country, and most prolific in its results and effects; for "Eye hath not seen, nor ear heard, neither have entered into the heart of man, the things which God hath prepared for them," in the inconceivable riches of the resources which that discovery developed. Thirty years ago, on the patriarchal demesne of a Swiss *emigré*, whose name has since become world-famous, a little speck of shining metal was found, and, like "a great matter a little fire kindleth," a stream of gold and silver began thenceforth to enrich the earth; succeeded by other wonders, scarcely less marvelous than those with which the fair Scheherezade beguiled her liege lord in the famed Arabian Nights. In the retrospect which each of us may take to-night, we behold a region superb in its physical features and attractions; delectable in its genial climate, and where

> " with lavish kindness
> The gifts of God are strewn"

in broadcast profusion and ubiquitous richness, needing only the touch of an energetic race of men to "pluck the ripe fruit and gather in the hollow of the hand." Broad plains stretching "many, many a league onward," the wealth of whose virgin soil was betokened by "the blackness of darkness" of purest loam; watered by noble rivers to which golden streams, mountain torrent and gentle rivulet paid tribute; picturesque valleys with graceful oaks in orchard regularity, and vast fields of indigenous grain—in winter of brightest green, in summer of dazzling gold: all hemmed in by mountain walls, whereon the lofty giants of the wood stood enthroned in majesty and beauty. Along the coast, amid charming pastoral scenes and surroundings, the humble *padres* of the missions of the grand old church of God taught to the Indian and his dusky mate the faith of Christianity, and the rudest arts of civilized life. Cattle stood upon a thousand hills, and the noble horse, in all the peerless beauty and strength of unrestrained freedom, pawed the earth over leagues and leagues of golden pasture. Peace and plenteousness were in the homely *adobe* abodes of the occupants of the soil, and undisturbed by the unknown pleasures and splendors of a higher civilization, a pastoral race, with their flocks and herds, enjoyed a life of calm repose and happy contentment:

> " Along the cool sequestered vale of life,
>   They kept the noiseless tenor of their way."

On slope and plain, the grape clusters, brilliant in bloom and luscious in flavor, gladdened the heart of man and filled the air with fragrance; the olive, in "its glossy bower of coolest foliage," mellowed its grateful fruit, beneath the bright sunlit or soft cloud-dimmed sky; and flowers, too, of exquisite hues and manifold variety,

> " Everywhere about us are they glowing,
>   Some, like stars, to tell us spring is born;
> Others, their blue eyes with tears are flowing,
>   Stand, like Ruth, amid the golden corn."

The antelope, the deer and the elk browsed upon the luxuriant herbage of forest and field; the grizzly, the lion and the *coyote* roamed through brake, and jungle, and *chaparral;* and the hunter, the trapper and the aborigine found their Elysium in its secluded wilds.

With the war with Mexico, and the alluring discovery which made us Pioneers and Pilgrims of the Golden Land, a wonderful, material change was inaugurated; a revolution wrought in the character, habits and pursuits of the *gentes* of the Californias, whether "native and to the manor born," or *los gringos* from other climes. "People of every nation, kindred and tongue" flocked to the golden shores, and the serene peace and pastoral beauty of the land was transformed to a scene of bustle, excitement, active life and industry. To the wondering eyes of the eager throngs, that gathered in her generous *placers,* California, her ample stores,

> "Rich with the spoils of Time, did *there* unroll;"

and the voice of the miner, as he smote the earth and rock with pick and drill, was heard in the land: "Eureka, aye, gold! glittering gold!" Beneath genial skies, and with lightsome toil, on the fallow of ages,

> " Hillside, ravine and *tulé* marsh
>   Soon blossomed as the rose,"

and the husbandmen, oft "reaping where they had not sown,"
in the assurance of a rich harvest,

> " How jocund did they drive their team a-field!
> How bowed the woods beneath their sturdy stroke!"

The scant coffers of the world soon shone with the splendor
and abundance of the precious ore from California's grand
treasure-house; and out of her horn of plenty she yet pours
her measures of corn, and wine, and oil, of wool and flax, of
rarest gems and richest metals, without stint, without abate-
ment. But, to rehearse the grand progress of our country, due
directly or indirectly to the effect of the golden discovery, to
rejoice over which I welcome you here to-night, and greet you
in the olden California spirit, time will not allow. Suffice it
to say, that the results of the influence of the riches of her
bounty are to be seen, in the wonderful impetus given to every
industry; in the solid and brilliant achievements or finer products of plough, anvil and loom, of forest and mine; in the
iron bands of commerce, binding the continent together; in the
marvelous feat of the modern Ajax, defying and controlling
the lightning, and saying, like Puck, "I'll put a girdle round
about the earth in forty minutes;" in "cities proud, with
spires and turrets crowned," rising in the wilderness as if by
magic; in States, "clothed and in their right minds," coming
forth out of the gloom of mountain and desert with "glad rejoicings and grateful praise"—"and all men did marvel!"
For, with "the victories of Peace no less renowned than War,"
the genius of California has added a brighter lustre to the
resplendent arms of the Republic; with new jewels set in its
proud diadem, new stars in the brilliant firmament of its
Union; in the radiant folds of "its glorious ensign, as it floats
over the sea and over the land." [Great applause.]

At the conclusion of General Gibson's address, the Secretary, Mr. Francis D. Clark, arose and announced the receipt
of letters of regret from General William T. Sherman, U.
S. A., General Joe Hooker, U. S. A., General Francis J.
Lippitt, General Joseph M. Revere, Bayard Taylor, Mark

Twain, ex-Governor Pacheco, Senator A. A. Sargent and Hon. Peter Dean, President of the "Society of California Pioneers," at San Francisco. The Secretary also announced that associates Hon. J. Sherwood, J. J. Hager and E. C. Kemble, were prevented from being present in consequence of recent family afflictions.

The President then called upon Mr. J. Berry, the elocutionist, who responded to the call and recited, with feeling and emphasis, the poem written by Mr. Samuel C. Upham, entitled, "THE LAND WE ADORE." This recitation elicited rounds of applause, and cries of "Upham! Upham!" brought that gentleman to his feet, who, in a few appropriate words, thanked his associates for their approval of his humble efforts to do justice to California. He said he had been so ably represented by proxy, that he feared anything he might say would fall upon their ears as "stale, flat and unprofitable." Nevertheless, if the poem, so eloquently recited by Mr. Berry, had in any way added to their enjoyment he should consider himself amply repaid for the time spent upon its composition.

The next gentleman called upon was Mr. Prentice Mulford, the California humorist, who spoke as follows about the "OLD GUARD PIONEERS OF THE DIGGINGS:"

MR. PRESIDENT:—An idea largely prevails among the generation born since the American occupation of California, that the pioneer element of the State was in character rude and uncultured. It is an idea which has been largely owing to the delineations of character given in California literature, so that the Eastern public will accept none other representative for the Pioneer, save the man in overalls and red shirt, knife and pistol at the belt, who uttered an oath at every other word and whose regular beverage was whisky. Yet this type was the exception in 1849. The element which rushed into the Territory on the announcement of the discovery of gold, embraced the pick of the energy, enterprise, education and refinement, not only of the Eastern States, but of Europe. It brought

with it the eloquence of a Baker; it called at an early period
for the brilliancy of a Starr King. Grant was a pioneer,
Sherman was a pioneer, and it is not impossible but that the
peculiar conditions of their California experience had much to
do in developing the tenacity and firmness of the one, and that
conciseness and directness of aim and action, the distinguish-
ing characteristic of the other. Out of this pioneer element
grew a new school of literature, the chief exponents of which
are a Phœnix, à Bret Harte, a Mark Twain, a Joaquin Miller
[and a Prentice Mulford]. And its energy and enterprise,
starting from a small inland city as a base, sent a thousand miles
of railroad over waste, mountain and desert, then as dangerous and quite as unknown as the interior of Africa.

I desire, however, to say a word in remembrance of another
and less known class of pioneers. I mean the men who went
to California in '49, who never came back, who never made
their fortunes, or who, if they did make them never kept them,
and who never will come back. I mean the Old Guard of
Pioneers still left in the "Diggin's." Travel through the
mines to-day and you will find it a country full of deserted
villages. Even the mountain roads and trails over which they
once packed their pork and flour, tobacco and whisky, from
store to camp, are now fading out and overgrown with *chaparral.* Even the deer and grizzly have in places resumed
their old haunts from which they were driven by the gold-
seekers' invasion. Travel along those rivers, now deserted, and
you will come here and there on lone, blackened chimneys—
all that remains of the pioneer's cabin: those chimneys about
which the "boys," full then of life, hope and energy, would
cluster in the rainy winter evenings and talk of their far-away
Eastern homes. But their fires were long since burned to
ashes, and the brilliant anticipations of that time are ashes
also. It is in some nook of the foot-hills, perhaps the only
cabin and the last man in the camp, that you find the pioneer
to-day. His coffee-mill is still nailed to the trunk of the over-
shadowing tree by his door; his clothes-line is still stretched,
and on it flutters his bachelor's washing; his little garden-patch
is fenced with old sluice lumber; he keeps a cat, a dog; he

sits at evening in his cabin-door, old, gray, grizzled, smoking his pipe and thinking of home—the home of thirty years ago, peopled in memory with faces fresh and blooming, now withered and wrinkled or long since laid in the dust.

These were the men who cooked their own meals, washed their own shirts and mended their own pants—with flour-sacks, the brand on the outside, so that often on passing the honest miner, did you turn your head, you might see prominently graven upon him the words: "Warranted 200 pounds Self-rising Genesee Flour." Such men as Justice Barry, the first Alcalde of Sonora, Tuolumne County, who, when once on the bench, was reproached by Lawyer Quint with the charge that he (Lawyer Q.) never could get justice in his (Judge Barry's) court, was told by Judge Barry that he (Barry) never intended that Lawyer Quint should get justice in his court. And my friend Shanks, of Red Mountain, still alive, not thoroughly sober since 1852, and never attired otherwise than in a gray shirt and duck pants, rope-yarned about the waist, who, when one evening at the bar-stove the conversation had taken a theological turn, assured his hearers that the New Testament seemed clear enough until he reached the book of Revelations. "John Second," he remarked, "had snakes when he wrote that book. And as for the beast of ten horns—can't scare me with that; been on the most familiar terms with him for the last ten years."

I don't claim for my Argonauts and the Old Pioneer Guard lingering in the foot-hills, that they came to California instigated by high and holy motives. They came to get gold, to get all they could, to get it as quickly as they could, and to get away with it as quickly as possible. But thirty years have passed away. Still they linger. Their friends and relatives in their native Eastern towns have quite forgotten them. The friends of former and more stirring days in California have departed. They have contracted none of those softer ties which make life happier. They are indeed alone. The country has, as it were, slipped away from beneath them.

A few years ago I made a pilgrimage to the old familiar ground on the Tuolumne. I found living between Jacksonville and Don Pedro's Bar, a stretch of 10 or 12 miles, about six white men. I found at Hawkin's Bar, once numbering near a thousand voters, one solitary miner still delving away at the same bank he worked in '50, and this man—the last man of the camp—his name was——Smith! The camp had dwindled from hundreds of houses and cabins to fifty; from fifty to ten, and then the river had rolled down a tremendous freshet, covering half the bar with a deposit of alluvium three feet in depth; on this the quickly-springing vegetation had taken root, and the camp site was a jungle of *chaparral*. Forty yards behind the last pioneer's cabin was a little inclosure—the camp graveyard. The fence was tumbling down. The wooden head-boards lying prone to earth, the inscriptions placed thereon by kindly yet stranger's hands quite erased by time and the weather. One familiar sound was still heard— the roar of. the Tuolumne over rapid and riffle below, roaring as it roared in the ears of those sleeping here when, for the first time from the summit of yon high red hill, blanket and pick on their shoulders, they caught their first glimpse of the long, winding, sun-glittering line of the river at their feet, while a thousand busy, excited men toiled along the banks, and the rattle of the gravel shaken in hundreds of rocker sieves sounded like the crash and din of a cotton-mill.

So it roared and murmured and seemed ever in their ears babbling some weird, monotonous story, as they lay sick and dying in their rude miner's bunks—still on and on it roars, babbles and sings an eternal requiem for the forgotten, nameless pioneers who sleep here, while still in some far-away home, wife, mother, sister, brother, friend, wait and weep and long for him in vain.

At the conclusion of Mr. Mulford's address, which was greeted with rounds of applause, the quartette sang "All Honor to the Miner." General Gibson said that they had with them a distinguished citizen of Brooklyn, who had been elected and re-elected to the Supreme Bench by the unanimous vote of the people He had known Judge Pratt in the field, and he was a distinguished soldier, lawyer and jurist. It gave him great pleasure to introduce him. [Applause.]

Judge Pratt, when the applause had subsided, spoke as follows :

I assure you that I had not the least idea that I should be called upon to make a speech, and I now feel very much as that young man in Brooklyn felt when he was informed that he would have to ride to the funeral of his mother-in-law in the same carriage with his wife. He replied : "I suppose I will have to do it, but it robs this occasion of all pleasure for me." [Laughter.] I can recollect the day when, if a California judge went to England, and was introduced to a gentleman, the latter always responded : "How do you do, Mr. Lynch?" [Applause and laughter.] Now, of course, it is not expected, that upon such a sudden call as this, I should be able to say much in favor of Brooklyn. Still, I can assure you that it is a city of some importance. We have the greatest park, the greatest bridge, we have had the greatest fire and the longest trial, at which my friend, Judge Neilson, presided. I presume he has left us for fear that he would be called upon to describe that trial. There is another thing about Brooklyn that will, no doubt, please a great many gentlemen here. In a large portion of it, the Heights—the best portion of it in my estimation —they have abolished hell. There is another thing about Brooklyn, and some gentlemen here may vouch for what I say, it is a place where there is more virtue and more honest office-holders than any other place in the world. [Laughter.] In proof of that, I refer to my friend, Mr. Strong. Now, gentlemen, permit me to say something about California. It was not my pleasure to go to that country. I was not blessed with a sight of it, but I regard the settlement of it, in its influence upon this country, in regard to the enterprise, hospitality and honesty of its people, of the greatest importance and benefit. It was a place where people could go to sleep at night and never fasten their doors, and where, if a stranger arrived at night the doors were thrown open to him and the best the house afforded set

27

before him. That, it strikes me, was one of the greatest countries under the sun. [Applause.]

Colonel T. B. Thorpe, a veteran of the Mexican war, and formerly on the staff of General Zachary Taylor, was introduced by the President and received with tumultuous applause. Colonel Thorpe stated that while employed as a journalist in New Orleans, several years before the discovery of gold at Sutter's Mill, a Swede, evidently far gone in consumption, called on him, representing that he was, in his own country, one of the "King's Orphans;"* that is, he had been educated at a government institution, one of the requirements of which was, that the pupil, after receiving a certain amount of schooling, should travel in foreign lands, record all he saw, put it in his manuscript, and on his return deposit it in the archives of the institution. In pursuance of this regulation, the Swede had visited California while under Mexican rule. He remained for several days at Sutter's Fort, enjoying the well-known hospitality of General Sutter. While there he had made a close examination of the surrounding country, the result of which was a conviction on his part that it abounded *richly in gold*. This opinion he had delivered in writing to Colonel Thorpe, who still retained the manuscript, and avowed his intention of depositing it in the archives of "The Associated Pioneers of the Territorial Days of California."

Before concluding his remarks, Colonel Thorpe called upon General Sutter to ascertain whether any memory of the Swede's visit remained with him.

General Sutter arose and said he did recollect the visit of the Swede, which occurred about thirty-four years ago; that he remembered, on his part, the expression of such opinion regarding the presence of mineral wealth in the neighboring hills. "But," added the venerable pioneer, "I

---

* See page 537.

was too much occupied at the time with other concerns to devote any time or attention to it.   My crops were ripe, and it was imperative that they should be gathered as quickly as possible.   *But I do recollect the scientific Swedish gentleman.*"

Colonel Thorpe also referred to the acquisition of California, its wonderful people, and its rapid march to greatness.   Eloquently he pictured some of the scenes of early days, and addressing General Sutter, paid him a most glowing tribute as a patriot, pioneer and philanthropist, whose name would live in history and be crowned with honors, not won on the battle-field, in the forum, or in political life, but as a benefactor and friend to humanity.

Colonel Edward F. Burton, " The man of '49," who is well-known in California, was brought to his feet by the unanimous call of the assembly, and proceeded to make a few " humble remarks."   He narrated his experience as an *honest* miner, a period when true happiness was to be found; when there were no rent or wash-bills to pay, no tax collectors to fret one's soul and eat up a man's substance; when there were no vile dyspeptic cooks, but every one prepared his morning and evening meal to suit his own taste.   His speech recalled the individual experiences of many present, and was in a continuous current of humor that kept the assemblage in a roar.

In honor of a number of ladies who had been invited into the hall to hear the singing and speaking, the quartette sang the " Toast to the Ladies."   General Gibson called upon Mr. Clark Bell, a distinguished lawyer of New York, to respond in their behalf, which duty he performed in his usual eloquent and pleasing manner, paying a most fitting tribute to the fair sex.

Mr. J. J. McCloskey, the California pioneer actor, next gave some interesting reminiscences of the drama in 1849. He said the time was too short to relate all of his experiences. It would take two or three weeks to do it.   The traveler from the East in visiting California is struck with the magnificence of the theatres. They have the finest appointments of any in the world. Brothers of the buskin in the Golden City now have their yachts, their base ball clubs, stop at the hotels, and wear purple and fine linen. It was not so in the days of '49. At that time, when traveling, they trusted to the back of *la mula* or walked. They had no scenery but that which was made by the local sign painter, who generally gave nothing but a daub of yellow sky. They had to fight against both fire and water, and move continually from camp to camp, following the miners wherever they went. Sometimes they gave a performance in the dining-hall of a hotel, and admitted the miners at $5 a head.

Mr. McCloskey next referred to Mrs. Lizzie Bingham, the pioneer actress of California, the first white woman who ever crossed the plains to that State. He spoke of her as a most remarkable woman, and described her entry into Downieville with her twin babies, in laughable terms. He also described the death of Mrs. Bingham in a battle at Nicaragua, and closed with a brilliant tribute to her memory.

Colonel Joe Lawrence, an old '49er and veteran newspaper editor, upon being called upon, arose and favored the company with a speech in a most humorous strain. He singled out of the guests prominent men of the early days, and related in an inimitable manner incidents connected with their early California life. He said he only intended to give their good points, and they need not tremble for fear of any revelations that might sound harsh. As the Colonel proceeded, he fairly warmed in his wit, and only that the orchestra broke in with some popular selection, he might have continued two or three hours longer. Of course, the President censured the leader of the orchestra for the interruption; but too late, the Colonel had resumed his seat.

Secretary Clark arose and said he had intended to have

made some remarks appropriate to the occasion, but that previous speakers having taken the "wind out of his sails," he would confine his remarks to one subject, and that was the claim of our venerated chieftain and associate, General Sutter, against the government for property of which he was unjustly deprived many years ago. Secretary Clark urged upon each individual member of the Society, and all other Californians, the duty that was imposed upon them to use all their personal influence, by all honorable means, to induce Congress to repay the old pioneer, and thus contribute to his comfort and smooth the pathway of his declining years. Mr. Clark's remarks were received at their close with three hearty cheers and a tiger for General Sutter.

Mr. Joseph S. Spinney delivered a very feeling and eloquent eulogy upon the late Henry Meiggs, of Peru. He believed if any man had ever repented of an error and tried in all possible ways to show his repentance by acts of charity and restoration, that man was Harry Meiggs, and he firmly believed he had gone to rest with the Saviour of all mankind in the realms above; and, in the words of Holy Writ, he would exclaim, "Let him that hath no sin cast the first stone." We must all remember that "to err is human, to forgive divine."

The President referred to the death of Colonel John A. Godfrey, late a member of the Society, and called on General Thomas D. Johns for a few words of tribute to his memory, to which the General responded as follows:

MR. PRESIDENT:—This would be a cold world, indeed, did we not sometimes recall the memories of departed friends; and this Society would not be true to one of its professed objects, did it fail to honor, in some befitting manner, the names of those associates who have been taken from us. During the early eventful years of California, we made the pilgrimage together, each in his allotted sphere. The varied experiences we have undergone, the excitements and dangers with which we have been surrounded, the trials and vicissitudes incident to that exceptional pioneer life, the almost magical changes of situation and of fortune, all tend to create a bond of union among us, and a sympathy which, perhaps, none but the early Californians comprehend and appreciate. I know, Mr. President, that I express not only the sentiments of the individual members of this Society, but those of the Californians present with us this evening, in thanking you for your eloquent, appropriate and touching remarks in announcing, in your Annual Report, the death of our late associate, Colonel John A. Godfrey. He was one of our most active and enthusiastic members, and took great pride in the welfare and success of our Society. One year ago, this evening, he occupied his accustomed place at the farther end of this table, in the flush of manhood, and leading in our festivities; his voice is hushed, that chair is vacant now and bears the emblems of mourning. We have no eulogy to pronounce here; but when we are called to follow him, may each of us have fraternal and friendly voices to speak of us as we now say of him, "gone but not forgotten."

During the evening, the quartette sang Mr. S. C. Upham's "*Song of the Argonauts; or, the Days of '49,*" the entire company joining in the chorus. Mr. William J. Hill sang the following serio-comic song, written by Mr. Samuel C. Upham, expressly for the occasion:

Y^e ANCIENT YUBA MINER, OF THE DAYS OF '49.

Air:—"Fine Old English Gentleman."

I.

To you I'll sing a good old song, made by a Quaker pate,
Of an ancient Yuba miner, who owned no real estate,
But who when asked where he belonged, this son of Uncle Sam,
He scratched his head a moment, then in accents clear and shrill, straightway ejaculated "*Yuba Dam!*"
Did this ancient Yuba Miner, of the days of '49.

Yᴱ ANCIENT YUBA MINER, OF THE DAYS OF '49.

II.

I'm told that simple was his food, he used no forks nor spoons,
And with old flour and coffee-sacks he patched his trouser-
loons;
He was saucy, lousy, ragged, lank, but happy as a clam,
And when interrogated in relation to the location from whence
he hailed, he invariably replied, "*Yuba Dam!*"
Did this grizzled Yuba miner, of the days of '49·

III.

On a prospecting tour one day, he struck it very rich,
'Twas on a little mountain stream, forninst the Yuba ditch;
Said he, "this claim of mine I'll sell, my purse the dust will
cram,"
But when questioned in relation to his antecedents, and from
whence he came, he articulated, "*Yuba Dam!*"
Did this lucky Yuba miner, of the days of '49·

IV.

He started down to 'Frisco town, this man of no estate,
On mule back first, by water then—but never mind the date,
And on his way they questioned him, this son of Uncle Sam;
They asked him the initials of his front name, the mine from
    whence he came, and then he placed his hand beside his
    mouth and roared out, "*Yuba Dam!*"
Did this jolly Yuba miner, of the days of '49·

V.

When he arrived in 'Frisco town, the mud was very deep,
Said he, " my equilibrium now, I surely mean to keep;"
But then the crowd they jostled him, and finally, in a jam,
He was pitched headlong into the mud, and when fished out
    and asked where he belonged, he sputtered, "*Yuba Dam!*"
Did this wilted Yuba miner, of the days of '49·

VI.

Into the " El Dorado " then, he went to try his luck,
Said he, " I'll show those gamboliers a little Yuba pluck,
I'll bust their cussed monte bank, for I am nary sham,"
But he soon emerged a wiser but a badly busted individual,
    and to every question asked him, he replied, " *Yuba Dam !*"
Did this busted Yuba miner, of the days of '49·

VII.

Soon on a stretcher he was laid, with his head all caved in,
For the way that they had walloped him, was a shame and
    awful sin ;
All mashed and shattered was his head, as if butted by a ram ;
The doctor felt his *corpus*, the parson sung a psalm, and when
    they asked him from whence he came, he faintly whis-
    pered, " *Yuba Dam !*"
Did this dying Yuba miner, of the days of '49.

VIII.

The coroner soon an inquest held, and then at his command,
They shoved old Yuba in a box, and dumped him in the sand,
At midnight hour they buried him, without show, or pomp, or
    flam,
And when at the last day Gabriel's trump shall sound, among
        the early risers, you bet, will be old "*Yuba Dam!*"
That defunct and ancient miner, of the days of '49·

The President called upon Hon. Demas Strong, ex-
Supervisor of Brooklyn, President of the *first* City Council of Sacramento City, and acting Mayor of that city after
the death of Mayor Bigelow, in the fall of 1850, for a speech.
That gentleman acquiescing, stated that, as it was past
midnight, and rather late for speech-making, he would
make his remarks brief. He described his voyage from
Panama to San Francisco in the first ship that left the
latter harbor after the discovery of gold. The crews of all
previous vessels invariably ran off to the gold-diggings.
The speeches of the evening had recalled memories to his
mind which would go down with him to the grave, but he
would refrain from putting them into words, as he merely
wished to ask those present to put the sentiments expressed
into practical form, and use every effort to enroll as members of this Society all the California pioneers throughout
the country, so that the Association should number thou-

sands instead of hundreds, and should become the chief bond of union among those who had settled California.

Among the notable gentlemen present, were ex-Mayor Vance, of New York; Donald McClellan, Esq., President of *Pacific Woollen Mills*, San Francisco; J. W. Simonton, Esq., *Associated Press;* Clark Bell, Esq.; Mr. B. C. Watson, President *Grocers' Bank,* a '49er; James F. Curtis, *ex-Chief of Police* of San Francisco; John McCullough, the *Tragedian;* Colonel Joe Lawrence and S. C. Upham, *Pioneer Newspaper Men* of Sacramento City; Prentice Mulford, the *California Humorist;* J. J. McCloskey and Clay Greene, *Playwrights;* Colonel T. B. Thorpe; and from Brooklyn were Hon. Calvin E. Pratt, *Justice of the Supreme Court;* Hon. Joseph Neilson and George G. Reynolds, *Judges of the City Court;* Hon. Demas Strong, *ex-Supervisor;* Mr. Maxwell, of the *Brooklyn Daily Times;* Mr. J. E. Edey, Mr. W. J. Hill, W. C. Bryant and James A. Sperry.

At half-past one o'clock, A. M., the quartette sang the following verses of the " *Song of the Argonauts; or, The Days of '49,*" the entire audience joining in the chorus:

> Fresh laurel-wreaths we bring to-day,
> To crown the Patriarch,
> Whose hand unlocked the golden ore,
> In gulch and cañon dark.
> Old Pioneer! thy name we still
> In all our hearts enshrine;
> God's blessing rest upon thy head,
> Dear friend of old lang syne!

> *Chorus.*—Oh, cherished be for evermore
> The days of auld lang syne,
> Those golden days—remembered days—
> The days of 'Forty-nine.

> Hillside, ravine and tulé marsh,
> Now blossom as the rose,

And 'round Diablo's verdant base
The crystal streamlet flows.
Now glory be to God on high!
Let this our pæan be—
And peace on earth, good-will to man,
Our prayer, O God, to Thee!

Chorus.—Oh, cherished be for evermore, etc.

At the conclusion of the singing, the orchestra struck up
" *Home, Sweet Home,*" and the company quietly dispersed,
well pleased with the evening's entertainment, and hoping
to meet again one year hence.

On Saturday, the day following the banquet, at the
special request of Mr. Sarony, the celebrated photographic
artist, of New York, General Sutter, Secretary Clark,
General Johns and Mr. Samuel C. Upham visited his
gallery and sat for imperial portraits. Mr. Sarony also
presented General Sutter with a fine picture of General
Albert Pike, of Arkansas, the aged veteran of the Mexican
war, and expressed himself much pleased by this visit from
so distinguished a personage as General Sutter.

RECEPTION TO GENERAL JOHN C. FREMONT.

Formal reception by General Fremont—Notables present—Decorations of the hall—The banquet—Vice-President Gibson's address of welcome—General Fremont's response—Letters of regret read by the Secretary—Speeches, etc.

GENERAL JOHN C. FREMONT, Governor of the Territory of Arizona, being on the eve of departure for his official post on the Pacific coast, was tendered a reception at the Sturtevant House, New York, on the evening of the 1st of August, 1878, by his friends and compatriots, " THE ASSOCIATED PIONEERS OF THE TERRITORIAL DAYS OF CALIFORNIA."

1843.   PIONEERS OF CALIFORNIA.   **1878.**

RECEPTION

—TO—

GENERAL JOHN C. FREMONT,

Governor of Arizona Territory,

PREVIOUS TO HIS DEPARTURE FOR THE PACIFIC COAST,

BY HIS OLD CALIFORNIA FRIENDS AND ASSOCIATES,

The Associated Pioneers of the Territorial Days of California,

AT THEIR HEAD-QUARTERS,

STURTEVANT HOUSE,

NEW YORK,

ON THURSDAY EVENING, AUGUST 1st, 1878,

AT 8 O'CLOCK.

FOR CARDS OF ADMISSION ADDRESS THE SECRETARY.

FRANCIS D. CLARK, *Secretary,*
16 Cortlandt Street.

JOHN A. SUTTER,
President.

(482)

The author is indebted to Secretary Clark for the following report:

From eight to nine o'clock, the General held an informal reception in one of the hotel parlors, after which about one hundred of the Pioneers sat down to an elegant supper. In the absence of the President of the Association, General John A. Sutter, the chair was occupied by General H. G. Gibson, U. S. A., the senior Vice-President. At his right sat the guest of the evening and his two sons, John C. Fremont, Jr., U. S. N., and Francis Preston Fremont. Among the members present were ex-Governor R. M. Price, of New Jersey; Joseph Evans, Colonel George D. Brewerton, William H. Rogers, Hon. Francis D. Clark, Charles J. McPherson and Colonel Geo. M. Leonard—the last six were members of the historic "Stevenson's Regiment;"—Hon. William Colligan, Deputy Surveyor E. F. Burton, Colonel E. C. Kemble, first editor of the *Alta California*, in 1846; Hon. C. Lydecker, Stephen L. Merchant, son of General C. S. Merchant; James J. McCloskey, the pioneer actor; Vice-President John Sickels, E. W. Crowell, Charles W. Schumann and William M. Walton. Among the guests were Colonel T. B. Thorpe, Dr. J. W. Morton, who had just returned from a trip through the Australian Diamond Fields; General W. L. Tidball, a Mexican war veteran; Colonel E. R. Goodrich, Judge Curtis, ex-Mayor of San Francisco; Major W. W. Leland, George B. Ammermon and General H. L. Burnett.

The dining-hall was handsomely decorated with mottoes and emblems appropriate to the occasion. At the head of the hall was an entablature with the following inscription: "Reception to Captain John C. Fremont by Captain John A. Sutter, at Sutter's Fort, California, March 6th, 1844." At the lower end of the hall was a large cuirass bearing the figure of a grizzly bear, with the word "California" above it and "Pioneers" below. The tables were profusely decorated with flowers. Before supper the guests arose and sang the long metre doxology—" Praise God from whom all blessings flow."

After the company had devoted over one hour to the viands set so temptingly before them, washed down with wines of California vintage of the famous house of Landsburgh & Co., San Francisco, and when coffee had been handed around, and cigars lighted, General Gibson, the chairman, arose and delivered the following eloquent address of welcome:

FELLOW-CALIFORNIANS:—In the absence of our grand old Patriarch and beloved fellow-Pioneer and President, the duty devolves upon me of welcoming our distinguished guest. I regret that he is not here to-night to express, though only in his tremulous and embarrassed utterances, the same cordial greeting which he gave to his worthy compeer and *compadre*, on the banks of the Sacramento thirty-four years ago. Though his speech might have been only silver, the welcome of his heart would have been golden.

We have met this evening to do honor to an eminent citizen of the Republic and a renowned pioneer, who, as the great Pathfinder of Empire, first disclosed to the nation a knowledge of the rich and attractive country bordering the Pacific, and whose name will, through all coming time, be identified with the exploration of a continent, and with the American occupation and development of the Golden Land. Traversing with his little band the trackless wastes, forbidding mountains and dense forests lying between the mighty Father of Waters and that magnificent region, whose

> " snow-sierras hide
> Huge crystalled rocks of virgin gold.
> Adown abrading torrents rolled,
> In lucid streams, by summer shoaled,
> A golden tide ;"

the youthful explorer in his first enterprise determined 'the physical geography of a vast, unknown territory, and contributed to science the wealth of his felicitous and valuable discoveries. Wending his way a second time to the then foreign provinces of the Californias, he inspired and aided the raising of the standard of revolt against the rule of the Mexican, on the oak-orchard plain of Sonoma, and thus made the initiatory step which led to the acquisition, consummated by the war with Mexico, of that beautiful and opulent domain, and which FREMONT and destiny had determined should be ours thenceforth and forever. Discovering, also, in his first expedition, a practicable route by the eastern base of the Sierra Nevada, from the valley of the Sacramento to the grand forest-crowned region "along the lone Columbia," his footprints became the unerring guide to all who followed after. For as to the fidelity and accuracy of his descriptions and observations, as he spied out the land, your chairman can testify from personal experience; that the itinerary of each day's journey, as we pursued the rough tenor of our way through the vast wilderness of lava bed, forest, plain, mountain and cañon—through "a land of fracture, violence and fire"—was pictured on the mental vision before as clearly defined as the actual vision beheld it thereafter. A portion of the country traversed by FREMONT had been imperfectly explored by the previous expeditions of Lewis, Clark and Long, as well as by Bonneville, whose crude narrative, enriched and embellished by the graceful pen of Washington Irving, charmed our childhood, and yet delights our mature years. These gave, however, but a faint idea of its magnificent character, and it remained for FREMONT to impart to us a full knowledge of its grand and peculiar features, its wonderful beauties and resources.

For his great and distinguished service to the State, the Government at Washington awarded him promotion in the army, and the new-born Golden State of California a seat in the Senate of the United States. In later years, bearing the standard of a great political party, he with knightly courage, courtesy and modesty, led it nigh unto victory, and *opened the path* to its subsequent success; and, at a critical period of its fortunes, contributed to its overwhelming triumph and continuance of power, by his graceful and opportune retirement from the field as the nominee, a second time, for the Presidency, of a great convention of his fellow-citizens.

In his military career, as an officer of engineers, he displayed rare ability, and remarkable fertility of resources and expedients; and as a field officer of the line, added to his fame by the joint conquest, with the gallant Stockton, of the territory of the Californias; and how far the crimes and blunders at Washington affected his usefulness, success and renown, as a leader and commander of our armies in the late civil war, as of other true and loyal soldiers, who bore the heat and burden of the day, and stood among their fellows high in reputation for wisdom and honor, impartial history must determine.* It suffices us, however, to know that his services came fully up to the official standard of "gallant, faithful and meritorious." But as an explorer, his name must ever be classed with those noble and illustrious names on that brilliant scroll, which embraces Marco Polo and de Soto, Mungo Park and Livingstone; with those who "in journeyings often, in perils of waters, in perils of robbers, in perils by the heathen, in perils in the wilderness; in weariness and painfulness, in watchings often, in hunger and thirst, in fastings often, in cold and nakedness," have exposed or sacrificed their lives in the cause of science and humanity; and whose marvelous sagacity, indomitable courage, patience and fortitude have reflected glory on our race.

But the full measure of reward for his brilliant and eminent services, whose

> "records half-effaced,
> Which with the hand of youth he traced
> On history's page,"

has never been conceded nor bestowed. It is an inherent, and

---

* The history of the war of the rebellion—written and unwritten—shows that McClellan, Buell, Fitz-John Porter and Stone (an old Californian) were victims of these crimes and blunders, and that Grant, Sherman (an old Pioneer) and Thomas came near being crushed in the opening of their careers, or at the zenith of their fame, by the ignorance, prejudice and imbecility at Washington. That the commanders in the valley of the Shenandoah and in front of Washington were likewise sufferers from these acts and influences must be the verdict of the honest and faithful chronicler of the war.

perhaps, ineradicable vice of all republics that their great benefactors and heroes are seldom dûly honored or rewarded while living—soon neglected or forgotten when dead; and our own Republic can claim no immunity from the vice. That it may cease to be its reproach and shame should be the fervent prayer of every true patriot;· and that when we have done with honoring with "storied urn and animated bust" the genius and heroism of antiquity and of other lands, we may find time and means to demonstrate to the world, that there are those of our own land who have "won a mural crown of towering glory." May the time yet come when as the golden orb of day sinks to his rest in the bosom of the mighty ocean beyond the portals of the Golden Gate, his parting rays shall shed their golden light on its pinnacles, whereon shall stand the sculptured forms of FREMONT and SUTTER, with the inscription on the one, "*The path he trod was the Path to Empire;*" and on the other, "*The golden heart that enriched the Golden Land!*"

General Fremont, you are about to depart for the vicinity of the scenes of your former labors and signal deeds, and we come as fellow-Pioneers and Californians, to offer to you our earnest congratulations and cordial good wishes. May health and happiness attend you, and in your new field of employment, may you ever enjoy the approving smiles and favor of a grateful, appreciative people. As your youth was adorned with fame, may your age be crowned with glory and honor. For myself, in the remembrance of a pleasant journey together in years gone by, through the beautiful valley of the San Joaquin, "on fields with daisies pied," and "gorgeous flowerets in the sunlight shining," through arid waste and cooling mountain grove—in the remembrance of a kindness done, but as soon forgotten by you, I tender to you the kindliest greeting and most earnest prayer that heart can feel, or voice or hand express. [Great applause.]

With evident emotion, General Fremont responded as follows :

GENTLEMEN :—You would no doubt think it strange if I did

are led moved by what has been so eloquently said by my friend, who speaks from a kindly remembrance of those events which opened California to us. We have seen what a commotion has been created in England by the annexation of Cyprus to Great Britain. But for the pioneers, California would also be a gem in the diadem of the Queen of England, and it is not to be denied that we dwell with pleasure on the fact. In those times the pioneers placed upon their flag the emblem of the grizzly. But before long this was exchanged for the Stars and Stripes of the United States. It may be remembered that the English Admiral Seymour at this time said that if he had arrived a few days sooner the flag of England would have floated over California instead of that of the Republic. The warmth of coloring with which General Gibson has painted some of my official acts is the result of the co-operation, the companionship and friendly thoughts of the early pioneers of California. The same friendly feeling was exhibited among the pioneers in California in its earliest days. I am profoundly gratified to find that I shall go out to my new field of labor with the recollections of what has occurred here to-night.

The Governor referred to Arizona as offering the most fruitful field we shall have for American enterprise for some time—a Territory that gives grand promises for the future—a sister that we shall feel proud to honor at no distant period in the galaxy of sovereign States. He gave as a sentiment: "Renewed life to the Society of Pioneers, and prosperity to our brethren wherever they may be found." [Applause and three cheers for General Fremont.]

Secretary Clark read the following letters from members

ciate and compatriot, the meridian of whose life was devoted
to deeds that have rendered his name famous wherever the
English language is read or spoken.

The "Great Golden Medal" for progress in the sciences,
sent to him by Baron Humboldt, on behalf of the King of
Prussia, his election as an honorary member of the Geographical Society of Berlin, the Founder's Medal, awarded him by
the Royal Geographical Society, of London, for his pre-eminent services in promoting the cause of geographical science,
attest the high estimation in which he is held by eminent men
of letters and of science in the Old World. His four exploring expeditions—the crowning efforts of his life—in the years
1842, '43, '45 and '48, the three latter being entirely across
that portion of this continent lying between the Father of
Waters and the Pacific Ocean, are grander in conception and
execution than any similar achievements of the present century, and have been prolific of results scarcely dreamed of by
their projector.

Westward, like the Star of Empire, the Pathfinder took his
way. His path was neither strewn nor embowered with roses.
Over arid plains, alkali deserts, through trackless forests and
yawning cañons, over the snow-capped Sierras, surrounded by
savage hordes, Fremont and his little band of modern Spar-
tans solved the great problem of a highway between the
Atlantic and the Pacific Oceans; and to-day, over a part of
this route, where lie the bones of many of those brave pioneers,
unmarked by mound or head-stone, the iron horse, with sinews
and nerves of steel and breath of steam, flies over the metallic
track so swiftly that space seems to be almost annihilated.

One of those brave Pathfinders, Charles Taplin, was my
fellow-townsman. When he left the old homestead, nestling
at the base of the Green Mountains, he was a wild, rollicking
youth, but when he returned home a few years later he was remarkably tame and docile; a striking exemplification of the
old adage that hunger and mule-steak will tame a crow.

General Fremont's identification with the early history of
California, having been elected Governor of that Territory by
the American settlers on July 4th, 1846, and his appointment

the same year by Commodore Stockton as military command-ant and civil Governor of that Territory, and his election by the Legislature of California, in December, 1849, as one of the two Senators to represent the new State in the Senate of the United States, render it meet and proper that we, his associates and compatriots, should congratulate him on his re-cent appointment as Governor of Arizona, the scene of a part of his early explorations.

His title to this office is not based upon mere political ser-vice, and the fact of his not being a "bloated bondholder," serves to show that he did not, while in office, prostitute his position to the purposes of private gain, and it must be grati-fying to the recipient to know that this somewhat tardy recog-nition by the government he has served so well meets with the general approval of the whole country.

In conclusion, I proffer the following sentiment, which I am quite sure my associates will heartily indorse: May the remaining days of our honored guest be as peaceful and tran-quil as his former have been active and illustrious.

Fraternally,
SAMUEL C. UPHAM.

WASHINGTON, D. C., July 30th, 1878.

FRANCIS D. CLARK, Secretary California Pioneers—*My Dear Sir:*—I thank you for remembering me in connection with the public reception tendered to General John C. Fremont, on the 1st of August, at the Sturtevant House, on the eve of his departure for his post of duty as Governor of Arizona.

It would afford me very great pleasure to form one of your guests on so pleasant an occasion, for General Fremont's name and fame are inseparably connected with the early days of California, the charm of which forms the bond of union to the Society of Pioneers, with its numerous branches all over the country.

As you foresaw, it will be impossible for me to come to New York on the 1st prox.; but I beg you to assure your guest of what he already knows, that he and his may always command

my office in any courtesy or assistance which will add honor to
his name or give him personal pleasure.

With great respect, your friend,

W. T. SHERMAN, General.

The reading of the above letters was interrupted by
shouts of applause and clapping of hands. The General
arose and made a special acknowledgment to the writers
of these two generous and warm-hearted letters.

Extract from a letter received from Mr. John Dolman,
of Philadelphia, one of the men of Commodore Stockton's
and General Fremont's command, in 1846, now a prominent lawyer of that city:

I am unfortunately unable to be with you to-morrow evening, at the Fremont reception. I had fully intended to be
present, but an argument fixed for three o'clock, P. M., to-
morrow, before a Master in Equity, will detain me beyond the
hour at which I could take the train for New York, and I
could not arrange for a postponement of the argument.

General John A. Sutter, President of the Society, writing
from his home at Lititz, Pa., said:

I think it is all right that our Society has tendered a reception to General Fremont, and greatly regret that a recent attack of rheumatism will keep me away.

Captain D. S. Babcock, President of the Pacific Mail
Steamship Company, wrote:

I regret exceedingly that circumstances will prevent my attendance at the dinner to General John C. Fremont, to-morrow
evening.

From Joseph Evans, Esq., of Newark, N. J., a former
member of Stevenson's regiment:

Circumstances may prevent my attending the dinner to
General John C. Fremont. It would afford me great pleasure
to assist in doing honor to the great Pathfinder, who is so pre-
eminently a Pioneer of California.

Thomas L. James, Esq., Postmaster of New York, replied as follows:

I thank you very cordially for your kindness in inviting me to the reception to General John C. Fremont by your Society, and unless prevented by some unforeseen official engagement, shall do myself the honor of being present.

Messrs. William R. Garrison, George Howes, John S. Ellis, Hon. Demas Strong, Hon. Jeremiah Sherwood, General James F. Curtis and several other members of the Society, sent their regrets, stating that absence from the city with their families would prevent their attendance upon so enjoyable an occasion.

At the conclusion of the reading of letters, the Chairman called upon ex-Governor Rodman M. Price for a speech, who, in response, related incidents about the occupation of Monterey in 1846. He spoke of the contemplated presence of General Fremont in Arizona as a promise of protection to all citizens. He felt sure that his former associate would serve with such distinction and prestige that thousands of emigrants would follow in his footsteps. He looked forward to the time when, in two or three years at the most, Arizona would cease to be a Territory and would become a State. Gov. Price also hinted at the possibility of the acquisition of the Mexican State of Sonora in the near future.

Colonel T. B. Thorpe, in answer to a call, made a very neat and complimentary speech, and in the course of his remarks compared General Fremont to Jason, put pointed out one great difference between the two. Jason was reported to have had the very worst wife ever known, while the General had the best that could have been chosen among the American people.

Secretary Clark, in a short speech, referred to the fact of this day being the thirty-second anniversary of "Stevenson's Regiment" going upon Governor's Island, New York harbor, preparatory to setting forth on the voyage to California, and that thirty-two years ago to-night the men took their first supper (bread and coffee) at the expense of Uncle Sam. Six of those men are with us to-night. [Secretary Clark always refers with pride to the old regiment.]

Hon. Wm. Colligan, who was present at the hoisting of the American flag at Monterey, was called upon for a speech, but said he *couldn't*. Mr. Colligan was attached to the command of Captain Fremont upon that terrible march over Saint Inis Mountains, December 25th, 1846, when the loss of animals was so great from the storm and cold. Colonel E. C. Kemble, another gentlemen present, was an officer in the same command.

Secretary Clark called attention to the fact that no name is so inseparably connected with the explorations of General Fremont as that of Kit Carson, but that gentleman had long since departed this life; but we had with us this evening a gentleman who made that celebrated ride, in company with Kit Carson, from California to New Mexico, in 1848. That gentleman was Colonel George D. Brewerton, a lieutenant in Stevenson's Regiment.

In response to the call of the assembled company Colonel Brewerton arose. In appearance he is tall and finely formed, with grizzled hair and whiskers, polished in his language, and would hardly be recognized as the same person whose portrait adorns the front of a work on Kansas published in 1856, dressed in buckskin shirt, cap and pants, with a rifle over his shoulder.

Colonel B. said he had sat listening this evening with intense interest to every word that had dropped from the lips of the speakers, and even now he could scarcely realize that it was not all a dream. Was he really awake, or was he once more amid the scenes of his younger days? days of so much pleasure and adventure upon the Pacific coast in the years of 1847 and '48· I am asked to speak of Kit Carson—not the Kit Carson we read about in the dime novels and other sensational literature of the present day, but Kit Carson as I knew him from close and intimate acquaintanceship amid the mountains and plains of the Pacific slope, and later, at his home, amid his family in New Mexico. In manner he was mild and gentlemanly, simple and childlike in his conversation, seldom or never speaking of himself or his exploits, but in an emergency as brave as a lion; cool, and betraying no sign of fear amidst the greatest dangers. That famous ride of Kit Carson's with his twenty companions, of which I was one, from California to New Mexico, in 1848, recalls an incident that transpired, which clearly shows the character of the man. One morning our small party was confronted by a band of two hundred and fifty hostile Apache Indians. Kit coolly surveyed his ground, and at a glance took in the situation. Drawing a line on the ground to their rear, he exclaimed, in that tone peculiar to Western trappers: "Thar, thar; let no man step across that line. Our business is in front of us!" And, after a short and determined fight the hostiles were dispersed. A few days succeeding this event I asked Kit how he felt at the moment of discovering the Indians. He replied: "I thought we should lose our ha'r before sundown;" and yet no one could detect in his actions the slightest sign to denote such a feeling. Colonel B. said he never tired of speaking of that noble and devoted associate of the Pathfinder, Kit Carson.

Colonel E. F. Burton, Deputy Surveyor of the port of New York and a member of the Society, being called upon for "a few remarks," said, "It was a great pleasure for this Society, the Associated Pioneers of—well, I cannot recall the balance of our title, but friend Clark over in the corner can give it to you, as he has studied it all by heart— to have General Fremont with us this evening, but he really did not think it was us that did the honor, for all the honor came from General Fremont himself. It was he that had honored us. He had a name that was famous the world over." Colonel Burton continued in his usual humorous strain, which caused the most deafening shouts of laughter and applause. His recollections of the "Days of '49," are always listened to with unusual interest.

Colonel E. C. Kemble, in answer to a call, made a short speech, in which he spoke of his arrival in California on July 31st, 1846, in the ship *Brooklyn,* in company with Mr. Samuel Brannan and the Mormon emigrants. He gave a very graphic account of that terrible march down the coast in the month of December, 1846, and of their sufferings on the night of Christmas, when officers and men laid down in a drenching storm without shelter or food. Colonel Kemble said that until Mr. Colligan arose he had supposed he and General Fremont were the only ones present who participated in that march. Colonel Kemble also spoke very feelingly of his old comrade and partner, Mr. Edward Gilbert, a lieutenant of Stevenson's regiment, both of whom were connected with the *Alta California* at the date of Mr. Gilbert's death, the circumstances of which are too well remembered by all old Californians.

Other speeches were made by Messrs. J. P. Curry, John P. Bidwell (nephew of Mr. John Bidwell, of Chico, California), Judge Curtis, a '49er, and Colonel W. L. Tidball.

Mr. James J. McCloskey, spoke of the recent death of Colonel Joseph E. Lawrence, a gentleman who was so well known in San Francisco, and referred to the fact that Colonel Lawrence was laid between the graves of one brother-in-law and one cousin, both of whom had occupied the position of Mayor of this great city.

Among the pleasant features of the evening was the sending from the festive board of a magnificent basket of flowers, with the name " Jessie " inscribed in floral letters, to Mrs. General Fremont at her residence in West Twenty-second Street, and in about one hour the following response was returned, written upon one of Mrs. F.'s cards:

My grateful thanks for the lovely form of remembrance
from the Pioneers.

JESSIE BENTON FREMONT.

The reception closed at a late hour, with long continued
cheers for the veteran American explorer and the chief
hero of the romantic history of the discovery, possession
and settlement of the gold regions of the great West.
The whole entertainment reflected great credit upon the
New York Society of California Pioneers, and General
Fremont will take fresh courage from this kindly greeting
of his old friends.

RECEPTION TO HON. PHILIP A. ROACH.

The banquet—General H. Gates Gibson's address of welcome—
Senator Roach's response—Letters of regret—Notables present
—Speeches, etc.

ON the arrival of Hon. Philip A. Roach, ex-President
of the "Society of California Pioneers," in New York, in
the summer of 1876, he was tendered a reception by "THE
ASSOCIATED PIONEERS OF THE TERRITORIAL DAYS OF
CALIFORNIA," at the Sturtevant House, in that city, on
the evening of June 19th.

RECEPTION
TO THE
Hon. PHILIP A. ROACH,
OF SAN FRANCISCO.

Ex-President of the Society of California Pioneers,

On his First Visit to the Atlantic Coast since the Spring of 1849, by

The Associated Pioneers of the Territorial Days of California,

At their Head-quarters, Sturtevant House, New York City,

Monday Evening, June 19th, 1876,

At 9 o'clock.

FRANCIS D. CLARK,	H G GIBSON,
Secretary and Treasurer.	*Brevet Brig.-Gen. U S A , President.*

The following account of the reception and banquet is
compiled from a report in the *New York Herald* of the
next morning, and memoranda furnished by Secretary
Francis D. Clark:

A reception was given last evening by the Pioneers of
California, at the Sturtevant House, to Hon. Philip A.
Roach, of San Francisco, this being his first visit to the

(497)

Atlantic coast since the spring of 1849. It is not at all likely that the people who knew Mr. Roach as a young man in this city previous to the memorable year of '49 will now recognize him. Twenty-seven years, under any circumstances, alter a man's appearance, but in the case of Mr. Roach they have worked additional wonders. They have left him as straight, as hale and as hearty as the day he set sail for the gold-land, but have turned his hair, which is long and thick, to a snowy whiteness, preserving withal his ruddy, rosy complexion—and have added many pounds to his weight. When he entered the parlor last evening, where were assembled from fifty to sixty of his old comrades of the territorial days, in spite of the evident advantage which was on their side, Mr. Roach seemed to have the best of them in the matter of recognition. The reception was unostentatious and without ceremony. General H. G. Gibson, U. S. A., President of the Society, took the veteran's arm and led the way to the supper-room, the others following. An elegant supper, provided under the direction of the Messrs. Leland, was devoured with a relish, the conversation at all points turning upon California, and many were the laughs and jokes of old times that passed down the table. Wine and cigars being brought, General Gibson arose and delivered the following eloquent address of welcome:

FELLOW-CALIFORNIANS:—You are aware of the purpose for which we have assembled this evening—to welcome our esteemed guest and brother-Pioneer, on the occasion of his return to the scenes of his boyhood, after an absence of twenty-seven years; and on a mission which commends itself to the approval of all, who have at heart the welfare of California and of our country. You will excuse me, therefore, whilst I address a few words of greeting and remembrance to my old friend and associate of the halcyon days of the Golden Land.

SENATOR ROACH:—As an old and honored citizen of California, and as one of her prominent Pioneers, the Associated

Pioneers of her Territorial Days have tendered you this reception; and in their name, I bid you a cordial, hearty welcome,
on this your first visit to the Atlantic coast, since you left it in
the heyday of youth, to participate in the exciting and glorious
scenes and events of 1849. This duty is especially grateful to
me, not only as your personal friend of auld lang syne, but also
as the friend and companion of your brother, who, in the early
days of California, perished in the wild mountain-stream, and
who sleeps in the ancient chapel of the Mission, founded by the
fathers of the grand old church of Christendom, and beside
whose tomb the praise of song, and prayer, and incense ever
ascend to the Almighty. In this greeting of mine to-night,
however, I would not recall aught save the delightful recollections, connected with him, with you, and with the many episodes
and incidents of our life in California in years long past. Familiar names, faces and scenes come to mind, with pleasurable emotions, and with almost vivid reality. Monterey and its old
redoubt—historic from association with the American conquest,
and where many of the noted and unnoted heroes of the nation
once quartered; the little social gatherings, at which with
"John Phœnix," Alfred Sully, Selim Woodworth, Jack Hamilton, Joe Boston, William Chevers and Theron Per Lee, the
wit and "fun grew fast and furious," amid "riot most un-
couth," though not unpleasant. And then, too, with Tom
Roach and Jack Durivage, traversing the beautiful valley of
the San Joaquin; with the hills and plains in rich verdure clad,
and "bright and shining flowers," of every hue and exquisite variety, "springing from out the silent ground;" or in the
graceful groves of oak, and on the borders of crystal, golden
streams, where in the quiet evening-camp, Tom Roach

> "lent to the rhyme of the poet
> The beauty of his voice;
> And the night *was* filled with music,
> And the cares that infest the day,"

were dispersed, by his sweet melody and song of "Ochone!
Widow Machree!" More I might revive of these

> "pictures of memory, long since hung away,
> And faded by age, or the dust of the past;"

more I might recall of "the friends so linked in love together;" but I forbear lest "chewing the cud of sweet and bitter fancies" and recollections, mingled as they are in human life, I should touch those tender chords of feeling, whose music "flows with" sacred and "sweet meanings for the heart alone." But our hearts must have become cold, indeed, from contact with the world, sadly hardened by the cares and sorrows of life, did they fail to respond to the thoughts and emotions aroused by your presence with us.

As the representative of the Pioneer element of California; as the last Alcalde and first Mayor of her ancient capital; as a leading journalist and distinguished Senator of the noble Golden State, we are glad and proud to do you all honor; but the memories of sweet friendships, formed and cemented, amid the novel and inspiring scenes of our youth in California, when the heart was fresh and sincere, and "unspotted from the world," require of us a greeting and welcome, as warm as that which I now give you, on behalf of this Society. If I have failed to express, in fitting language, all that I feel on this occasion, or to convey to you, in glowing words, a most cordial welcome, you must attribute it to the poverty of the brain, not the poverty of the heart. May God bless and prosper you all the days of your life; may greater honors in the future await you, and may you ever find in the hearts of your friends in California and elsewhere, a corner as fresh and green, as that which you find in our own to-night. [Great applause.]

When Mr. Roach arose to respond, tears filled his eyes and his voice was husky with emotions he tried hard to conceal. "Fellow-pioneers," said he, "I have lived an active life in California, and I have not often been so much taken by surprise as to lose my speech, but the General has surprised me to that extent just now; he has recalled memories and awakened old feelings in my heart that check my utterance. I see before me many of the men who assisted in making the State of California. I see the first editor, I see the old Collector. My mind wanders back to the time when we were all brothers together. I feel twenty-seven years younger to-night. Gentlemen, you must excuse me until I can collect my thoughts and quell this emotion." And Mr. Roach sat down amid a storm of applause that quite frightened the waiters, and made it appear that the guests were still hardy young pioneers instead of quite middle-aged and sedate old men.

The Secretary, Mr. Francis D. Clark, next read many letters of regret. General Joe Hooker sent his greeting and his sympathy. General Sherman regretted that a recent visit to West Point made it impossible for him to leave his post at this time. Colonel Burton, General Edward F. Beale and Mark Twain likewise sent regrets.

The following is General Beale's letter:

LAFAYETTE SQUARE,
WASHINGTON, D. C., June 17th, 1876.

FRANCIS D. CLARK, Esq., Secretary of the Society of "The Associated Pioneers of the Territorial Days of California," New York—*Dear Sir:*—It is with much regret that I am compelled to deny myself the pleasure of meeting you at the head-quarters of our Society, on the 19th, to honor the return to the East, after so prolonged an absence, of the Hon. Philip A. Roach.

The high respect I have for Mr. Roach, his eminent services to the State we all love so much, and his honorable career during so many years' residence in California, all combine to render my regret at not being able to attend the more keen. I have had the honor, pleasure and satisfaction of Mr. Roach's acquaintance for very many years and, although I do not agree with him in political sentiment, I believe there is no purer or more patriotic citizen on the Pacific coast, and I think we can well honor him who has so long and so ably stood as one of the best representative men of dear old California.

With great respect, your friend and obedient servant,

E. F. BEALE.

A letter was also read from Samuel C. Upham, of Philadelphia, extending an offer from that gentleman to write an appropriate song to the air of " Auld Lang Syne," to be sung at the grand re-union of Californians, which is to be held at Philadelphia on the 9th of September next, which offer was received with applause. After this, speeches followed fast and furious. Mr. E. C. Kemble, an early Californian editor, one of the founders of the *Alta California*, made one of some length, in which he referred to a thousand things dear to the memory of his listeners, anecdotes of "Bob" Semple, who thought "California was governed too much," and of old "Bob" Parker, sending the table off in roars of laughter, and others of a different kind, exciting tenderer emotions.

At one end of the room hung the old pioneer banner, and until late at night the gentlemen sat at the table gazing upon the emblematic bear, telling tales of long ago and discussing the present and future prosperity of the "land of gold." Among the guests were Mr. John Sickels, Mr. W. B. Farwell, General Thomas D. Johns, John A. Godfrey, O. H. Pierson, W. M. Walton, Colonel James E. Nuttman, John J. Hager, General James F. Curtis, E. C. Kemble, Hon. J. Sherwood, J. H. Butler, H. B. Hawkins, Hon. Beverly C. Sanders, Benjamin W. Jenness, E. W. Crowell, John Gault, Robert W. Dowling, Alfred T. Goodell, and other '49ers.

Later in the evening, Mr. Roach was again called to his feet in response to some remarks made by gentlemen present, who had referred to the fact that, notwithstanding Mr. Roach was a bachelor, he had always been the champion of the female sex, and had fought hard in the legislative halls of California to insure to them all just and womanly rights, and that as far back as 1852 he had been the author and advocate of a law, still in force in the Golden State, permitting women to transact business in their own name, and to enjoy the fruit of their industry; the law protecting them against the abuse or extravagance of dissolute husbands, and that during the past winter, as Senator from San Francisco, he had obtained the passage of a law punishing wife-beating with the lash. The response of Mr. Roach was listened to with marked attention, and when he again resumed his seat, the very walls resounded with applause.

Hon. Beverly C. Sanders, who was one of the early Collectors of the port of San Francisco, arose in response to the call of the company, and made some very humorous remarks. Among other things, he said that when he was an officer of the government, the officers, as a general rule, considered that the money which came into their hands belonged to the government, but they had arrived at a much higher degree of intelligence since that time.

The banquet was an enjoyable affair, and will long be remembered by the '49ers of the Atlantic coast.

DEDICATION OF THE LICK MONUMENT AT FREDERICKSBURG, PA.

En route to Fredericksburg—Reminiscences of the town—Genealogy
of the Lick family—The house in which James Lick was born—
The old graveyard—Cedar Hill Cemetery—Unveiling and dedication of the monument—Addresses by Colonel J. P. S. Gobin, of
Lebanon, and Samuel C. Upham, of Philadelphia—Knights Templar inauguration ceremonies.

THE following report of the dedication of the Lick
Monument was prepared expressly for, and published
originally in, *The Pioneer*, at San José, California :

PHILADELPHIA, April 25th, 1878.

FRIEND MURGOTTEN :—Presuming that an account of
the unveiling and dedication of the Lick Monument, at
Fredericksburg, Lebanon County, Pennsylvania, on the
22d instant, will interest the readers of *The Pioneer*, I will
endeavor to perform the task as briefly as possible. I left
Philadelphia on Saturday last, 20th instant, at half-past
three o'clock, P. M., on the Reading Railroad, and at Lebanon took the Tremont branch road for Jonestown, 7 miles
distant, where I arrived at eight o'clock the same evening,
and remained over night. Jonestown, situated on both
sides of Swatara Creek, is a thrifty inland town, consisting of a single street and a population of about eight
hundred inhabitants. After breakfast on the following
(Sunday) morning, I engaged a team, and with Mr. Simon
Desh as guide and interpreter, started for Fredericksburg,
about 4 miles distant, and 85 miles from Philadelphia,
where I arrived at about ten o'clock, A. M. A *patois*,

(504)

called by the natives "Pennsylvania Dutch," is spoken almost exclusively in Lebanon and Berks Counties, and an interpreter is required by any one not familiar with that language. The scenery *en route* was magnificent. Large fields of waving grain gladdened the eye in every direction, and the apple and pear-blossoms perfumed the air with their fragrance. The land between Jonestown and Fredericksburg is mostly owned by the Dunkards, a thrifty but parsimonious sect. Mr. Desh, my companion, informed me that whenever a coin of the realm came into their possession, they squeezed it so tightly that the Bird of Freedom invariably shrieked.* Whatever may be said of their religious and social habits, they certainly own the most magnificent farms I have ever seen, and their double-banked Swiss barns and other outbuildings are in keeping with their farms. In fact, the entire Lebanon Valley, 60 miles in length by 20 miles in breadth, is the garden-spot of the Keystone State.

Fredericksburg, formerly Stumptown, is one of the oldest towns in the Lebanon Valley, and was founded by Frederick Stump, a pioneer and Indian-fighter, in 1755. In after years, as the town increased in wealth and population, the old burghers dropped the name of Stumptown and dignified it with the title of Fredericksburg, derived from Stump's Christian name. The old villagers don't like to be reminded of the former name of their town. If any one desires to know whether "cuss words" are obsolete, let him say Stumptown to a Fredericksburger. It is said of Stump, that while on a hunting expedition in the vicinity of Harrisburg, he amused himself one morning by slaying, single-handed, ten drunken Indians, whose bodies he shoved

---

* Since the above was written, I have been informed by Mr. John H. Lick, that on Dedication day, Mr. Gible, living on the Jonestown road, and Mr Oberholtzer, residing in the eastern part of the town, dined one hundred and fifty persons, for which they declined to receive any remuneration; thus verifying the aphorism, that the devil is not as black as he is sometimes painted.

under the ice and they floated down the Susquehanna River to their happy hunting-grounds.

Fredericksburg contains at this time nine hundred inhabitants, and, like Jonestown, is surrounded by a rich farming country. Several of its citizens count their wealth by hundreds of thousands of dollars. The brothers J. W. and E. Grove, who own the largest ironworks in Pennsylvania, located at Danville, are natives of this town, and I visited them at their spacious mansion on its southern outskirts. The Groves own one of the largest, if not the very largest, farm in Lebanon County. It is about a mile in width and extends several miles in length. They are millionaires. John H. Lick, before the death of his father, was reported to be worth $25,000, made in the mercantile business in this quaint old town.

The town is mostly built on Main or Market Street, a quarter of a mile in length, running east and west, in the centre of which there is a small square or market-place. Centre, Mechanic and Pinegrove Streets cross Market Street at right angles, running north and south. The buildings are mostly frame, with an occasional brick front blushing between its whitewashed neighbors, and forming an agreeable contrast. At the south-west corner of Market and Pinegrove Streets, is a large plot of ground surrounded on two sides by horse-chestnut trees with whitewashed trunks, owned by John H. Lick.

About midway, and on the north side of Market Square, stands a two-story red frame house, somewhat rickety with age, in which James Lick's father kept a hotel some fifty years ago. Against the small glass window over the front door is "J. Lick," formed of rudely-carved letters. Half a square east of the old Lick Hotel, on the same side of the street, stands a recently-built two-story brick building, on the site of the house in which the mother of James Lick died in the year 1812. The old house was destroyed by a conflagration in the year 1827, in which more than one-

From a Photo by Bradley & Rulofson, San Francisco

half of the buildings of the town were burned. James Lick was born on the 25th of August, 1796, in a log or block-house, still standing, about two miles west of the village of Fredericksburg.* Some ten or fifteen years since, Mr. Lick wrote to one of his old friends in Fredericksburg, asking if the old house in which he was born could be taken down and shipped to California. He said he desired to show the people of the Golden State the house in which he was born. On examination, the logs of the old structure were found to be too much decayed for removal, and the project was abandoned.

John Lick, father of James, was born on September 13th, 1765, in Montgomery County, Pa., and removed to Fredericksburg, then Stumptown, when a young man. He was a carpenter and joiner by profession, and one of the most ingenious workers in wood in that section of the state. He married in Fredericksburg, and both he and his wife died there. James inherited his father's mechanical talent. Their remains lie in the old Reformed and Lutheran graveyard, on the east side of Pinegrove Street, on a slight eminence, commanding a fine view of the village. Their graves are some twenty feet apart, without headstones, each being inclosed by a plain iron railing, erected by their grandson, John H. Lick, in the year 1867.

During the afternoon, I made the acquaintance of John Desh, a hale old man of seventy-eight years, who never enjoyed the luxury of a law-suit in his life. He smokes and chews tobacco, and occasionally indulges in a glass of lager for his stomach's sake. Jacob Weaber, also aged seventy-eight years, is a chum of Desh, and the two old

---

* The house in which James Lick was born, like the birthplace of Homer, seems to be a mooted question. I have the authority of George Brutzman, John Desh and Jacob Buchmoyer, old residents of Fredericksburg, for stating that James Lick was born in the old block-house, two miles west of the village of Fredericksburg. John H. Lick is of the opinion that his father was not born in that house. *Quien sabe?*

burghers are fast friends. They are the men whom the poet probably had in his mind's eye when he wrote—

> "Their hours in cheerful *smoking* flew,
>   Nor envy nor ambition knew."

James Lick visited Fredericksburg only once after his departure in the year 1819, and no one living in the old town at this time can say positively in what year he returned, but incline to the belief that it was in the year 1832—"thar or tharabouts." One old burgher informed me that he was loaded down with doubloons, which he carried in belts around his body. He came to Fredericksburg with a horse and buggy, which on his departure, about two weeks after his arrival, he presented to his brother William. The horse died soon after; the buggy was then sold, and the proceeds, $100, were given to John H. Lick when he attained his majority. This amount represented one-third of the capital with which he started business. His education was paid for by one of his uncles. Jacob Buchmoyer, a cordwainer, now in his seventy-eighth year, was an intimate friend and schoolmate of James Lick. I had, with the aid of an interpreter, a long talk with the old gentleman, who showed me a relic he had preserved many years and which he still treasures highly. It was a piece of oné of the leg-bones of the horse James Lick presented to his brother William, on his visit to Fredericksburg in the year 1832.

John H. Lick lived in Lebanon and Centre Counties from the time of his birth, June 30th, 1818, until he joined his *paterfamilias*, in California, in 1855. On his first visit to the Golden State, John remained with his father about three years. In about one year after his return to the old homestead he again visited his father in California, who sent him on a tour in Europe; after visiting Germany, France and England, he returned to California, where he remained with his father until August, 1871, when he re-

From a Photo by Houseworth & Co, San Francisco

John H. Lick

turned East, where he remained until the death of his father, in the fall of 1876, when he again visited California, where he now resides. When John received his father's summons from California, in 1852, he was engaged in mercantile business in his native town, and replied that he could not dispose of his store and settle up his business without great pecuniary sacrifice. The following characteristic reply was soon afterward received from the senior Lick : "*If you can't sell your store, give it away. Come at once. I have enough for both of us!*" It is perhaps needless to add that John went, but not until the summer of 1855.

From the fall of 1859 until 1863, John had the entire supervision of his father's flour-mill, near Alviso. The net profits during those three years were $52,000. In consequence of ill-health, John returned East in the year 1863, and during his absence, owing to some trouble with his successor, his father closed the mill. In 1868, the old gentleman offered to sell the property, which had cost him $500,000, for $250,000, but could not find a purchaser, and in the year 1872 he donated it to the "Tom Paine Society," of Boston. The Paincites, finding that they had an elephant on their hands, sold the property to Pfister & Waterman for $18,000, who converted it into a paper-mill. The sale of the mill displeased Mr. Lick very much.

John H. Lick is highly respected by his fellow-townsmen, and his return from California will be hailed by them with exceeding great joy. I am indebted to Mr. George Brutzman, of Fredericksburg, for the following genealogy of John, father of James, Lick's family :

John Lick, father of James Lick, born September 13th, 1765, and died June 13th, 1831.

James Lick, the eldest son, born August 25th, 1796, in Stumptown, now Fredericksburg, Dauphin County, Pa. (Lebanon County, in which Fredericksburg is situated, was formerly a portion of Dauphin County.)   Mr. Lick's sponsor or godfather was John Gettel.

The second child was born July 25th, 1797.   It died in infancy.

John Lick, born May 24th, 1798, in Bethel Township, Dauphin County, Pa.   The sponsors were Christian Long and Molly Gettel.

Catharine Lick, born January 8th, 1800, in Bethel Township, Dauphin County, Pa.   Catharine Licken was her godmother.

Sarah Lick, born August 27th, 1802, in Bethel Township, Dauphin County, Pa.   Sponsors, Conrad Reinoehl and wife.

Jacob Lick, born January 25th, 1804.   Baptized March 1st, 1804.   Sponsor, Jacob Weaber.

Margretta Lick, born September 27th, 1806, and baptized on the 6th of the following March.   Margretta Weaber officiated as godmother.

William Lick, born February 11th, 1808, in Bethel Township, Lebanon County, Pa., and baptized April 16th, the same year, by the Rev. George Lochman.   His sponsors were his parents.

Margretta Lick, born April 11th, 1816, in Bethel Township, Lebanon County, Pa.

Cedar Hill Cemetery, in which the Lick Monument is erected, is situated on an elevated piece of ground, embracing about four acres, about a quarter of a mile north-east of Market Square.   William, brother of James, was the projector of the cemetery.   The land was purchased and inclosed in the year 1869.   The first person buried in the cemetery was Daniel H. Eisenhaur, September 20th, 1869.   Since that time, to April 22d, 1878, one hundred and sixty interments have been made in the cemetery. About one hundred feet west of the Lick Monument, in a plot of ground inclosed by a tasteful iron railing, lie the remains of William Lick.   A plain obelisk of Italian marble, about ten feet in height, bears the following inscription:

> ### WILLIAM LICK,
> BORN FEBRUARY 11TH, 1808,
> DIED DECEMBER 21ST, 1872.
> Aged 64 years, 10 mo's, 10 days.

The Lick Monument stands in the eastern section of the cemetery, in a commanding position, and its symmetrical shaft, surmounted by the Goddess of Liberty, resting her right hand on a shield and grasping with her left a partially-folded flag, can be seen for many miles. It stands on a secure foundation, composed of no less than sixty-five perches of stone laid in cement. The interior is solid brick work—ten thousand bricks being used to fill it up. The monument contains one hundred and fifteen pieces of Scotch granite, from the famed Aberdeen quarry, several of which weigh over two tons each, and its entire weight is one hundred and seventy-five tons. It also contains nine statues of Italian marble, the Goddess of Liberty being eight and a half feet in height. There are also four large urns of the same material. The contractor and sculptor, Mr. Robert Reid, of Montreal, Canada, shipped the monument by rail to Jonestown, four miles distant from Fredericksburg, it was transported from that place to the cemetery by wagons and other vehicles, furnished by the farmers of the neighborhood. Three experts came with the monument, and were engaged about two months in its erection. The monument is sixteen feet square at its base, and its extreme height is thirty-five feet and six inches. At the four corners, a few feet above the base, standing on projections or pedestals, are four life-size female figures, each holding a scroll, on which is engraved respectively the following appropriate Scriptural mottoes: At the south-east corner, "Blessed are the dead which die in the Lord;" south-west corner, "He being dead, yet speak-

eth;" north-east corner, "He giveth His beloved sleep;"
north-west corner, "Blessed are they that do His com-
mandments." On the south or front side, four feet above
the base, is the word "LICK," in raised letters, six inches
in length, with polished surface. In niches on each of
its four sides, some twelve feet above the base, are life-size
statues of a Continental soldier in uniform, and Faith,
Hope and Charity. Above the head of the soldier are the
words "VALLEY FORGE," in raised letters, with polished
surface. On the four corners, two or three feet lower than
the statues, stand four large and partially-draped urns.
On the south or front side, midway between the word
"LICK" and the statue of the Continental soldier, is a
tablet three by five feet, with polished surface, bearing the
following inscription in gilt letters:

COMMEMORATIVE
of the services rendered by
WILLIAM LICK,
(GRANDFATHER OF JAMES LICK,)
AT VALLEY FORGE
and in other struggles of the Revolutionary War
for American Independence:
Who died in Montgomery County, Pa.,
at the age of
One Hundred and Four Years.

There is a tablet of the same size on each of the three
other sides. The one on the east side bears the following
inscription:

IN MEMORY OF
CATHARINE LICK,
(SISTER OF JAMES LICK,)
Who was born at Fredericksburg, Penna.,
January 8th, 1800;
Died at Manheim, Penna.,
April 10th, 1862.

LICK MONUMENT, FREDERICKSBURG, PA.

On the north side :

IN MEMORY OF
JOHN LICK,
(FATHER OF JAMES LICK,)
Who was born September 13th, 1765 ;
Died June 13th, 1831.
Also in Memory of
SARAH LICK, (HIS WIFE,)
Who died at Fredericksburg, A. D., 1812,
Aged Forty Years.

On the west side :

THIS MONUMENT, ERECTED IN 1876,
BY
JAMES LICK,
WHO WAS BORN AT
FREDERICKSBURG, PENNA.,
August 25th, 1796 ;
DIED, AT SAN FRANCISCO, CALIFORNIA,
October 1st, 1876.

The monument was erected at a cost of $20,000, and, as a work of art, reflects great credit upon the sculptor. For beauty of design and elegance of finish, it is unequaled by any monument of its size in the United States, and the gentlemen composing the Lick Trust have shown excellent judgment and taste in their selection of a design which has been so skillfully and artistically executed by the contractor.

During Sunday the wind blew a gale from the north-west, and Mr. Reid was fearful that he would not be able to keep the monument covered until the time for unveiling arrived, but fortunately the wind went down with the set-

ting sun, and he retired to his couch a happy man. Mr.
Reid and myself stopped at the same hotel—"The Traveler's Repose"—and occupied the same room. We retired
early, and before performing our evening devotions, put a
little old Otard, furnished by Mr. R., where we thought it
would do the most good. I slept soundly until midnight,
when a discordant fife and dilapidated kettle-drum awoke
the whole town and rendered the remainder of the night
perfectly hideous. My room-mate was uncharitable enough
to wish that the persistent fifer would blow his "blarsted"
head off, and your correspondent seconded the motion.

At an early hour on Monday morning, the people from
the adjacent towns commenced flocking into Fredericksburg, and the old town was thoroughly awakened from its
sleep of one hundred and fifty years. At noon there were
over six thousand persons present, and the two hotels, private
residences and streets were filled to their utmost capacity.

The dedication ceremonies were under the supervision
of a committee of citizens of Fredericksburg, with Colonel
J. P. S. Gobin, of Lebanon, as chairman. Colonel Gobin
was the head and front of the affair, and most admirably
did he perform the duties intrusted to him. In addition
to being chairman of the committee of arrangements, he
was orator of the day, and also Commander of the Hermit
Commandery, Knights Templar, of Lebanon. Chief Marshal, Dr. A. W. Shultz, assisted by Augustus Behney, J.
Kephart and I. J. W. Fox, formed the procession on Pinegrove Street, at one o'clock, P. M., in the following order:

1 Committee of Reception.
2. Committee of Arrangements.
3. S. C. Upham, representative of "The Society of California Pioneers," and Mr. Robert Reid, contractor and sculptor of the
   monument.
4. Perseverance Band, of Lebanon, Pa.
5. Grand Lodge Officers, Knights Templar; Grand Recorder, Chas.
   E. Meyer; Grand Treasurer, M. Richards Mucklé; Grand Prelate, Rev. D. Washburn.

6. Hermit Commandery, No. 24, Knights Templar, 76 men, Adam Rise, Eminent Commander.
7. Invited Guests.
8. Fredericksburg Band.
9. Thirteen girls dressed in white, with blue sashes and red ribbons, carrying a flag.
10. Millersburg Band.
11. Citizens, four abreast.
12. Choir, composed of twelve ladies and six gentlemen.
13. Pinegrove Band.

The procession marched down Pinegrove Street to Market, down Market to Centre, out Centre to Locust, down Locust to Mechanic, down Mechanic to Market, up Market to Pinegrove, and out Pinegrove to the cemetery.

CEREMONIES AT THE CEMETERY.

1. Music.
2. Prayer by the Rev. Daniel Washburn, Grand Prelate of the Knights Templar, of Pennsylvania.
3. "Star Spangled Banner," by a choir of ladies and gentlemen.
4. Address by Colonel J. P. S. Gobin, of Lebanon, Pennsylvania.
5. Music.
6. Address by Samuel C. Upham, of Philadelphia, representative of "The Society of California Pioneers."
7. Dedication of Monument, by Hermit Commandery.
8. Music.
9. Benediction, by Grand Prelate Washburn.

At the conclusion of the music by the Perseverance Band, the Knights were ordered to uncover, and Grand Prelate Washburn delivered, in a deep and sonorous voice, the following impressive and appropriate prayer:

Almighty Lord and Saviour, before the mountains were brought forth, or ever the earth and the world were made, Thou art God from everlasting to everlasting. In Thy name we assemble, even the name of Immanuel, under the auspices of the Masonic Brotherhood of Knights Templar of Pennsylvania, to dedicate this monument of James Lick, with his ancestors and kindred. To Thee, O God, in whom we live, do we give thanks for our being, our reason, and all the faculties of our souls and bodies. We thank Thee for all the blessings of this land of plenty, of liberty, and of peace. We thank Thee that rising from this mountain site of our Keystone State is seen this splendid token of a perpetual Union extending unbroken from the Atlantic to the Pacific. With Faith, Hope and Charity, its defender stands aloft in grateful presence under the ægis of triumphant Freedom. To Thee for the State, for the Church, for the family institution so potent in its beneficence, and the filial affection that in consequence has enshrined itself here in marble, we give thanks, and humbly pray their blessings upon all our generations. Be with us, O God of our fathers, this day and ever. Bless everywhere our fraternity. Bless the President and Governor, and all in authority. Let the Gospel of our redemption shine unto all nations, and may as many as have received it live as becomes it. Bless the work of all who are here, making these valleys stand so thick with corn that they shall laugh and sing. And finally, our God of Peace who brought again from the dead our Lord Jesus Christ, the Great Shepherd of the sheep, through the blood of the everlasting covenant, make us all perfect to do Thy will, working in us that which is well pleasing in Thy sight, through Jesus Christ, to whom be glory forever and ever. Amen.

At the conclusion of the prayer, the "Star Spangled Banner" was rendered in fine style by the choir. Colonel J. P. S. Gobin, orator of the day, being introduced by Hon. F. M. Bachman, delivered the following eloquent address:

FRIENDS AND FELLOW-CITIZENS:—The occasion of our assembling at this time and in this beautiful cemetery, is one fraught with more than ordinary interest. Representative men from the far distant shores of the Pacific; officials from our own and other States; numbers of those who bear the banner of the cross, rendered immortal by the martial deeds of the Knights of the Temple of old, amid the sands of Syria— a vast concourse of our fellow-citizens from the surrounding country, have gathered to show their appreciation of the heart

feeling evidenced by these ceremonies. And beautiful, graceful, enduring as is the monument that rises before us, and
which we are about to dedicate, it is but typical of the sentiment which its erection illustrates. That sentiment is love of
home—love of the spot which gave you birth, and with which
every thought of your childhood's days are identified; and
above all, that holy, undying love for father and mother, for
brother and sisters, for family ties and the old hearthstone,
which time, with all its attendant vicissitudes, cannot obliterate
or drive from the soul, but which, amid prosperity or adversity,
is the green spot toward which the pilgrim's mind is ever
directed. Aye, as each revolution of the grand cycle carries
us nearer our ultimate goal, bringing with it increased age and
additional responsibilities, it is the thought of those who gave
us life, perhaps dwelling afar off in some distant clime, whose
loved forms we have not beheld, save in our dreams, for many
years, but whose images are impressed indelibly upon our
hearts, that causes the blood to course more rapidly and all
the better feelings of our nature make themselves manifest.
Could we but look into the mind of him whose memory is to
be commemorated by our ceremonies to-day, as, after many
days of weary wanderings upon unknown seas, and amid
storms and sunshine, he beheld accumulating around him the
fruits of his industry, energy and genius, doubtless we would
have beheld there a longing for you grand old. mountains,
those green fields, the streets of your quiet, beautiful village,
the familiar greeting of the friends of his boyhood, and more
prominently than all others, the desire to fulfill to the utmost
the Divine injunction, Honor thy father and mother. As the
result of this we have the beautiful structure before us, and the
interested concourse of people to witness its dedication.

Another thought suggested, and which cannot fail to impress
the most casual observer, is in the fact, that in the erection of
this monument we have so striking an illustration of the wonderful growth of our nation, and what is susceptible of being
done by a citizen within it, of energy, genius and pluck. In
imagination, and passing before you as a panorama, you can
behold the boy James Lick, the child in your village streets,

30

gamboling amidst your fields, indulging in all the sports of merry boyhood's days. At an early age he sallies forth to test the world, to be the architect of his own future, and in the Golden State we behold him in his mature age, reaching out as it were into the old world for the products of their skill and art, with which to beautify and adorn the graves of those of his own blood. It is the greeting of the man in the young East to the boy in the older West; of the man of accumulated wealth in California to the memory of the aspiring boy of the old Keystone State.

From a work entitled "Representative Men of California," we learn some facts relative to him :

James Lick was born in the village of Fredericksburg, within a short distance of where we are now assembled, on the 25th of August, 1796, of German ancestry. His grandfather was one of that worthy race who found a home in the infant colonies, to be devoted to freedom, and soon, thereafter, upon the battle-field of the Revolution, proved his courage and patriotism. The sufferings of this aged veteran at Valley Forge evidently made a deep impression upon the young lad, as he listened to their recital—impressions which were never effaced, and which we find, to-day, transferred to the monument upon which his name stands so prominent. The Continental soldier is before you as the representative of the acts of his ancestors in the days which tried men's souls. Near this historic ground— Norristown—the father of James Lick was born. He married, at an early day, a Miss Long, and emigrated to Fredericksburg, the birthplace of James. His education was such as was taught in the small towns of the interior of that day—sufficiently meagre, none can doubt. We next find him working as an organ-maker in Hanover, Pa., already exhibiting the energy and desire for adventure which distinguished his after life. In 1819, he obtained employment in the establishment of Joseph Hiskey, a prominent piano manufacturer in Baltimore. While here he met a young man named Meyer, in search of employment, and between the two was formed a friendship which lasted through life. The lad Meyer, of 1819, is Conrad Meyer, of Philadelphia, to-day, the celebrated piano manufacturer, who, while accumulating fame and fortune in Pennsylvania, never ceased to rejoice over the success of his friend in other and varied fields. In 1820, young Lick went to New York to go into business. The want of capital interfered with his success, and at the end of that year he joined an expedition to Buenos Ayres. As this country had but recently become independent, it promised a grand future. Although earnestly solicited to accompany him, his friend Meyer refused, and Lick made the journey alone. For ten years in this new country, he followed his business, manufacturing pianos, and began to reap the reward of his industry. In 1832, he surprised his friends by a visit to his native State, bringing with him $40,000 worth of valuable South American skins and hides. This return gave him for a moment a desire to remain, and he even rented a house on Eighth Street, in Philadelphia, with the intention of going into business in that city. His ardent temperament could not brook the quiet life this promised. His thoughts, doubtless, reverted to the freedom and greater scope of action which the southern hemisphere afforded, and relinquishing his leased premises, he again sailed for South America. In a few months after arriving there he had settled his business in Buenos Ayres and sailed for Chili. In 1833, his home is in Valparaiso, and he is hard at work at his old trade, in addition to engaging in other ventures. In 1837, his restless spirit looked out toward other scenes of conquest in his line, and he selected Peru as the place of his future operations. To determine was to act, and he at once repaired thither with all his worldly goods. Pursuing the even tenor of his ways, he is about given up for dead, when his friend Meyer received a package from him, containing some $1,400 in gold doubloons, and an order for the inside work or action for twelve upright pianos, which he wished forwarded to Lima, Peru. About this time, his attention was directed toward California, now coming into prominence, and after due consideration he determined to proceed to the new *El Dorado* to be. Influential friends endeavored to dissuade him from this step. He was assured that the United States could not hold California; that the inhabitants were a set of cut-throats, who would murder him for his money; in short, that he was very well where he was and that it would be folly to go elsewhere. To this James Lick gave answer, that he knew the character of the American government and its people, and it was not in their nature to give up a country it had once laid hold of, and as for the other reasons, he had implicit confidence in his ability to take care of himself. A new difficulty presented itself, however, the surmounting of which shows the character of the man. He had on hand a contract for a number of pianos, when his workmen suddenly left for California. To violate his word was not for a moment to be considered—his contract must be fulfilled—and he personally did the work, although it cost him two years of hard labor to perform it. His pianos finished, everything is converted into money at a great sacrifice, and he is possessed of $30,000 in gold doubloons. With this he sailed for California, in the ship *Lady Adams*, arriving at San Francisco in the latter part of 1847. In the spring of 1848, San Francisco contained barely a thousand inhabitants. It had just emerged from its pristine condition and primitive name of Yerba Buena, and was becoming, under American rule, a valuable sea-port. Rumors of the discovery of gold filled the air, and tens of thousands flocked into and flooded out of the new metropolis of the Pacific. The vast majority, irrespective of class, rushed to the mines; the sagacious minority remained in the city. Among the latter was James Lick. His shrewd insight told him that a great city would arise on this peninsula; it would be the inlet and the outlet, not only of the commerce of California, but eventually of the whole Northern Pacific coast. The sand-hills which stretched out from the coast, and the *chaparral*-covered eminences, his prophetic vision converted into broad streets and avenues, lined with handsome and enduring structures. He foresaw the population streaming from every quarter of the globe to this focus of attraction; the ships laden with the necessaries and luxuries of life, and he took his measures accordingly. Quietly and carefully he invested his money, sowing his gold broadcast over many a piece of ground, the sellers jubilant and exultant at the price he paid them. During 1848, he pursued this course. Keeping his own counsel, as was his wont, none knew the extent of his purchases, or the amount he paid for any of them. The usual contests over titles were encountered, and frequently he was compelled to enforce his rights through the persuasive eloquence of leveled revolvers. Squatters would respect these arguments, and instances are reported of their houses disappearing almost as rapidly as the tenants. The risk was great but he accepted it, and having planted his money in the ground, he serenely awaited the harvest. It came, and rapidly. As the city increased, in the heart were observed large vacant, unimproved lots, apparently forsaken, but which the inquirer found belonged to James Lick. Meanwhile he branched off in other pursuits. In 1852, he purchased a property in San José, and had erected a mill, which was probably never equaled in the world. The wood was of mahogany, and the machinery of the finest description. It cost him $200,000, and by some was regarded as a folly, but it turned out the finest flour in California, and Lick's brand commanded the market. Around the mill, with his own hands, he planted a splendid orchard of fruit trees, which in those early days was itself a fortune. During all this, he did not forget his handiwork, and in 1872, he addressed a characteristic letter to his old friend Meyer, discussing some of the peculiarities of piano making, and giving his own views as to their relative merits. The Lick House, in San Francisco, was another of his enterprises. It covers nearly an entire block, and in the floor he displayed the knowledge which he had gathered while working at the bench. He composed it of many thousand pieces of inlaid wood, highly polished.

When the fraternity of Free Masons wished to erect a temple in San Francisco, they found the only site which would suit them belonged to James Lick, and was a part of the square upon which he designed to erect the Lick House. Of course it was not for sale. However, one of the brethren frankly approached him, and in a straightforward manner told him it was the only spot which suited them. The result was that the ground now covered by the handsome temple, in which our brethren of the Golden City greet their fraters from abroad so cordially, was secured, and the Lick House was to that extent curtailed in its proportions. Those only who knew the man, could fully appreciate the sacrifice he made in this transaction.

Although reluctant to sell, he was lavish in his gifts. The Pioneer Society, an organization which has so ably represented the State on different occasions, and over which he presided, received as a donation, the land upon which their hall is situated, and subsequently a larger and more valuable property. The California Academy of Sciences received a lot of great value also, and erected their building upon it.

But now he is approaching the sere and yellow leaf. The years usually alloted to man, have long been passed, and he announces what was evidently the result of a life's purpose—a plan conceived in a spirit of philanthropy, and which only increased in magnitude in proportion as the means and power of the donor increased. Selecting seven trustees from among the distinguished of his fellow-citizens he ceded to them his immense property—the accumulations of an unusually successful life—for the benefit of his adopted State, and for other noble purposes. To enumerate these purposes were needless. Suffice it to say that the exquisite work of art before us, the granite and marble, the life-like statues and enduring pyramid, the grateful tribute to those he loved, form a part.

Like our own Girard, the pervading aim or idea which attached to him during life, culminated in this act. It was the desire to benefit his kind. And now, having performed his life mission, he gathered the drapery of his couch around him, and patiently awaited the summons to appear before the Eternal throne where all men are judged impartially.

Around his eventful life, let us throw a halo of pleasant memories. He sleeps quietly in his narrow bed by the blue waters of the Pacific. May the flowers which spring so plentiful in the Golden State of his adoption, bloom upon his grave, winter and summer, and may we all, in the further performance of our duties, as we dedicate his work, and expose for all time to God's sunshine and storms, this monument to his memory, say as a requiem:

"Farewell! the early dews that fall
Upon thy grass-grown bed,
Are like the thoughts that now recall
Thine image of the dead.
A blessing hallows thy dark cell—
I will not stay to weep—Farewell."

Mr. Samuel C. Upham, of Philadelphia, an Argonaut of '49, being introduced by the Chairman, spoke as follows

MR. CHAIRMAN, LADIES AND GENTLEMEN:—I appear before you under peculiar and somewhat embarrassing circumstances. The Hon. John S. Hittell, Historian of "The Society of California Pioneers," selected to represent that Society on this occasion, finds it impossible to be with you to-day, and at the urgent request of the Hon. Peter Dean, President of the Society, and of Mr. Francis D. Clark, Secretary of "The Associated Pioneers of the Territorial Days of California," of which Society I have the honor to be a member, I have, at a few hours' notice, consented to act as the representative of our parent Society in San Francisco. The following letter will more fully explain the matter:

THE SOCIETY OF CALIFORNIA PIONEERS, ⎫
808 Montgomery Street, ⎬
SAN FRANCISCO, CAL., April 10th, 1878. ⎭

FRANCIS D. CLARK, Secretary Pioneers, etc., New York—
Dear Sir:—You are aware that the Lick Monument, at Fredericksburg, Pa., is finished, and will be dedicated on the 22d inst., and that the Hon. John S. Hittell, the Historian of this Society, was selected to represent the Pioneers on that occasion. To-day Mr. Hittell has informed me that he cannot leave until the 17th inst. It will, therefore, be impossible for him to participate in the dedication ceremonies on the 22d. Under these circumstances, Mr. Dean, our President, has requested me to ask you if you will not do something toward having the Pioneers represented on that day. He desires me to ask if there are not some of your members who will take a run over to Fredericksburg and represent the Pioneers and assist in the ceremonies upon that interesting occasion. If

you can do anything in this matter, Mr. Dean will feel under
many obligations, and the Pioneers also.

Very truly,   A. C. BRADFORD,

Sec'y Society Cal. Pioneers.

As your orator has so ably and eloquently portrayed the life
and services of the noble man whose memory we delight to
honor, my remarks will be brief.

In the year 1819, a young man, in the vigor of manhood,
and in whose lexicon there was no such word as FAIL, left his
boyhood's home in this beautiful valley, and the endearing
associations of the old hearthstone, to seek employment in one
of our large cities. He obtained a situation in a piano manu-
factory in Baltimore, and a year later started in the same
business for himself in the city of New York, but failing to
succeed for want of capital, went soon after to Buenos Ayres,
and then to Valparaiso, where he devoted himself to his business of piano-making for four years. He then visited different
places in Peru, remaining in that country eleven years. Mr.
Lick arrived in California in the year 1847, with about
$30,000, which he invested in real estate in San Francisco and
vicinity, and its rapid advance in value, caused by the discovery of gold at Sutter's Mill, in that State, in the month of
January, 1848, and the large emigration thither, soon made
him a second Crœsus. His great wealth did not dry up the
fountains of his noble, generous heart, which was ever susceptible to the emotions of sympathy for his fellow-men.

In the year 1874, he placed his entire property in the hands
of seven trustees, to be devoted to public and charitable purposes. In the spring of 1875, a year previous to his death, the
bequests, aggregating several millions of dollars, were changed
in some respects. To the "Academy of Natural Sciences," and
to "The Society of California Pioneers," which latter I have
the honor to represent, and whose honored President Mr. Lick
was at the time of his decease, in the fall of 1876, he bequeathed
a one-hundred <i>vara</i> lot, at the corner of Fourth and Market
Streets, in the city of San Francisco, and also the residue of
his vast estate, to be equally divided between the two Societies

after his various legacies had been paid. For this munificent bequest to " The Society of California Pioneers," and for his other benefactions, we honor his memory, and our children and our children's children shall in after years rise up and call him blessed. Among his many bequests he did not forget the far-off home of his childhood, and the loved ones whose dust was mingling with the soil of the old Keystone State; and we are assembled on this beautiful April day to unveil and dedicate the sculptured marble, erected at his request to the memory of his devoted mother and father, loving sister and honored grandfather.

The mortal remains of the great benefactor whose memory we honor to-day, lie mingling with the dust of that far-off land he loved so well, and which is so dear to the heart of every true Californian—the land where

> " The vine and the fig-tree are laden with fruit,
>   And the breezes blow soft as tones of the lute."

There, in that beautiful, silent City of the Dead, near the portals of the Golden Gate, with the roar of the waves of the mighty Pacific ever singing his requiem, he shall lie until the final day, when earth and ocean shall give up their dead, and this globe shall dissolve with fervent heat and leave not a rack behind.

At the conclusion of Mr. Upham's address, the following letters were read by a member of the Committee of Arrangements:

OFFICE OF THE JAMES LICK TRUST,
 SAN FRANCISCO, April 12th, 1878. }

COLONEL J. P. S. GOBIN, Chairman Committee of Arrangements Dedication of Lick Monument, Lebanon, Pa.—*Dear Sir:*—I am instructed to say that it is a matter of great satisfaction to the Trustees of The James Lick Trust to know that the people of Mr. Lick's old home have shown so much interest in the monument that he has erected to the memory of his family, and that they have made such appropriate arrangements to honor its dedication.

It was hoped that one of the Trustees, at least, might be able to attend the ceremonies, but circumstances have obtained which prevent all of them that pleasure.

They have instructed me to express to you, sir, their sincere appreciation of the sentiment which actuates your people in recognizing, through the ceremonies you propose, the honorable distinction deserved by a man who has devoted all of a large fortune to the noble purpose of benefiting his fellow-men.

I have the honor to be, sir, very respectfully, yours,

HENRY E. MATHEWS,
Secretary of The James Lick Trust.

By order of the Trustees of The James Lick Trust.

ALTA CALIFORNIA OFFICE,
SAN FRANCISCO, April 9th, 1878.

COLONEL J. P. S. GOBIN—*Dear Sir:*—I regret, on my account as well as that of the Society of California Pioneers, which I was to represent, that circumstances render it impossible for me to reach Lebanon before the 23d inst.

With respect, JOHN S. HITTELL.

EXECUTIVE CHAMBER,
HARRISBURG, PA., April 18th, 1878.

DEAR COLONEL:—I regret very sincerely that I am unable to accept your very kind invitation to attend ceremonies attending the dedication of monument at Fredericksburg, Lebanon County, on Monday next.

Yours, very truly, J. F. HARTRANFT.

Adam Rise, Eminent Commander, then ordered the Hermit Commandery to form in a hollow square around the monument. Buglers were stationed in the rear of the lines—one each to the North, South, East and West. One Sir Knight was placed on each side of the monument, the covering of the statues being so arranged that at the proper signal—a sound of the trumpet—one pull would unveil each side. The E. C. then announced:

In pursuance of the duty assumed by Hermit Commandery, No. 24, Knights Templar, of Pennsylvania, and by the authority of the Right Eminent, the Grand Commander of Pennsylvania, we have assembled to dedicate this monument with Knightly honors.

The C. G. commanded—"Present swords."

The E. C. asked—"Sir Knight, is it well in the East?"

The Sir Knight, John Matthes, stationed on the East, replied:

> "The sunbeams from the eastern sky,
> Flash from yon blocks exalted high,
> And on their polished fronts proclaim,
> Our worthy brother's widespread fame."

E. C.—"Sir Knight, is it well in the West?"

The Sir Knight, Simon G. Boltz, stationed on the West, replied:

> "The chastened sun adown the West,
> Speaks the same voice and sinks to rest;
> No sad defect, no flaw to shame
> Our worthy brother's lofty fame."

E. C.—"Sir Knight, is it well in the South?"

The Sir Knight, C. H. Shank, stationed on the South, replied:

> "Glowing beneath the fervid noon,
> Yon granite dares the southern sun;
> Yet tells that wall of fervid flame,
> Our worthy brother's honest fame."

E. C.—Sir Knight, is it well in the North?"

The Sir Knight, P. L. Zimmerman, stationed on the North, replied:

> "Perfect in line, exact in square,
> The works of all our craftsmen are;
> They will to coming time proclaim
> Our brother's worthy, well-earned fame."

E. C.—"Sir Knights, our Warder will make proclamation."

Warder, C. H. Killinger, announced: "I am directed to proclaim, and do proclaim, that the monument of our deceased brother, James Lick, is now dedicated to the uses designed, and to the memory of those whose names are inscribed thereon.

This proclamation I make to the East, to the West, to the South, and to the North. Due notice being given, let all govern themselves accordingly."

When the Warder pronounced the word East, the bugler on the eastern side gave one blast of his trumpet, and the Knight uncovered that side of the monument. When the word West was pronounced by the Warder, the bugler on the western side gave two blasts of his trumpet, and the Knight stationed there uncovered that side of the monument. Three blasts of the trumpet from the bugler stationed on the southern side was the signal to uncover that portion of the monument. As the word North was proclaimed by the Warder, a general salute of all the buglers was the signal for uncovering the northern side and the statue of the Goddess of Liberty on top of the monument.

C. G.—" Carry swords."
E. C.—" Uncover, Sir Knights. Our Prelate, will you lead in our devotions?"

PRELATE W. G. WARD'S DEDICATORY PRAYER.

O Thou Supreme Architect of the Universe, in Thy name have we assembled upon this day, and we lift up our hands and hearts unto Thee, our Creator and Father. Deign to look upon us, the unworthy suppliants of Thy favor. Thou hast taught us to look unto Thee in all the undertakings of life; to count upon Thy help in every laudable enterprise. We invoke Thy blessing upon the work of our hands this day.

O Thou God of our Fathers, remember us as Knights Templar, who have been called to the performance of the important duties of unveiling this monument and dedicating it to the uses for which it is designed. May it not only be a monument to perpetuate the memories of those whose names are inscribed thereon, and whose bones lie mouldering under the clod in the valley; but may it be an immutable memorial to remind every visitor to this sacred spot, that

" Honor and fame from no condition rise,
Act well your part, there all your honor lies."

As Templars, may we here learn a lesson and from it receive Wisdom from on high in all our doings, Strength of mind in all our difficulties, and the Beauty of harmony and holiness in all our communications and work. Let Faith be the foundation of our Hope, and Charity the fruit of our obedience to Thy revealed will. As we display the Standard of the Cross, may we follow the symbolic banner, whose inscription, "*In hoc signo vinces*," should animate us all to wield our swords manfully in the cause in which we have enlisted.

Grant, Heavenly Father, that we may so conduct ourselves during our earthly pilgrimage, that at its close we may be found worthy, through the merits of Him who has gone before us, to enter that Asylum of rest which He has prepared for all those who put their trust in Him.

And unto Thee, the only living and true God, we will ascribe power, and majesty, and dominion, now and evermore. Amen and amen.

E. C.—" Cover."
Music—" Old Hundred."

The following benediction was then pronounced by the Rev. Daniel Washburn, Grand Prelate of Pennsylvania:

Praise God from whom all blessings flow.
Praise Him all creatures here below,
Praise him above, angelic host,
Praise Father, Son and Holy Ghost.

The Lord bless us and keep us; the Lord mercifully with His favor look upon us and be gracious unto us; the Lord lift up His countenance upon us, and give us peace both now and evermore.

The procession again formed, marched into town and was dismissed in Market Square, at half-past three o'clock, P. M.

Among the prominent persons present were ex-Senator

Simon Cameron, State Superintendent Wickersham, G. Dawson Coleman, Senator Meily, William Calder, of Harrisburg, Henry S. Eckert, of Reading, Grand Recorder C. E. Meyer and Grand Treasurer M. Richards Mucklé, K. T., of Philadelphia.

Through the kindness of Mr. Jonathan See, of Philadelphia, who invited me to occupy a part of his seat in a crowded vehicle, I was enabled to reach Jonestown in time to take the 4.40 P. M. train for Philadelphia, where I arrived at nine o'clock same evening, wayworn and weary.

In conclusion, I desire to return thanks to the following gentlemen for courtesies extended to me during my brief visit to Fredericksburg: Colonel J. P. S. Gobin, Grand Prelate Daniel Washburn, Dr. A. W. Shultz, Levi Shiffler, Hon. F. M. Bachman, George Brutzman, Simon and John Desh, and several Sir Knights whose names I cannot call to mind.

Au revoir,

SAMUEL C. UPHAM.

VISIT OF THE "KING'S ORPHAN"* TO CALIFORNIA IN THE YEAR 1843.

Upper California—Its climate, agricultural and mineral resources—Gold and silver discovered in 1843—Fort and port of San Francisco—Military barracks of San Francisco—An Indian feast—Sonoma—Colonel Valléjo—Yerba Buena—New Helvetia—Captain Sutter—Russian fort at Bodega—Messrs. Sinclair and Grymes.

THE following sketch, alluded to on page 470, has been compiled from the manuscript of the "King's Orphan," kindly placed in the hands of the author by Colonel T. B. Thorpe.†

Upper California is geographically situated west of the United States, beyond the Rocky and other mountain

---

* The "Orphan's" name was Mafs or Mass.

† Colonel Thomas Bangs Thorpe, better known to the literary world as "Tom Owen the Bee Hunter," died in New York city on the morning of September 20th, 1878, aged sixty-three years. Colonel Thorpe was in several respects a remarkable man. In addition to his fine literary attainments, he was an amateur naturalist and an artist in oil colors of no mean ability. His *chef-d'œuvré*, "Niagara Falls," was sold in London for $5,000. He was an able journalist as well as a fluent and eloquent speaker. During the Mexican war, Colonel Thorpe was first attached to the staff of General Worth, and afterward appointed aid to General Zachary Taylor. He is said to have been the first correspondent who wrote his descriptions from the battle-field, and his letters published in a New Orleans journal added much to the fame of "Old Rough and Ready," a *soubriquet* given to him by the Colonel. He was also the author of the laconic order attributed to Old Zach—"*A little more grape, Captain Bragg!*" Colonel Thorpe, at the time of his death, held a position in the Law Division of the New York Custom-house Although not a member of "The Associated Pioneers of the Territorial Days of California," he was always a welcome guest at their re-unions, and the decease of the "old man eloquent" has caused a void in their circle which can never be filled. A delegation of the California Pioneers attended his funeral, and accompanied his remains to their last earthly resting-place—Greenwood Cemetery. Peace to his *manes!*

> "None knew him but to love him—
> None named him but to praise."

(537)

ranges, between the thirty-second and forty-second degrees of north latitude; bounded on the south by Lower California, on the north by Indian territories and Oregon, and on the west by the Pacific Ocean. The extent of the country is 600 miles from north to south, and about 300 miles from east to west, embracing an area of about 200,000 square miles, being nearly twice as large as Great Britain and as large as the New England and Middle States.

The Cordilleras are of extraordinary elevation, there being peaks among them from ten to twenty thousand feet above the level of the sea, from which they are seen at an immense distance. The higher mountains are almost destitute of vegetation, except stunted trees and shrubs. In the valleys is found the richest soil, varying from a rich alluvial to a deep black vegetable loam, upon a strata of sand, gravel, clay and trap-rock. The hills are generally of a more loose and gravelly nature than the mountains, while some are composed entirely of basalt, slate and marble. The Californias are *rich in minerals*. *Gold, silver*, lead, oxide of iron, manganese and copper ore are met with throughout the country, *the precious metals being the most abundant.*

Upper California is naturally divided into two great sections, the cultivated and the wild country. The former may be said to be that portion which lies along the Pacific, already populated to a considerable extent. The latter, or the Indian country, part of which is called the *Tulares* or marshy plains, intersected by lakes and swamps, occupying a valley of 500 miles in extent, running north and south. The climate is variable, as is that of all mountainous countries, but the mean temperature of the country in the spring is 66°; summer, 70°; autumn, 67°, and winter, 61°. Warmest month, 74°; coldest, 48° Fahrenheit.

The productions of the country are timber of the finest quality and all fruits and grains peculiar to the tropical

FORT AND PORT OF SAN FRANCISCO, 1843.

SCATTERGOOD-ENG.

From a Sketch by the "King's Orphan."

and temperate zones; among which are apples, pears, peaches, oranges, lemons, figs, plums, cherries, grapes and almost every tropical fruit, in the southern portion of the country. Wheat, rye, oats, barley, beans, peas, hemp, flax, tobacco, coffee, corn, Irish potatoes and sugar-cane. Vegetables of all kinds can be raised in the greatest abundance, frequently two or three crops a year. Wormwood and wild mustard abound as weeds. Oats grow wild, and the cultivated grow to an enormous height. Wheat crops, sown in the fall, early the following year have yielded *one hundred and fourteen bushels* to the acre. At the Mission of St. Joseph it was ascertained that the yield was *one hundred and twenty bushels to the acre, and the spontaneous crop the following year was sixty bushels to the acre.* The wheat of Taos has six distinct heads. Clover and the grasses are extraordinarily fine and productive. Indian flax grows wild all over the country. Horses, cattle, sheep and hogs thrive well, and are possessed in greater or less quantities by all the inhabitants, and are tended by herdsmen.

*   *   *   *   *   *

An opportunity occurring, I embarked on board a small trading schooner to pay a visit to the Mission of San Francisco, on the most splendid bay in all California, and surrounded by the richest country. A pleasant run of two days [from Monterey], brought me to the mouth of the bay, which is peculiar, and will always attract attention, both for its easy adaptation to defense at little cost and for its very picturesque appearance. The entrance to the bay is excellent, being fully a half mile wide. On the south side, rises a high, rocky point, on the top of which are the ruins of an old fort. On the north side, is a high and bold coast, at the foot of which are some perforated sandstone rocks, that looked precisely as would the remnants of castles of which remained only their porticoes and archways. After you pass well into the bay, you meet with various small islands, or round bold rocks, one of which is known

as Bird's Island, from the vast quantities of the feathered
tribe that make a home upon it.   This island is most admirably calculated for a light-house, or a fort, as it perfectly commands the harbor, and could not have been
better situated for the purposes named had it been placed
there by a skillful engineer.   Such is the entrance to San
Francisco Bay, the best one on the Pacific coast, and not
surpassed for beauty of surrounding country, for ease of
defense, or safety of shipping at anchor, by any in the
world.

The port of San Francisco presents a very pleasant appearance.   It has a bold shore, and high hills for a background.   The main entrance to the bay, viewed from the
ruins of the fort, looking out toward the sea, is most
beautiful, bounded as it is on both sides by bold rocks,
while its high precipice on which you stand, brings the
waves of the ocean below you, and gives to shipping
the appearance of a well-arranged panorama.   The Mission of San Francisco, as is generally the custom of the
country, is situated in the interior, and, after leaving the
schooner, I journeyed to it by land.   At this mission I
became acquainted with Colonel Valléjo, whose relatives I
met with in Monterey.   He is the commander on the
frontier, and resides at Sonoma, on the north side of the
bay.   While at this place, the venerable Father Alviso,
whose restoration to health, under my professional skill, had
been so much credit to my reputation, visited me, having
ridden from Santa Clara for that purpose, a distance of
42 miles.   Having made arrangements favorable to
the visiting of the more northern portions of the bay of
San Francisco, I declined Father Alviso's pressing invitation to visit Santa Clara for the time being, and promised
to accept of his hospitality at some future period.

I sailed, with most beautiful weather, up the magnificent
bay, and toward evening entered a curious stream called
the Devil's Creek; no doubt so named because, its mouth

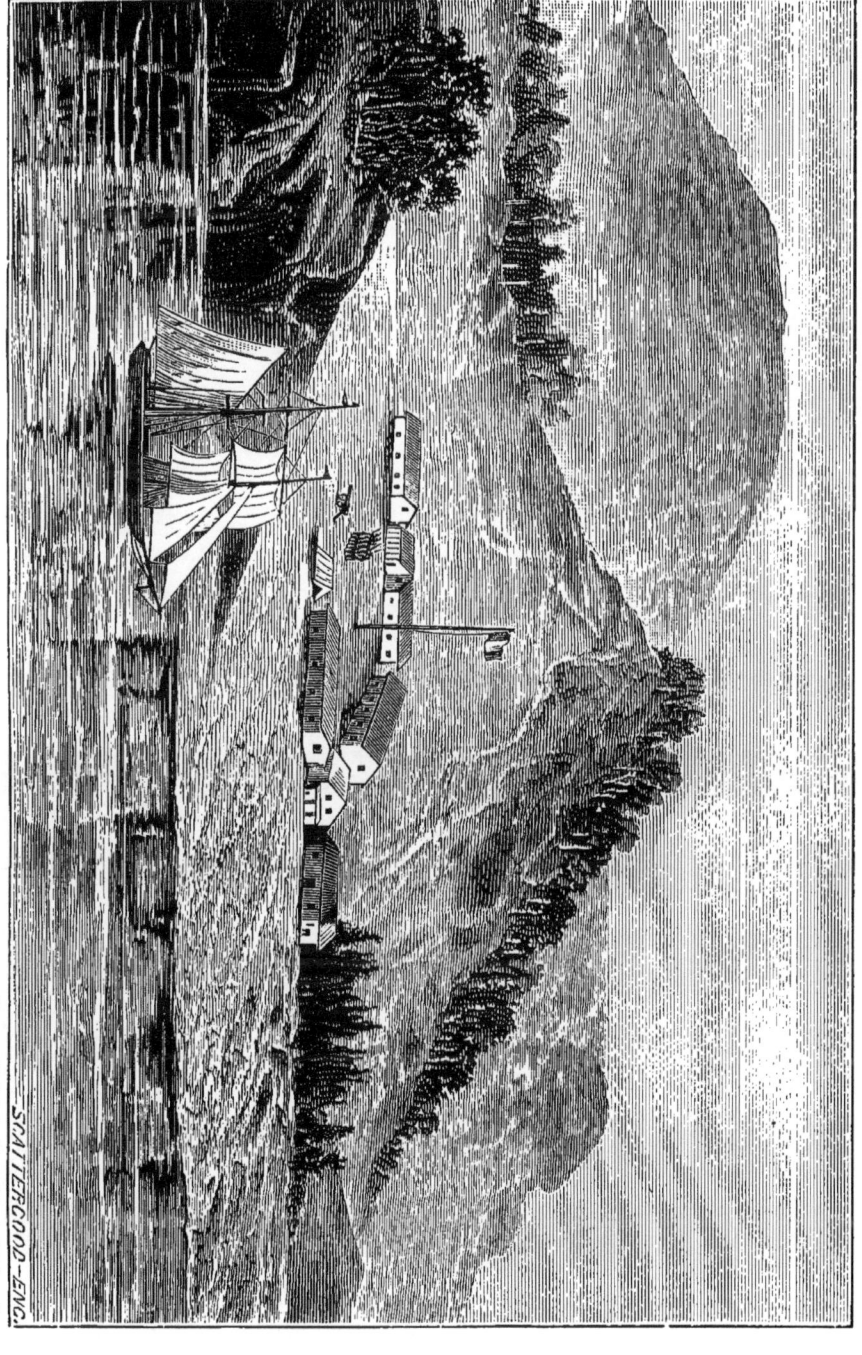

MILITARY BARRACKS OF SAN FRANCISCO, 1843.

From a Sketch by the "King's Orphan."

SCATTERGOOD-ENG.

being lost in the low marsh, its channel is difficult to discover. A gentleman having a ranch on this creek, had contracted with the owners of the schooner to deliver some lime, and he was on shore to show us the proper place to enter the creek. The Indians who formed the crew of the schooner, knew nothing about it, nor did they perceive a ranchman who was perched on a high hill in the background, endeavoring also to point out the way. Unfortunately, the undergrowth of portions of the country was on fire, and a dense smoke clouded the atmosphere in some directions. After much delay and confusion, the ranchman came on board the schooner to act as pilot, and brought us safely up a winding but beautiful creek. We were often so near to the land that the cattle, deer and antelopes could be seen flying before the devouring element. The flames finally reached the *tulé* rushes of the marshy places, and ran along the sides of the creek, making our passage dangerous and awful to look at, as we frequently appeared to be enveloped in the flames and in dense columns of steam and smoke. A favorable wind hurried us through this appropriately-named creek, or the schooner and its inmates might have been consumed. It must have presented an extraordinary spectacle, as our little schooner disappeared in a sheet of fire, and then emerged beyond it unharmed by the ordeal ; a scene entirely harmonious with the superstitious feelings that surrounded the creek and the traditions that are reported of Mount Diablo to which it leads.

The schooner came to anchor in a beautiful bend in the creek, and as night set in the fire exhibited one of the most singular sights I ever witnessed. The larger brush, which had now become ignited, sent up long tongues of forked flames behind the green canopy of willows and the moving branches of the trees. The effect was as if myriads of living creatures were struggling in the flames, and the illusion was horribly carried out by the howling of wolves, and

bears, and other wild animals that resounded in the confusion of the crackling and falling trees.

To occupy the time consumed by the delay of loading
the schooner, I went up to the *original* Mount Diablo in
search of fresh water. I found this celebrated place a small
eminence, overgrown with beautiful willows and other
trees, that were nourished by a gurgling stream of water
that flowed at their roots. It is said that the persons who
first discovered this place camped by the running water,
and at nightfall they were saluted by hideous noises and
lamentations, mingled with frightful groans, and the place
thus got a bad name. One family, possessed of more than
common intelligence, many years ago, built a house, now
in ruins, on this beautiful eminence, and stocked the surrounding country with cattle.

From policy, no doubt, this family kept up the " hob-
gobblin " stories and circulated new ones, and they were
thereby enabled to hold sole possession of the surrounding
country. At length, in an incursion of a hostile tribe of
Indians from the mountains, this family was murdered,
their settlement robbed of its wealth, the Indians escaping
without detection. This atrocity confirmed the stories so
much circulated about it, and as a consequence the country,
until quite recently, has been entirely deserted.

To extend my excursions, I procured an easy-riding
horse, and after having examined the limekilns, I rambled
about the country quite alone, and, as is customary with
me, searching for minerals and rare plants, examining the
direction of the hills and their geological formations. In
the course of my ride I ascended to a considerable distance up the side of the mountain, known by the Californians and Indians as Mount de Barbones. This mountain,
although not more than sixteen hundred feet above the
level of the sea, is so situated in regard to the surrounding
country, that it can be seen further at sea than those of
much higher elevation.

While climbing the steep sides of this mountain, the sun at times almost disappeared amongst the thick smoke, yet tinged the distant forest and cliffs with a most singular light. My hopes of obtaining any specimens for my herbarium were vain, as all the delicate plants that had escaped the fire were destroyed for my use by the heated air and smoke. I therefore paid more particular attention to the geological character of the mountain.

De Barbones is similar to all mountains of this country, being composed of soft sand-stone, quartz, with occasional exhibitions of lime-stone and porphyry, with the evidences of such minerals as manganese, oxide of iron and lead ore. But for the smoke I should have been able to see, while up on the mountain, the celebrated rocks, or, as the Canadian hunters term them, the Butes, and many other mountain ranges.

The continued repetition of these fires does great injury to the country. The undergrowth that springs up in the "burns" is always inferior to that growing where no fire has injured the soil. Very often the ground becomes loose, the fire penetrating deeply into it, following the roots; then sets in the dry season, the winds blow off the soil and leave an arid desert where before was luxurious vegetation. The causes of these fires are various. Sometimes they are accidental, sometimes purposely made to destroy the insects that infest the undergrowth; but, most often they are the work of the Indians, who gather grasshoppers, a favorite food, by setting fire to the grass which they inhabit. They also kindle fires to place a barrier between themselves and the whites. The Indians, too, use fires for the purpose of conveying information, and they may be said to form the telegraphic system of the red man. They are ingenious in the manner of forming their signals. A hole is dug in the ground, much wider at the bottom than at the top; this hole is filled with combustibles and set on fire; once well ignited, the hole is nearly closed at the opening. By this means the smoke rises to a considerable height in a column, and thus information is conveyed to different tribes of the approach of an enemy or friend, or whether they are coming in large or small bodies.

It was well-nigh sundown when I returned to the schooner, where I found the Indians busily engaged in skinning a yearling heifer, presented to them by the owner of the limekilns. The captain of the schooner had been well provided with game, among which I noticed the body of a large elk. The Indians that formed the crew of the schooner, having been rather stinted in food for a day or two, determined on a feast, as a recompense for their previous fasting. They presented on the occasion a spectacle I had never before witnessed of disgusting sensual indulgence, the effect of which on their conduct struck me as being exceedingly strange. The meat of the heifer, most rudely cooked, was eaten in a voracious manner. After gorging themselves they would lie down and sleep for a while, and get up and eat again. They repeated this gluttony until they actually lost their senses, and presented in their conduct all the phenomena peculiar to an over-indulgence in spirituous liquors. They cried and laughed by turns, rolled upon the ground, dozed and then sprang up in a state of delirium. The following morning, they were all wretchedly sick, and had the expression peculiar to drunken men recovering their reason after a debauch.

I should, perhaps, mention that the land on the northern side of the Devil's Creek is lower than is elsewhere to be seen, and is principally settled by California creoles, many of whom are owners of immense herds of cattle. The soil is remarkably fruitful, suffering less than most other places from the drought, in consequence of its being flat, and through it flow many small rivulets, that come down from the hills, communicating with handsome bayous that, in every direction, intersect the ranches, thus affording easy transportation of their produce to the bay for sale or exportation.

The schooner, after having been loaded, was navigated with great labor out of the creek, against a head-wind, but the moment we reached the bay the wind became favorable for our voyage, and we dashed over the bounding waves most merrily. It was a short run across the Bay of San Pablo, the northern arm of San Francisco Bay, and much resembling a lake. The schooner passed close to the western shore, through a narrow strait made by small islands, continuing on until it dropped anchor in the vicinity of Sonoma, the residence of Colonel Valléjo, the commandant of the frontier. Sonoma is situated on a creek, three miles from its entrance into the bay. In this neighborhood are several settlements. San Gabriel, near the bay, is an old mission, at present nearly destroyed. The administrator of the place is a Mr. Murphy, formerly of Peru. He has accumulated by his industry a small property, consisting of horses and cattle. I saw, as I passed on from San Gabriel, beautiful bottom-land with clumps of trees, mostly oak. An Indian chief is settled here, assisted by some of his tribe. His ranch is well laid out, and his house quite comfortable. This chief betrays much intelligence and has a good character. He was formerly, with those about him, attached to the " Valléjo ranch." Fine deep creeks everywhere thread the country here, resembling in their appearance natural canals. They are invaluable to the agriculturist; for independent of the facilities of transportation, they seem to irrigate the land in the dry season of summer. The ranch of Colonel Valléjo is situated upon an eminence; is possessed of rich land, and portions of it are under fair cultivation. Having passed this estate, I came to the military station of Sonoma and the residence of Colonel Valléjo.

Sonoma, originally called St. Solona, was by its founders laid out with great taste, and had the enterprise of the

people built it up according to the first intent, it would have
been one of the handsomest places in California.   The
military barracks extend along under the high hills, running parallel with them, and in front is a magnificent
Plaza for military parades, or place of resort and recrea-
tion for the citizens.   At the time of my arrival, a flag was
flying at the staff, and a few ragamuffin soldiers were wan-
dering about after the heels of a horse carrying the officer,
who had just returned from a successful military expedition, to which we will allude again.

This station has a garrison nominally consisting of one
hundred and fifty men, rank and file, but never mustered
more than *thirty*, including all the hangers-on and loafers
generally, whose professed business it is to ravage the country to keep the Indians in check.   Attached to the garrison is a friar who is dignified with the title of chaplain.
Enough of agricultural enterprise is exhibited about Sonoma to show the capacity of the rich soil if it were in the
hands of an industrious population.   Fruit was growing
finely, such as it was; wheat and corn gave evidence of an
abundant yield, though badly planted and tended, in every
particular.   The stock looked better than any I had seen,
the horses being particularly fine.   In the vicinity of Sonoma are hot springs, remarkably effective in curing rheu-
matic complaints.   A water-mill for grinding wheat was
standing on the creek that runs near the station, but the
ignorant Indian who had it in charge could not manage the
machinery, simple as it was, and there was not a Yankee
about who could attend to it; so the mill stood still and
the people satisfied themselves with eating *frijoles* and
meat, spending more time in one day in beating corn for
tortillas, when they indulged in luxuries, than would have
been necessary to have fixed the machinery of the mill.

The commandant of Sonoma, at the time of my arrival,
was sick and needed medical attendance.   He bears the
character of a haughty man, being full of the Spaniard;

but I found him affable and polite. I was struck with the military reputation of this officer, it being so much like all those of Mexico holding distant commands. The story always is, that the commandant does not faithfully apply the revenues of the government, but appropriates them to his own use. The moral is, that no confidence exists among the rulers themselves, and no character can be above suspicion. There were very many things at Sonoma to destroy the pleasure of my visit, as they gave me a train of thoughts relative to the lawlessness of the people and the miserable government under which they live. As I have before stated, on my entrance to the *Plaza* in front of the barracks of this station, I beheld a military company just returning from what was termed a "successful expedition," and near by were the prisoners and the happy conquerors. This expedition was commanded by the brother of Colonel Valléjo and was so characteristic of similar ones in California that I give its particulars.

A small tribe of Indians, inhabiting an island in the northern part of the Bay of San Francisco, was reported to have threatened the settlers in their neighborhood that they would steal some of their cattle as payment for contributions denied them, for occupying their lands. Upon this shallow pretext, Colonel Valléjo permitted his brother, who is a blood-thirsty man, to take the "soldiers" and a number of Indians and march against these poor people, who had made threats that they were going to steal cattle from people indebted to them for land. Advantage was taken when the Indian men were away from home fishing and gathering roots for subsistence. These armed men were very brave when they found no resistance but from old men, women and children, who were unconscious of any danger until an indiscriminate massacre commenced that spared nothing but the women for prisoners. Not contented with this barbarous shedding of blood, a poor negro blacksmith, a deserter from the United States sloop of war

Cyane, was found hidden away on this island, whom the commander had brought out, pompously proclaimed an enemy to Mexico, and then shot in the back, and only killed after repeated discharges of fire-arms. Having thus accomplished their work, the expedition made a hasty retreat, fearing the Indians would gather *en masse* and destroy it, which would have been the case.

These barbarous incursions into the Indian territory are often made from mere wantonness, or result from the Indians being cheated out of their lands or the reward of their labor. As a consequence, they retaliate by stealing cattle; never, as far as I could learn, by committing murder. Advantage is taken of these misunderstandings by the Californians, who, joining with the military force, scour the country, committing every cruelty that can be imagined. By a *wise provision* of the Mexican government, as if to make *barbarousness* a subject of reward, the officers receive as *remuneration for heading these expeditions the prisoners that fall into their hands;* so, whenever a ranch requires laborers, you hear of some Indian outrage, followed by the taking of prisoners by the Californians.

The prisoners I saw at Sonoma were mostly females and young children. They were huddled together like beasts, nearly naked, and seemed to create no sympathy. Some were good-looking. They maintained a sullen expression, and bore up under their misfortunes with a stoicism peculiar to the aboriginal inhabitants of this continent. The Indians belonging to Sonoma station, that had accompanied the expedition, seemed to have revived within them, by the shedding of blood, all the bad traits of their savage nature. They celebrated, through the whole night of my arrival, their victory with dances and songs. They painted their bodies coarsely, and showed less variety and spirit in all they did than you will meet with among the real savages, who have not, like most of the California Indians, been, by years of degradation, deprived of their original character.

TOWN AND PORT OF YERBA BUENA, IN SAN FRANCISCO BAY, 1842.

From a Sketch by the "King's Orphan."

After a visit of some days at Sonoma, visiting most of the places in the vicinity situated on the beautiful bay, I left for Yerba Buena, a small and growing town on the south-west side of San Francisco Bay, and near the town of that name. The harbor offers great facilities for the unloading of vessels of all descriptions; but, like many other places bordering on the sea, in California, it suffers from want of good water, which cannot be obtained—the wells being rather brackish. Vessels, therefore, are obliged to cross the bay for a supply of wholesome water. As this country becomes more thickly settled, and facilities are created for traveling, there will be still another port opened further south than Yerba Buena, which will no doubt become of great importance as a place of business. I found three "whalers" in the bay at Yerba Buena, and occupied my time most pleasantly in conversation with their officers —two of them being American vessels.

  *   *   *   *   *   *

It was with great pleasure I witnessed the preparations which, when completed, would, without further delay, permit me to sail for New Helvetia, the most interesting portion of California, and destined to become thickly populated with American residents.

I shall never forget the morning following my departure for New Helvetia. A landscape of beauty burst upon my view, such as I never before witnessed. A view containing every soft and delicate feature, yet bounded by the sublimest exhibitions of nature. The mouth of the San Joaquin opened to my view on the south, presenting a far reach inland, that grew dim by the distance. Before me was the Sacramento; a rich green canopy was suspended from the noble trees that lined its borders, casting deep shades that seem to invite the wanderer to its hospitable shores. It was Sabbath morning, and I thought I never saw more fit temples for praise and worship than everywhere presented themselves. The green grass came down in graceful descent to the water's edge, and groups of splendid oaks, as if of gorgeous parks, were scattered about in rich profusion. The crystal dew-drops glistened upon the leaves, and a thousand feathered songsters that flitted about appeared to join in the universal hymn of praise.

The day was consumed in our passage up the river, nothing occurring to break the pleasant thoughts the scenery around suggested. Occasionally a deer would betray itself among the tangled vines that hung in profusion from the larger trees; or cattle, almost as wild as the deer, would rush along with heavy tread, crushing the undergrowth making it sound singularly loud. No signs of civilization were to be seen, and a deserted hut made the landscape look more quiet, perhaps, than it would otherwise have done. I arrived in the evening at the *Embarcadero*, or port of New Helvetia, the schooner coming to anchor in a fleet of smaller craft. Here were a few huts situated upon elevated ground, nestling beneath the protection of lofty sycamore and oaks. The settlement of Captain Sutter is nearly three miles from the landing-place, the road leading over a beautiful country, constantly rising as you leave the Sacramento.

Captain Sutter, who is the most enterprising citizen of California, *and who is destined to play a prominent part in the future history of the country,* is a native of Switzerland, and was at one time an officer in the Royal Guards of France. By making friends, from his enterprising character and by extensive traveling over the Rocky Mountains, North Mexico and the Sandwich Islands, he was enabled to commence a farming establishment on the Sacramento on a large scale.

Captain Sutter obtained a grant from the Mexican government of a large tract of land on the Sacramento, on condition that he would keep the Indians in check and punish them if they interfered with the settlement. He displayed wonderful energy of character, and came so un-

RUSSIAN FORT ROSS, BODEGA, CALIFORNIA, 1843.

From a Sketch by the "King's Orphan."

expectedly on his enemies, that they soon became convinced that they all would be destroyed if they did not remain at peace with the white inhabitants. Captain Sutter acted with great judgment in securing the good-will of the tribes immediately about him, and thus managed to form them into a protection against his more distant enemies. All prisoners taken in war were brought to his establishment and set to work, thereby increasing his force and modifying the cruelties of war.

To carry out his extensive plans, Captain Sutter purchased the movable property of the abandoned Russian Mission of Ross at Bodega, agreeing to pay for it in a certain number of years in agricultural products. He then, with great difficulty, managed to make laborers out of the Indians, paying them fair prices in beads and blankets, and by these Indians has been performed the greater part of his agricultural labor.

Captain Sutter's establishment has more the appearance of a fort than a farming establishment. It is protected by a wall, ten feet high, made of *adobes*, or sun-dried bricks, having a turret with embrasures and loopholes for fire-arms. Twenty-four pieces of cannon of different sizes, can be brought to defend the walls. Against the walls, on the inside of the fort, are erected the storehouses of the establishment, also a distillery to make spirits from the wheat and wild grapes, together with shops for coopers, blacksmiths, carpenters, saddlers, granaries, and huts for the laborers. At the gate-way is always stationed a servant, armed as a sentinel. I arrived at the establishment early in the morning, just as the people were being assembled for labor by the discordant notes of a Mexican drum. I found Captain Sutter busily employed in distributing orders for the day. He received me with great hospitality, and made me feel on the instant perfectly at home under his roof. The magical sounds of the drum had gathered together several hundred Indians, who

flocked to their morning meal preparatory to the labors of
the day—reaping wheat. The morning meal over, they
filed off to the field in a kind of military order, armed
with a sickle and hook.

Breakfast was by this time announced for the family,
which was served up in an out-house adjoining the kitchen.
The breakfast consisted of wholesome corn-bread, eggs,
ham, an excellent piece of venison and coffee. In the rear
of the fort is a large pond, the borders of which are planted
with willows and other trees, a most valuable acquisition as
well as ornament. This pond furnishes water for the necessary wants of domestic use, and for irrigating the garden.
Owing to the drought, the vegetables as well as the wheat
had suffered; the latter proving almost a failure. The
want of rain is the greatest evil that befalls the country.
In the front of the fort, there are inclosures for horses and
cattle, and places to deposit corn and wheat. The manner
of threshing which I witnessed was conducted on the most
patriarchal plan, the grain being strewn upon the floor, and
then trodden out by horses or cattle, which causes it to be
much broken and mixed with the earth, and almost impossible to clean.

The raising of wheat, corn, horses and cattle, constitutes
the principal business of Captain Sutter; but he has realized
considerable income from the salmon fisheries of the rivers;
the fish being unequaled in flavor and found in the greatest
abundance. He also organized extensive hunting and
trapping expeditions for the skins of the beaver, otter, elk,
deer and antelope, but in this he was greatly interfered
with by the Hudson Bay Company, who sent their hunters
upon his grounds. He complained to the proper authorities, but they paid no attention whatever to the matter.
His enemies, not content with thus injuring him, informed
the suspicious Mexican government that Captain Sutter
was concocting revolutionary plans, and that he encouraged
deserters and other disorderly people to live at his settle-

ment. Captain Sutter replied to these charges by stating, that he had received the grant to his lands on condition that he would obtain settlers, the principal portion of which he expected from Europe. To make amends, he had encouraged all the stragglers of the country to flock to his central position, and they being principally unmarried men, and some rather lawless spirits from the mountains, they soon formed a very independent set of men, and were quite competent to defend themselves.

The government at Monterey was not satisfied with Captain Sutter's explanations. Urged on by envious neighbors, it was prompted to send to Captain Sutter a committee of investigation. The Captain was so enraged at the idea of such a thing that he treated the committee with great contempt, and said he could defend himself against any force or means that might be employed against him. Whereupon the government at Monterey threatened to send a force against him, but thought better of the matter when they found out the character of the men Captain Sutter had about him, and of the Russian armament he had mounted on the walls of his fort; but annoyed him with legal suits, and after a great deal of difficulty he was acquitted of any treasonable design against the government.

The Hudson Bay Company's hunters having destroyed his trade in furs, and thus disappointed him in his income, he retaliated upon them by erecting a large distillery, with the product of which he secretly purchased from the hunters of the company the greater part of their furs, and managed to make more by the operation than if he had kept up a large hunting establishment of his own.

Mr. Sinclair, a partner with Captain Sutter in farming pursuits, and a Mr. Grymes, have large and productive farms on the American Fork, a tributary of the Sacramento. Mr. Sinclair is from Scotland; is a very interesting gentleman in conversation, and possesses great enterprise in business. He was a hunter for many years among the Rocky

Mountains, acting as a clerk to one of the Hudson Bay Company's expeditions.   Mr. Sinclair treated me to a rural breakfast, and, in accordance with his old habits, broiled his meat on a ramrod stuck up before the fire.   The limpid and beautiful river near which his house is situated is made doubly attractive when compared with the sultry plains in the vicinity, upon which good water is not always to be obtained.

MAKING AND RAISING THE "BEAR FLAG."

THE author is indebted to Mr. Francis D. Clark, Secretary of "THE ASSOCIATED PIONEERS OF THE TERRITORIAL DAYS OF CALIFORNIA," for the following correspondence, which settles the matter as to the date of raising the "Bear Flag" at Sonoma, Cal. Secretary Winter deserves the thanks of the Pioneers for his persistent and painstaking efforts in settling for all time this mooted question:

OFFICE OF THE "TERRITORIAL PIONEERS
OF CALIFORNIA,"
No. 103 Montgomery Street,
SAN FRANCISCO, August 30th, 1878.

Dear Sir:—Inclosed please find a list of "Pioneer" Associations, with their places of meeting and the names of their presidents and secretaries; and, as well, a copy of a communication from James G. Bleak, Esq., to me, of date April 16th, last, giving the date of the raising of the "Bear Flag" at Sonoma.

I am prompted to send these papers to you, because I think them valuable to the Society you represent, for reference and preservation; and more than this, because WE ARE REGARDING THE NEW YORK SOCIETY—SO CLOSELY RESEMBLING OUR OWN, IN NAME AND SENTIMENT, DECLARED OBJECTS AND ACCOMPLISHED WORK—AS MUCH NEARER AKIN TO OUR ASSOCIATION than any other existing organization.

The list of "Pioneer" organizations, etc., sent is the result of considerable examination of Directories and correspondence, with a desire to make it as complete and correct as practicable; yet, it is possible, you may be able to suggest some additions, in which case you will please do the favor.

32

I transmit the copy of James G. Bleak's letter, for the reason that it is esteemed important in SETTLING THE QUESTION AS TO DATE OF RAISING THE "BEAR FLAG" at Sonoma, in 1846, upon which there has hitherto been so much contradiction, both among the "Bear Flag" Party and in History.

Mr. John S. Hittell, Historian of the Society of California Pioneers, S. F., in his Report of 7TH JANUARY last, fixed the Date as the 12th of June, 1846. Bancroft, the Pacific Coast Historian, intended to publish it as on the 15th June, etc.

To Wm. L. Todd (Maker of the Flag and one of the party) I was indebted for the information that Captain Wm. B. Ide, in command of the party, kept a Diary during that eventful period of California's early History, and this Diary must henceforth be received as THE MOST RELIABLE DATA EXTANT and, I think, conclusive on that point, in view of the treachery of human memory.

Yours fraternally,
WM. WINTER, Secretary.

FRANCIS D. CLARK, ESQ., *Secretary Society of "The Associated Pioneers of Territorial Days of California,"* Head-quarters, N. Y. City.

ST. GEORGE, Utah, 16th April, 1878.

To WM. WINTER, Esq., Sec'y of Association of "Territorial Pioneers of California"—*Dear Sir:*—Your communication of 3rd inst. is placed in my hands by the widow of a departed friend—James M. Ide—as I have at present in my charge some of his papers.

In reply to your question asking for "the *correct date*" of *raising the "Bear Flag"* at Sonoma in 1846, I will quote from the writing of Wm. B. Ide, deceased:—"The said 'Bear Flag' [was] made of plane [plain] cotton cloth and ornamented with the red flannel of a shirt from the back of one of the men, and christened by the words 'California Republic' in red paint letters on both sides; [it] was raised upon the standard where had floated on the breezes the Mexican Flag aforetime; IT WAS THE 14TH OF JUNE, '46. Our whole number was 24 all told. The mechanism of the Flag was performed by Wm. Todd of

Ill. The Grisly Bear was chosen as an emblem of strength and unyielding resistance."

I will quote a few lines more, though not pertinent to the fact of raising the Flag; still I believe the few following words cannot fail to be gratifying to the companions in arms of Wm. B. Ide:

" The men were divided into two companies of 10 men each. The 1st Artillery was busily engaged in putting the cannon in order, which were charged doubly with grape and canister. The 1st Rifle company were busied in cleaning, repairing and loading the small arms. The commander after setting a guard and posting a sentinel on one of the highest buildings to watch the approach of any persons who might feel a curiosity to inspect our operations—directed his leisure to the establishment of some system of finance—whereby all the defenseless families might be brought within the lines of our garrison and supported. Ten thousand pounds of flour were purchased on the credit of the *Gov.* and deposited within the garrison. And an account was opened on terms agreed upon for a supply of beef and a few barrels of salt, constituted our main supplies. Whisky was contraband altogether. After the first round of duties was performed, as many as could be spared off guard, were called together and our situation fully explained to the men by the Commander of the Garrison. It was fully represented that our success—nay, our very life depended on the magnanimity and justice of our course of conduct, coupled with sleepless vigilance and care. (But ere this we had gathered as many of the surrounding citizens as was possible, and placed them out of harm's way, between 4 strong walls; they were more than twice our number.) The commander chose from these strangers the most intelligent, and by the use of an interpreter went on to explain the cause of our coming together—our determination to offer equal protection and equal justice to all good and virtuous citizens, that we had not called them there to rob them of their liberties, or to deprive them of any portion of their property, or to disturb them in their social relations one with another nor yet to desecrate their religion."

Here I will desist as my time is much occupied and perhaps

I have written full as much as you care to read, or the association to hear.

Before closing I beg leave to refer to a newspaper clipping I find among the papers: it is from the "Daily Alta California" of 20 Jan'y 1846. Appended to a copy of the "Proclamation" is a certificate from Señor Joachin Torres stating the Flag was hoisted on the date of the Proclamation, June 15th, 1846. This you will perceive is incorrect. I have been careful to give you VERBATIM COPY OF IDE'S WORDS AS WRITTEN BY HIMSELF.

Respectfully,

JAMES G. BLEAK.

The foregoing is a true copy of a Letter received by me, from James G. Bleak, Esq., of St. George, Utah.

WM. WINTER,

Secretary Association of "Territorial Pioneers of California,"

SAN FRANCISCO, August 30th, 1878.

PIONEER ORGANIZATIONS.

"THE SOCIETY OF CALIFORNIA PIONEERS,"

Hall, 808 Montgomery Street, San Francisco, California.

S. C. HASTINGS,   FERDINAND VASSAULT,
President.   *Secretary.*

ASSOCIATION OF "TERRITORIAL PIONEERS OF CALIFORNIA,"

Hall, 103 Montgomery Street, San Francisco.

WM. T. GARRATT,   WM. WINTER,
President.   *Secretary.*

SOCIETY OF "THE ASSOCIATED PIONEERS OF THE TERRITORIAL DAYS OF CALIFORNIA,"

Head-quarters, New York City.

JOHN A. SUTTER,   FRANCIS D. CLARK,
President.   *Secretary.*

No. 16 Cortlandt Street, N. Y.

SOCIETY OF "SANTA CLARA COUNTY PIONEERS,"
San José, California.

COLEMAN YOUNGER,
President.

ALEX. P. MURGOTTEN,
Secretary,
Room No. 1, Commercial Bank Building.

"SACRAMENTO SOCIETY OF CALIFORNIA PIONEERS,"
Rooms, 7th Street, between J and K, Sacramento City, Cal.

A. B. OSBORN,
President.

ASA P. ANDREWS.
Secretary.

"MARYSVILLE PIONEER ASSOCIATION,"
Marysville, California.

WM. G. MURPHY,
Secretary.

"SAN JOAQUIN SOCIETY OF CALIFORNIA PIONEERS,"
Pioneer Hall, 174 El Dorado Street, Stockton, California.

W. F. FREEMAN,
President.

ALONZO RHODES,
Secretary.

ASSOCIATION OF "OREGON PIONEERS,"
Salem, Oregon.

W. J. HERRON,
President.

J. HENRY BROWN,
Secretary.

SOCIETY OF "PACIFIC COAST PIONEERS,"
Hall, B Street, Virginia City, Nevada.

A. J. TYRRELL,
President.

S. D. BAKER,
Librarian.

"PIONEERS OF AMADOR AND CALAVERAS COUNTIES,"
Jackson, California.

JAMES MEEHAN,
President.

JEFF. DAVIS,
Secretary.

"VALLÉJO PIONEERS ASSOCIATION,"
Valléjo, California.

"SOCIETY OF CALIFORNIA PIONEERS, FOR THE DISTRICT COMPOSED OF SONOMA, NAPA, MARIN, MENDOCINO AND LAKE COUNTIES."

J. CAVANAUGH,
President,
Petaluma.

CAPT. ANDREW HENRY,
Recording Secretary,
Petaluma, Sonoma Co., Cal.

KINDRED ORGANIZATION.

———

SOCIETY OF "NATIVE SONS OF THE GOLDEN WEST,"
Hall, 320 Post Street, San Francisco.

JOHN H GRADY,
President.

H. LUNSTEDS,
Secretary.

———

"TRUCKEE," THE INDIAN GUIDE.

The following letter, which explains itself, is deemed worthy of a place in this volume:

OFFICE OF THE ASSOCIATION OF "TERRITORIAL
PIONEERS OF CALIFORNIA,"
No. 103 Montgomery Street,
SAN FRANCISCO, September 26th, 1878.

SAMUEL C. UPHAM, Esq., Philadelphia—*Dear Sir:*—The following is a copy of a recent communication in which is contained an *interesting* fragment of our Pioneer history, which I have caused to be unearthed, and believe may, at *this* moment, to be of service to *you*.

I have thought it only an act of courtesy due you from this Association to give you the copy.

Yours, very respectfully,
WM. WINTER, *Secretary.*

"OAKVILLE, NAPA COUNTY, CAL.,
"August 26th, 1878.

"WM. WINTER, Esq., San Francisco—*Dear Sir:*—In answering your inquiries, I have a request to make of you, which is, that if in future you meet with James M. Harbin, you will write a biographical sketch of the Indian Truckee, as Mr. Harbin can give all the particulars better than any one else, judging from the following facts:

"In 1845, Harbin and a few others were on their way to California, *via* Overland Route, and on arriving at the Sink of the Humboldt, they met with an Indian and employed him to pilot them across the desert. While *en route* Harbin noticed a resemblance in him to a Frenchman he had formerly known, and therefore bestowed the name of the Frenchman (Truckee) on the Indian, and on arriving at the river (Truckee), they were greatly elated at their good fortune, and named it 'Truckee's River.' 'Truckee' and two of his brothers came to California with the emigrants, in 1846, and served in Fremont's Battalion until the end of the war, and 'Truckee' was admitted to be as brave, if not the bravest, man among *us*, and was certainly far superior to most Indians in intellect.

"I am glad that you met with Mr. Wm. L. Todd, and hope the controversy concerning the Bear Flag will soon be settled, not that in itself it is a matter of great importance, but as it will form a part of history, the story of it should be correctly told. I have several times published truthful accounts of it, and, in every instance, other persons, who of their own knowledge could have known absolutely nothing about the circumstances narrated, but who happened to be better writers than myself, would prove to their own satisfaction, and that also of most people, that my statements were false and theirs correct.

"Yours, etc.,

"Wm. Baldridge."

THE LAND WE ADORE.

Song and Chorus

WORDS BY

SAMUEL C. UPHAM.

AIR—*"Flow Gently, Sweet Afton."*

The gleam of the camp-fires of em-i-grant trains Is sel-dom now seen on the far-a way plains,

From his ey-rie the ea-gle looks down in dis-dain, As the steam-whistle shrieks out its startling refrain.

Our camp-fires no lon-ger il-lume the ra-vine, The Pan and the Rocker are rare-ly now seen,

Fri-joles and flap-jacks, our di-et of yore, Like a vis-ion have flown to re-turn nev-er-more.

CHORUS.

Now fond rec-ol-lec-tions of long a-go times, Come ech-o-ing back like the mu-sic of chimes,

Our thoughts wander back to the land we a-dore, Be-yond the Si-er-ras—Pa-cif-ic's lov'd shore

570

II.

The Tom and the Sluice-box, once sparkling with gold,
No longer wash out the auriferous mould;
The Quartz Mill and Crusher have taken their place,
And steam 's declared victor again in the race.
Our cabins now roofless and gone to decay,
Like their tenants of old, are fast passing away;
The grave on the hillside, with head-board decayed,
Marks the spot where a comrade we long ago laid.

Cho.—Now fond recollections of long-ago times, etc.

III.

O woman, dear woman! pure as gold without dross,
The first at the tomb and the last at the cross,
Thy presence ne'er cheered us in camp nor in mine,
In those long-ago days, the days of lang syne—
When the toils of the day had drawn to a close,
And wrapped in our blankets in silent repose,
Our thoughts wandered back to our sweethearts and wives,
The loved ones for whom we had periled our lives.

Cho.—Now fond recollections of long-ago times, etc.

IV.

Now hamlets like magic to cities have grown,
The *ranchero* has reaped the grain he has sown,
The vine and the fig-tree are laden with fruit,
And breezes blow soft there as tones of the lute;
The orange-tree blossoms and fruits in the vale,
The date and pomegranate, 'mid sand and 'mid shale,
The filbert and almond, and manna of yore,
Abound in the land that we love and adore.

Cho.—Now fond recollections of long-ago times, etc.

V.

The Tuolumne rolls on as in ages of yore,
The Stanislaus laves its auriferous shore,

The Bear and the Yuba flow down to the sea,
Bright flowers are still blooming, and green is each tree;
The Sierras tower up in their helmets of snow,
And the wild rose and tulé still wave to and fro;
Diablo, proud monarch, all grizzled and gray,
Looms up in the distance his realm to survey.

Cho.—Now fond recollections of long-ago times, etc.

VI.

Now fond recollections of long-ago times,
Come echoing back like the music of chimes;
Our thoughts wander back to the land we adore,
Beyond the Sierras—Pacific's loved shore.
But where are our comrades of long-ago days?
Some with us are crownéd with laurels and bays,
And others are here with locks frosted by age,
Whose names add new lustre to history's page.

Cho.—Now fond recollections of long-ago times, etc.

VII.

And Stevenson's veterans are present to-day,
From Sonoma, La Paz, and from old Monterey—
Heroes, who helped add to the Red, White and Blue
A bright golden star, ever loyal and true.
And others lie mouldering on the plains of the West,
Their spirits have soared to the land of the blest,
Where soon we shall meet on that far-distant shore,
Shall meet, and shall greet, and shall part nevermore.

Cho.—Now fond recollections of long-ago times, etc.

A TRIBUTE TO GENERAL JOHN A. SUTTER, AND A TOUCHING REPLY.

New York, March 1st, 1878.

General John A. Sutter, President, etc., Washington, D. C.—*Dear General:*—At a special meeting of "The Associated Pioneers of the Territorial Days of California," held in New York on the 18th ult., reference was made to the coming birthday anniversary of our esteemed friend and associate, General John A. Sutter; and, by a unanimous vote, the officers of the Society were requested to prepare some appropriate memento of this anniversary, to be presented to yourself.

With the greatest pleasure, we hasten to fulfill the honorable duty assigned us by our associates, and hand you the accompanying cane, wrought specially for the occasion, of California gold and of California rosewood; it is but a feeble token of our respect and fraternal regard for one who has, during these long years, not only been our friend, but the friend of all Californians; who has illustrated, by his life and by his signal benefactions, the Divine precept of "charity." On behalf of our . associates, we tender our congratulations that, in health and strength and surrounded by friends, you are able to celebrate this seventy-sixth birthday and anniversary, and that you may long be spared for similar annual congratulations, is our earnest prayer.

Very truly, yours,

Francis D. Clark,

Secretary.

(573)

GENERAL SUTTER'S REPLY.

WASHINGTON, D. C., March 2d, 1878.

FRIENDS AND COMPANIONS of "The Associated Pioneers of the Territorial Days of California," New York City— *Gentlemen:*—I received yesterday, by express, as an appropriate memento of the seventy-sixth anniversary of my birth, a beautiful cane, " wrought specially for the occasion, of California gold and California rosewood," symbolizing, at one and the same time, the generous gratitude of my contemporary pioneers and the acts of my life which signally marked my humble career as one of the hardy adventurers of the Pacific slope.   For your kind allusions to my early services to the pioneers of California, you will, one and all, gentlemen, please accept my grateful acknowledgments, and the assurance that in such manifestation on the part of those I may have served, I have my reward.

We are now hastening onward to our final resting-place, but the romance of our history as California pioneers, with its reverses and its successes, will tend, for ages to come, to stimulate the energy of our posterity.

Thanking you for the new honors, and for the many past favors received at the hands of the Society, collectively and personally, I am, truly and sincerely, your friend and obedient servant,

JOHN A. SUTTER.

HISTORY

OF THE

INAUGURATION AND ORGANIZATION

OF THE

ASSOCIATED PIONEERS

OF THE

TERRITORIAL DAYS OF CALIFORNIA.

HEAD-QUARTERS IN THE CITY OF NEW YORK.

THE annual re-union of old Californians, now resident of the city of New York and its immediate vicinity, was inaugurated on the evening of the 6th of March, 1872, by a party of gentlemen, former members of that pioneer regiment to the Pacific Coast in 1847, known as "Stevenson's California Regiment of New York Volunteers." The party assembled at the residence of a former comrade, John Wolfe, Esq., on West Twenty-third Street, and upon the invitation of that gentleman. Of the regiment there were present: its former surgeon, Dr. Alex. Perry, Captain James M. Turner, Lieutenant Jeremiah Sherwood; Privates Russell Myers, Francis D. Clark and John Wolfe, the host. Among the guests were Mr. O. H. Pierson, an old '49er, and John A. Sutter, Jr., grandson of that old pioneer, General John A. Sutter. The evening was the twenty-fifth anniversary of the arrival of the ship *Thos. H. Perkins*, the pioneer ship of the fleet which conveyed the regiment to California. Letters of regret were received from absent comrades, Major-General Jas. A. Hardie, Inspector-General U.S.A., formerly major of the regiment; Generals Nelson, Taylor and Francis J. Lippitt, formerly captains; Hon. Sherman O. Houghton, House of Representatives, formerly a member of Co. A, as also letters from other distinguished gentlemen residing away from the city. It was at this little gathering that the subject was discussed of the organization of a "Society of California Pioneers of New York City," all Californians of 1849 and prior, to be eligible, the Society to act in concert with the one at San Francisco.

On the following year, in the month of March, the second re-union took place, and there assembled at the residence of Mr. Wolfe, Dr. Perry, Captain Turner, Lieutenant Sherwood, Privates Myers, Clark, Wolfe, as also the following who were not among those present upon the former occasion, Privates Jacob J. Schoonmaker, Wm. H. Rogers, James E. Nuttman, Jacob W. Norris and John Taylor, and thus was another evening passed in a joyous re-union of these early pioneers.

In the month of March, 1874, the members of the regiment decided to hold the re-union of that year at one of our hotels in consequence of sickness in the family of their comrade, Mr. Wolfe, himself also an invalid, and while arrangements were being effected for that purpose, the proposition was made to those gentlemen having the matter in charge, by a number of '49ers, to join the two elements upon the present occasion, and have a re-union of California Pioneers, on the evening of the 26th of March, 1874, celebrating the twenty-seventh anniversary of the landing of Stevenson's Regiment of New York Volunteers at San Francisco, and the following circular was issued and addressed to all pioneers known to be residents of this and adjoining States:

1847.   RE-UNION OF CALIFORNIA PIONEERS.   1874.

NEW YORK, March 16th, 1874.

The undersigned take pleasure in announcing that arrangements have been completed for a re-union of California Pioneers, to be held at the STURTEVANT HOUSE, Broadway, Twenty-eighth and Twenty-ninth Streets, on Thursday evening, the 26th instant, at eight o'clock, being the twenty-seventh Anniversary of the landing of Colonel Stevenson's Regiment of New York Volunteers, at San Francisco, Cal.

Should you be pleased to participate in the re-union, a response addressed to the Secretary will meet with attention.

COMMITTEE OF ARRANGEMENTS.

Surg. ALEXANDER PERRY,		Maj -Gen. H. GATES GIBSON, U.S.A.,	
Lieut. J. SHERWOOD,	_Stevenson's Regiment._	" FRANCIS E PINTO,	_California Pioneers._
JAMES E. NUTTMAN,		Hon. JAS. S WETHERED,	
RUSSELL MYERS,		JOHN SICKELS,	
FRANCIS D. CLARK,		O. H. PIERSON,	
JOHN WOLFE,		JACOB P. LEESE,	

ALEXANDER PERRY, M. D., *Chairman.*

LIEUT. J. SHERWOOD, *Treasurer,*

1172 Broadway.

GEN. FRANCIS E. PINTO, *Secretary,*

106 Wall Street.

Upon the evening indicated there assembled at the Sturtevant House a large and enthusiastic gathering of Californians of the early days—among the number being Commodore C. K. Garrison, General Thos. B. Van Buren, Willard B. Farwell, William Colligan, William M. Walton, Jas. F. Curtis, John Lambier, H. P. Townsend, G. A. Mendon, James Stark, the old pioneer actor, E. W. Crowell, and besides the gentlemen composing the committee of arrangements there were some fifteen former members of the regiment present, and among the guests were Rufus Hatch, Esq., Vice-President of the Pacific Mail Steamship Company, and Clark Bell, Esq., Counsel to the Company, who represented the old pioneer Steamship Company of California. This assemblage unanimously voted that the re-union so worthily inaugurated by the little band of Stevenson's regiment should henceforth assume a permanent character, and upon the motion of Mr. O. H. Pierson, the present company adjourned to meet again, if alive, during the coming winter, and in furtherance of that resolution the following circular was issued, calling a meeting of old Californians at the Sturtevant House, on the evening of the 28th January, 1875

RE-UNION OF OLD CALIFORNIANS.

MEXICAN AND AMERICAN.

NEW YORK, January 21st, 1875.

A meeting of gentlemen who were residents of California prior to its admission as a State into the Union September 9th, 1850, will be held at the STURTEVANT HOUSE, Broadway, Twenty-eighth and Twenty-ninth Streets, on Thursday evening, 28th instant, at eight o'clock.

The object of the meeting is for the purpose of selecting a Committee of Arrangements for a proposed Re-union Banquet, at an early day, as also to obtain the views of those intending to participate upon the occasion.

The re-union of the 26th of March last was attended with so much pleasure and satisfaction, that those who were participants, as also many who were unable to be present, have expressed a desire for its repetition the present winter.

Californians of 1851 and 1852, the early days of the Golden State, are cordially invited to participate.

You are requested to be present upon the evening indicated, or may address a communication (giving your views and expectation of participating) to the Chairman, California meeting, Sturtevant House.

Respectfully, etc.,

JACOB P. LEESE,	1833.
RODMAN M. PRICE,	1846.
WILLIAM COLLIGAN,	"
ALEXANDER PERRY, M. D.,	1847.
JEREMIAH SHERWOOD,	"
FRANCIS D. CLARK,	"
O. H. PIERSON,	1849.
E. W. CROWELL,	"
S. D. JONES,	"
WILLARD B. FARWELL,	
WILLIAM M. WALTON,	
JOHN SICKELS,	
FRANCIS E. PINTO,	
J. A. SPERRY,	"
THOMAS D. JOHNS,	1850.
JAMES F. CURTIS,	"

This circular was addressed to all old Californians, known to be residents of the city of New York and vicinity, and to many residing in distant States, and in response there assembled at the Sturtevant House, on the evening of the 28th of January, the following-named persons: Lieutenant Jeremiah Sherwood, George M. Leannard, Russell Myers, Francis D. Clark and James E. Nuttman, of Stevenson's Regiment, 1847; General H. Gates Gibson, O. H. Pierson, John Sickels, William M. Walton, Thomas McSpedon, H. Barnard, Edw. F. Burton, Willard B. Farwell, pioneers of 1849; S. L. Merchant, Thos. D. Johns, George W. Stanton, J. A. Prior, of 1850, and James H. Butler, of 1852.

The inclement state of the weather, a heavy storm prevailing, caused many to be absent who otherwise intended to have been at the meeting.

The meeting was called to order by Mr. Willard B. Farwell, and on motion of that gentleman, General H. Gates Gibson, U. S. A., was chosen chairman, and on motion of Mr. O. H. Pierson, Mr. Francis D. Clark was selected as Secretary.

The Chairman stated the object of the meeting, which was to make arrangements for the annual banquet of old Californians resident of the city of New York and vicinity.

On motion of Mr. Pierson it was resolved that the banquet should take place on Thursday evening, the 11th of February, at the Sturtevant House.

The Chair announced the following committees in connection with the banquet, and who were instructed to make all necessary arrangements for the same.

COMMITTEE OF ARRANGEMENTS.

VICE ADMIRAL S. C. ROWAN, U. S. Navy,
MAJ.-GEN. JOSEPH HOOKER, U. S. Army,
    "   H. GATES GIBSON, U. S. Army,
HON. RODMAN M. PRICE,
ALEXANDER PERRY, M. D.,

JACOB P. LEESE,
JEREMIAH SHERWOOD,
JOHN SICKELS,
WILLARD B. FARWELL,
FRANCIS D. CLARK.

33

MAJ.-GEN. RUFUS INGALLS, U. S. Army,   JOHN SICKELS.

RECEPTION COMMITTEE.

GEN. FRANCIS E. PINTO,   WILLIAM M. WALTON,
EDGAR W. CROWELL,   O. H. PIERSON.

COMMITTEE ON DECORATIONS.

JAMES F. CURTIS,   MAJ. RUSSELL MYERS,
WILLIAM COLLIGAN,   COL. JAS. E. NUTTMAN.

Mr. Clark moved that this meeting proceed to take the necessary steps for the immediate organization of a permanent association, to be known as the "Associated Pioneers of the Territorial Days of California."

Mr. Pierson moved that the Chairman appoint a committee to frame a Constitution and By-Laws for the purpose of such an organization.

The Chair appointed as such committee Messrs. Johns, Sickels, Walton, Farwell, Colligan, Myers, Sherwood, Clark and Nuttman, with instructions to make their report on the evening of the banquet.

After a full exchange of views on the part of those present, in relation to the subjects brought before the meeting, on motion of Mr. Merchant the meeting adjourned until the evening of the 11th of February.

At a subsequent meeting of the Committee of Arrangements, the resignation of Dr. Alex. Perry was received, in consequence of his inability to attend the banquet.

On motion of Mr. F. D. Clark, the same was accepted, and Mr. S. L. Merchant was chosen to fill the vacancy.

On motion of Mr. John Sickels, Major-General H. Gates Gibson was chosen Chairman of the Committee.

REPORT OF COMMITTEE.

NEW YORK, February 11th, 1875.

At the meeting of Old Californians, held at the Sturtevant House, in this city, on Thursday evening, the 28th of January last, the undersigned were selected as a committee to prepare a suitable plan of organization for a permanent Association, through which the memories of their pioneer experiences in the settlement and development of California, during its territorial and early days, may be perpetuated to the members of such association and their posterity.

Believing that the best way to perfect such an organization is to approach the subject in the simplest and most concise manner, and to act without unnecessary expenditure of time, the committee have prepared the subjoined brief articles of association, which they hereby submit, with the recommendation that they be accepted and signed by all who desire to become members, and by that act thus calling the desired association into immediate existence.

THOS. D. JOHNS, 1850, Chairman.
JOHN SICKELS,
WM. M. WALTON,   } 1849.
WILLARD B. FARWELL,
WILLIAM COLLIGAN, 1846,
RUSSELL MYERS,   Stevenson's
J. SHERWOOD,   Regiment
FRANCIS D. CLARK,   1847.
JAS. E. NUTTMAN,

General Francis E. Pinto moved the acceptance of the report, and on being seconded by ex-Governor Rodman M. Price, the same was unanimously received.

Thomas D. Johns here presented, as Chairman of the Committee, the following:

ARTICLES OF ASSOCIATION.

1st. This organization shall be called "The Associated Pioneers of the Territorial Days of California."

2d. It shall be composed of all residents of California prior to its admission into the Union, September 9th, 1850.

3d. All former and present citizens of California, who resided there subsequent to September 9th, 1850, shall be eligible to "*honorary membership* on the same terms as other members, and shall enjoy all the rights and privileges of the Association."

4th. The officers shall consist of a President, Vice-President and a Secretary (who shall also be Treasurer); they shall constitute *ex officio* the Board of Trustees, and shall have the executive management and direction of the Association.

5th. All persons eligible to membership as above, shall be and become members of the Association on subscribing to these Articles of Association, and paying to the Treasurer the sum of *ten* dollars, and without payment of any further dues whatsoever.

6th. The sums received for membership as above, or from any source whatever, shall be invested by the Trustees in United States Government bonds, and placed for safe keeping in the vault of a reliable *Safe Deposit Company*, not to be withdrawn or appropriated except by vote of the Association. The interest on such bonds to be expended from time to time as may be in the judgment of the Trustees requisite for expenses of printing, stationery, etc., on behalf of the Association.

7th. The annual meeting shall be held on the 18th day of January, the anniversary of the discovery of gold in California. But when that day falls on Saturday or Sunday, the meeting may be held on such other day as the Trustees may select.

The articles above enumerated, with the exception of the seventh, as above stated, were unanimously adopted.

An election of officers for the ensuing year was then proceeded with, and General H. Gates Gibson, U. S. A., was chosen President; John Sickels, Vice-President, and Francis D. Clark, Secretary and Treasurer.

OFFICERS OF THE SOCIETY,

Chosen at the Annual Meeting, held January 18th, 1878.

PRESIDENT.
General JOHN A. SUTTER, *Litiz, Pa.*

VICE-PRESIDENTS.

Gen. H G. GIBSON, *U. S. A.*
JOHN SICKELS, *N Y. City*
GEORGE HOWES, *N. Y. City.*
JOHN J. HAGER, *Rhinebeck, N. Y.*
Hon. DE N AS STRONG, *Brooklyn, N Y.*
SA N'L C UPHA N, *Philadelphia, Pa.*
GIL N OR N EREDITH, *Baltimore, Md.*
Gen EDW. F BEALE, *Washington, D C.*
Hon ROBERT H. N CKUNE, *Scranton, Pa.*
W N. N. WALTON, *Newark, N. J.*

TRUSTEES.

Gen. THOS. W. SWEENY, *U. S. A.*
Gen THOS. D JOHNS.
Col EDW. F. BURTON.
Hon. C LYDECKER.
GEO. F SNIFFEN
JA N ES A SPERRY.
EDW. R. ANTHONY.
E. W. CROWELL.
WM. C. ANNAN

SECRETARY.
FRANCIS D. CLARK.

TREASURER.
Hon. JEREMIAH SHERWOOD.

AMENDED AND REVISED

ARTICLES OF ASSOCIATION.

ARTICLE 1. This Society shall be known by the name of " THE ASSOCIATED PIONEERS OF THE TERRITORIAL DAYS OF CALIFORNIA," and is declared to be a social organization. Its objects are to form a more perfect union of the Pioneers of California, now residents of the Atlantic States, and to cultivate social intercourse between them.

ART. 2. To collect and preserve historical facts and information, in connection with the early and subsequent history of the Pacific Coast, and to perpetuate the memory of those whose wisdom, valor and enterprise advanced civilization to the shores of the Pacific.

ART. 3. The members of the Society shall be classified as follows: Those elected under Art. 6 to be designated *Territorial* members. Those elected under Art. 7, to be designated *State* members. Those elected under Art. 8, to be designated *Honorary* members.

ART. 4. It shall be the duty, as it will be the interest, of every member of the Society, to use all laudable efforts to collect and procure such relics, incidents and facts connected with the history and settlement of California, as may be interesting and useful to the Society; and so soon as it is prepared to provide for the care of the same, donations of such articles and information will be received.

ART. 5. It is declared to be the further purpose of the Society, at such period as its financial strength will warrant, to support a permanent hall in the city of New York, which shall contain the journals and periodicals of the Golden State, a library for the diffusion of useful knowledge among its members, a museum containing valuable records of interest, and curiosities pertaining to the early days of California; as also a head-quarters for residents of California visiting the city of New York.

ART. 6. All persons who were for any period in California

prior to the 9th day of September, 1850 (the date of the admission of the State of California into the Union), all who served in the Navy of the United States on the Coast of California during the conquest of that then Mexican Territory, and the male descendants of all such, of lawful age, shall be eligible to *Territorial* membership.

ART. 7. All persons whose residence in California dated subsequent to the 9th day of September, 1850, and who were residents of the State for the period of one year, shall be eligible to *State* membership on the same terms as other members, and shall be entitled to all the privileges of the Society, except to hold office; *provided*, however, that this Article shall in no wise change the status of the State members who were enrolled prior to the 18th day of January, 1876.

ART. 8. Any person who, previous to the 9th of September, 1850, the date of the admission of California into the Union, is recognized as having been prominently identified with, or prominently connected with, California in direct business or commercial relations, and is not eligible to *Territorial* or *State* membership, may, by vote of two-thirds of the members present at an annual meeting of the Society, be admitted to *Honorary* membership, without the payment of the membership fee or other dues, and shall be entitled to all the privileges of the Society except to vote or hold office; *provided*, however, that the names of such persons shall have been presented in writing to the Secretary of the Society at least thirty days before said annual meeting.

ART. 9. Any person qualified as prescribed in Articles 6 and 7, desiring to become a member, shall make application to the Secretary of the Society, giving name, place of residence, occupation and date of his arrival, or that of his ancestor, in California; and within ten days after the receipt of such application the Secretary shall transmit the same to the Board of Trustees, and upon the return of the application by them, as approved, the Secretary shall notify the applicant of his election.

ART. 10. All applicants for membership to this Society must

be of good character and gentlemanly deportment, and in every way entitled to the respect and confidence of the Associated Pioneers; and in any case where the facts obtained by the Board of Trustees are to the contrary, the application shall be rejected.

ART. 11. Each person, on admission as a member of the Society, shall pay into its treasury the sum of *ten dollars*, and an annual assessment of *five dollars*, payable semi-annually in advance, and shall sign the Articles of Association with his name in full, and the day of the month and year of his arrival in California; and if any person residing in the city of New York, for two months after his notification by the Secretary of his election, or if residing outside of the city of New York, for three months after said notification, shall neglect to pay his membership fee and sign the Articles of Association, he shall be considered as having declined to become a member; indebtedness for six months after the semi-annual assessment shall have become due, shall render the member liable to be suspended from all privileges of the Society until said indebtedness has been paid. This Article *shall not apply* to any member who was elected prior to the 18*th day of January*, 1878, unless he shall have notified the Secretary of his willingness to abide by its conditions.

ART. 12. Any member who shall be accused of moral turpitude or misconduct inconsistent with his obligations as a member of the Society, or who shall make a false representation of the time of his arrival in California, shall be notified to appear before the Board of Trustees, and if found guilty, shall be reprimanded or expelled by said Board, and notice thereof shall be given to the members by the Board, through the Secretary, stating the reason of said action: *provided*, the member shall have the right to appeal to the next annual meeting of the Society, by filing in the Secretary's office notice of his intention so to appeal within one month after the service upon him of the notice of the judgment of the Board. And unless the decision of the Board be affirmed by a vote of a majority of the members present, the action of the Board shall be of no effect.

ART. 13. The officers of the Society shall consist of a President, ten Vice-Presidents, Secretary, Treasurer, and a Board of Trustees, to consist of nine members.

ART. 14. The annual meeting of the Society shall be held on the eighteenth day of January, that being the anniversary of the discovery of gold at Sutter's Saw-mill, by James W. Marshall, an employee of General John A. Sutter.

ART. 15. The election for officers, all of whom shall be qualified members of the Society, shall be holden at the annual meeting, and their election shall be by ballot.

ART. 16. The officers of the Society shall hold office for one year, or until their successors have been elected and qualified.

PRESIDENT.

ART. 17. The President shall preside at the meetings of the Society, and of the Board of Trustees. He shall preserve order and decorum, and shall announce the order of business, and decide questions, subject to an appeal by any two members. He is also empowered to call a special meeting of the Society at any time that it may, in his opinion, be deemed necessary; the call to be made through the Secretary of the Society by written or printed notice to each member.

VICE-PRESIDENT.

ART. 18. The First Vice-President shall preside and perform all the duties of the office of the President in the absence or disqualification of that officer; and in the event of the death or resignation of the President, he shall succeed him during the remainder of his term; and in the absence of the President and the First Vice-President the senior Vice-President present shall perform the duties of the office.

SECRETARY.

ART. 19. The Secretary shall keep a record of all the proceedings of the Society, and of the Board of Trustees. He shall record its Articles of Association in a book to be kept solely for such purpose. He shall register the names of members, and shall have charge of the roll of members.

He shall be responsible for the safe-keeping of all books of record and papers belonging to the office of the Secretary.

He shall, whenever directed by the President, give the members of the Society and Board of Trustees proper notice of all meetings, and shall perform such other duties as may be assigned to him by the Board of Trustees.

TREASURER.

ART. 20. The Treasurer shall collect the admission fees and dues, and shall hold all the money, evidences of indebtedness, and valuable documents of the Society. He shall not pay any money except upon an authorization signed by the President and countersigned by the Secretary of the Society. He shall make a report every six months to the Board of Trustees, and exhibit in detail his receipts and payments, and the balance in the treasury, and if invested, how; *provided*, that the Treasurer is not authorized, nor are the Board of Trustees empowered, to appropriate or direct the payment of any money from the funds held by the Treasurer from *membership fees.* Such money shall be held as a permanent fund of the Society, the interest, *only* therefrom, to be at the disposal of the Board of Trustees for the necessarily-incurred expenses of the Society.

He shall keep a regular account of the financial affairs of the Society, an abstract of which he shall exhibit, accompanied by satisfactory vouchers, at each annual meeting of the Society; at the expiration of his term of office he shall deliver to his successor all moneys, evidences of indebtedness, valuable documents, books, vouchers and other papers in his possession belonging to the Society.

LIBRARIAN.

ART. 21. It shall be the duty of the Librarian to keep a full and accurate catalogue of all the books, magazines, maps, charts, relics or other property belonging to the Society, and arrange them in proper order. He shall make a record of all books or other donations presented to the Society, in a book provided for that purpose, with the names of the donors, and to make suitable acknowledgment of the same.

The Secretary shall be, *ex officio*, Librarian of the Society, and perform all the duties as Librarian until the Board of Trustees shall appoint one, and under such regulations as the Board of Trustees may from time to time direct, which instructions shall be given to the Librarian in writing, under the signature of the President of the Board.

BOARD OF TRUSTEES.

ART. 22. The Board of Trustees, of which the President and Secretary shall be members by virtue of their respective offices, shall meet for the transaction of business at such time and place as the President of the Society shall direct.

The President of the Board shall, upon the receipt of an application for membership from the office of the Secretary of the Society, make inquiry as to the moral character and social standing of the applicant; and if the information received be satisfactory, the application shall be returned with the indorsement *Approved*, if to the contrary, it shall be indorsed *Rejected*, and shall be signed by at least three other members of the Board.

A majority of the members of the Board shall constitute a quorum to transact the business of the Society.

The Board shall have charge and control of the personal property of the Society.

The Board shall direct the investment of the funds received by the Treasurer from the membership fees, or from any special donation to the permanent fund of the Society, in United States Government bonds, where the amount in the hands of the Treasurer is sufficient for that purpose, such bonds to be placed by the Board in a reliable *Safe Deposit Company*, not to be withdrawn or appropriated except by the vote of two-thirds of the members present at an annual meeting of the Society; the interest, however, derived from said bonds, to be subject to appropriation by the Board for the current expenses of the Society.

The Board is empowered to fill vacancies occurring in any office, except that of President, until the next annual meeting.

The Board shall have power to appropriate the funds of the Society, *not otherwise prohibited*, but shall not create any debt or liability in the name of the Society, or in any manner use its credit.

The Board shall examine all bills paid by the Treasurer, as otherwise provided, at least once in every three months.

ART. 23. The President, on the decease of any member in good standing, shall call a meeting of the Society; and the obituary and resolutions passed at such meeting may be published in a newspaper published at the place of residence of the deceased, and the Secretary shall communicate the proceedings to the family or relatives of the deceased.

ART. 24. When the Board of Trustees shall be satisfied that any worthy member of the Society is unable, for the time being, to pay the yearly dues hereinbefore prescribed, it shall have power to remit such dues. But if any member of this Society, having the ability to pay the yearly dues hereinbefore prescribed, shall refuse to pay the same, and shall not, at the time of such refusal, render an excuse that shall be satisfactory, he shall be debarred from all privileges of the Society, the Secretary shall cause his name to be erased from the roll, and he shall not again be admitted as a member except by two-thirds vote of the Board of Trustees, and upon such conditions as the Board shall deem fit to impose.

ART. 25. It shall be the duty of the Board of Trustees to create a Relief Fund; and they shall cause to be transferred thereto, from time to time, from the General Fund, any surplus money there may be therein, beyond the estimated current expenses of the Society for the year. And all moneys obtained by the Society from any and all sources for charitable uses, shall be paid into said Relief Fund, and be disbursed under the direction of the Board of Trustees, to aid such members as shall, in their judgment, be entitled thereto.

ART. 26. The Articles of Association may be amended at

any annual meeting of the Society, upon the vote of two-thirds of the members present.

ART. 27. These revised Articles shall take effect immediately upon their passage, and shall supersede those in force heretofore.

Examined and approved.

JAMES A. SPERRY,
THOMAS D. JOHNS, } *Committee.*
JOHN GAULT,

The above Committee was appointed at the annual meeting held January 18th, 1878, to revise the foregoing Articles. Their action to be final.

FRANCIS D. CLARK, *Secretary.*

ROLL OF MEMBERS.

JANUARY 18th, 1878.

TERRITORIAL MEMBERS.

1833.

Jacob P. Leese, ... San Antonio, Texas.

1839.

Gen. John A. Sutter, ... Litiz, Lancaster Co., Pa.

1843.

Gen. John C. Fremont, ... Arizona Territory.

1846.

Hon. Rodman M. Price, ... Ramsey, Bergen Co., N. J.
Gen. Edw. F. Beale, ... Washington, D. C.
Gen. Joseph W. Revere, ... Morristown, N. J.
William Colligan, ... 58 Monroe St., N. Y.
John Dolman, ... 727 Walnut St., Phila , Pa.

Edward C. Kemble,	312 E. 79th St., N. Y.
Dr. George McKinstry,	Old San Diego, Cal.

1847.—(Stevenson's Regiment.)

Francis D. Clark,	16 Cortlandt St., N. Y.
Joseph Evans,	70 High St , Newark, N. Y.
Russell Myers,	3 West 27th St., N. Y.
Charles J. McPherson,	604 9th Ave , N. Y.
James E. Nuttman,	Newark, N J.
William H. Rogers,	1363 Fulton St., Brooklyn, N. Y.
Judge Theron R. Per Lee,	Baltimore, Md.
Hon. Jeremiah Sherwood,	1180 Broadway, N. Y.
John Wolfe,	114 West 23d St., N. Y.

1848.

Hon. James S. Wethered,	100 East 23d St., N. Y.

1849.

William C. Annan,	160 Fulton St., N. Y.
Edw. R. Anthony,	70 Wall St., N. Y.
Col. Edw. F. Burton,	Custom-house, N. Y.
Russell W. Benedict,	102 Wall St , N. Y.
Mark Brumagim,	9 Nassau St , N. Y.
Stephen M. Barbour,	154 N. 9th St., Phila., Pa.
E. W. Crowell,	40 Pine St., N. Y.
David M. Chauncey,	140 Joralemon St., B'klyn, N.Y.
Henry K. Cummings,	205 N. Water St , Phila., Pa.
Robert W. Dowling,	105th St. and 11th Ave., N. Y.
John S. Ellis,	96 Wall St., N Y.
Willard B. Farwell,	New York.
John H. Fisher,	97 First Place, Brooklyn, N. Y.
John Gault,	71 Broadway, N. Y.
Gen. H. G. Gibson, U. S. A.,	Fort Wadsworth, N. Y.
A. T. Goodell,	451 East 57th St., N. Y.
R. R. Griffith, Jr.,	202 McCullough St., Balto., Md.
Gen. Joseph Hooker, U. S. A.,	Garden City, L. I.
H. B. Hawkins,	35 Broad St., N. Y.
John J. Hager,	Rhinebeck, Dutchess Co , N. Y.
John H. Harris,	90 Broadway, N. Y.
John G Hodge,	San Francisco, Cal.
Joseph B. Hill,	Great Neck, L. I.
George H. Johnson,	747 Broadway, N. Y.
Benjamin W. Jenness,	220 Lewis St., N Y.
John Laimbeer,	245 West 50th St , N. Y.
R. J. Paulison,	Hackensack, N. J.

Hon. Cornelius Lydecker, ... Englewood, N. J.
Hon. Robert H McKune, ... Scranton, Pa.
Gilmor Meredith, ... 43 Franklin St., Baltimore, Md.
Com'r Richard W. Meade, U. S. N., . Huntington, L. I.
James J. McCloskey, ... 113 Spencer St , Brooklyn, N.Y.
Gen. Francis E. Pinto, ... 37 Pearl St , N. Y.
Oliver H. Pierson, ... 59 West Ninth St , N. Y.
Joseph M. Pray, ... 179 Montague St., B'klyn, N. Y.
Silas H. Quint, ... 14 S. 4th St., Philadelphia, Pa.
John Sickels, ... 25 Pine St., N. Y.
Joseph S. Spinney, ... 66½ Pine St. N. Y.
A. A. Selover, ... 52 Broadway, N. Y.
George F. Sniffin, ... 239 Broadway, N. Y.
James A. Sperry, ... 145 Broadway, N. Y.
Gen. Thos. W. Sweeny, U. S. A., . 314 East 120th St., N Y.
Hon. Demas Strong, ... 67 Broadway, Brooklyn, N. Y.
Robert J. Tiffany, ... San Francisco, Cal.
Samuel C. Upham, ... 25 S. 8th St., Philadelphia, Pa.
William M. Walton, ... 19 Dey St , N. Y.

1850—(Prior to September 9th)

Gen. James F. Curtis, ... 50 Pine St., N. Y.
George Howes, ... 82 South St., N. Y.
C. C. Hastings, ... 51 West 46th St., N. Y.
Gen. Thomas D. Johns, ... 95 Liberty St., N. Y.
Beverly C. Sanders, ... 71 Broadway, N. Y.
Capt. Joseph Spinney, ... 338 Pearl St., Brooklyn, N. Y.

STATE MEMBERS.

1850—(Subsequent to September 9th)

*Gen. Charles S. Merchant, , . . . Carlisle, Pa.
*Stephen L. Merchant, ... 53 Broadway, N. Y.
*Charles R. Thompson, ... 73 Broadway, N. Y.

1852.

*James H Butler, ... 9 Maiden Lane, N. Y.
*Charles W. Schuman, ... 24 John St , N. Y.
Capt. James H. Merryman, . . . 16 Broadway, N, Y.

1853.

Hon. C. K. Garrison, ... 40 Park Ave , N. Y.
William R Garrison, ... 5 Bowling Green, N. Y.

* Enrolled prior to January 18th, 1876.

1859.

George W. Gilbert, ... 25 Wall St., N. Y.
Lewis Leland, ... Sturtevant House, N. Y.

HONORARY MEMBERS.

Reuben Lord, ... Stapleton, Staten Island, N. Y.
Effingham B. Sutton, ... 82 South St., N. Y.

Lightning Source UK Ltd.
Milton Keynes UK
UKHW022318221118
332795UK00019B/1739/P